Torah with a Twist of Humor

Published by DEVORA PUBLISHING COMPANY

Text Copyright © 2004 *Down Under Publishing, LLC*
Cover and Inside Design: David Yaphe
Editors: Uriela Sagir, Yaacov Peterseil

Library of Congress Cataloging-in-Publication Data
Bobker, Joe.
Torah with a Twist of Humor / by Joe Bobker
p. cm.
ISBN 1-930143-96-6 (hc : alk. paper) – ISBN 1-932687-15-7 (pbk : alk. paper)
1. Bible – OT. 2. Weekly Portion – interpreted and analyzed, interspersed with jokes and anecdotal humor. I. Title.

Library of Congress Control Number: 2004116061

Cloth ISBN: 1-930143-96-6
Paper ISBN: 1-932687-15-7

Email: publisher@devorapublishing.com
Web Site: www.devorapublishing.com

Printed in Israel

ACKNOWLEDGMENTS

First things first.

I would like to thank my wife Miriam who gives new meaning to the words patience and understanding, without which this book would still be on my shelf instead of yours; and my four sons — Eli, Avi, Benny, Dovi — who were, and are, a continuing inspiration to me.

Without their probing questions, this book would never have gotten started.

I thank their Torah teachers and all the role models they found inside their academies of learning ranging from *Emek*, *Tores Emes* and *Yeshiva Gedola* in Los Angeles, to *Ner Israel* in Baltimore, and the *Mir* in Jerusalem.

I am constantly awed by my sister Chanale who, despite being cruelly deprived of her teenage years in the Holocaust, remained true and faithful to her faith.

My rabbeim from Sydney, the late and saintly Rav Gedaliah Hertz *z'tl*, Rabbi Osher Abramson *z'tl* and Rav Barzel *z'tl*, of blessed memories, and from Melbourne, the charismatic Rabbi Yitzchak Groner — all deserve special credit for imbuing in me a permanent *yiddishkeit*.

Finally, I have reserved for last the most important: My parents, by far, the most single searing influence on my Jewish being. My mother and father were two Holocaust survivors from Poland; two simple *yidden* who saw over 131 family members turn into genocidal ashes yet never swayed in their belief system. In God's dictionary, they can be found under *"emunah un bitachon."*

The Heavens should be both proud and appreciative that there still existed, in the doubting aftermath of a bloody Auschwitz, Jews of the caliber of my parents — Chaskel *z'tl* and Ida Bobker, whose faith was clearer than sight.

Joe Bobker
Rosh Hashana, 2004

TABLE OF CONTENTS

Introduction   7

─────────────── BEREISHIS • 11 ───────────────

Bereishis: Murder in the First   12
Noach: A Hard Rain a' Falling   25
Lech Lecho: Coming or Going?   33
Vayera: Houseguests and Fish   46
Chayei Sarah: Aging Gracefully   55
Toldos: Battle of the Blessing   67
Vayetzei: Man on the Run   79
Vayishlach: From Yaacov to Israel   90
Miketz: From Prison to Palace   98
Vayeishev: Begin Worrying. Details to Follow.   105
Vayigash: Pathos, Poignancy, Passion   112
Vayechi: Live and Let Die   119

─────────────── SHMOS • 131 ───────────────

Shmos: So, What's in a Name?   132
Va'eira: It's About Time   144
Bo: Up Close and Personal   153
Beshalach: Say a Little Prayer for Me...   163
Yisro: Go With the Goy   170
Mishpatim: And Justice for All   179
Terumah: Giving is Receiving   184
Tetzaveh: From Rabbis to Robes   192
Ki Sisa: All That's Gold, Does Not Glitter   198
Vayakhel/Pekudei: From Golden Calf to Golden   205
                      Opportunity

─────────── VAYIKRA • 213 ───────────

Vayikra:	Big Aleph, Little Aleph	214
Tzav:	Leviticus at Its Most Levitical	223
Shemini:	The Agony and the Ecstasy	230
Tazria/Metzora:	Death as Part of Life	236
Acharei Mos/Kedoshim:	Hermits and Holiness	244
Emor:	Being Holy or Looking Holy?	251
B'har/B'chukosai:	Love at First Fright	259

─────────── BAMIDBAR • 267 ───────────

Bamidbar:	How One Counts Also Counts	268
Nasso:	Hair and There	274
B'ha'aloscha:	The Kvetching Sedra	282
Sh'lach L'cho:	I Spy With my Little Eye	289
Korach:	Rebel, Without a Cause	298
Chukas:	The Mother of all Mystery Mitzvos	307
Balak:	The Prophet Motivated by Profit	318
Pinchos:	Where There's a Will, There's a Relative	325
Mattos/Maaseh:	Green Belts and Open Spaces	332

─────────── D'VARIM • 339 ───────────

D'varim:	Déjà Vu	340
V'eschanan:	Back to the Future	347
Eikev:	Not By Chance Alone	353
Re'eh:	Tithes and Taxes	359
Shoftim:	Justice by Just Means	366
Ki Setzei:	A Medley of Morals	378
Ki Savo:	Rewards and Warnings	384
Nitzavim:	High Days and Holy Days	391
Vayelech:	May You Live to be 120 Years!	399
Ha'azinu:	Song, Song, Song	407
Zos HaBrocho:	Breaking Up is Hard to Do	415

Introduction

A young married couple was having serious problems and went to see Rav Shimshon Pinchus. The rav interviewed the couple but couldn't find any underlying reasons for the acrimony and bitterness, certainly not enough to warrant granting a divorce. So he decided to speak to them individually, and asked the wife what had convinced her that she could never be happy with her husband.

"I can't take it anymore. I've been married nearly two years and I've never seen my husband smile. I'll never be happy!"

The rav then called in the husband, and asked, "How come you never smile?"

"Well," he replied embarrassed, "I have very crooked teeth and when I grin or laugh, they distort my face and make my smile ugly."

"Why don't you get them fixed?"

"I would love to have good teeth, be able to smile, make my wife happy...but I can't afford it; orthodontic work is costly."

Rav Shimshon then took his entire life's savings, about $2,500, and gave it to the man to pay for the dental work, waving his hand with a word of advice, "Start smiling! It'll save your marriage!"

The pursuit of comic relief was recognized by Judaism centuries before it crept into Greek theatre, Shakespeare, and Henry James's exhortation, "Dramatize, dramatize! Show us, don't tell us! Get out of the way and let the story speak for itself!"

No, advised the rabbis of the Talmud: those who wish to "tell the story" should begin each *d'var Torah* with a joke. Why? It is wise, no matter what you are doing, to *enjoy* what you are doing; and laughter is relaxing, a unifying force for the audience, and, according to Tehillim, God's presence doesn't dwell in a place where there is no joy — in fact, the Jew "shall have to give account for every legitimate pleasure that came his way and on which he turned his back since despair, the antithesis of joy, comes to be seen as denial of God."

Laughter is thus serious business.

Like the Torah, it "nourishes" the soul, creates an internal equilibrium; and, as a "universal bond," notes Ausbel, it "draws all men closer." And more: it throws up a comforting "psychological buffer" between expectations and reality, as so brilliantly utilized by Sholem Aleichem's comic-philosopher Tevye whose audience was his horse and his God.

Yes, say our Sages: the study of Torah is a sober exercise, but laughter can lead the way.

In fact, happy Jews are God's *nachas*; under the fundamental principle articulated by Rav Moshe Isserles (*Ramo*), the Ashkenazi voice in the Shulchan Oruch, as *shivisi Hashem lenegdi somid,* — *hu klal gadol Batorah,* that "God is always watching."

But not too much jolliness.

The Yiddishists of Eastern Europe suggest that the Jew "weep before God, laugh before people;" King David praises the Jew who does not sit among jokers; meanwhile Rav Yosef Karo of Shulchan Oruch fame, forbids reading "nonsense" books. Why? Because it leads one to mix and mingle with "jokers and scoffers."

Yet the centrality of Sinai is the mitzvoh of being happy ("*some'och*"), especially on certain Jewish festivals (e.g.: on Shmini Atzeres the Jew must be immersed in a mood of *v'hayiso ach some'och*), and, in a startling Talmudic piece, Yochanan ben Nappaha, in an attempt to mandate a life-sustaining atmosphere of high spirits, advises Jews to greet each other with warm smiles rather than with food or drink.

The question is obvious: how does a smile fill an empty stomach?

The answer comes courtesy of those same Yiddishists ("A smile is a small curve that sets many things straight") who, despite their cynicism, instinctively understood that jokes perform a social function, that a smile is an essential ingredient in the health and continuity of a community, that good cheer was an emotionally sound and stable platform, a warmth that helped the Jew function properly, as necessary as food and drink — and that, in the pursuit of Yiddishkeit, time was to be associated with joy and laughter, happiness and gratitude. Why? Because the religion of Israel is essentially a *Toras Chayim,* a "law of life," intended to cultivate a happy frame of mind that pulsates with the joy of existence.

Torah giants took note: the veritable Yochanan ben Zakkai made it a point, no matter how busy or preoccupied he was, to be the first to greet another Jew affably; Reb Nachman of Breslov warned his followers to be aware of sadness, a sneaky ruse of the "evil spirit" (*yetzer horo*) which could only be mitigated by a shield of Judaic cheerfulness; the Rambam defined happiness as the "highest form of prayer," ominously cautioning that "the Jew who does not rejoice, deserves to be punished" (based on the Biblical verse, "Because you did not serve your God with joy"); while Rabbi Shlomo Wolbe compared the happy face (defined by the Mishna as a *reshus horabim,* existing in "a public domain") to the existential need of plants for the warmth of the sun, in the belief that Jews transform euphoria into energy, and simcha into strength, without which they wilt, wither, and wane (an echo of Louis L. Mann's adage, that "happiness is a perfume which you cannot pour on others without getting a few drops on yourself.")

"Smile," sang the brilliant Charlie Chaplin, "and the world smiles with you;" or as the Yiddish idiom puts it, *platsn fun gelechter,* literally, "to explode from laughter" (colloquial Hebrew derives its verb *l'hitpalets,* "outrageous laughter," from Job's *yitpalatzun,* "to shudder," or "tremble" from fear). Hopefully, this book will assist both the teacher and the student.

And so Rav Avrohom Grudzinsky, famous mussar master, taught himself to smile through the stress of Hitlerian ghettoes, knowing his radiance helped and comforted other Jews through their sufferings; he was inspired by Jewish history itself — as his colleagues wept at the sight of a broken Jerusalem, Rabbi Akiva, the greatest sage of the times, laughed, secure in the knowledge that if the prophecy of destruction was being fulfilled, so then must the Prophet's forecast of a holy city being rebuilt.

In an eye-catching counsel, Rava tells Jews to make a blessing from "a posture of simcha" (*hatov v'hameitiv*) even on bad news (e.g.: *Dayan ho'emes*, when informed of a death). Why? Rashi, the brilliant 11th century French commentator, comes to the rescue: *simcha*, in the context of this Mishna, means *b'leivav sholeim*, with a full heart ("wholeheartedly") in order to generate a simcha of serenity, the same sensation that our sages urge be installed in the Jew *before* he studies Torah.

And more: being happy is the antithesis of anger, rage, hostility — the very qualities that blinded the otherwise soft and humble Moshe to slander his folk as "rebels" (*shimu na hamorim*), causing him to lose his calm, hit a rock (*twice*), thus forfeiting his life-long dream to enter the promised land.

Stunned at the severity of Moshe's punishment, Rabbi Yehuda Loew (*Maharal*) from Prague concludes that since anger and faith (*emuna*) cannot co-exist, the presence of such qualities as antagonism, rage, or bad temper poisons the atmosphere for proper Torah study.

Being in a good mood is thus a part of the *yiddishe zeitgeist*; so sit back and enjoy this book in laughter and amusement, hilarity and jollity.

Joe Bobker

Bereishis
(GENESIS)

Torah portions do not have names; they are instead identified by their first important Hebrew word.

Thus the first book and parsha of the *Chumash* is Bereishis, not necessarily because of its contents but because it begins, *B'reishis boro Elokim*, "In the beginning God created."

This is the starting salvo of 54 parshas that together embody the Five Books of Moshe, opening with a calm yet awe-inspiring narrative of the dawn of history; the dramatic genesis of how a perfectly planned universe began, a melodious process deliberately depicted in a mere 31 verses and 469 graphic words (*ma'amaros*).

By listing each individual in the ten generations (*toldos*) from primary man (Adam, who lived 930 years) through to Noach's 500th birthday, Genesis sweeps through 1,500 years, a longer time span than all the other Torah portions combined (the entire Five Books covering 2,488 years).

Murder in the First

> "Can I help you?" the secretary asks Izzie.
> "Yes. I'd like to see the psychiatrist."
> "What seems to be the problem?"
> "I think I'm God."
> She returns a few moments later, "The doctor can see you now."
> "I don't think so."
> "Why not?"
> "I'm invisible."

A rabbinic adage: we do not begin with a tale of woe...and so this parsha's opening pictorial immediately catapults us from unfathomable emptiness and chaos (*tohu vavohu*) to an intricate "something" (*yesh*) of balance and beauty; wherein everyone and everything is suddenly gifted with a defined and defining individual purpose.

It is here that time begins, space is shaped, matter is molded.

The "spirit of God hovers" above a theological assembly plant whose physical, chemical, and biological components fall into three categories: separation (day from night, land from water), occupation (trees, plants, fish, birds, creatures), and population, wherein Man (*ish*) arises from *ho'adomo*, the "dust of the ground," in a wondrous garden, east of Eden.

Jewish mystics take the Hebrew root *dom* ("blood") from *adomo* to indicate man's transformation, via the breath of a Divine kiss, into a *nefesh chayoh* (a "living soul"), and link the numerical value of *odom* to *mah*, which has a double meaning for the potential of mankind: either "How small!" or "How great!" — the former as low as insignificant dust; the latter as high as an elevated soul.

Highs and troughs can be hard to distinguish...

> *A police officer pulls over Yankele one night after he sees him weaving in and out of the lanes, and says, "Sir, I need you to blow into this breathalyzer tube."*
>
> *"Sorry, officer, I can't do that," replies Yankele, "I'm an asthmatic. If I do that, I'll have a really bad asthma attack."*
>
> *"Okay, fine. I need you to come down to the station to give a blood sample."*
>
> *"Sorry officer, I can't do that either. I'm also a hemophiliac. If I do that, I'll bleed to death."*
>
> *"Well, then, we need a urine sample."*
>
> *"I'm sorry, officer, I can't do that either. I am also a diabetic. If I do that, I'll get really low blood sugar."*
>
> *"All right, then I need you to come out here and walk this white line while counting to ten."*
>
> *"Sorry, I can't do that either, officer."*
>
> *"Why not!?"*
>
> *"Because I'm drunk."*

The word *Bereishis* seems simple to transliterate: it comes from *b'kadmin,* which means "genesis" or "beginning," but as *the* sole originator, the "mother of all words", serving as a prelude to the entire Torah, it has naturally attracted intense scrutiny from an army of Torah scholars.

Rabbi Shimson Raphael Hirsch, 19th century founder of modern Orthodoxy, was of the opinion that the Hebrew root of Bereishis was *boro*, a Chaldean word which means "health," or "outside" (taken from the traditional expression *"breishis boro"*), indicating that "bringing something out into the open" was a healthy spiritual exercise, in the spirit of Ben Sira's advice: if one has health he has everything!

> *"Have you seen any other doctor?" the medic asks Chanale.*
> *"Yes, why?"*
> *"Well, what foolish advice did they give you?"*
> *"They told me to come to you!"*

All serious students of Torah are intrigued not on the *when* or *how* the world was created but also on the *why*; embracing the Books of Moshe not as history lessons but as a *Toras Chayim*, a "Living Torah," the term Torah being derived from *horo'oh* ("guidance") with a twofold purpose: to impart universal moral messages by inculcating *yiras shomayim* ("fear of Heaven"), while simultaneously establishing the pivotal message of monotheism ("Know that it was I, God, who created the sun, moon, planets, stars...").

Since Judaism accords deep significance to every letter, word, and phrase in the Torah, even if seemingly superfluous, many Torah scholars have had field days with the symbolic exegesis (*remez*) of this first parsha.

> *After the English teacher asks for a methodology on how to spell "potato," Yitzi puts up his hand, and explains,*
> *"If gh can stand for p as in hiccough; and if ough can stand for o as in dough; and if phth can stand for t as in phthisis; and if eigh can stand for a as in neighbor; and if tte can stand for t as in gazette; and if eau can stand for o as in plateau; then the right way to spell potato is, "ghoughphtheightteeau."*

The first opening letter *beis* alone, was granted no less than four connotations: "for the sake of"; "with"; "house"; and "two:" the latter implying two beginnings, two Torahs, etc; this then became the foundation for the Judaic concept that "double" was a sign of blessing, an idea bolstered by the fact that *beis* is also the first letter of *b'rocho* (blessing) — as opposed to *alef*, which stands for *orur* (curse) — and that each of the root letters in the word *b'rocho* are all double (*beis* is double one; *reish* is double a hundred; *chof*, double ten).

Having the ability to analyze letters into words is not so easy…

The very first verse in the Torah describes time ("there was night and morning"), and the first thing declared holy was its measure ("God blessed the seventh day"), a heralding in of the world's first grandeur of a day of rest, the Sabbath ("to cease"), whose 3-letter Hebrew root also spells *shevah* ("seventh"), and *sovai'oh* ("satisfaction, completion"), a linguistic signal that this day represents both satisfaction (of creation) and completion (of the work-week).

Scientists, physicists and cosmologists agree that the universe was created *ex nihilo,* but are unable to grasp the Torah's version of creation; that, for example, the sun and moon resulted from a Godly command ("Let there be luminaries"), and prefer either the blind watchmaker thesis, or "Big Bang" conceptions, and a world age of 15 billion years vs. the Torah's 6 days; despite the fact that the Genesis term for day (*yom*) is not necessarily a 24-hour day.

Alexander Pope put it succinctly: "Nature and nature's laws lay hid in night. God said, 'Let Newton be,' and all was light" (How many scientists does it take to change a light bulb? Two: one to hold the bulb, the other to rotate the universe).

Rabbi Samson Raphael Hirsch, a contemporary of Darwin, claimed that the most convincing evidence of a Creator lay not in six days of physical construction, but in the 7th day, the spiritual Sabbath zone that proves the existence of an Authority that consciously limited (*va'yichulu*, "finished") the forces of creation; a nod to the Midrash that traces one of the names of God (*El Shaddai*) to this very power: "It is I who said to My world, *'dai'* [enough!] for had I not said '*dai!*' the heaven and earth would still be spreading and expanding to this very day."

The Rambam, one of the leading Torah scholars of the Middle Ages, took a bold approach: rejecting any ideas of a chasm between them, he asserted that the study of science is a prerequisite to the comprehension of Torah, arguing that since the laws of mother nature are "the will of God" (as per the Psalmist's song, "How manifold are Thy deeds, O Lord"), the natural sciences must be studied in order to come closer to God.

When asked why the world was constructed round, the formidable Rav Chaim Volozhiner replied that a circular world was necessary to create different time-zones that ensured a spot of daylight, *always*, in order that Torah learning not stop for a moment.

French Rabbi Shlomo Yitzchaki (Rashi), the fundamental Torah commentator, elaborates on this creation-Torah linkage by first noting that the Torah's term for creation's completion (*vayechal*) reappears *only* at Sinai when Moshe completes (*k'chaloso*) receiving the Torah.

To Rav Tzvi Hirsh Meisels, the Veitzener Rav, Bereishis is an acronym for *bris eish*, a "Covenant of Fire", implying that each Judaic heart, mind, and psych carries within it a Jewish spark (the *pintele yid*) just waiting to connect, to help "shed a light," and ignite the people of Israel into an aspiring "light unto the nations."

When God fashions the first couple, two naked (*arumim*) genders in His own spiritual image (*b'tzelem Elokim*), the Daas Zekeinim, a 13th century French Tosafist commentator, crowns this description as the most fundamental verse in the entire Torah (in contrast to Rabbi Akiva's preference, "Love your neighbor like yourself").

> *"How come," a curious visitor to the Jerusalem Museum asks, "one of these antique Bibles is two-foot thick and the other only an inch square?"*
> *"Because," replies the guide, "the big Bible contains everything Eve said to Adam."*
> *"And the little one?"*
> *"Everything Adam said to Eve."*

The rise of Eve is the *grande finale*, a biological female (*isha*) that is miraculously fabricated from Adam's "side, rib (*tzela*);" thus it is natural, writes Dosetai ben Yannai, a second-century sage, "for a man to woo a woman." Why? Because "he seeks what he lost [i.e.: a rib]."

> *Moishele is captivated when his cheder rebbe relates this tale. A few days later the little boy isn't feeling well.*
> *"Where does it hurt?" asks his concerned mother.*
> *"Here," Moishele points to his side.*
> *"What do you think is the problem?"*
> *"I think I'm going to have a wife."*

God's decision to create man-woman was based on pure pathos, a concern for relationships and human feelings, a sensitivity for matehood that became the *raison d'être* for the matchmaking concept of *shidduchim*, bringing a couple together for marriage (Remember: the difference between in-laws and outlaws is that outlaws are wanted!)

> *Fearing that he is not assertive enough, ol' Mr. Teitelbaum sees a psychiatrist who concludes that the fault lies in the home. "You don't have to let your wife bully you. Go home and show her you're the boss!"* ▶

> *So the newly-confident Teitelbaum runs home, slams the door, shakes his fist in his wife's face, and growls, "Listen, from now on you're taking orders from me! I want my supper right now! You hear?! And then I want my shirt ironed 'cause tonight I'm going out with the guys! You understand!? And you're gonna stay home where you belong! And another thing, guess who's gonna polish my shoes!?"*
> *"The undertaker?" she replies calmly.*

Thus was human conflict born, from the very first Torah command (a negative one; not to eat from a certain tree whose knowledge oscillates between good and bad).

So, was it really an apple?

No: not only do apples not grow in that part of the world but the Torah later advises (*Song of Songs*) that apples are *good* for one's health. And so the Midrash searches for other "fruits," suggesting a fig, grape, wheat, quince, pomegranate, nut, or the seductive-sounding "apple of paradise."

Rabbi Moshe ben Nachman (*Ramban*) from 13th century Spain, identifies it as the citron, influenced by the fact that its Hebrew term, *esrog*, is derived from an Aramaic root denoting "passion, desire."

Perhaps the "fruit" was allegorical? A moral lesson, an analogy that underlies such common idioms as "the fruit of one's deeds," which is not literally a reference to any specific fruit category, but a Torah teaching that some kinds of indulgence are halachically out of bounds.

> *The elderly rabbi walks up to a young lady in a miniskirt, greets her politely and hands her a fruit.*
> *"What's this for?"*
> *"Well, Eve didn't know she was naked either, until she ate a fruit."*

This early inquisitive instinct was to plague human nature: a trend, right from the get-go, to gravitate towards the negative, to hop on board the chariot of curiosity and always gallop towards "the enemy," known as the *yetzer horo* ("evil inclination.")

In Eden this came in the form of a crafty (*arom*) walking, talking serpent who tricks Eve to stumble into sin, dragging Adam with her.

The result?

In less than a single day, humanity goes from grace to disgrace, from innocent utopia to banishment; from sheltered existence to the grind of reality (Adam to Eve, "Don't forget! I wear the *plants* in this family!")

Not one of the principal players expresses remorse. A discomfited Adam recoils in humiliation, hides among the trees, and makes history with the first recorded communication from God to man: "Where are you?" — leading the Talmudic sage Rabbi Eliezer to declare that all of human history begins with these three words, the discovery of shame.

In history's first finger-pointing exercise, now known as "passing the buck," Adam blamed Eve and Eve blamed the primordial snake. Who did the generic serpent blame? Himself? God?

Our sages call the expulsion from Eden, God's first recorded failure, *vayehi miketz yomim*, the "end of a privileged era." And it is about to get worse.

We are stunned by how fast a potential has unraveled: six chapters later a pagan civilization arises, a decay of decency begins, and God, His heart broken, has serious second thoughts ("I am sorry I made them"), especially when sibling insecurity in the world's first family leads to the rage of fratricide.

Since that moment every Jewish parent has felt the disciplinary limit of parental omnipotence.

> *"Tata, tata," shouts the little boy as he runs into the house after cheder, "Can you write in the dark?"*
> *"Sure,* mein kindt. *What do you want me to write?"*
> *"Your name on my Hebrew grammar test."*
> *"Hey," says the father sternly, "How come you got such a low mark!?*
> *"Because of absence."*
> *"You were absent the day of the test?"*
> *"No, but the boy who usually sits next to me was."*

Adam and Eve have twin sons, the farmer-murderer Cain (an *oved adomoh*, "worker of the ground"), and his brother-victim Abel (a *ro'ay tzon*, "shepherd.")

Nothing prepares us for this sudden murder: in fact, when Cain is born he seems privileged.

The Torah explains his name immediately (*Kayin*, meaning "acquisition," a gift from God), but when his twin brother Abel is born, only minutes later, the parsha gives no reason for his name: in Hebrew it is *Hevel*, which means either "breath" or "nothingness," suggesting that right from the start, Abel is "nothing," just the brother of Cain.

Rabbeinu Bachya, the classic 14th century commentator, interprets *hevel* as meaning "vanity" (as in King Solomon's famous Ecclesiastes', "Vanity of vanities; all is vanity"), implying that Abel was humble.

What caused this murder in the first?

No one knows; but there is a census that jealousy over sacrifices is the culprit — the rejection by God of Cain's puny *p'ri ho'odomoh* ("fruit offering"), in favor of Abel's more generous sheep offering.

The lesson? All is in the eye of the beholder…

> *One afternoon Abie's son comes running home from school puffing and panting, sweat rolling down his red face. As he collapses exhausted on the couch, he says to his father, "Boy, will God be proud of me today!"*
> *"How come?"*
> *"I saved $1 by running behind the bus all the way home!"*
> *"Oh yeah. Well you could have made Him even more proud by running behind a taxi and saving $20 dollars!"*

Inexplicably, the parsha does not record the emotional reaction of Adam and Eve to their son's death; but it does go into great detail in presenting history's first ever court case.

Cain's defense?

Philosophical *chutzpah* ("Am I my brother's keeper?" — a question that God simply ignores), and, according to Meir Yehuda Leibush ben Yechiel Michal (*Malbim*), the great 19th century Russian rabbi, a feeble attempt at reverse psychology, "Since *You* created the *yetzer horo*, why blame me!?"

The sentence?

Cain is lucky: there are no lightning bolts of retribution for brutally beating a brother to a pulp, only a relatively lenient curse to be an eternal "homeless wanderer," let loose in a kind of twilight zone, detached from mankind and inaccessible to God's grace.

Cain's appeal ("I cannot bear my sin") is denied: although the Midrash, in the first application of the rabbinic concept of *midda k'negged midda*, "measure for measure," claims that the world's first murderer is himself murdered several generations later by his own descendant, Lamech (father of Noach, grandson of Adam).

> *"Doctor," asks the lawyer, "Before you performed the autopsy, did you check for a pulse?"* ▸

> "No," replies the witness.
> "Did you check for blood pressure?"
> "No."
> "Did you check for breathing?"
> "No."
> "So, then it is possible that the patient was alive when you began the autopsy?"
> "No."
> "How can you be so sure, Doctor?"
> "Because his brain was sitting on my desk in a jar."
> "But could the patient have still been alive nevertheless?"
> "It is possible," replies the doctor, "that he could have been alive and practicing law somewhere."

Cain eventually concludes that a lack of proper education (*middos*) caused him to kill his brother in cold blood, that character development relies solely on cognitive knowledge, which is why he names both his son and city "Chanoch," derived from *chinuch* ("education.")

God grants them two blessings: to "be fertile and multiply," and to "rule and guard" (*l'avdah ul'shomrah*) the earth; the former creating an ongoing co-creator partnership (*shutfis*) in conceiving more life via procreation, the latter an order to shape the environment in a way that will protect and nurture that same life.

That is why the Torah, according to *Yismach Moshe*, uses the plural expression of *na'aseh odom*, "let us make man," to teach that the effort to create more worthy humans is a joint one; or as the charismatic Chassidic master, the Kotzker Rebbe put it: "God created the beginning; the rest He left for man to accomplish." To emphasize his role as active and not passive, the Heavens immediately assign to Adam the right to distinguish (*lir'os*, "to see") the animals from each other, and confer upon them names; it is here that he calls Eve *Chavoh* from *chai*, which means "life," since she is about to enter world history as the mother of all people.

Mankind thus became a joint-venture partner in God's most ambitious project (*tikkun*), to "improve" the world, known as the "anthropic principle," from the Greek *anthropos* (which means Man).

> *One day Moe, the manager, his secretary, and a worker are walking through the Jerusalem Park on their way to lunch, discussing how to improve the world, when they suddenly discover an ancient old antique oil lamp. Moe picks it up, rubs it, and a genie comes out in a huge puff of gray-blue smoke, and invites each one of them to make a wish.*
>
> *"Wow!" says the secretary, "I want to be in the Bahamas, driving a speedboat, without a care in the world!"*
>
> *And poof! She's gone.*
>
> *"I want to be in Hawaii," the worker wishes, "relaxing on the beach with my personal masseur, an endless supply of food, drink and the love of my life."*
>
> *And poof! He's gone.*
>
> *Moe the manager then calmly adds, "I want those two back in the office after lunch!"*

Moshe ben Maimon (*Rambam*), the 12th century leading Torah scholar of the Middle Ages, notes that the Heavens do not trumpet *ki tov* ("this is good") over Man as immediately as over the rest of creation because the "goodness" of man was yet to be seen.

"It was good" suddenly became "no comment (for the time being)."

Human responsibility had only just begun, and the jury of history was still out; it was up to man to decide whether being created would ultimately be "good," since part of humankind's DNA was the free will to choose not to.

It was this expectation, to "do the right thing," to be righteous and diligent in Torah, that caused the book of Genesis to become known as *Sefer Hayoshor,* the "Book of the Straight," a title that the forceful 19th century Rabbi Naftali Zvi Yehuda Berlin (*Netziv*), Lithuanian rosh yeshiva of Volozhin, used in support of his attacks against false piety.

This helps explains the chronology of creation: specifically why humankind was deferred until late in the sixth day, erev Shabbos; the rabbinic consensus is that everything that had been created beforehand had been created inherently incomplete. Man on the other hand came fully formed with spiritual power, skill, capability; "equivalent," according to a Midrash, "to all of creation," in fact the only cog in creation imbued with *ko'ach ha'dibur*, the unique power of intelligent speech, a *nishmas chaim* (soul), defined as a *ru'ach memalela*, "a speaking spirit."

The end of the first parsha thus establishes mankind as a joint-venture partner in God's most ambitious project (*tikkun*), to "improve" the world...

> *An ambitious Jewish farmer purchases an old, run-down, abandoned farm in Poland. The fields are overgrown with weeds, the farmhouse is falling apart, the roof leaks, the fences are collapsing...but he is determined to turn it into a thriving business. He rolls up his sleeves, gets down on all fours and starts the difficult task of repair.*
>
> *On the first day the town Rav comes by to give him a brocho, "May you and God be matzliach and work together to make this the farm of your dreams!"*
>
> *Several months of hard back-breaking toil and labor go by. The Rav returns and is pleasantly surprised: the farm house has been completely rebuilt, cattle and other livestock roam happily munching on feed in well-fenced pens, the fields are brimming high with healthy-looking crops planted in neat rows.*
>
> *"Amazing!" the Rav says, "What tikkun! Look what God and you have accomplished together!"*
>
> *"Yes, rabbi, but remember what the farm looked like when God was working it alone!"*

NOACH
A Hard Rain a' Falling

> *One buzzing bee asks the other bee, "Hey, do ya know where I can get something to eat around here?"*
>
> *"Well," the second bee replies, "I hear Noach is putting on a party in the hull, and there'll be plenty of flowers and pastries 'n stuff."*
>
> *The bee buzzes off merrily and returns later, with a bloated belly of fresh flowers, sweet pastries, and a yarmulke on his head.*
>
> *"Hey!" asks the other bee, "What's with the yarmulke? Did you convert?"*
>
> *"No, I wore it so they wouldn't think I was a WASP!"*

This week's parsha is titled after Noach, one of only six personalities to have their own parsha dedication; an "honor" not accorded to either Avraham or Moshe, but to a man who is both witness and survivor of the planet's watery apocalypse.

The transition from last week is abrupt, startling, disturbing. From a bright hopeful genesis, all is suddenly in turmoil.

God, suffering from a post-Garden of Eden remorse, is about to erase mankind from the young earth, having decided to de-create creation by way of a hard rain a' falling.

The parsha paints a spiritually decayed generation with a deficiency brush of "violence, thievery, vulgarity;" unworthy of the very essence of humanity, in contrast to Noach who surges ahead as a *tzaddik* and a *tomim*; a "righteous" and "perfect" person," the former by way of deeds, the latter via character traits.

Noach is one of only two Biblical men to *his'halech*, "walk with God;" the other is Enoch, a mysterious, converted sinner who dies "alive," Elijah-like.

The Torah's description is intriguing. Why? Because *holech* refers to a knowledge of astronomy, a salute to Noach's continuous spiritual growth (*holchim*) that he gets from observing the celestial bodies (in contrast to angels who *omdim*, "stand still").

Rain falls for 40 days and 40 nights, and when the flooding subsides, Noach sends out two emissaries, a raven and a delicate white dove who returns with a fragile "olive leaf" clenched in its beak.

> As the animals file out of the ark, Noach tells them to "Go forth and multiply," but notices that two snakes stay behind, curled in a dark corner.
> "Hey! You guys, didn't you hear me? You can go now... go...go forth and multiply!"
> "We can't."
> "Why not?"
> "We're adders."

To ease the anxiety God illuminates the chaos and heralds in a new dawn with a rainbow ("My bow in the clouds"), a post-flood symbol of corrective "repair" which Moshe ben Nachman (*Ramban*), one of the leading Torah scholars of the Middle Ages, sees as the bow of an archer minus the string, pointed not to send arrows of destruction downwards but upwards, towards the Heavens, turning it permanently away from its human adversary.

The climax is a Godly *condicione sina qua non*, a covenant of "natural laws" with humanity-at-large, known as the "Seven Noachide Laws," and a promise to never resort to flood again as a universal weapon.

Don Isaac Abarbanel, the insightful 15th century Spanish Torah commentator, notes how the previous system of reward and punishment, based on judging the deeds of mankind, has now significantly changed: from collective punishment to individual sentences.

Noach thus acts as *the* hinge in history, between equal sets of ten generations (from Adam to Noach, Noach to Avraham) who openly defy and anger God; the first motley world being destroyed by a primordial flood of terror, the second being spared.

Why the difference in Divine punishment?

The answer lies in behavior: the former society was quarrelsome and vindictive towards each other, the next generations lived in communal harmony, friendship, respect...

> *Chaim tries to be a good neighbor to Eric but every time Eric rings his front door bell Chaim knows that he wants to borrow something, so one day he tells his wife, "Enough is enough! I've had it with being nice to neighbors! Today, it's going to be different, he's not going to get away with it anymore!"*
>
> *A few minutes later, Eric rings the doorbell, and sure enough he asks, "Hey Chaim, I was wondering, are you going to be using your tools, power-saw and hammer this morning?"*
>
> *"Actually yes, Eric, I am. I'm going to be using them, all of them, all day!"*
>
> *"Oh, then you won't be using your golf clubs. Mind if I borrow them?"*

The tragedy of Noach?

He exists in a selfishly self-satisfied state, an island unto himself, indifferent to the destruction of civilization, a simple soul whose "righteousness" is defined not from what he does (the Torah is silent on this) but from what he does *not* (participate in the breakdown of the fabric of society), thus receiving Heaven's reprieve through omission, *not* commission.

His resume is thus mixed: the Kotzker Rebbe mocks him as a *"tzaddik* in Peltz," and the prophet Yeshayahu describes the terrifying flood as *mei Noach,* "the waters of Noach," insinuating that

Noach bears some responsibility for the watery carnage.

Torah scholars (Sforno, Vilna Gaon, Rabbi Levi Yitzchak from Berditchev) write critically of the man, concentrating not on his portrayal as savior of humanity but on his failings and foibles, accusing him of ambiguous morality, of failing to set the right tone of manners and middos, an example of the rabbinic saying, "Where there is no *derech eretz* there is no Torah."

Noach (a word which means "rest"), may have found "favor" in the eyes of God as "a good just man, pure in his generation," confirmed by Jewish mystics who spell his name backwards to get *chen* ("goodness, decency"), but his virtue is elusive and relative to his shortcomings, so stapled to the caveat of *that* time and *that* place, that his tzaddik-status borders not on credit but discredit.

This leads Rashi, the great 11th century Torah commentator, to make a startling claim: "Had Noach been living in the generation of Avraham [the apotheosis of righteousness] he would have been considered worthless."

But wait: hasn't Rashi forgotten the chronology?

Avraham *did* live in Noach's generation, and, at age 48, started his one-man war against paganism during the towering Babel construction. Yes, but Jewish history sees Avraham as having to make a lonely, singular entrée because Noach's absolute passivity had rendered him a useless partner in his colleague's religious renaissance.

> Sammy, the oldest member in shul, introduces himself to the new rabbi, boasting, "Rabbi, I'm 90 years old, and, Boruch Hashem, I haven't a single enemy in the world."
>
> "That's beautiful," replies the rav, approvingly, "a credit to you."
>
> "Yes rabbi, I'm outlived every single one of 'em nasty, no-good, miserable ......"

The drama of this parsha lies in its embarrassing exposure of Heaven's disappointing human experimentation.

Noach enters the cosmic laboratory of history as a "second" attempt at creation after Adam has failed, only to have it flunk once again, courtesy of a tower of babbling dispersion.

God, ever the realist, openly admits that the flood did not have its desired effect, that "the imagination of man's heart is evil from his youth" and cannot be so easily "washed" away from the world.

The catalyst for this depressing conclusion is a disobedient generation that ridicules Noach for 120 years as he builds a life raft to mitigate a Divine decree of destruction. Who are these folks? Immigrants from the east, led by chief instigator Nimrod of Kush, a sinister misanthropic "mighty hunter" and spiritual mentor to Esav.

Nimrod means to "rebel," and he is the first person in the Torah to lead others astray, using his brutish strength and "manipulating" demagoguery to spread fear, "ensnaring people with his words." His determined goal? To turn God's original ideal sense of the world into a primordial mess. Does he succeed? Yes.

Instead of behaving as partners in restoring the Eden foliage, his contemporaries transform the art of language into a fanatic refractoriness, a backdrop to a new societal swamp that elevates materialism over holiness, polluting creation with such cruel *chamas* ("lawlessness, depravity, injustice") that the indifferent folk weep more over the loss of a brick than the bricklayer.

Their city of Babel becomes a legend; its ultimate symbol of status and power an infamous tower-skyscraper whose spire aims to penetrate and wage war at the Heavens themselves, a breathtakingly ambitious platform of self-centeredness intended to "unseat" God with a "throne of human might [in order to] make a name for ourselves [*lanu*]."

> *A tourist from Babel is boasting to a Manhattan cab driver how tall his tower back home is, but the driver is unimpressed.*
> *"Big deal," he says, "We have a building in this country that's so tall, it took my friend 72 hours to fall off it!"*
> *"Wow, surely he died?!"*
> *"Of course. He was without food or water for three days!"*

The Heavens, of course, strike back, and, incredibly, God spurns the traditional utopian unity of peace and brotherhood and chooses the weapon of diversity, separating what was a mosaic of folks bound by one common language into different nations with divergent languages. The result? Their power of speech and mannerisms are confounded into a neat "babble" (from which the tower gets it name); one that causes a bewildered community to scatter around the globe, ensuring that they never again collaborate in their amoral, corrupt ways.

From Noach to Babel the punishment has changed: from total drenched annihilation to babbling speech, communication breakdown, talking at cross-purposes …

> *The frustrated judge is examining Mrs. Bornstein on the stand, "What are the grounds for your divorce?"*
> *"About four acres on which sits our nice little home."*
> *"No, I mean what is the foundation of this case?"*
> *"It is made of concrete, bricks and mortar."*
> *"No, no, no. I mean, what are your relations like?"*
> *"Well, I have a nice aunt and a great uncle who live near us."*
> *"No, ma'am! I want to know, do you have a real grudge!?"*
> *"Oh no, sir, you see, we never really needed one so we only have a large carport."* ▶

> *"Please, Mrs. Bornstein," the judge tries again, "Is there any infidelity in your marriage?"*
>
> *"Oh yes, your honor, both my son and daughter have stereo sets."*
>
> *"Ma'am, does your husband ever beat you up?"*
>
> *"Yes, several times a week he gets up earlier than I do."*
>
> *"Lady," the judge says, giving up, "Why don't you just tell the court why you want a divorce?"*
>
> *"Oh, I don't want a divorce, I've never wanted a divorce. It's my husband who does. He says he can't communicate with me."*

Noach lives for some 300 years after the flood, witnessing the birth of numerous descendants and countless future generations.

Jewish tradition credits his three sons as the father-founders of the nations of the world: Shem, of the Middle-Eastern nations; Chom, of the African and Far-Eastern nations; Yefes, of the European nations. Shem means "name" (as in, "a good name"); *chom* means "hot" (as in, this son's licentious nature); and *yefes* means "beautiful" (as in, conveying his beautiful streak of goodness).

From whom do the Jews trace their descent? Shem. Why? Because this son, unlike his brothers, reacts with respect (by covering him up) at the unseemly sight of his naked drunken father, who sprouts his very first words against his children only after awaking from a drunken stupor.

> *Dovid is worried that his father's drinking problem is causing a hearing loss and takes him in for an examination. The doctor concurs, and advises him to immediately stop drinking.*
>
> *"I see you stopped drinking," the doctor says several weeks later when his next check-up shows that his hearing is perfect.*
>
> *Two weeks later, the doctor bumps into Dovid's* ▸

31

> *father in the street and is shocked to see him drunk, with his hearing regressed.*
>
> *"What happened?! Are you back on the bottle?"*
>
> *"Yesh, doctor, I yam," he burps.*
>
> *"But why? I told you, if you drink you won't be able to hear!"*
>
> *"Yesh, doctor, that is true, but I must tell you, I like vat I drink better than vat I hear."*

Is Noach the only Torah personality who hit the bottle?

No; there is Lot, the "very drunken" husband of Abigail, Jeroboam, a king of Israel, a prodigious drinker who "sinned and made Israel sin" (and who even has a wine named after him), and all those scholars who Ben Sira, the early Palestinian Sage, describes as "frequenting taverns."

Why was Noach drunk?

The Torah is mute: no one really knows what drives people to excessive drink (as the old saying goes, before you criticize some-one, you should walk a mile in their shoes; that way, you're a mile away and you have their shoes).

Everyone knows: a drunk is not in control of his senses…

> *A drunk goes up to a parking meter, puts in a quarter, the dial goes to 60, to which he responds, "Hey! I just lost 100 pounds!"*

LECH LECHO
Coming or Going?

The rabbi decides to invite the local minister to his Shabbat table and offers him some of his favorite hot, pure, homemade horseradish.

His guest takes a big spoonful and suddenly clutches his throat and slinks off his chair. His face turning red, he gasps, "Rabbi, I've heard many ministers preach hellfire, but you are the first one I've met who actually passes out samples."

The historic adventures of the ancient worlds of Babylon, Egypt, Greece and Rome begin with tales of wars and warriors, blood and barbarity, murder and mayhem.

Not so the story of the Jewish people: their epic begins with a single expression, *lech*, "go," a pro-active term that symbolizes the history of a Jewish people whose first step lies in Avraham's migration.

Travel, notes Benjamin Disraeli, teaches tolerance: and, in case it was not obvious, the Midrash adds, it's also "hard on clothes, person, and purse."

The parsha's title is derived from God's monumental encounter and opening words to Avram, *Lech lecho m'artzecho* "Go for yourself from your land," a seemingly random yet compelling directive to abandon an entire way of life and step forward into the unknown, unexplored, unfamiliar, "to the land that I will show you," with no road-map, no exact coordinates, no cell-phone,

God was thus the original author of Zionism, at the time when the Promised Land was called Canaan, a generic term that included seven indigenous nations between two "great rivers."

In those days, to "walk the length and breadth of the land," was not a nature hobby, but a legal custom that signified ownership of the property traversed. Early Roman law required the acquirer of land to walk through it; ancient records from Mesopotamia describe how land was transferred: the seller would literally lift his foot off his property, and physically put the buyer's foot on it. To reconfirm their "ownership," Egyptian and Hittite kings would leave their palaces for ceremonial walks through the countryside.

Similarly, the rabbis of the Talmud saw Avraham's God-ordered sojourn — compared by Rav Yochanan to a "vial of perfume" which only gives fragrance when moved — as his symbolic possession of the land bequeathed to his descendants as an eternal possession.

Rashi notes the contrast: "Unlike Noach, who 'walked *with* God,' Avraham 'walked *before* God;'" in other words, he paved the way of morality, proclaiming "one world;" this is why the founder of monotheism is the first person in history to be called an *Ivri*, "Hebrew," from *la'avor*, the ability "to cross" borders.

In geographic terms, Avraham's journey had already begun the day his father (Terach, descendant of Shem) left Ur for Haran; however the Heavens now place the compass squarely in the son's hands, and ensure that this week's parsha becomes the opening premiere of Jewish history, *the* most significant chapter of the Torah, when God's spiritual relationship with Israel is set in motion, thus allowing the exciting adventures of the Jewish people to begin.

The similarity between *lech* and *l'cho* is only in sound, for they mean different things; the former is an instruction ("to go") because God said so; the latter ("for yourself") — an admission that the journey is for Avram's own benefit. The Zohar, the magnum opus of Biblical mysticism, interprets the order as "Go to your self," an *inner* road map, a metaphysical guide wherein every crucial step in life requires listening to an inner call.

Read together, the dual commands represent two distinct expeditions: one obligatory, one freely chosen, yet together they are an integration of individual needs within a Divine imperative.

Rabbi Samson Raphael Hirsch, the 19th century neo-conservative Orthodox giant, regards the twin motives as both a lesson and a legacy; the never-ending journey of spiritual growth begins with a first step, taken alone, but within three concentric "casings" of Jewish survival: an outer geographical circle of nationalism ("your country"), an inner one of immediate family ("your father's house"), both being dependent on the connecting link of community ("*moladesecho*").

> *One day Chaim Mendelbaum decides to go ice fishing. As he begins to drill a hole in the ice, he hears a sudden booming voice from above, "Heeey! There are no fish down there!"*
>
> *So Chaim packs his gear, walks several yards away, drills another hole, peers inside, only to be interrupted by the same roaring loud voice from above, "There are no fish down there!"*
>
> *Chaim packs up again, walks fifty yards away, and begins to drill another hole — but again, the loud voice booms from above, "I told you twice already! There's no fish down there!!"*
>
> *Chaim looks up to the sky, and yells, "God, is that you?"*
>
> *"No, you idiot, I'm the rink manager!"*

This parsha covers Avraham's life from his 75th until his 99th year (out of a lifespan of 175), one huge leap of faith that follows the itinerary of *etzba Elokim*, the "finger of God."

The journey is the first of ten trials which Avraham confronts (successfully), demonstrating an unequivocal certitude in God; the Torah uses the word *nisayon* for "tests," from *neis* which means "to lift up," as opposed to the traditional test of knowledge, *bechina*, which means "to discern."

The final test, which makes it *the* most pivotal parsha of fundamental faith, is the startling command from God to a parent to bind and sacrifice ("as a whole burnt offering [*veha'alehu le'olah*]") his own child (*Bni*, "your favored one, Yitzchak, whom you love"); this command, known in Hebrew as *Akedas Yitzchok* (an obvious contradiction to God's recent promise that a great nation would descend from Avraham) suddenly forces a father and son to emotionally connect; a problem that has faced many a parent and child....

> *"You kids have it so easy," the father says to his son, "When I was your age, I couldn't have music blaring while my father did my homework."*

Ultimately, the sacrifice did not take place, courtesy of another 11th-hour Godly order commanding Avraham not to harm his traumatized son; the boy then breaks his three-day journey of silence, only once, with a nervous query ("Where is the sheep for the burnt offering?"), showing that despite being old enough to resist, to run away, to just say "no," he remains with an incredibly unwavering trust in his father.

And yet there is no denying it: this powerful tale of terror has created a spiritual dilemma for every major Torah scholar.

Saadia Gaon, the Egyptian-born early Babylonian rosh yeshiva, said it was God's way to publicly display Abrahamic righteousness; however, the Torah is clear: no one else was present. And so Ibn Ezra, 12th century Spanish commentator, concluded that this traumatic saga was witnessed by "every Jew, past, present, and future" (based on translating Avraham's reply of *yadaati*, "I know," to *hodaati*, "I have informed.")

Meanwhile the Rambam, in a famous philosophical work

(*Moreh Nevuchim*), claims the Akeida episode as *the* epitome of total spiritual belief (the "fearing of God," *yiras shomayim*); while others (the *Gro*) learn from the patriarch's two-day preparatory period the lesson of actively "toiling," in advance, for mitzvos; and what does Rashi say?

The French sage makes the startling claim that God had to test Avraham's fidelity in order to convince a doubting Satan; a "necessary progression of belief," according to Sforno, 16th century Italian commentator, which the mystical Ramban characterizes as *min hako'ach el ha'poal*, "transforming the potential to the actual."

Not all commentators are so kind: a Midrash whispers that a "confused" Avraham, fundamentally misunderstood what was being asked of him, and therefore the lesson is to listen more carefully; French Rav Shmuel ben Meir (*Rashbam*), 12th century sage, goes a step further, claiming that the Heavens were "criticizing" Avraham's faults, specifically his relinquishing of the (Divine-given) Negev during his inappropriate peace overtures to the Philistine King Avimelech.

Jewish mystics note that going from Avram to Avraham required adding the letter *heh*, the same letter which created the world; and whose numerical value (5) not only symbolizes the five basic Torah elements in the path to repentance, but increases the gematria of 'Avraham' to 248.

This is a significant number in kabbalistic circles. Why? Because it matches *ramach*, the number of limbs (248) in the human body, suggesting that the first patriarch was *sholaim*, "whole and complete, without any deficiency or blemish."

This parsha thus acquaints the Jews with a new custom, the changing of names: Avram to Avraham, Sarai ("my princess") to Sarah ("princess for the entire world.") Why? In order that "your destiny (*mazel*) will be changed."

The question is obvious: why is it forbidden to refer to Avraham by his previous name (Avram), yet it's OK to call Yaacov by either name (Israel)?

To 18th century Rabbi Eliyahu of Vilna (*Gro*), the former's name change was an instant and irreversible transformation, "with immediate effect (*v'hoyo*)," whereas Yaacov's transformation came only "later (*yihye*)," thus either name is permissible depending on its context.

What's in a name? Plenty...

Chaim Ber, on tour, is fascinated by a sign in San Francisco's Chinatown, "Reb Yankel Dudek's Chinese Laundry," and asks the old Chinese man standing at the door, "'Yankel Dudek?' What sort of a name is that!?"
"Is name of owner," replies the old man, "Me!"
"You? How did that happen?"
"Is simple. Many, many years ago when come to this country, stand in line at documentation center. Man in front is Jewish man from Poland. Lady look at him and go, 'What your name?' He say, 'Reb Yankel Dudek.' Then she look at me and go, 'What your name?' I say, 'Sem Ting.'"

Avraham *nee* Avram is rewarded by becoming the forefather of the Jewish nation, the *rosin homa'aminim,* the first and greatest of the believers, an instigator of total self-sacrifice; the ultimate optimist; a walking-talking vital role model of benevolence, propelled forward in a pilgrimage with a universalistic spirit.

Who was Avraham's mother?

The Torah does not say but the Talmud (which also gives us the names of the mothers of Haman, David, and Samson) does. According to Rav, a 3rd century Babylonian sage, her name was Amatlai bat Karnevo.

Avram and his two brothers (Nahor and Haran) are born into a world of polytheism, and raised by a father whose brisk trade was purveying toys of idolatry; like Moshe, the Torah says not a word about his childhood, other than his lineage, leaving the void to be filled by Aggadic tales.

Avraham, writes the Rambam, knew not "his Creator" until he turned 40, an age when, having experienced the world differently than others, he was able to digest, comprehend, emulate and teach that there exists something beyond mother nature, something more meaningful than nouveau riches and material possessions (*chemdas homamon*, like "cattle, silver, gold"), something that cried out for a new principle of purity.

The founder of Judaism had reached his belief in God by rational means, a religious methodology, and a commitment to use the mind, a sagacious approach that the future Rambam was also careful to follow.

Remarkably, Avraham had no precedent on which to base these conclusions on, relying solely on the courage of his own convictions; yet his logic transformed the world by abruptly ending the dark ages of multiple deities.

> *"What would you do," the sea captain asks his young naval student, "if a sudden storm sprang up on the starboard?"*
>
> *"Throw out an anchor, Sir."*
>
> *"Tell me, what would you do if another storm sprang up aft?"*
>
> *"Throw out another anchor, Sir."*
>
> *"And if another terrific storm sprang up forward, what would you do then?"*
>
> *"Throw out another anchor, Sir."*
>
> *"Wait a minute! Where are you getting all these anchors from?"*
>
> *"Sir, from the same place you're getting your storms!"*

One can be forgiven for associating this great pioneer of faith with ophthalmology; and yet that is exactly what our sages do.

In the tradition of pure rabbinic symbolism, they praise the first patriarch as a man with a "good eye," a reference not to eyesight but to his *middos* (character traits), contrasting the "good eye, humble mind, lowly spirit" of the disciples of Avraham to those of Balaam who posses "an evil eye, haughty mind, proud spirit."

This is the source of the Yiddishist belief that eyes can be evil, which led to the introduction of the expression *einahora* into the Jewish lexicon, which means not wishing someone ill fortune; that "looks can kill!" is why my mother would often say, "*kein einahora,*" in that no evil eye should affect us.

The belief in an *ayin horo* ("evil eye") dates back to ancient days and symbolizes the evil power of covetousness, envy, hatred. The concept is found nowhere in the Tanach and first appears in the post-Biblical period: "He cast his eye on him and he died," is straight from the Talmud (after Rav visits a cemetery, he concludes that, "Ninety-nine die through an evil eye for each one who dies from natural causes!")

Its scare even infiltrated synagogue practices, making it "superstitious" to call up two brothers, or a father and son, to the Torah one after the other; and kick started an entire magic industry of mystical Jewish amulets, *kameyos*, that supposedly warded off the evil eye. The arch-rationalist Rambam, aware that the Torah bans "diviners, necromancers and soothsayers," because *hakol biy'dei shomayim,* "everything is in the hands of Heaven," was against this practice (claiming it borders on idolatry) but even he had to concede that amulets gave psychological comfort to the wearer (which is why the great 19th century German halachist, Rabbi David Hoffman, allowed amulets to be hung in rooms where Jewish women were in labor).

The Vilna Gaon and obviously the Zohar ("There is not one blade of grass in the whole world over which a star or planet does not preside") disagreed with the Rambam, insisting that some amulets and incantations are rooted in the Divine (often quoting the Song of Deborah, "The stars fought against Sisera," and the words of the great Rava, Talmudic sage, that "life, children and sustenance depend not on merit but on the stars"); and, don't *all* Jews say *mazel tov*, which means literally, "May you have a good planet!" — although the Rambam rationalists insist that the term *mazel* consists of the letters from *makom, z'man, la'asos*; i.e.: being in the right place (*makom*) at the right time (*z'man*) which leads to achieving something (*la'asos*), a nod not to heavenly "co-incidence" but to historical forces.

"The eye of the universe is man," wrote Perdichevsky, poet from Podolia-Germany, while the rabbis of the Talmud related to man's "stumbling" as "only with the eyes" (which led to the Rambam reminder in his 1195 *Letter to Marseilles*, "A man's eyes are in front, not behind!")

"Better to believe one eye more than two ears," mumbles a Yiddish proverb...

> *The Rosenberg's are driving down the road when they see two teenagers standing on the sidewalk holding up a sign, "The end is near! Turn yourself around now before it's too late!"*
>
> *Mr. Rosenberg instead speeds past them as his wife yells out the window, "Leave us alone you religious nuts!"*
>
> *Suddenly, from around the curve there is the sound of screeching tires, screams, and a big splash.*
>
> *"You know," one teenager says to the other, "Maybe we should change our sign to say, 'Bridge Out' instead?"*

The first seeds of universalism are beautifully enunciated in this parsha ("*All the families of the earth shall bless themselves by you*") with an echo of God's eternal unabrogated message to Jews and Gentiles, "I will bless those who bless you and he who curses you I will curse."

This is an interesting chronology: the Heavens curse the curser only *after* the fact, and bless the blesser *before* he blesses.

This powerful clarion call is sounded hundreds of years before the rise of the Hebrew prophets and their prophetic literature, making Avraham the "father of a multitude of nations," buttressed by a courageous advocacy of chutzpa that passionately argues universal justice and fairness. His soul-searching does not end in private meditation, or insulated academia; but as a self-appointed advocate for human rights, even in towns of hatred.

In his plea to God not to destroy the standard-bearers of coerced "sameness," the corrupt and immoral cities of Sodom and Gomorra, his legendary questioning ("Will You sweep away the innocent along with the guilty?") and criticism ("Shall not the Judge of all the world deal justly?") inspires a Divine agreement to partner with Avraham's earthly ethic: to desist if ten righteous people are found in the evil cities.

Are ten found? No (did you hear about the guy who sent ten different puns to friends, with the hope that at least one of the puns would make them laugh? Unfortunately, no pun in ten did).

The obvious question is this: why Avraham?

The Torah never explicitly explains Heaven's selection process that chooses only one person over ten generations (since Noach) to become the progenitor of the Jewish people — but leaves plenty of clues.

After establishing Avraham's prime role, the first outreach program in Jewish history, known as *koreh b'shem Hashem*, to call out in God's Name, the Haftarah has God calling Avraham, "my friend;" this is an unusual title reserved only for this patriarch, but apropos considering that its Hebrew root also forms the word "love."

Aguila, the English novelist, describes love as "the voice of God,

42

the rule of Heaven; "To live," shouted Ludwig Boerne, "is to love!" while Immanuel, 13th century poet of Rome, writing in his treatise *Machberet*, sees love as "the pivot of the Torah."

Thus it comes as no surprise that God gives practical marital advice to Avraham, "Whatever Sarah says to you, listen to her" — and *voila*, the rules of who-is-the-boss-in-the-Jewish-household are laid down forever.

> *Little Pinchas comes running home from classes, all excited that he got a part in the school play.*
> *"Mazel tov, that's wonderful," says his mother, "Tell me, mein kindt, what part are you playing?"*
> *"I'm playing a Jewish husband."*
> *"Pinchas," the mother scowls, "next time, make sure they give you a speaking role!!"*

The credo and protocol of Abrahamic teachings was pure *emunah*: that all will end well, that he is only a small cog in Tevye's vast eternal master plan, that life's travels and travails come with both fortune and misfortune, that all obstacles and adversaries are to be met with faith — and occasional quick thinking (as in passing his wife off as his sister when in danger of her being abducted into Pharaoh's harem.

God's new best "friend" earns his humble title by leading an unassuming life, treading a paragon path of humility (regarding himself as *afar v'eifer*, only "dirt and ashes"), punctuated by an ever-ready alertness (*zrizus*), a term for liveliness that is derived by combining the Hebrew *zehirus* ("meticulous care") with *neki'us* ("cleanliness"), to imply a life totally detached from sin, animated only with concern for others to whom he rushes to offer help.

Typical was Avraham's third day after his *bris milo*, when, even in pain, he refuses to designate tasks to a servant and runs to greet his guests in the sweltering heat with a determination of *ki hem chayeinu*, "without the slightest doubt."

He then "runs" again, to tell his wife to prepare a meal, and runs to the herd to choose a bull; showing an impressive old-age alacrity.

> *Beryl and Shmeryl, two elderly Jews are sitting in their rockers on the nursing home porch.*
>
> *Beryl decides to leave so he pushes himself out of the chair, slipping, grunting, groaning and straining for about ten long minutes, until finally getting up.*
>
> *As he begins to shuffle away, Shmeryl yells out, "Hey Beryl, ver ya running to?"*

All this runnin' around had a single purpose: to produce, and more important, accept sincere converts; which is why the Midrash uses this parsha as its basis for declaring that "God loves converts greatly."

What is truly surprising is that there is no "Complaints Department" in this week's parsha of obedience: Avram does not protest at a destiny that requires leaving his "land and kindred, birthplace and father's house" for a distant *terra firma* ("to the land I will show you"); nor does he rumble when told that his descendants will be enslaved for 400 years; nor when confronted by a terrible famine in his land of destiny, forcing him to descend to the licentious peninsula of Egypt; nor when that country's King, taken by his wife's beauty, makes advances at Sarai; nor when he is suddenly thrust into a regional conflict between the four marauding kings of Elam, Goyim, Shinar, and Ellasar (the causes of which remain unknown) in order to rescue, without thought of personal benefit, his brother's captive son Lot.

The daily Amida prayer, which matches each blessing with

a different Patriarch, reserves its conclusionary *brocho* ("And you will be a blessing") only for Avraham, causing the sainted Rabbi Elchanan Wasserman, a martyr of the Nazis, to conclude that only when Avraham's unique character traits are widespread will the Messiah arrive; however, the absence of complaining does not mean that Avraham was infallible: he was not, for like all humans the first Jew was human.

The classic 13th century Medieval commentator (*Ramban*) accuses him (of "accidental sin") for leaving God's land of "promise" (Israel) when faced with famine, and for placing his own wife in danger from Pharaoh's wiles (saved only by *nissim giluyim,* "open miracles"); in fact, it is no coincidence that the once affectionate dialogue between God and Avraham comes to an abrupt halt, resumed only after Avraham returns to the Holy Land.

This parsha also gives us the Torah's first armed conflict, a difficult but successful military battle in which Avraham frees his nephew Lot from terrorist captivity; an episode that lays the Halachic basis *against* a philosophy of pacifism, and leads to a famous Talmudic adage: *shluchei mitzvoh eynan nizokin,* that those who are in pursuit of a Godly command will come to no harm.

> *Ernie goes hunting in the jungle and stumbles on a huge dead dinosaur with a pigmy standing beside it.*
> *"Wow!" he says, amazed, "Did you kill that?"*
> *"Yep! Sure did!"*
> *"How? You're just a little guy! How'd ya kill such a huge beast?"*
> *"I killed it with me club."*
> *"How big is your club?"*
> *"There's about 60 of us."*

VAYERA
Houseguests and Fish

The title to this week's parsha is *Vayera*, "appear," which is what God does to Avraham, "in the plains of Mamre."

Why? What brings on this visit?

Avraham is convalescing, three days after his circumcision (*miloh*), Judaism's oldest ritual, the first mitzvoh given to the first Jew, and the only mitzvoh the Jews perform communally prior to entering the Holy Land

God's visit does two things: it "honors" Mamre, Avraham's close associate who makes his one and only appearance in the Torah for encouraging Avraham's act (in contrast to the negative attitude of his two other friends, Oner and Eshkol); and lays the Halachic foundation for the central mitzvoh of *bikkur cholim*, visiting the sick.

The numerical value of *bris* (which means covenant) is 612, add to that the commandment of *miloh* (from the verb *la'mul*), makes 613, the number of commandments in the Torah.

The Greek term for circumcision was *peritomei*; in early Latin *recutitus* (from the prefix *re-*, "back from," and *cutis*, "skin"); in the 4th century, Jerome invented a new Latin word *circumcisio*, from the verb *circumcaedere* ("to cut around"), which led to the English "circumcised."

The ritual was universally recognized as uniquely Judaic; Gentiles were known as the "uncircumcised ones."

The Latin poems of Horace have a fictional Jew called *Apella,* a bilingual pun that means "foreskinless" (from the Latin *pellis*, "skin," and the Greek prefix *a-*, "not"). Juvenal, a first-century satirist who called Jews "cloud worshipers" and Judaism a *superstitio* ("superstition") described the many Roman converts to Judaism as *quaesitum ad fontem solos deducere verpos*, "the circumcised [*verpus*]" who are accepted in their "desired fountains [i.e.: *mikvos*]."

And the opposite was true too: Martial, another first-century Roman satirist, describes how Menophilus, an assimilated Jew, *Dum ludit media populo spectante palaestra, delapsa est misero fibula: verpus erat!* "While he was in the middle of a game in the gym, off fell his jock strap in front of everyone: the poor man was circumcised!"

> *After Yossele moves into a Catholic neighborhood his neighbors are up in arms over his habit to barbecue steaks on Fridays, the day they are forced to eat fish. So they tell him if he wants to continue he should convert. So Yossele dutifully goes with them to the local priest who sprinkles holy water over him, solemnly intoning, "Born a Jew, raised a Jew, now a Catholic...born a Jew, raised a Jew, now a Catholic...."*
>
> *The Catholics return home ecstatic: no more tempting smell of delicious meat on Fridays.* ▶

> *But on the very next Friday they are shocked at the scent of barbecue again drifting through the neighborhood. They rush to Yossele's house to remind him of his new vows, and find him sprinkling water over a cooking steak, solemnly intoning, "Born a cow, raised a cow, now a fish…born a cow, raised a cow, now a fish…"*

A second mitzvoh, known as *hacnosos orchim*, welcoming the stranger with receptive enthusiasm, also has its basis in this week's parsha.

The Biblical equivalent of a welcome mat? Avraham sitting at his tent door under a blaring sun with open flaps on all sides, generously inviting passing strangers to enter, determined not to miss any opportunity of cordiality and hospitality.

"A dish tastes best, when shared with a guest," writes the 19th century German scholar Daniel Sanders, obviously influenced by the earlier sagely advise from Jose ben Kisma, "a little refreshment goes a long way; it's denial alienated two tribes, Amon and Moab" (adds Calvin Trillin, "The remarkable thing about my mother is that for 30 years she served us nothing but leftovers. The original meal has never been found!")

> *A mother was preparing pancakes for her three and five-year-old sons. When the boys begin to argue over who would get the first pancake, she sees an opportunity for a moral lesson. "Kinderlach! If Avraham were sitting here, he would say, 'Let my brother have the first pancake, I can wait.'"*
>
> *"Mum's right," says the older brother to the younger one, "You be Avraham!"*

The Midrash translates the term *eishel* in the verse, "And he planted an orchard [*eishel*]," as "a guest-house" erected for weary travelers, and sees it as an acronym of *achilah, sh'siyah, linoh,* to "eat, drink, and stay overnight" (an advantage, according to the insightful Yiddishists, who advise, "Fill your house with guests, and you'll marry off your daughter!")

Avraham's attitude was more than just good manners: in the harsh desert climate this bed 'n breakfast refuge saved nomadic lives, and served as the motivating factor for the rabbinic sage Huna to start each meal by shouting, *kol dichfin yaysay v'yechul,* "Let all who are hungry, come and eat" — an open invitation that opens the Haggadah, penned in Aramaic in order that the Aramaic-speaking masses would understand, and respond.

Avraham, now an active ambassador for the Jewish God, would gently explain to his satisfied guests that their scrumptious meal and unleavened "cakes" (*ugos matzos,* linguistically similar to Pesach food), was a gift from Heaven that deserved a hearty "thank you" (*yasher ko'ach*) not to man but to God. He exerts himself with not just "a morsel of bread" but an entire festive meal, displaying a willing-to-please attitude unheard of today.

When God's visit is interrupted by the sudden showing of three angels (*malochim*) masquerading as human messengers (*malach* implies "a messenger," or "agent"), the question is obvious: who needs them to advise Avraham of his future family when God was in the middle of His own conversation, about to relay the same message?

The rabbis explain that, in the aftermath of Avraham's circumcision, God was "checking up" on His recuperating "patient," simply to be there, *b'chvodi* (in His own glory), and witness the "new walk" of Avraham as a *yedid Hashem* (friend of God); the timing thus required the three angels to deliver their specific messages.

> *A Russian Jew goes into a new car dealership and buys a car. Knowing of the long delays, he asks, "Nu, how* ▶

long will it take for delivery?"
The salesman looks up his schedule and replies, "On May 17, 2009."
"Morning or afternoon?"
"Does the time matter?" the angry dealer snaps back, "It's five years away!"
"Sure it does! The plumber's coming that day!"

This parsha, the critical midpoint of the Avraham chronology, has more metaphysical angelogy than other parshas, as angels appear as guardians (saving Lot from a mob, leading Hagar's son to water); as healers (comforting Hagar during her terrifying experience); as preventors (stopping Avraham from sacrificing his son); or as messengers (telling Sarah she's with child, warning Lot of Sodom's imminent destruction, relaying God's intent to bless Avraham and his descendants; assuring Hagar that, despite being banished, "I will make a great nation of him [Ishmael]").

As "agents" of Heaven, this opens the debate as to what God's primary duties were: guardian, healer, preventor...?

An accountant, surgeon, philosopher, biologist and architect find themselves in a theological debate over what was God's real profession.
"God created Eve from Adam's rib," explains the surgeon, "so obviously God is a surgeon and thus medicine is the oldest profession."
"Not so," interrupts the philosopher, "first and foremost, God must be a philosopher because He created the principles by which man is to live."
"That's ridiculous!" argues the biologist, "let's not forget that before all of that, God created man, woman and all living things so clearly He was a biologist."
"Wrong, wrong!" the architect shouts, "God was a builder first! Before man He created the heavens and ▶

> the earth. Remember, in the beginning there was only com-
> plete chaos!"
> "And who," says the accountant proudly, "do you think
> helped Him arrange the chaos?"

The visiting angels are described by the Midrash as pagans "from the marketplace (who) bow down to the dust of their feet."

Does this bother their gracious host? No. In a benevolent mixture of the holy and the mundane, Avraham welcomes them into his home with such a natural manner that he proves that men and angels can coexist; subconsciously setting forth a revolutionary Torah maxim: by asking God to wait until he welcomes his guests, Avraham places the mitzvoh of hospitality on a greater level than maintaining the presence of the Divine (*kabolas p'nei Shechinoh*).

"Nowhere," notes Rabbi Leib Kagan, "does the Torah say, 'Invite your guest to pray;' but it does tell us to offer him food, drink, and a bed."

Mankind is divisible into two great classes: hosts and guests, writes Max Beebohm, 19th century British cartoonist, echoing Yehoshua ben Hanania's observation: the poor does for the host more than the host for the poor!

The Yiddishists were, as usual, cynical: "houseguests and fish," they declared, "spoil on the third day."

> A little ol' Jewish guy drops by Avraham's tent and asks
> for the soup du jour, which his host serves him with two
> slices of bread.
> "Nu, how was it?"
> "Vas goot," the ol' man replies, "but next time you
> could give a little more bread."
> The next day Avraham makes a point of giving him
> four slices, and then gently inquires, "Nu, how was ▶

> *your meal today?"*
>
> *"Vas goot, but next time you could give a little more bread."*
>
> *So the next day Avraham generously serves eight slices, and asks, "Nu, how was it today?" to which the reply is, again, "Vas goot, but you could give a little more bread."*
>
> *The following day Avraham is ready: he shleps out a giant ten-foot-long whole loaf of bread, cuts it in half, butters the entire length of each half, and serves it with a huge bowl of hot soup.*
>
> *The ol' man sits down, and devours it all.*
>
> *"Nu," asks a nervous Avraham, "How was it?"*
>
> *"It vas goot as usual...but I see you are back to giving only two slices!"*

This parsha also contains a lesson in humility when judging others: when raising the possibility of virtuous people in Sodom, Avraham uses the word *tzaddikim* ("righteous") but the Torah leaves out a letter (*yod*), implying that even the non-perfect pious deserve recognition ("There is no righteous person on earth who is completely righteous and never sins"); a point he emphasizes by cleverly urging God to look for them *not* in the shuls *nor* study halls but "in the city (*b'soch ho'ir*)."

This is thus the real test of righteousness: how one behaves in public, amidst the temptations; recognition that there is no such thing as infallibility...

In the opening scene of this parsha, God lays the groundwork for Avraham's propagation into a great nation, and a future of ethical monotheism.

God promises an aging Avraham, a man well into his 90's, a progeny from a childless Sarah, who is long past her child-bearing years ("Count the stars if you are able to count them; so shall be your descendants.")

> *Mimi marries at a late age and is concerned, so she asks her grandma, "Bubba, should I have a baby after thirty-five?"*
> *"No, thirty five children is enough!"*

God "took note [*pakad*] of Sarah" and lets Avraham in on a little secret: "Your wife shall bear you a son," a word of compassion to ease the anxiety that neither Rivka nor Rachel, who were also both barren, receive prior to their pregnancies.

The great Yisroel Meir Kagan (*Chofetz Chaim*) describes this episode as the basis for a latter rabbinic belief: *ma'aseh ovos siman l'bonim,* that what happens to the Founding Fathers is a sign of what will happen to their descendants (Remember: if your parents did not have any children, chances are you won't either!)

> *"I have great news for you," says Rosy, the excited newlywed, to her husband, "Pretty soon, we're going to be three in this house instead of two!"*
> *Her husband gives her a big hug and a kiss, glowing with happiness at the news.*
> *"Honey," she says, "I'm so glad you feel this way. Tomorrow, my mother moves in with us."*

Avraham, the stunned father-to-be, is then advised, a year in advance, to "name him Yitzchak," a term that Samson Raphael Hirsch notes is derived from *tzochek* ("laughter"), in that the very idea of such a late childbirth is laughable (or as the Yiddishists put it: "Blessed are those who laugh at themselves because they can never cease to be amused!")

Shmuel ben Meir (*Rashbam*) links the name 'Yitzchak' to the "joy" that must have surrounded such an astonishing turn of events, while his grandfather (*Rashi*) diverts the expression *mi* from, "Who

[mi] would believe that Sarah would suckle children," away from its derogatory cynical tone and places it in the complimentary context of deference and praise — as in mi chamochoh, "Who is like You, God!"

> "Wish me mazel tov," Mr. Kestenberg, a 95-year-old, tells his doctor during a routine checkup, "I just re-married and intend to have children."
>
> "Oh really? Tell me about her, is she recently widowed?"
>
> "Nope, never been married."
>
> "Is she in good health?"
>
> "She oughta be, she's only twenty three."
>
> "You know, Mr. Kestenberg, you gotta be careful, marrying a girl that age could be life threatening."
>
> "Well," he sighs, "If she dies, she dies."

CHAYEI SARAH
Aging Gracefully

> *"Tell me," the father asks a young yeshiva bochur who wants to marry his daughter, "How do you intend to support her? You have no profession, no trade, no skills?"*
>
> *"Zog zachnt nisht, don't worry," he replies, "Got vet helfen, God will provide."*
>
> *"But what about an apartment? How will you pay rent?"*
>
> *"Don't be concerned. Got vet helfen, God will take care of everything."*
>
> *"And personal affects? Jewelry, clothes, food, a car, baby things? Who will pay?"*
>
> *"Have no fear, Got vet helfen."*
>
> *"You know," the father says to his wife, "I'm taking this boy. He's called me God three times already!"*

Don't let the title of this parsha fool you: the *chayei* suggests a focus on the "life of" Sarah, however we are exposed more to her demise; a Judaic teaching that awareness of death gives meaning to life.

The Torah places Sarah's death in-between two joyous milestones: the birth of Rivka and the marriage of Yitzchak; a reminder to temper joy with a nod and a wink at the fragility of Life…

> *The Greenberg's go to see a popular Broadway play and manage to get prime front row seats. Surprised that the seat in front of them is empty, they lean over and ask the well-dressed woman, "Pardon me, but seats are in such demand, we were wondering how come this seat next to you is empty."*
>
> *"Oh," she replies, "That's my late husband's seat."* ▶

> *The Greenberg's, embarrassed, apologize for being so insensitive, and ask, "Surely you have a close friend, a relative or neighbor who would have loved to see the show with you?"*
>
> *"Oh, yes, I do, plenty…but they're all still at the shiva."*

When the parsha describes the 127 inspirational and exemplary "years of Sarah's life," it divides her righteous womanhood into three parts: "100 years, 20 years, 7 years."

Isn't this redundant? Technically, yes, but it is the Torah's desire to emphasize certain distinct qualities: that at 100, Sarah's lofty spiritual purity was "equal to a 20-year old," and at 20, her pristine physical beauty was "as wholesome as a seven-year-old."

There is nothing more enviable, notes 19th century Rabbi Daniel Sanders, than to have an old head and a young heart; to which Oscar Blumenthal, the German playwright, adds, "A man is as old as his wife looks!" Solomon Ibn Gabriol, an 11th century Spanish poet, described "folly" as disgraceful in an old man, while the Yiddish proverbs were adamant: an old man in a house is a burden; an old woman, a treasure!

> *"What are you doing, dear?" asks the husband to his wife who has been sitting in front of a mirror for hours.*
>
> *"Oh," replies Bettie, "I'm trying a new 'miracle' cosmetic, guaranteed to make me look years younger. Tell me honey, honestly, how old do I look?"*
>
> *"Well," he replies, "Judging from your skin, I'd say 20…your hair, mmmm, about 18…and your figure, twenty five."*
>
> *"Oh, you're so sweet!"*
>
> *"Wait! I'm not done yet. I need to add them all up!"*

This parsha advances a Judaic concept of aging; a stance against worthlessly swaying in rocking chairs, and a search for active grace and gentility.

Remember: both Avraham and Sarah's significant accomplishments are not in their youth but during the last quarter of their lives; fulfilling an old rabbinic adage, *ben orboyim l'vinoh, ben chamishim l'etzoh, uben shmonim l'gevuroh,* "At 40, one is fit for discernment; at 50, for counsel; at 80, for special strength."

> *"I'm worried," the aging Leah confides to her close friend Shifra, "I don't think my husband finds me attractive anymore. What about you?"*
> *"I guess I'm lucky," replies Shifra, "My husband says I get more beautiful every day I get older."*
> *"Yes, but your husband's an antique dealer!"*

Sarah is the only Jewess in the Torah who has both her age, and details of her burial place, revealed even though it has become politically incorrect to ask a woman her age...

> *When the lawyer asks Mrs. Rottenberg on the stand how old she is, she stubbornly remains silent. He asks her again, and again, to no avail.*
> *"You know," says the judge, "The longer you wait, the worse it gets!"*
> *But she remains mute, so the judge gives up, and declares, "The witness will state her age, after which she will be sworn in."*

This parsha is a boon for Jewish mystics and feminists: the numerology of the opening term *Vayih'yu,* (37) "And they were," is the same as the difference in Sarah's age from the time she gave birth to Yitzchak (90) to her death (127): thirty-seven intervening years that were surely the best years of her life, when she was raising a child, a blessing all parents can identify with.

That the parsha is named after Sarah speaks volumes of her importance to Jewish history; she is in fact the *only* woman in the entire Torah to be so honored: the others are all men; Noach, Yisro, Korach, Balak, Pinchos. And more: this parsha has a whopping impressive ratio (33%) of Jewish women in highly active roles, in comparison to the average number (7%) of female names in the Torah.

In general, other than in laws of inheritance (the daughters of Zelaphchod), the only Jewish women mentioned are either directly relevant to the story (e.g.: Rivka, Dina), or help differentiate sons born to different mothers (e.g.: Hagar, mother of Ishmael son of Avraham; Haggith, mother of Adonijah, son of David, etc); or, as in this week's parsha and Haftarah, their lives have specific important roles (e.g.: Rivka, Keturah, Avishag, Batsheba).

Sarah's demise occurs "in Kiryat Arba," and Avraham comes running from Beersheba, causing Rashi, the fundamental commentator on the Torah, to grapple with geo-chronologic difficulties.

Other Torah scholars interpret "Avraham arrives" not literally, but as a euphemism for immediately turning his attention to the task at hand: funeral arrangements. And since Sarah's is the first funeral recorded in the Torah, all future scholarly eyes are on her grieving husband to set the traditional Halachic tone.

The first thing Avraham does is eulogize, and only *afterwards* does he cry; and by using a miniaturized letter *kaf* within *livkos* ("to cry"), the innuendo, according to the 14th century Halachist Jacob ben Asher (the *Baal Haturim*) is that weeping be restrained, grief subdued, sorrow kept to a bare minimum.

> *The championship golfer is at a highly important point in his game, when he suddenly sees a funeral hearse drive by. He stops, lowers his head, puts his hat over his* ▶

heart, stands silent for a full minute — and then vigorously resumes the play.

The crowd is stunned; this sports star is not known for his sensitivity, so at the end of the game, a reporter shoves a microphone in front of him, and asks, "Hey, how come you stopped your game at such a critical moment?"

"You know, we were married for 35 years, it's the least I could do."

Avraham's life is also divided into three parts, to accentuate the continuity of a flawless spiritual repute, but this parsha does not use similar language (e.g.: *shnei chayei Avrohom*, "the years of Avraham's life") to illustrate his death at 175 years. Why? Because the passing of Sarah has a special "closing" and meaning, laying the Midrashic foundation that for righteous people, death is the pinnacle of perfection, in that the pious die with a peaceful certainty of eternal reward in a world to come (*olam habo*).

Avraham's singular search for spirituality has been shared by Sarah, his partner and equal, a woman always ready for self-sacrifice — whether criss-crossing the countryside, uprooted from her native country, childless till 90, subjecting herself to sexual advances, held captive by Gentiles kings (*twice*) even allowing another woman, her maid (Hagar, an Egyptian woman of royalty) to bear her husband's child in order that he have a son.

And she even subjects herself to her husband's lies: Avraham calls his wife his sister as a form of self-protection, afraid that her beauty would motivate the King's gangs to kill him in order to take her. Our sages (*Ramban*) are horrified, and castigate the first patriarch for a deception that puts a wife's honor at risk; Avraham's attempt at self-justification, "She is indeed my sister, the daughter of my father but not the daughter of my mother, and so she became my wife" (a "half-sister marriage" that is prohibited by Jewish law but not by the Seven Noachide Laws) but this is, according to Rashi, only metaphorically correct. Why? Since grandchildren are considered one's children, she is regarded as Terach's child and therefore Avraham's "sister."

How was Sarah able to sustain such die-hard endurance?

By approaching life with a basket of optimism, and an inner core of tranquility that helps her deal with adversity.

Sarah's absence is followed by three stories, told in painstaking detail, in stark contrast to the Torah's traditional rule of terseness: Avraham's acquisition of a burial plot in Hevron's Cave of the Couples (*Ma'aras Hamachpeloh*, Tomb of the Patriarchs, the world's most ancient Jewish site and, after the Temple Mount in Jerusalem, the second holiest place for the Jewish people), his search for a daughter-in-law, and a second marriage to Ketura (with whom he has six more sons).

This trio of tales is all we know of the last 38 years of Avraham's vigorous life, yet they share a common theme: continuity, the securing of the future.

Ensuring a wife for his son guarantees an ongoing family; by sending his six children from his second wife away ("eastwards," toward Mesopotamia) he dramatically announces that Yitzchak, and Yitzchak alone, is his *only* spiritual heir; and finally, the buying of a grave site, the critical first parcel of real estate ever purchased in the promised land, is an act which inaugurates Israel's foothold in the Holy Land for generations to come.

The death of Avraham's wife is more than just a transition of matriarchs (from Sarah to Rivka) and patriarchs (from Avraham to Yitzchak); it represents the death of an alliance, for despite his relative longevity, the shadow of the first patriarch and his leadership begins to disappear after Sarah's death.

"Without Sarah," writes J.B. Soloveitchik (the *Rav*), "Avraham takes leave of the world stage."

Sarah's composure had helped ensure the successful future of the Abrahamic dynasty, which is why she was such a perfect mate — in both life and in death, for it was her passing that forces Avraham to set his house in order.

Marriage equates to a Judaic future which is rooted in a past, requiring grandchildren to follow the faith of their grandparents; thus the Torah insists on characterizing deaths in terms of the living (e.g.: "the life of Sarah," and *Vayechi*, "he [Yaacov] lived"), and derives the name Rivka from the same Hebrew root as *hakever* (*kever* in Hebrew meaning both "grave" and "womb").

The lesson is this: when deciding on a spouse, one must step back and absorb the larger picture. One is marrying not just an individual but a family package.

How to find your bashert?

> *There are 3,292,393,157,375,253,593 beings in this universe.*
>
> *3,292,393,151,307,561,583 of those are angels, seraphim, aliens, creatures, cartoon characters, and imaginary friends. That leaves 6,067,692,010 available human earthlings you can date! Jews currently represent 1/5 of 1% of the world's population. That leaves about 13,000,000 people you can pick from. Of the 13,000,000 Jews available, 50% are not quite the gender you're looking for. That leaves 6,500,000. Plenty of Jews are currently dating, plenty of Jews are already married, plenty others aren't dating yet. So we can eliminate 2/3 of what's available. That leaves about 2,166,666 people.*
>
> *There are several categories of Judaic practice. In no particular order whatsoever, they are: Reform, Conservative, Orthodox, Yeshivish, Litvish, Chassidish, Black hatters, Kippa Srugarians and Young Israelites. Since no one should be dating outside of their category — lest they suffer from community gossip — we can eliminate 8/9 of what's left. That leaves 240,740 people. 4/5 of what's left don't have the funds, transportation or* ▶

61

desire to date anyone not from their continent. 48,148 left over. 3/4 of what's left are nowhere near your age. That leaves 12,037 people. 2/3 of those are too lazy to date anyone located more than 50 miles away. That leaves 4,012 people. Of those 1/2 are waiting for love to find them. They can wait. That leaves 2,006 people. 6 Jews are too cheap to pay the tolls. Of the 2,000 people left over, you will never hear of 3/4 of them. 500 people are left over. Let's assume that 500 is the maximum amount you'll ever get "ret" to you in your entire lifetime. Of these 500, 50 will be too tall for you to ever go out with, 50 will be too short, 50 won't go out with you because some friend of theirs told them not to go out with you, 50 won't go out with you because some friend of YOURS told you not to go out with them, 40 are too Reform/Conservative/Orthodox/Yeshivish/Litvish/Chassidish/Black Hatty/Kipa Srugy/Young Israeli.

40 aren't Reform/Conservative/Orthodox/Yeshivish/Litvish/Chassidish/Black Hatty/Kipa Srugy/Young Israeli enough/and 10 simply give your mother a "bad vibe."

Now let's assume that 200 people is the maximum that a person will ever date. Of these 200, 9/20 will reject you, and you'll never know why, 1/20 will dump you with a pretty good reason. 100 left. Let's assume that with what's left over, YOU get to decide what to do. 10 are too dumb, 10 are too smart, 10 have an attitude, 10 you have hashkafa problems with, 10 you're not attracted to, 10 you have nothing in common with, 10 are too self-centered, 10 are hyper, 10 did weird stuff on your date that you didn't approve of. Of the remaining 10, 5 you share no chemistry with, one is a fruitcake, one is nutty, one scares you for no particular reason, one should be locked up, and one belongs in Bellevue.

That leaves your bashert!

Avraham's preferred method to find a daughter-in-law was to send "the oldest servant of his house," an unnamed faithful emissary, who the Midrash reveals as Avraham's confidante, the imposing Eliezer of Damascus, to return to his former Mesopotamia home (Aram Naharaim.)

Eliezer becomes the first shadchan of Judaism, a term which means "to persuade," or "to negotiate."

As a distinct profession, *shadchanus* ("matchmaking") dates from the time of the Crusades, when Jewish life was so disrupted that parents worried that their children, especially daughters, would remain unmarried or kidnapped.

The shadchan's little dog-eared book ("the social register of the shtetl") became his most valuable asset. It was a perfect side-line for rabbis in the Middle Ages who received no salaries and had to seek "subsidiary" income (e.g.: the Maharil was a highly esteemed marriage broker), and the Halachic responsa of the times shows an increase on the subject (e.g.:, how much of a fee should a shadchan claim? what happens if the marriage is canceled? etc).

> *Frankie bumps into his rabbi on the way home from shul one evening, "Nu, rabbi, how was your day?"*
> *"Today, boruch Hashem, I made seven hearts happy."*
> *"Wow, that's great! Seven hearts? How'd you do that?"*
> *"I performed three marriages."*
> *"Three weddings? Isn't that six hearts?"*
> *"What do you think? I do this for free?!"*

This process is obviously important to God. How do we know?

Because the search for a bride is long and drawn-out: in fact, more space is dedicated in this week's reading to the patriarch's re-petitive conversations with his right-hand man, a *"z'kan baiso,"* than the sections of laws and rituals.

The Midrash, acknowledging that this focus seems disproportional, makes the stunning statement that at times "stories" (i.e.: narrative) take precedence over "teachings" (Torah laws); especially so in the case of Eliezer, described as *Damesek Eliezer,* from *doleh u'mashkeh*, in that he "drew up the waters" of Torah and gave others to drink (the Midrash credits him with being one of only nine who do not die but ascend to Heaven, alive).

Eliezer's daily routines were within the spiritual stratosphere of Avraham and thus the words, acts, and animation of this "servant" are momentous "clues" to the very genesis of authentic Judaism, prior to Sinai.

That it takes 67 Torah verses to describe Avraham's efforts to find a daughter-in-law, implies that fathers should take an active involvement in their children's dating habits.

What was Eliezer looking for?

Turning aside the traditional position of Proverbs ("grace is deceptive, beauty illusory"), the rabbis choose the eyes ("Any bride who has goodly eyes, need not be checked regarding the rest of her.")

Why?

Rabbi Shlomo Ephraim Lunschitz (*Kli Yakar*) explains this metaphorically: Eliezer was out to see if Rivka "looked" kindly on others, an act of goodness that dovetails into the Hebrew *ba'alas ayin yafo*, "the possessor of a good eye," an expressive interpretation of the Talmudic dictum that one who has "goodly eyes" is sure to be kind.

Avraham's sole criteria in choosing a wife, the future mother (*eim*) of the Jewish people, centers not on the physical nor material (known as *gashmius*) but on the spiritual (*ruchniyus*); specifically that she not only have *chesed*, but be a *lover* of chesed, an indication of the presence of complete grace, selflessness, kindness, benevolence (*gemilas chassadim*).

> • "Yeshiva bochur, Torah scholar, long beard, payos. Seeks same in woman"
> • "Female graduate student, studying Kaballah, Zohar, exorcism of dybbuks. No weirdoes, please" ▶

> • *"Jewish businessman, manufactures Sabbath candles, Chanukka candles, Havdala candles, Yahrzeit candles. Seeks non-smoker"*
> • *"Jewish princess, 28, seeks successful businessman of any major Jewish denomination: hundreds, fifties, twenties"*
> • *"Orthodox woman with get, seeks man who got get, or can get get. Get it?"*

Rivka, granddaughter of Milcah, wife of Avraham's brother Nahor, displays these qualities the moment she compassionately draws water not only for the "road-weary servant," but also runs to quench the thirst of his ten camels. Another lesson? Actions speak louder than words.

Against her family's wishes the bride-to-be accepts the offer, using an aggressive Torah term, *aileich* ("I will go") rather than a straight "yes" (*hein*), a response which convinced the Mizrachi, an insightful commentator on Rashi, of her forthright decisiveness, an important quality in maintaining spousal communication ...

> *Sammy comes home from work angry at his wife that dinner's not ready, "You're gonna be sorry," he yells at her, "I'm gonna leave you one day!"*
> *"Make up your mind! Which one's it gonna be!" she yawns back.*

In the Torah's first real estate transaction Avraham buys not a commercial building or an apartment complex, but one field and a double cave in Hevron ("an estate for a burial site.")

And, wonder of wonders, the first Jew pays retail! — or as the Torah puts it, *kesef molei*, the "full price," after turning down an offer from Efron the Hittite (the seller) for a free site.

Efron, in a phony display of graciousness, then inflates the price, which, according to Yehudah ben Pazi, a famous homilist and 3rd-generation Amora, was paid in weight, the equivalent of "400 silver shekels".

The seller's greed does not escape the Torah terminology: when his name first appears it is spelled with the letter *vav,* but not this time; the gematria of Efron less a *vav* is 400, which equals the gematria of *roh ayin* ("evil eye"), an observation of his low moral stature, derived from the Mishna's *ayin horoh* which according to Rabbi Joshua describes the evil power of human selfishness and envy (the opposite is "*ayin tovah*", a good eye).

Avraham strangely introduces himself to his new neighbors, the children of Heth, as, "I am an alien and a resident among you" (*ger v'soshav anochi imochem*), a self-definition that is an inherent contradiction: either a local citizen or a stranger: which one was it?

The formidable J.B. Soloveitchik (the *Rav*), a 20th century American Torah giant, sees in the patriarch's overture the dual nature of Jewish existence: nothing less than *the* fundamental guideline of non-Jews as to how a Jew should function in modern society; as a physical "resident" he is assuring non-Jews that he intends to be a fully functioning, affiliated, law-abiding citizen (a "*soshav*"), within the context of remaining a spiritual "stranger," inherently distinct, courtesy of the monotheistic laws and lores of the Jewish God.

> *Peering over the fence, Izzie tries to strike up a good ol' neighborly conversation with his neighbor's little boy filling a hole in the garden.*
> *"Hey Eli, what are you up to," he asks.*
> *"My goldfish died and I've just buried him," Eli yells back.*
> *"So how come you need such a big hole for a little goldfish?"*
> *"Because he's inside your cat!"*

Battle of the Blessing

One hot day, a hat-seller in Poland gets tired shlepping his basket of hats to the market and stops to take a short nap in the woods. When he wakes he discovers that all his hats are gone, and sees a group of monkeys in the tall tree above him wearing them. As he thinks of how to get his hats back, he notices that when he scratches his head the monkeys do the same. So he takes off his own hat, and they copy him and take off their hats. He then throws his hat on the ground and the monkeys do that too. So he quickly runs around, picks up all his hats, and runs off to the market place, laughing as to how stupid the chimps are.

Fifty years later, his grandson, also a hat-seller, hears this tale from his grandfather. Then one day, the grandson is on his way to the markets and passes through the same forest. It is very hot so he takes a nap under the very same tree, and awakes later to discover his hats stolen. He looks up and lo and behold, the monkeys had taken all the hats. He remembers his zeida's words, starts scratching his head and the monkeys follow. He then takes off his hat and starts fanning himself, and again the monkeys follow. He then throws his hat on the ground, just like his grandfather did, but to his shock the monkeys do not copy his movement, and instead start clutching their hats.

One chimp then climbs down the tree, grabs the hat on the ground, gives him a slap, and says, "Hey! You think you're the only one who had a grandfather?"

This week's parsha, *Toldos*, means "descendants" and is derived from the Hebrew root, to "bring forth," or "beget," as in producing progeny.

Yitzchak is last seen under his father's sharp blade atop Mt. Moriah, but suddenly reappears, quietly digging wells in Gerar, the capital of Philistine.

In fact, he is busy *redigging* (and renaming) the same wells his father once dug on his way to Beer Sheva. Yitzchak is making a powerful case: that, despite the trauma of his *Akeida* episode, tradition must be reclaimed in order to preserve tradition (*shalsheles hakabboloh*).

This symbolism is powerful and deeper than any well: the Philistines had intentionally filled the water holes with earth, a physical barbaric act in a desert landscape, in order to keep Yitzchak away from wells named after God. Avraham's desire was to remind a heathen populace that whenever they needed water, obviously a common occurrence in the desert, to first recognize the existence of God.

The Midrash thus sees Yitzchak's "digging" as a metaphor for "sowing," nourishing the seeds of Torah with the sustenance water of his father's religious insights.

Is Yitzchak an innovator, originator? No. But a guardian, yes; charged with conveying a paramount didactic Torah principle that the life-giving examples of forefathers are to be "impressed upon children."

By honoring his father's memory, notes 13th century Egyptian Chief Rabbi Avraham ben HaRambam, Yitzchak displays a clear purpose in life: not just to amass wealth from flocks and sheep, but to become a faithful covenantal carrier and servant of God (*eved Hashem*), trusted with one legacy and one legacy only, Jewish continuity.

This parsha is a dramatic tale of family and kinship, of intrigue and jealousy; a unique snapshot of the fractious, complex world of the house of Yitzchak as it erupts onto the opening stages of our national history.

Yes, the illustrious Yitzchak may have lived in an *ohel* (tent), yet it was Yaacov, father of 12 sons, whose tribes ultimately merge into the House of Yaacov (now known as "the Jewish people"), who used his skills to move his people into a more solid structure, a *bay-is* (house), thus founding a nation out of the family that Avraham had initiated and Yitzchak had guarded.

Yet despite all the attention, we never really get to know Yitzchak, the world's first second-generation Jew and most passive of the three patriarchs; the rabbis of Pirkei Avos crown this spiritual Jew as *the* personification of might (*gevurah*); his strength being defined in Torah terms, as self-control, discipline, "one who conquers his passions."

Incredibly, his entire biography is condensed into this one parsha, and even here Yitzchak seems to be playing a cameo "walk-on" role, cast as an unlikely hero whose needs are always being subordinated to those of others. Rabbi Moshe ben Maimon (*Rambam*) calls him a loner, uninterested in maintaining a circle of disciples, satisfied with a single student: his son, Yaacov.

This is understandable: Jewish history finds Yitzchak sandwiched between an intense father figure (Avraham) with a revolutionary new spiritual vision, and a determined son (Yaacov-Israel) who is busy reconstructing a family into nationhood; Yitzchak's primary claim to Judaic fame is thus generational: he is *the* biological progenitor of the entire Jewish nation, and the only patriarch who never leaves Israel.

The 19th century *Mei Hashilo'ach*, a charismatic Chassidic Rebbe, credits the contemplative Yitzchak as being the source of a rabbinic concept known as *ma'aseh ovos siman l'bonim*, that the actions of forefathers pave the way for descendants (the shortened adage being, *z'chus ovos*, "the merit of our forefathers"); a "trickle down" theory, that God's stream of compassion continues to spill out into less worthy generations *only* because of the inherited spiritual excellence of their forefathers and mothers.

"You know," says the happy bride to her new husband after the chuppa, "one of the reasons I married you was because your father is so thoughtful, generous and compassionate. It's so wonderful to see, after thirty years of marriage, that he still brings your mother a hot cup of coffee every morning in bed."

"Yep, that's my dad."

"Isn't that an inherited quality?" asks the newlywed.

"Yep, sure is," he replies, "Luckily however, I take after my mother."

The parsha begins with Yitzchak pleading "on behalf of his wife" (*l'nochach ishto*) for the wonderful gift of life.

To refrain from begetting, notes Eleazar ben Azariah, a Palestinian *Amora* from the fourth century, is "to impair the Divine image;" while the rabbis of the Talmud pitied "a childless person" who they likened "to the dead," and the Psalmist sang, "Lo, children are a heritage of God: happy is the man that has his quiver full of them!"

Yitzchak uses an expression of prayer (*vaye'etar*) which the Talmud compares to the way a pitchfork (*eter*) "turns the grain over," in that the tears of a childless patriarch so penetrated the "far side" (*yarkesayim*) as to shake up Heaven's mercy and reverse ("turn over") the harsh reality of a 20-year barrenness.

Rivka is one of seven in the Torah's "childlessness" club (*akoros*) who all eventually bear sons by special grace; their impending births disclosed either by an angel, prophet, or God. Why? Because offspring "from heaven" have a special calling in life — yet, Rivka's case is significantly different.

The Torah consistently details the misery of mothers, but spares not a single word of sympathy for her. And more: whereas Sarah suggests a surrogate, Rivka does not; Hannah cries and prayers to God, Rivka does not; compare Rachel's heartbreaking, "Give me children, or else I die," a despair of life itself to Rivka's heavyhearted, "If so, why do I exist?" despair of barrenness.

In fact, this is the only incident in the entire Torah where the father, and *not* the mother, actively agitates for a son. Why is Yitzchak so anxiety-ridden? Unlike the other patriarchs who had secondary wives, Yitzchak's unique monogamous relationship threatens to terminate the family line.

After Rivka realizes she is pregnant and will give birth to twins; she is faced with a painful, rambunctious fetal motion ("the children agitated within her"), she is as frightened at the idea of having and raising children than not having them at all. She is obviously aware, notes the Kli Yakar, a 16th century Torah commentator, that Hagar had given birth to a non-righteous son (Ishmael), but in Avraham's case the heir was predetermined.

Not so in her case, wherein a successor becomes much more problematic since, with only one wife, either son of Yitzchak's is a legitimate claimant to be the bearer of Jewish destiny.

> *Getting away from her messy divorce Saidie goes on vacation to a desert island where, while walking along the sandy beach, she accidentally kicks a magic lamp, and out pops a genie.*
>
> *The genie patiently listens to Saidie as she vents her troubles. He then tells her that he will give her three wishes to help cheer her up but, since he is against divorce, he cautions her that he will give her ex-husband ten times whatever she wishes.*
>
> *Saidie thinks this is harsh yet goes ahead anyway: her first wish is for a billion dollars (her ex gets ten billion dollars); her second wish is for a beautiful mansion on the beach (her ex gets ten mansions).*
>
> *Saidie is beside herself in anger at the sight of her ex-husband's sudden good fortunes, so she takes her time contemplating her final wish, and then, with a smile on her face, turns to the genie and says, "For my last wish, I'd like to give birth to twins!"*

Rivka's maternal concerns come tragically true.

The struggle in the womb and the birth of twin sons (Esav and Yaacov) is the origin of a deadly sibling rivalry that continues to reverberate in history. Rashi, the father of all Torah exegetes, derives "struggle" from the Hebrew root of "run" ("and her sons ran [*vayisrotztzu*] around in her womb"), and traces the genesis of disorder to each fetus's natural tendencies; Yaacov "struggles" to emerge when his mother passes synagogues or schools, in contrast to Esav's longing which stirs towards idolatrous temples.

This is why Yaacov is described in glowing terms, an *ish tam*, a *yoshev ohalim*, a respectable man of "wholeness" (or "perfection") who "dwelt in [the Torah-enveloped] tents of Shem and Ever."

The charismatic Reb Nachman of Breslov concluded that the womb struggle symbolizes conflict between people's predispositions and their souls; Yaacov's propensity was to do good (*yetzer tov*), Esav's to do evil (*yetzer horo*)." Not so, claims the 16th century Maharal of Prague, a seminal figure in Jewish thought, who, in contradiction to the Rambam's embrace of free will, denies that any inclinations, good or evil, appear before birth, arguing that the twins represent not in-born personality traits but opposing cosmic forces entwined since creation and destined never to coexist (like fire and water.)

Meanwhile, the 16th century halachist, Moshe Isserles (*Rema*), sees the Yaacov-Esav clash in the womb (followed by only two face-to-face meetings in the entire Torah), as a timeless environmental lesson in logic that the dominant culture *always* dominates: children raised in an atmosphere of idol worship will become idol worshipers; children surrounded by Torah will become Torah scholars.

The names of the twins reflect their essence.

Esav's name is derived from a Semitic root *seir* meaning "thick-haired," however the Midrash links it to the Hebrew *asui*, which means "fully formed, complete [at birth];" a reference to his emergence from the womb as a "mature" infant, with a full head 'n body of hair, whereas 'Yaacov' relates to the Hebrew word *eikev* (Yaakov), which means "heel."

Ovadiah Sforno, 16th century Italian Torah commentator, relates to "heel," being at the end of the body, as a positive Yaacov attribute, a nuance for, "he will remain at the end," suggestive of persistence and adaptation; grabbing his brother's heel symbolizes Yaacov's tenacious and prolonged struggle to win the birthright.

> *One day a Jew runs across the street and taps another Jew on the shoulder, "Yossie, Yossie! Remember me? It's so good to see you after all these years! But Yossie, look at you! What happened? You used to be short and fat, and now you're tall and thin!"*
>
> *"I'm sorry," replies the man, "you must be mistaken, my name is not Yossie, it's Cliff."*
>
> *"So, Yossie, you changed your name, too?"*

The Midrash develops this prenatal struggle into a lethal ideological conflict filled with perpetual strife, independent of time and circumstance, between the two nations that the twins will beget. This leads to the rabbinic practice of using eponymous ancestors as the symbolic source of the eternal anti-Amalekite struggle of Israel, seeing the gory hand of Esav's descendants in Hadrian Caesar's Rome, expulsions in England, tortures in Spain, genocides in Germany, intifadas in the Holy Land.

All Torah commentators rely on God's (unexplained) hostile attitude to Esav ("I loved Yaacov, but Esav I hated"), as proof that the Israelite is the chosen one; and justify Yaacov's birthright "swindle" as a matter of sheer national existence.

Rabbeinu Bachya, a classic 14th century Torah commentator, summarizes Esav's misanthropic personality problems in one word: priorities, the subordination of serving God to impulsive love, thereby becoming a skilled *ish yodea tzayid ish sadeh*, "man of the field who knows hunting;" in contrast to his brother who embraces spirituality as *the* predominant goal.

> *One day a little ol' Jewish man is sitting on a park bench, minding his own business, reading the morning paper — when suddenly a great big dude walks up and whack!!, knocks him to the floor, boasting, "That was a karate chop from Korea!"*
>
> *The little ol' Jewish guy tries to ignore the incident, picks himself up, sits back down and resumes reading the paper — when suddenly, whack!!, another knock from the big dude returns him to the ground again, boasting, "That was a judo chop from Japan!"*
>
> *So the little ol' Jewish guy gets up, brushes himself down, and quietly walks away. A few minutes later he returns, walks up to the bid dude and wham!!, knocks him cold, saying, "That was a crowbar from Sears!"*

Blessings play a major role in this brief 106-verse parsha, its Hebrew root (*boruch*) appearing no less than 34 times.

But this week's "Battle of the Brocho [Blessing]" (*boruch* is derived from *braicha*, "wellspring;" a proclamation that God is the source of everything) over who has rights to primogeniture benefits, one of the most controversial and complex episodes in the entire Torah, with such major anti-Torah behavior as shameless lying (Yaacov to his father), bold defiance (Rivka to her husband), deceit, theft and the glorification of false and misleading representation.

Yitzchak had only one last dying wish, to confer the *noblesse oblige* blessing to his beloved "nature boy," the son with a ruddy complex and ravenous appetite. And why not? Wasn't Esav the first born? Didn't he have the stronger claim? Yes and no.

Torah linguists have pored over the parsha's syntax, and find it ambiguous, specifically Rivka's prophecy (*verav ya'avod tzair*) which can be read as either, "the elder will serve the younger," or "the elder, the younger will serve him;" but the Ramban sees no ambiguity. He claims that Esav's subservience to Yaacov is unequivocal; a conclusion not shared by Rabbi David Kimhi (*Radak*) who is intrigued by the Torah's absence of an *es* (the "object" which usually precedes the subject), thus making multiple interpretations of the words *rav* (older) and *tza'ir* (younger) possible.

Blind, and approaching death, Yitzchak was aware of three things: that his days were numbered ("Behold, I have become old"), that "I know not the day of my death" — and *im lo achshav eimosai*, "if not now, when?"

> *"How old was your father when he died?" asks the insurance agent of Mendel.*
> *"He was 65."*
> *"And what did he die of?"*
> *Mendel was embarrassed, his father was a no-good thief who had been hung, so he slowly replies, "My father came to his end…uh, mmm, while participating in a public function when the platform suddenly and tragically gave way."*

It is unclear from where Yitzchak gets the motivation for pre-death, first-born blessings, which only transfer rights and responsibilities for the clan's material and spiritual welfare to the eldest child.

Did Yaacov receive a first-born blessing from his own father? No.

Are there any other parental blessings prior to this parsha? Yes, but only one: when Rivka is about to leave home to marry a man sight unseen, her mother (and brother) see her off with, "O sister! May you grow into thousands of myriads; may your offspring seize the gates of their foes." This is still the traditional pre-nuptial

blessing given today for Jewish brides, expressing similar conflict-
ing parental emotions of hope and fear, in seeing their girls leave
the familial nest.

Is the fact that Yitzchak was blind significant? Yes; it is a deprivation of an important sense, a tragic personal tension that coincides with his family's disintegration. How did he go blind, and
when? No one knows. One Midrash traces it to the smoke of the
neighborhood's idolatrous practices, another even refuses to accept
his blindness as a "medicinal" (physical) fact, claiming the patriarch, helpless in old age and facing a confrontational, dysfunctional
family, retreated into a self-inflicted "spiritual" blindness;

> *"Doctor, I need your help," complains Yossele, "I think
> I'm losing my sight, and rather than meet people and be
> embarrassed, I end up talking to myself a lot."*
>
> *The doc examines Yossele and finds nothing wrong
> with his eyes. "Do you suffer any pain?" he asks.*
>
> *"No."*
>
> *"Well, in that case, go home and don't worry. Millions
> of people talk to themselves..."*
>
> *"But doctor," cries Yossele, "you don't know what a
> nudnik I am!"*

Yet there is no denying it: taking advantage of a vulnerable
"blind father" was a mischievous act that the Torah, surprisingly,
neither condemns nor justifies. The Heavens had reaffirmed the
spiritual larceny ("The voice is the voice of Yaacov, yet the hands are
the hands of Esav"), but they leave us wondering whether morally
dubious means in order to achieve righteous ends is acceptable, but
not without hinting that Yaacov's problematic performance represents a contradiction, desecration and corruption of his very existence as a flawless man of "special purity" (*ola temimo*).

Perhaps that is why history is not kind to the third patriarch, who does not escape retribution. Yaacov's life becomes complicated, his problems exasperated by…deceit! Not surprisingly, worry was Yaacov's middle name; the bearer of the mantle of Avraham didn't have it easy: he was forced to leave his fathers house, never to see his mother alive again, destined to struggle with his brother, his father-in-law (Lavan), troublesome children, and an angel. Yet, against all the odds, he quietly prevails.

> *The folkspeople of Chelm were natural born worriers so they called a meeting to discuss what to do about the problem. They decided to hire Shmuli, the town cobbler, to be the sole Jew in town authorized to worry on behalf of the whole community. They then agreed to pay him a weekly salary of 5 rubles when suddenly the rebbetzin stands up and objects, "If Shmuli earns 5 rubles a week, what would he have to worry about?"*

In an ironic taste of his own medicine, Yaacov is tricked into marrying the wrong woman (Leah, not Rachel), and then "sentenced" to spend twenty long, exploitative years with the master deceiver of them all, Lavan, his father-in-law.

To return to the blessing: isn't this the most bizarre bidding in history?

Esav barters away eternal spiritual values to satisfy a transitory physical hunger, reducing the value of a birthright to a bowl of lentil stew (*adoshim*), a traditional food of mourning which Rashi links to the *seudas havoroh* following the funeral of Avraham; its color being the source of the term, Edomite (from *adom*, "red.")

This incident concludes: "And he ate, and he drank, and he got up and he left," four verbs in a row; the Yiddishists interpret it pejoratively for anyone who "eats like Esav: he breaks bread without washing, he drinks wine without a blessing, he gets up without the grace after meals, he leaves without saying thank-you."

By paying attention only to the gratification of the moment, the Steipler Gaon, a 20th century Torah giant, claims that Esav later regrets his choice, and cries "a great, bitter cry" in anguish; Yitzchak demands "savory food" before he gives his blessing, and the Torah records that his request comes from the soul. Yet, Yitzchak, in his desire to bless and transmit his spirituality to the next generation, wanted to do so with all his strength, which required eating beforehand.

> As Saul lay dying he smelled a familiar aroma waffling in to the bedroom from the kitchen. "Zissale," he cries out to his wife, "is that your famous kugel that I smell? The one I have always liked?"
> "Yes," she responds from the kitchen.
> "Zissale, my dear Zissale," cries out the dying husband, "can I please have just one last piece of my favorite food before I die?"
> "No," she yells back, "it's for after the levaya! (funeral)."

Man on the Run

This weeks parsha is called *Vayetzei*, "and [Yaacov] left," a rather passive way of describing a man on the run, in flight from his parents' home in Beersheba, terrified of what his enraged brother (Esav) might do to him for his betrayal.

The Torah's terminology is purposeful: Yaacov might be running to Lavan's house, as in "escaping," but the literal translation is also true: the third and last patriarch has in fact "left" the fold and is about to confront destiny, "arriving" on the stage of Jewish history as the leader of a great nation.

The Ramban, the master 13th century Spanish Torah commentator, views this parsha as a classic story of spiritual awakening, a glimpse of the future relationships between the nations of the world and the Jewish people Yaacov (symbolic of the Jews) comes across a well covered by a large stone, surrounded by thirsty sheep whose shepherds (symbolic of the nations) are not strong enough to lift the stone. Despite his weariness, Yaacov lifts it and shares the water (symbolic of Torah) which satisfies their thirst (of God's knowledge).

Why is he fleeing? Yaacov is concerned not to expose his children to the seductive influence of Lavan's nefarious culture. Yaacov's uncompromising faithfulness to the (613) mitzvot; a conclusion of such theological significance that it finds its way into the Haggadah ("Pharaoh sought to annihilate only the males, while Lavan sought to uproot everything.")

This parsha is one of only two (the other is *Mikeitz*) that is presented in a continuous narrative form, without any breaks, except before the initial, and final, word. It describes the formative events in the life of a lonely Jew who leaves his familial familiarity, a warm and loving home for the still nights and the silence of the woods.

The umbilical cord from Yitzchak's oasis of spirituality has been cut.

Since metaphors are an integral part of the Torah, Yaacov's journey is immediately embraced by Torah scholars as a model of uncertainty in the journey of life, similar to Avraham's order to "go forth [*lech lecho*]."

Yaacov's time has come to face a "real" world, where materialism competes with religiosity, morality with the profane, where the days are full of challenges and obstacles, and the nights filled with doubts and confusion; that Yaacov's destination is called Charan is relevant: its Hebrew root is related to *charon*, "anger," a common trait for the traveler into the unknown.

> One morning Sophie arrives at the airline counter and asks the girl if she can buy a ticket that will fly her to Hawaii and her luggage to Dallas.
> "Sorry, miss, we can't do that."
> "Why not? You did it last time I traveled!"

Perhaps no other episode in the Torah has attracted such a wide range of interpretive philosophical exegesis as that of the illustrious ladder apparition ("Jacob's ladder"), a singular experience in the stillness of sleep that begins with ascending and descending angels, and ends with Yaacov finding God, "standing [*nitzav*] at the top of the ladder."

> *Izzy and Yankie are laying roof tiles one late afternoon when, all of a sudden, a gust of wind comes and blows away their ladder.*
> *"Now what do we do?" cries Izzy, "We're stuck!"*
> *"I have an idea," says Yankie, "I'll throw you down, and then you can put the ladder back up."*
> *"Hey, what do you think I am? Stupid? I have a better idea. I'll shine my flashlight, and you can climb down on the beam of light."*
> *"Oh no! Do you think I'm stupid? You'll just turn off the flashlight when I'm halfway there."*

It is Yaacov's first night in his brave new world, and ironically, although laden with fatherly blessings, he finds himself with no place nor shelter in all of Canaan, forced to form a "pillow" from several small stones and sleep on the hard ground.

This ladder episode has been a magnet for the greatest Torah minds, collectively grappling for its meaning: the Rambam sees a ladder of wisdom, the descending angels symbolically "bringing down" God's knowledge; the Abarbanel, 15th century scholar from Spain, disagrees, and imagines the ladder as an upward-moving vehicle for Jewish prayers; Rabbi Yisroel Meir Kagan (*Chofetz Chaim*) saw the continually ascending-descending ladder movements as suggestive of the constant flux of one's spiritual rise and fall, symbolizing the human frailty of growth and decline.

Rashi relies on a Midrash that places the ladder on the borders of Israel, wherein the "ascending" angels are leaving holy ground towards heaven; the "descending" ones bringing God's presence down to "guard" the Jews who find themselves outside of Israel (*chutz l'aretz*); to Ibn Ezra the presence of angels "proves" that they, and not (inferior) man, are central to creation, an opinion not shared by Meir ben Gabbai, grand kabbalist, nor by Prague Rabbi Yehuda Loew ben Betzalel (*Maharal*), who both view man as *the* quintessential of all creatures formed "in the image of God."

And in one of the rare occasions of chassidic-misnagdic accord, both the great Chassidic leader Shneur Zalman of Lyady and Hayyim of Volozhin, a disciple of the Vilna Gaon, explain the up-down movements (*olim ve-yordim*) as humanity's attempt to join the spirit (*ru'ach*) to the soul (*nefesh*); the ladder resting not on the ground (*b'aretz*) but *towards* the ground (*artzah*), implying that its principal anchor is above.

Rav E. E. Dessler interprets the ladder sequence as the preferred "incremental" method of spiritual growth, as in a step-by-step, rather than one large leap, in life.

> *One day a Catholic priest and a rabbi are talking about job prospects. "There's a good chance," says the priest, "that I'll be the next Bishop, maybe in the next year or two."*
>
> *"Wow, a Bishop!" marvels the rabbi, "and after that?"*
>
> *"Well, I don't know. It's possible I could become Archbishop, given some luck, and God's blessing."*
>
> *"Wow, an Archbishop! And then?"*
>
> *"Ha! Well, you know, it's Cardinal after that, but it's really very unlikely. But in theory, I could become a Cardinal."*
>
> *"Wow, so what's after Cardinal?"*
>
> *"After Cardinal?," the priest smiles, "well, I guess it's Pope, but I'm hardly likely to become... hmmm, oh well, I guess it is a possibility."* ▶

"Wow, and after Pope?"
"After Pope?" the priest replies in surprise, "there's just
God above the Pope, and obviously I can't become God!"
"Why not? One of our boys made it!"

A more intriguing analysis comes to us via Pirkei de-Rabbi Eliezer, a homiletic collection of Midrashim, which claims the stairway to heaven as a hint of world domination: the nations are the angels, the number of steps equaling the number of years a nation rises to, and maintains, influence and power; each nation succumbing to the next "ascendancy" of new world powers (e.g.: Babylon gives way to Persia, Persia to Greece, Greece to Rome, etc).

Yaacov's vision is thus a prophecy of the rise and fall of empires and is intended, according to the Ramban, to alert future builders of the house of Israel that their ultimate destiny is guided by the One who stands above the ladder.

Yaacov awakes in wonder and fear ("How awesome is this place!"), and notices that his multiple "pillow" stones have been joined into one big stone, reflecting unity. The Torah calls it *even*, extracted from *av-ben,* "father-son," the symbol of family continuousness.

The patriarch quickly erects this one-stone into a "cornerstone" monument (*matzeiva*), an act of spiritual ground-breaking, symbolically transforming this "place" (*ba'makom*) into an *ad hoc* House of God, becoming the first Jew to establish the principle of a *matzeiva* as a spiritual gateway to heaven.

He calls this "place," his last stop before leaving the Holy Land, *Beis-El* ("House of God"), a spot where Judaism's third daily evening prayer (*ma'ariv*) is initiated. Why here? Because in the fields outside Luz, Yaacov is the epitome of helplessness, exposed to the wilderness, completely alone and cold, uncertain of the future, surely more forsaken than blessed.

The parsha uses the phrase va-yifga bamokom, he "encountered the place [at night]," to symbolize, according to Rav Eliyahu Mizrachi (Ram), loneliness, darkness and fear, in the category of hester ponim, the "hiding of God's providence."

Our sages have a general rule: in order to ascertain a word's importance one must retreat to its first appearance in the Torah and examine it in its original context; the word "place" first enters Jewish scripture during creation, on the third day, when water was "separated" from dry land.

The same connotation exists here: both this "place" is detached as a holy mokom, a euphemism for God's abode, from its surroundings, and the stone (even sh'siyyah) is set aside as the "foundation of the world," center of civilization. And more: the Torah repeats the term no less than 7 times in this weeks first 10 verses, indicative of mankind's constant bodily movement, from mokom to mokom ("place to place") in a perpetual search for a lofty Godliness (symbolic of Yaacov, a man in constant motion, always changing, ever-growing.)

Avraham, the originator of faith, prayed at dawn; Yitzchak, the passive, content contemplator prayed in the afternoon as the sun set; Yaacov got the night portion. Why? Because of the three patriarchs his is a life of trauma and tragedy, family tensions, societal strife; Yaacov's extraordinary transformative moment, an unexpected encounter with God ("Surely God is in this place, but [v'anochi lo yadati] I did not know it!") caused the Chassidic masters to read, "And I did not know" as a lesson to stay spiritually awake in order to recognize sacred moments.

This paradigmatic Jewish story of awakening to the presence of the Divine results in a simple rock becoming synonymous with synagogues, as the third patriarch establishes the first mikdash m'at, a "miniature sanctuary."

> *Several months after opening their respective syna-gogues, three rabbis get together to discuss their progress.*
>
> *The orthodox rabbi complains, "Oy! We have such a problem with mice, the shammes keeps putting out all kinds of baited traps but they keep coming back."*
>
> *The second rabbi, a Conservative, immediately chips in, "We have the same problem at our shul, we've spent all kinds of gelt on exterminators but the problem still persists."*
>
> *"You know," says the third rabbi, a Reform, "I had the same problem. We tried traps, exterminators, prayers and baseball bats. Nothing worked. Then one Shabbos morning I had a brilliant idea. I laid out a huge kiddush spread of yellow cheese and then called up all the mice, and dozens came out of nowhere, and while they were busy feasting on the cheese banquets, I bar-mitzvohed them all — and I never saw one of them in shul again!"*

In this parsha Yaacov, now a man in his upper 70's, finds his "shapely and beautiful" young *bashert* at a well. The Zohar is blunt: an unmarried man is deficient ("blemished"), and nothing blemished may approach the altar.

"A man without a wife?" muses Eleazar ben Pedat, "is not a man."

To Judah Hanasi, home and wife were synonymous (although Ben Sira must have had a bad dating experience: "I'd rather dwell with a lion and dragon than keep house with a wicked woman.")

"Enjoy life," writes the otherwise morbid Koheles, "with the woman you love."

The Torah's episode of marriage provides the Halachic basis of its sanctification (known as *kiddushin*), based on the hermeneutic principle of "purchase," in that the legality of betrothal occurs only when the bride is "acquired" by the groom's "payment" of a silver ring.

> *Avimelech takes Esther out to a kosher Chinese res-*
> *taurant on their fifth date. Studying the menu, he asks his*
> *date, "How would you like your rice — fried or broiled?"*
> *Looking him straight in the eye, she replies, "Thrown."*

Yaacov is mesmerized by the girl of his dreams, a shepherdess who turns out to be his cousin Rachel, daughter of his wily Uncle Lavan.

Every story needs a villain: so this parsha introduces us to the despicable, detestable Lavan.

Yaacov and Lavan, surely the oddest couple in the Torah: the former a paragon of ennobled spirituality, the latter a master con-artist and serial chicanery abuser, are now family, for good or for worse.

In addition to all his other bad habits, Lavan is the epitome of bad employee-employer relations; constantly changing the terms of their work agreement, even forcing Yaacov to work for nothing.

Our sages trace the term *lavan* to the color "white" (as in "glowing with wickedness"), and link his nickname "the Aramean" not just to the place of his birth (Aram) but to the Hebrew word *rammo'i*, which means "impostor, "deceiver" and a fraudulent thief: he cheats Yaacov both financially and emotionally by marrying him off to Leah instead of Rachel and forcing him to labor for years before marrying his first love.

> *As Yossele the merchant drives his wagon into a Polish*
> *shtetl a potential customer yells out, "Hey, what are you*
> *selling?"*
> *Yossele beckons the guy over, bends down, and whis-*
> *pers, "Oats."*
> *"Oats? So, why be so secretive?"*
> *"Sssh! Not so loud! I don't want the horse to know."*

The Yaacov-Rachel sparks are love-at-first-sight and quantitatively different than his father and grandfather's spousal unions, who deferred revealing their feelings until *after* they established a relationship.

Which direction is right?

They both are, says the Midrash, approving the active enthusiastic Yaacov-style ("he went forth"), and the passive appreciative Yitzchak-style ("And he saw the caravan approaching"); disapproving only of those who procrastinate, delay and dilly-dally in marriage.

Yaacov is so instantly smitten and passionately energized that he agrees to seven years of hard work in return for Rachel's hand in marriage — and claims it "seems like only a few days."

The secret to a good marriage? Communication…as overhead in a movie theater:

> *Husband: "Can you see, dear?"*
> *Wife: "Yes."*
> *Husband: "Is there a draft on you, dear?"*
> *Wife: "No."*
> *Husband: "Is your seat comfortable?"*
> *Wife: "Yes."*
> *Husband: "Good! Let's change seats."*

Does Yaacov's instant-love syndrome automatically translate into the traditional subsequent requisite, that "they all lived happily ever after?"

No: for Yaacov, domestic life is about to become intricately complicated, and exponentially compounded. The Heavens had decreed that Yaacov, unlike Avraham who had one primary partner, and Yitzchak one wife, should have not just any two wives, but sisters!

As they say, marriage is when a man and woman become as one; the trouble starts when they try to decide *which* one.

When the big day for Yaacov comes, Lavan, the trickster's trickster, decides that his older daughter (Leah, also beautiful but with "weak-tender eyes [*rakkos*]") should get married first, based on the custom of not marrying off the "younger child before the elder," and switches the veil-covered bride.

Yaacov doesn't notice until the morning after: and the original love couple wait seven more years before consummating their wedding. Yaacov's second marriage (this is the genesis for three patriarchs, four matriarchs) is an arrangement (the marrying of two sisters) that Halacha now forbids.

Remarkably, Yaacov shows a superhuman equanimity; there is no anger, no outrage over his servitude, loss, pain and betrayal. But the more blatant question is this: how could Leah stay married, knowing her relationship was not built on courtship nor love, but on deceit?

The Torah is mute, but our Jewish mystics file it under "Secretive Divine Planning" as the Zohar allocates to the patriarch two schizophrenic-style missions for Yaacov-Israel, the former being obligated to marry the primary wife (Rachel), the latter, his alter-spiritual ego, to marry Leah; and by linking *b'nos* ("daughters") and *banos* ("builders"), Jewish linguists credit these two "rival sisters" as silent partners for a greater purpose, *the* architects of God's spiritual "construction firm," laying the foundations for the destiny of the nation of Israel.

This parsha also introduces us to an elaborate concept of name-giving as a family empowerment, an act that is a child's' first Jewish life-cycle event.

It is the Jewish mother, not the father (nor God), who bestows names on 11 of Yaacov's children, who all make their debut in this parsha. Unlike today's custom of naming children after ancestors, the early Torah practice was to give the child a name reflective of hope, or of the mother's emotional state of mind, ranging from love to despair (for example: Reuven's name is based on "seeing;" Shimon's on "hearing;" Levi's on "touching," and when Rachel's second boy is born, the mother dies in childbirth, but not before naming her boy, Ben-Oni, "the son of my distress.")

That is why the Midrash advises parents, "Examine names carefully in order to give a child a name that is worthy so that the child might become a righteous person."

Why does the Torah switch back-and-forth between the names Yaacov and Israel, especially after Yaacov is *twice* told that he has a new name? (and why is he *still* referred to in our siddur prayers as "Yaakov," his former name?)

The name *Israel* is symbolic of the "struggle" between man and angel, its essence is thus *ongoing*, whereas Yaacov's name remains, on the threshold of life's ups and downs, setbacks and disappointments — its essence thus being the Jews' permanent potential to improve. The Hebrew root of Yaakov is *ayin, kuf, beis*; it also forms "skill," a necessary quality of life itself, in contrast to the root of 'Yisrael' which connotes "honor, nobility, virtuousness," the spiritual results of overcoming adversity through a Torah way of life.

Sam Schwartz, the oldest of 7 children, had to quit school before he could even learn how to read or write in order to work to help support his younger siblings. He opens up a bank account but, being illiterate, is forced to sign checks with an "XX." Sammy soon prospers and becomes a very rich man and then, one day, he gets a call from his bank, "Mr. Schwartz, I wanted to ask you about a check we just got. We aren't sure this is your signature, it has three X's instead of your usual double X."

"Ah yes," he replies, "you see, since I became wealthy my wife thought I ought to have a middle name."

From Yaacov to Israel

> *"I have to have a raise," the man demands of his boss. "There are three other companies after me."*
>
> *"Is that so?" asked the manager, "what other companies are after you?"*
>
> *"The electric company, the telephone company, and the gas company."*

The title of this week's parsha, *Vayishlach*, comes from its opening verse, "Yaacov sent [*vayishlach*]," and refers to his dispatching of "messengers" to his brother (Esav), as the sibling drama, whose stories we follow from the womb itself, bubbles to the surface.

Rabbi Judah the Prince views this entire Yaacov-Esav saga as a prototype, a pre-enactment of the history between Jews and nations, to the extent that he would first study this parsha whenever summoned to see the Roman consul to glean insights on how to present his people's cause.

> *A couple of centuries ago the Pope decided that all Jews had to leave the Vatican, a dictate that caused a huge uproar in the Jewish community. To quell their anxiety the Pope offered to conduct a religious debate wherein if the Jews won, they could stay; if the Pope won, they would leave.*
>
> *To make the challenge more interesting, the debate is to be mute; with signs, no words. The Jews have no choice, so they search for the most learned amongst them but every Torah scholar turns them down, afraid of the responsibility.*
>
> *The only one willing to confront the Pope is Moishele, a Jew with little intellectual stamina and even less seichel. But they have no choice as Moishele is the only volunteer.* ▸

The day of the Great Debate arrives, and the Jew and the Pope sit opposite each other. The Pope begins by raising his hand and showing three fingers. Moishele quickly raises his hand but shows only one finger. The Pope then waves his fingers in a circle around his head to which the Jew responds by pointing to the ground where he sits.

The Pope suddenly pulls out a wafer and a glass of wine; to which Moishele hesitates, then reaches into his pocket and pulls out an apple. The audience is stunned at the Pope's reaction. He stands up, exasperated and humiliated, and surrenders, "This man is too good. The Jews can stay!"

The shocked cardinals crowd around the Pope for an explanation.

"Well, let me tell you what happened," the Pope explains. "First I held up three fingers to represent the Trinity, and the Jew responded by holding up one finger to remind me that there was still one God common to both our religions. Then I waved my finger around me to show him that God was all around us, and the Jew responded by pointing to the ground and showing that God was also right here with us. So I pulled out the wine and the wafer to show that God absolves us from our sins, and he pulled out an apple to remind me of Original Sin. He had an answer for everything. What could I do?"

Meanwhile, an elated and surprised Jewish community wanted to know how their Moishele had beaten the theological leader of a billion Catholics.

"What happened?" they ask.

"Well," replies Moishele, "First he told me that the Jews had three days to get out of here, so I told him that not one of us was leaving. Then he tells me that this whole city would be cleared of Jews, so I let him know that we were staying right here." Moishele then stops.

"Well, what happened then?" they ask.

"I'm not sure. The Pope suddenly got hungry and took out his lunch, so I took out mine."

Yaacov has extricated himself from his father-in-law's "wicked ways" with great difficulty, and is returning to his ancestral homeland of Canaan in order to resume the spiritual mission of his grandfather and father; but the 500-kilometre trip requires him to go through Edom, which is Esav-controlled territory.

Thus he has no choice but to confront his past as well as an estranged and presumably still adversarial, and powerful, brother. It has been 22 years since he obeyed his mother (Rivka) and, disguised as a goat-skinned Esav, stole his brother's first-born blessing from his father.

The parsha ignores Esav's state of mind, but tells us how Yaacov feels: "greatly frightened and distressed."

"All worries are forbidden, except worry about worrying" was a favorite *vort* of Mordechai of Lekhovitz, Chassidic Polish Sage. In English slang: You don't get ulcers from what you eat, but from what's eating you.

The *Yalkut Shimoni*, a 13th century Midrashic anthology that delves into the character of the patriarchs, defines Yaacov as "the choicest of the patriarchs," crediting him with radiating *tiferes* (glory) by creating his own reality over time, and being responsible for unparalleled successes and achievements, even greater than his father and grandfather's (which is why Jews are known as the house of Yaacov, not that of Avraham or Yitzchak).

It is here that the Torah, for the first time, uses the term *ho'om*, "the people," as in nation and no longer as "family," to describe those who are with him.

The parsha's dramatic centerpiece occurs at a river's edge, the night before Yaacov confronts his brother. He seeks privacy but the solitude is short-lived; he finds himself in a lonely mysterious struggle, "wrestling" [*vaye'avek*] an unknown assailant, a "stranger" that the Torah only identifies as *ish* (a man). Rashi interprets the term *vaye'avek* as to "fasten on to," as in the cleaving of two opponents; the Ramban notes its similarity to *vaye'havek*, which means, "and he embraced."

This closes the circle for Yaacov: a baby who began his life's journey by wrestling in the womb now wrestles his way into adulthood, and nationhood.

The physical winner may be the anonymous opponent who leaves Yaacov with a permanent disability that "strains" his sciatic thigh nerve (*gid hanasheh*), but Yaacov leaves the ring spiritually invigorated, transformed, empowered.

This famous all-night tussle ("until the break of dawn") has provided study fodder for centuries of Torah commentators; Yaacov has either come face-to-face with God (which is why he names the site *Peniel*, the "Face of the Divine"); or perhaps an angel of God (Michael, protector of the Jewish people, sent to test his courage); or the disguised evil guardian angel of Esav (*saro shel Esav*) whose intent, notes the saintly Rabbi Elchanan Wasserman, is to destroy the Jewish people.

Jewish mystics claim Yaacov fought a mirror image of himself, a reflective type of "homecoming" that forces him to confront his own demons of deception, wrestling a guilty conscience over having usurped birthrights and blessings for which, the Midrash reminds us, he has never accepted responsibility nor asked for forgiveness.

The inner struggle is thus necessary to transform Yaacov into a "new creature" (Israel, limping) via the vehicle of repentance (*tshuva*).

It is a Chassidic custom to read this tale of "spiritual wrestling" during the motzei-Shabbos *Havdoloh* services; a reminder that the spirituality of Shabbos is over, and one must now be prepared to "take on" the secular week ahead.

Yaacov, displaying enormous strength and indefatigable will, refuses to release this superhuman power until he is blessed with a new Hebrew name, *Israel*, which literally means "he who struggles with God" ("and man, and won"), a name-change that trickled down to the people as *Israelites*, and whose homeland became known as the land of Israel.

Unlike Avraham and Sarah whose name changes were insti-tuted via only one letter, Yaacov's is a total new name altogether: the contrast is dramatic — from one word 'Yaacov,' derived from *akev*, a "heel" (suggesting a "supplanter") to 'Israel,' derived from *sar*, a "prince" (suggesting superiority).

The old Yaacov attempted to succeed by deceitfully seizing blessings; the new Yaacov intends to earn his kudos and glory through his own efforts. Interestingly, during Talmudic times vari-ous Torah monikers (e.g.: Avraham, Adam, Isaiah, Israel), which are now common, were considered too holy to use, and only be-came popular in the Rhineland in the Middle Ages.

As Esav approaches with his entourage of 400 men, a reticent Yaacov resorts to an intense and elaborate diplomatic etiquette to appear *motzei chain b'einecho*, "favorable in his brother's eyes."

He first sends messengers of appeasement (*melochim*), and then spends over half of this entire parsha gathering an incredible array of gifts; flocks, cattle, camels, which the Torah calls a "*mincha*," the name reserved for one of the sacrifices, a caravan of gifts that Rashi describes as stretching "as far as the eye can see."

One of the lessons of Yaacov?

The righteous handle money differently, using material pros-perity as successful tools for the service of God, in this case to make *sholom* with a brother.

Yet Yaacov also hedges his bets: he prays for a *kappara* ("atone-ment") while preparing for battle, struggling to overcome his fearful apprehension.

When the two brothers finally meet in an epic showdown and dramatic reunion, an excited Esav makes the first overture: he runs, kisses and embraces his brother in an effort to dispel the tension. Both admirably seek rapprochement and brotherly reconciliation, and do their best to break down old walls of recrimination, suspi-cion, anger.

Esav has nurtured his rage well, no longer harboring hatred in his heart (although he never actually "forgives" his brother), whereas Yaacov, bowing seven times in submission, as if to a king, uses candid expressions of deeply felt humility stirred with a touch of flattery (*chanifus*), determined to create an atmosphere more reflective of *d'rachecha darchei no'am*, "Its [Torah] ways are ways of pleasantness."

There is no question about it: Yaacov is now older, wiser, more polite; and this reunion becomes *the* Torah's epitome of a later rabbinic saying, *ayze hu gibor?* ("Who is a true hero?"), *ha'oseh sonehu ohavo, ha'kovesh es yitzro* ("The one who turns an enemy into a friend.")

But although Yaacov and Esav are (briefly) reunited, they are never truly reunited for there is not a single future reference in the Torah to the brothers ever getting together again; Esav goes to Seir, Yaacov settles in Sukkot — and, to this day, the children of Yaacov and Esav are still hostile to each other, perpetuating a 4,000-year-old grudge.

> *One day Yitzie and Feigie try to book a hotel room in the fancy upscale French Riviera, but are denied.*
> *"Sorry," says the snobby concierge, "there's no vacancy." Just then, a man checks out.*
> *"Good, now you have a room," points out Feigie.*
> *"No, I'm sorry," the concierge admits openly, unashamed, "this hotel is restricted."*
> *"And what does that mean?"*
> *"No Jews allowed!"*
> *"Well what makes you think we're Jewish?"*
> *"I know you are!"*
> *"Well, we're...we're...we're Catholic!"*
> *"Oh yeah! So tell me, did God have a son?"*
> *"Sure."*
> *"What's his name?"* ▸

> *"Jesus."*
> *"And, where was he born?"*
> *"In Bethlehem, in a stable!"*
> *"And, why was he born there?"*
> *"Because some pea-brained idiotic moronic shnook like you wouldn't rent his parents a room!"*

This week's parsha also has a real-estate transaction: Yaacov buys a grave site in Shechem from the children of Hamor for 100 kesitahs.

How much is a kesitah? No one knows for sure: in the science of numismatics, "coins" only became a method of payment during the 7th century BCE, in Lydia, Asia Minor.

Commercial Biblical transactions were conducted either via units of metal (brass, silver, or gold, which were in the forms of a bar that was then broken down into smaller pieces of fixed weights, from where the Hebrew terms *beka* and *betza kesef*, "coins" and "greed" are derived from), weight, or barter; the latter method (one *kesitah* equaling one sheep) being the form of Yaacov's purchase, according to the Targum Onkelos.

This transaction introduces us to the Torah's first, and only, specific tombstone on a specific grave (Rachel's), the concept of a post-death "memorial marker" (Absalom's memorial in the Valley of the King, doesn't count as a "tombstone" because he erected it himself before he died.)

> *One Rosh Hashanah morning, the rabbi notices little Alex staring up at a large plaque hanging in the shul foyer, covered with names with small American flags mounted on either side.*
> *The rabbi goes over to the pensive seven-year old, and says quietly, "Good Yom Tov Alex."* ▶

> *"Good Yom Tov rabbi," replies the boy, fixated on the plaque, "Tell me, what is this?"*
>
> *"It's a memorial, in holy memory to all the young men and women who died in the service."*
>
> *After standing together for a few minutes, staring at the large plaque, little Alex asks, "Which one, the 9:00am or 10:30am service?*

The question is thus obvious: why then did Yaacov put up a tombstone over the righteous Rachel's gravesite?

According to Rabbi Hayim Elazar Shapira, the Munkatcher Rebbe, the grave of Rachel, "on the way to Bethlehem," would be passed by future generations of Jews on their way to exile.

How did Rachel die? We're not exactly sure.

> *...but we know how ol' Freddie died. Lying in hospital he was visited by the rabbi who stands next to his bed, holding his hand, watching as Freddie's condition deteriorates.*
>
> *Unable to speak, Freddie begins to frantically motion for something to write on. The rabbi lovingly takes out his pen and some paper and hands it to the patient who then uses his last bit of energy to scribble a note...and then he dies.*
>
> *The rabbi puts the note in his pocket at the laveya he begins his eulogy, "We all know how smart and wise the deceased was. He wrote his last dying words on a note just before he died. I haven't looked at it, but knowing Fred, I'm sure there's a word of inspiration for us all."*
>
> *The rabbi slowly opens the note with all eyes upon him, the family weeping in the front row, as he starts to read, "You idiot! You're standing on my oxygen tube!"*

From Prison to Palace

> Three men are sentenced to 25 years of solitary confinement. As a concession, the governor allows each of them to take one item into his cell.
>
> The first guy asks for a pile of books; the second for his wife; the third for 100 cartons of cigarettes.
>
> At the end of the 25 years, the first prisoner is released and says, "You know, those books proved immensely invaluable. I've studied so hard I can now enter into any profession. I'm really happy."
>
> The second man steps out of his cell, with his wife and 11 children, smiling, "My wife and I have never been so close. This saved our marriage! I have a beautiful new family. I'm so happy."
>
> The third guy steps out of his prison cell, turns to a guard, and says, "Hey, anybody got a match?"

The title to this week's parsha comes from the opening salvo, *vayehi mikeitz*, "and it was at the end of," suggesting that Yosef is, finally, after two years, approaching "the end of" his prison ordeal.

This is also *the* parsha of Chanukka, which arrives during the longest nights of the year, when darkness needs light, and mankind needs additional comforting

Chanukka's timing is appropriate because it commemorates the spiritual-physical salvation from the Greeks; a liberation also evident in this weeks parsha wherein Yosef survives both the (physical) shenanigans of his brothers and the (spiritual) temptation of the seductress wife of his boss (Potiphar) who is attracted to the *na'ar* ("young lad").

It is here that Yosef enters Jewish history as *the* role model of generations, as *Yosef Hatzaddik*, "Yosef the Righteous."

The saga of Yosef in Egypt is one of the most compelling stories in the entire book of Genesis, recalled in a dazzling literary display of irony, symbolism, jealousy, hatred, and dramatic juxtaposition: witness Yosef's unexpected dizzy ascent from prison to palace — as his brothers plunge from great heights to misery.

> *Two guys are sharing a prison cell and one asks the other, "So, what are you in here for?"*
> *"I stole some paintings from the Louvre."*
> *"So, how'd ya get caught?"*
> *"Well, after planning the crime, getting in and out past security, I was captured only two blocks away when my Ford Econoline ran out of gas."*
> *"Wow! So how come you can mastermind such a daring, brilliant crime and then make such an obvious error?" asks his baffled cell mate.*
> *"Well, because I had no Monet to buy Degas to make the Van Gogh."*

In the beginning, Yosef sits isolated, invisible, alone in a forgotten prison, as he once did in a bottomless pit, eerily reminiscent of how his brother Reuven once described him, as *einenu,* "nonexistent." Yet it is here, after staring at the wall of a Pharaoh dungeon, that Yaacov's youngest and most favored son finally allows the God of his ancestors to enter his life to the point where, when called upon to interpret the Egyptian ruler's disquieting dreams, Yosef begs off, "Not I; God will see to Pharaoh's welfare."

> *"I had the strangest dream last night," Zalman, lying on the couch, tells his psychiatrist. "Maybe you can help me understand it. My mother came into my room and when she was up close I saw your face, not hers. Isn't that strange? I was so shaken that I couldn't go back to sleep so I just lay there all night until morning. Then I got up,* ▶

> *drank a can of diet coke, and came right over here for my appointment."*
>
> *"A diet coke!" the psychiatrist screams, "Zalman! You call that a breakfast!?"*

Welcome to the Parsha of clairvoyance, one of augury and foretelling, wherein Yosef becomes the first Jewish psychic of the Diaspora and a pioneer in the trade of prophecy. The dream, declared Hanina ben Isaac, Babylonian *Amora* of the third century, is the "incomplete form of prophecy." Others were not so kind: "No wheat without chaff," says Simeon bar Yohai, adding, "No dream without nonsense." Dreams? They are "of no consequence," concludes Rav Meir. Don't depend on them, warns the insightful *Sefer Hasidim*; and yet there is no doubt that the Torah is fond of dreams: ranging from King Solomon in this week's Haftarah (searching for the difference between "good and evil"), Pharaoh (and his cows and wheat), Yaacov (and angels), Yosef (and his sun, moon, and stars), Jeremiah (of Temple's destroyed, exile in Babylon, Rachel weeping for her children); and King Nebuchadnezzar (desirous of statues whose "heads are made of gold, arms of silver, legs of iron.")

> *Shmeryl once tossed 'n turned all night dreaming of the number "five."*
>
> *The next day he goes to a dream interpreter who tells him not to worry, that "five" is his lucky number; especially now that he had just turned 55, was born on the fifth day of the fifth month, been married for 5 years with 5 children, and earned $55,555 a year.*
>
> *The very next morning Shmeryl receives a phone call from his dream analyst with a hot tip that a horse named Lucky 5 is running in the fifth race at the local track that day.* ▶

> *This must be* bashert, *thinks Shmeryl, who runs to the bank, withdraws his entire life's savings, and bets it all on Lucky 5.*
> *Sure enough: the horse comes in fifth!*

According to tradition, Yosef's *ketones passim*, "coat of many colors," made especially for him by his father, represented all those peoples who had played a part in his fate.

The Hebrew term *passim* stands for "stripes" and its four letters are an acronym for Potiphar (the Egyptian minister who bought Yosef as a slave), *Socharim* (merchants), *Ishme'eilim* (Ishmaelites) and *Midyanim* (Midianites); however none of these "strangers" destroyed Yosef's coat but his own brothers, who "were unable to speak peaceably to him."

In their blind fanaticism, the sons of Yaacov had convinced themselves that they acted for the "sake of Heaven," that the means justifies the end.

This parsha is a treasure trove of relationships, often dysfunctional; and a discomforting truth, that even righteous people are not immune to grievous fallible failings, as predicted by a future Solomonic observation, "There is no man who does not sin."

Abandoned as a 17-year-old teenager, and sold to a camel caravan of Ishmaelites, Yosef is now thirty; yet the lost years have taken a toll. His brothers do not recognize him. Why should they? Yosef not only "acts like a stranger" but covers his face (*Ramban*) and changes his voice (*Rashbam*, grandson of Rashi).

In a potent display of God's ability to direct events towards a specific goal (known as *hashgocho perotis*), Yaacov's son Yosef was, unbeknownst to the family, alive and well. And more: he was no longer a lowly Hebrew slave-boy but a powerful and skillful vizier, second in command, in charge of Egyptian food supplies; a national hero for rescuing an entire country from a future famine.

Yosef's true talent lay not in marketing but in his spectacular ability, combined with resilience and ingenuity, to interpret dreams: transliterating Pharaoh's famous apparition sequence (of 7 robust and 7 poor cows, of 7 full and 7 poor ears of grain), into 7 great years of abundance and 7 disastrous years of famine..

Yosef's dream interpretation requires courageous temerity. Why? He had to publicly disagree with Pharaoh's entire cabinet, his entrenched sorcerers, and the wisest men of the land (whose visions, that the king would bury 7 daughters, or that 7 countries would rebel against him, were, for obvious reasons, unsatisfactory to the throne).

It is then that one of the most incredible metamorphosis in the Torah takes place, as Yosef's version catapults him from degrading slavery into the seat of power; rewarded with an official signet ring, fine robes and gold chains, a new name (Yosef Zaphenath-Paneah) and a wife (Asnat, daughter of Potiphera, powerful priest of On).

Rashi, the "prince" of Torah commentators, traces the name Zaphenath to *tzephunot,* which means "hidden," suggestive of his uncanny capacity to explain the clandestine.

The comfortable Yosef, son and grandson of patriarchs, now seems fully assimilated: he dresses like an Egyptian, marries an Egyptian, and answers to an Egyptian name; a disturbing turn of events that led Rav Shalom Schwardon to see Yosef's dream sequence as a metaphor for life itself: that in the cycle of the Jew there are years of spiritual abundance (when one is young, active, ambitious) and spiritual famine (when one is aged, no longer possessing the drive and energy to succeed at self-growth).

> *Etti and Estie, two elderly Jewish women, go out for a drive one morning in a large car, both barely seeing* ▶

> *over the dashboard. They cruise up to an intersection*
> *where the stoplight is red but go straight through.*
>
> *Ettie, sitting in the passenger seat, thinks to herself, "I*
> *must be losing it, I could have sworn we just went through*
> *a red light."*
>
> *A few minutes later they drive straight through another*
> *intersection stop light.*
>
> *Etti is now getting nervous, and when it happens again,*
> *she screams, "Estie! We just ran through three red lights in*
> *a row! You could have killed us!"*
>
> *"Oh," replies Estie, "Am I driving?"*

The entire history of the Jewish people takes a dramatic turn in this week's parsha — all over food, or more accurately, the lack of it.

Faced with a devastating shortage in the Holy Land, the people are desperate. For "rations" or "food," the Torah uses the word *shever* repeatedly, a term which attracts a lot of attention from our Kabbalists. Noting that the tribe of Ephraim suffered from a speech defect, unable to say the "*sh*" sound (thus pronouncing the word as *sever,* which means "hope"), our Jewish mystics saw in Yaacov's ten sons' shopping expedition to *chutz l'aretz* (Egypt) to buy corn, not just a search for food (*shever*) but for hope (*sever*) as well.

> *One day Mrs. Rosenblum goes into the butcher shop*
> *inquiring about the price of lamb chops.*
>
> *"$5.50 a pound," the butcher replies.*
>
> *"What!," she screams, "the guy next door sells them for*
> *$2 a pound!"*
>
> *"Nu, so go buy from him!"*
>
> *"I can't, he's all out!"*
>
> *"Well, Mrs. Rosenblum, when I'm out of lamb chops*
> *they'll only be $1.50 a pound."*

Why were only ten sons of Yaacov sent to Egypt?

To Rashi it symbolized a *minyan*, the traditional quota of unity and the pursuit of a common purpose. But to Yosef it meant failure, the miscarriage of his explicit dream which would remain unfulfilled until "eleven" sheaves of wheat bow to him. That is why Yosef lures Benjamin, his youngest brother (and the missing "eleventh") to Egypt in the hope of making his dream finally come true.

Ultimately Yosef wants only one thing, "My brothers do I seek; tell me, please, where are they?"

His words have haunted every member estranged from family, detached from kindred. Yaacov "turned away and wept" — above all, he just wants to be at one with his siblings, to fill the deep void in his life, to finally vent some intense, suppressed emotions.

And so another destructive relationship comes together, in the spirit of Malachi, "We are sons by the same father. Did not one God create us?"

Yet we are still startled at the scorn between parents and children: why do "these things always happen to me!" cries the new voice of Israel-Yaacov, a painful parental cry that motivates a future prophet (Malachi) to promise that "God shall reconcile parents with children and children with their parents."

> *Four Jewish grandmothers are sitting around their retirement home playing cards, when the first bubba suddenly sighs, "Oy..."*
> *The second nods, sighs, and adds, "Oy vey!"*
> *The third goes, "Oy veys meer!"*
> *"Okay, Okay," interrupts the fourth bubba, "enough talk about the children, let's get back to the game!"*

VAYEISHEV
Begin Worrying.
Details to Follow.

"How long do you intend to teach here," the principal asks the young Bais Yaakov girl.
"From here to maternity," she replies.

In this week's parsha, the Torah describes how Yaacov, with his twelve sons and one daughter, finally settles down "in Canaan," an ancient Egyptian term that refers to the territory between the Phoenician-Lebanese coast extending southward to Palestine.

After the era of the patriarchs, it becomes known as the "Holy Land," or *Eretz Yisroel*, "the "land of Israel," with Canaan being derivative of *kena'anim*, a local ethnic group.

The Torah uses the Hebrew verb *yeshev*, "settled," to emphasize that this was a true "sinking roots" attempt, and not just a temporary act of *m'gurei*, to "dwell" (*m'gurei* being a derivative of *ger*, "stranger," implying only a transitory stopover between wanderings).

Rashi stretches the simple meaning of *Vayeishev Ya'akov*, "Yaacov was settled," to mean "Yaacov, at the end of his life, desired to live in peacefulness" (*shalva*). But was it *bashert* (fated) for him to finally "settle down?"

It is late one night and Aaron, a puny little guy, is sitting at a bar staring at a full glass of drink when a group of unsavory rowdy bikers come in. Wanting to separate himself, Aaron picks up his drink and moves down to the other end of the bar. A biker sees easy prey, so he goes ▶

> *over to the little puny Jewish guy, grabs his glass, guzzles down half the contents, and laughs, "Ha! So what'ya gonna do about that, little man?"*
>
> *"Nothing," sighs Aaron despondently, "I guess it's bashert." He picks up his cup, and moves even further away. Another big biker then straddles over, grabs his glass, and guzzles down the rest of the drink, laughing, "Now what'ya gonna do, little Jew boy?"*
>
> *"Well, nothing. It's all fate, bashert!"*
>
> *"Whaddya mean?"*
>
> *"Well, you see, today has been the worst day of my life. This morning I overslept and was late for an important meeting. My boss was furious and so he sacked me. I cleared my desk, went to my car, only to discover that it wasn't there — somebody had stolen it. So I got a taxi home, but when it came to paying the driver I realized I'd forgotten my wallet. I went home only to discover my wife having an affair with the gardener. So I left home and came to this bar. And just when I was thinking about ending it all, you and your mates show up and drink my poison!"*

Yaacov's spectrum of horror and harrowing experiences cannot be understated.

Talk about *tzorres*!

His brother tries to kill him; his nephew steals from him, his father-in-law deceives him; he marries the wrong woman; his wife dies during childbirth; his daughter is seduced; he is maimed by a fight with an angel; he loses his sight; and finally, his spiritual serenity is shattered by the inconsolable grief at the sight of his missing son Yosef's bloodied tunic, an image that caused such despair that when his "sons and daughters sought to comfort him, he refused to be comforted."

Sounds like the typical Jewish telegram: "Begin worrying. Details to follow."

No wonder Yaacov is disconsolate when he meets Pharaoh, and

admits, "few and bad [*ro'im*] have been the days of my life," a summary of a long spiritual winter in the history of the Jewish people, a portrait of estrangement, a series of episodes of endurance so offensive as to warn us that no one goes through life unscathed...

> *One day the rabbi of a Polish shtetl drops in to visit a poor Jew who was bitten by a stray, rabid dog and finds him sitting up in bed writing furiously.*
>
> *"Yiddle," says the rabbi in a quiet voice, "rabies can be cured, you shouldn't concern yourself with writing a will."*
>
> *"Will, what will!? I'm making a list of all the people I'm gonna bite!"*

This parsha details the growth of Yosef, Yaacov's most favored son, from adolescence to adulthood; a Jew who is allotted more text than any other person in the Bible (except for Moshe).

Yosef begins as a shepherd and dreamer, which he sees as "prophecies" (*n'vua*); and, wonder of wonders, after interpreting Pharaoh's dreams and forecasting the impending years of plenty and famine, he is catapulted into an interpreter *extraordinaire*, economic wizard, polished statesman, a "discerning and wise man" (*ish navon v'chochom*).

Usually dreams (and wishes) are treated as private, intimate moments, personal and secretive, yet to Rabbi Bana'a a dream is "a prophecy in miniature;" the Torah, for example, is the story of how the dreams of God for a better world, are transformed into human reality; the Ultimate Dreamer "partners" with the earthly dreamer Yosef saves the entire Jewish people.

That is why the kabbalistic term associated with Yosef is *Yesod*, meaning "foundation," as in *tzaddik yesod olam*, meaning "a good and just man is the foundation of the world."

"The dream that is not interpreted," notes the Talmudic sage

Rabbi Chisda, "is like a letter that is unread."

> *During their vacation in Europe Mr. and Mrs. Greenbaum come upon a wishing well, so they lean over and the husband makes a wish and throws in a penny.*
> *His wife suddenly falls into the well, and the husband, stunned, begins to smile, and says, "It works!"*

The value of true friendship is hinted at in this week's parsha, the first time that the Torah uses the word *re'a*, "friend," in describing Judah's chummy Adulamite *chaver* Chirah (*re'aihu ha'adulami*).

What makes Chirah such a close buddy?

Because Judah feels comfortable enough to disclose such innermost secrets as the immoral sin he commits with Tamar, his strong and determined daughter-in-law who he did not recognize (like the man who met his wife at a party and was shocked, *shocked*, because he thought she was at home with the kids).

The theme is brotherhood and sibling rivalry, and incredibly, it is the first time in the Torah that Judah, the fourth son and future leader, actually speaks.

It is he who decides not to kill Yosef ("he is our brother and our flesh") but to sell him as a slave instead.

The story of Yosef and his brothers, the "sons of [concubines] Bilhah and Zilpah," who fail in their perfidious attempt at fratricide, is surely one of the most bewildering episodes in the Torah; the 14th century Rabbeinu Bachya, shocked that the future tribes of Israel would behave so poorly, especially after God testifies to their righteousness and attaches His name to theirs (*shivtei Ka*), interprets Reuven's plea, "Shed no blood, but cast him into this pit," as a generic plea against killing.

The brothers then casually and callously sit down together to eat, ignoring the cries of their brother from the pit. But this doesn't absolve them of the endless misery and suffering they cause for their aging father.

The question is obvious: why do they hate Yosef so much?

Resh Lakish blames their father for showing favoritism by giving his son a special *kesones pasim,* "coat of many colors." The 16th century Italian Rabbi Ovadiah Sforno agrees: a father's lavish attention has spoilt Yosef who, in turn, feels, and acts, superior...

> *One day Michael, the boss of a large clothing factory calls all of his employees into the company auditorium and announces, "Ladies and gents. I've called this meeting to introduce my young son, Billie, who will be coming to work here. I want you to show him no favoritism and treat him like any other employee — and not like the man who will be taking over this factory in two weeks."*

But surely there is more to this unbridled sibling hatred?

The clue lies in the complicated makeup of the family. There are four wives; the status of each is so complex that the fallout trickles down into the next generation, a perfect example of the rabbinic concept of *ma'aseh ovos simon l'bonim,* "the actions of the forefathers serve as a portent for their descendants."

The tension in Yaacov's marital life rises when one realizes that one wife (Bilhah) is her mother-in-law's servant, and her children feel that they must act in a serf manner despite Yosef's pleas that they consider themselves of equal status.

Meanwhile, the children of Leah, who consider themselves more exalted, act abusively to the children of Bilhah and Zilpah, which, according to the 12th century Rabbi Shemuel ben Meir (*Rashbam*), a member of the Tosafos school which flourished in the early middle ages, spreads to a hatred of Yosef who they see as being "too friendly."

Even a monogamous marriage can be stressful, which is why thousands of words have been written about how to maintain *sholom bayis* in the home (consider: in the first year of marriage, the man speaks and the woman listens; in the second year, the woman speaks and the man listens; in the third year, they both speak and the neighbors listen).

> "I have a problem at home," confides Menachem to his rabbi.
> "What's the difficulty?" the rabbi asks sternly.
> "It's my wife, rabbi. She has a very bad habit."
> "What, Menachem?"
> "She stays up every night until 1 or 2 o'clock in the morning, and I can't break her of the habit."
> "Well," asks the rav, "What is she doing all that time?"
> "Waiting for me to come home."

Add to this the fact that Yosef is a man with faults: he succeeds in uniting his brothers, *against* him!

Jewish aggadah then goes one step further in the "Faults Department": Yosef's immaturity, his vanity, his role as gossiper and talebearer (about his brother's misbehavior to his father), and his assimilation into the Egyptian lifestyle.

And yet, at the same time, our sages describe him as righteous and wise; his wisdom being the quality that his father loves most. How do we know this? Because the parsha describes Yosef as a *ben z'kunim*, a term often mistranslated as "the child of his [Yaacov's] old age," which is technically incorrect (because Binyamin was). The Targum Onkelos, *the* Aramaic translation on the Torah, translates *z'kunim* as *chakim* ("wisdom"); Rabbi Naftali Zvi Yehuda Berlin (*Netziv*), the great 19th century Lithuanian commentator, claims that it means, "to be subservient."

> *"Typhoid! Measles! Tetanus!" the priest shouts.*
> *Puzzled, Devorah asks her neighbor, "Why is he yelling like that?"*
> *"Well, he likes to call the shots around here!"*

VAYIGASH
Pathos, Poignancy, Passion

> *One day Mr. Levine, dressed as Napoleon, walks into a psychiatrist's office, and the doctor asks him, "What's your problem?"*
>
> *"I don't have no problem," he replies, "I'm one of the most famous people in the world. I have a great army behind me, I have all the money that I will ever need, and I live in great luxury."*
>
> *"Then why are you here?"*
>
> *"It's because of my wife, she thinks she's Mrs. Levine."*

The title to this week's parsha, *Vayigash*, means to "draw near" (or "approach"), a reference to the dramatic and emotional confrontation between two mighty sons of Yaacov: Yosef, powerful and autocratic viceroy of Egypt, and the future *gur aryeh Yehudah*, "Lion of Judah."

Judah is portrayed in densely syntactic poetry ("Judah is a lion's cub, from the prey you have risen. He crouches, lies down like a lion, and like a lioness, who dares arouse him?"), enduring lyrics of strength, calm, and dignity that aptly describe the future people of Israel.

The story of Yosef uniting with his brothers after many years of separation flows into the Haftarah, which speaks of the eventual reunion of the Northern and Southern Kingdoms of Israel after their return from exile.

The Bnei Yissoschor ties these exiles into four specific periods of history where the souls of Jews were exiled (in Babylon), their bodies subjugated (in Persia), their intellect challenged (by the Greeks), and the current Roman-Edom exile, which combines the worst elements of all three.

Jewish history considers this early brotherly antagonism the forerunner to the split of Israel into two kingdoms (Judah, Israel), although Jacob ben Asher (the *Baal Haturim*) is convinced that the "approach" was between equals, based on the fact that the three final letters in the parsha's opening words spell *shaveh* (equal).

It is this "approach" from a transformed Judah, an appeal to Yosef's sense of justice to save his brother Benjamin (falsely accused of stealing Yosef's goblet), that overwhelms Yosef with a tidal wave of longing to finally come "home."

> *A Jewish gangster is shot while dining in a mob restaurant. He staggers and stumbles out into the street, crawls several miles to his mother's apartment, a woman he has not seen nor spoken to in years.*
>
> *Clutching his bleeding head and stomach, he crawls up seven flights of stairs and bangs away on his mother's door, screaming, "Mama, Mama! Help me, Mama!"*
>
> *His mother opens the door, eyes her son up and down, and says, "Bubbeleh, come in, first you eat, then we'll talk!"*

This parsha begins with Judah taking center stage as the eloquent spokesman for his penitent brothers, displaying confession and regret, thus fulfilling the Rambam's minimum requirement of *tshuva*, a near magic word in the Torah thesaurus; a halachically precise belief whose power is so strong that it can reduce yesterdays "deliberate sins" into mere "errors," even merits.

Judah becomes a true hero and an impressive *ba'al teshuvah sheleimoh*, "master of complete repentance," emerging from the evil of his youth to become the progenitor of Israel's most enduring tribe.

And it is from his name (Judah) that Jewish history derives the words "Jew" and "Judaism."

Judah succeeds in keeping the family intact, and is rewarded with twins (Zerach and Peretz) from his wife Tamar.

> *Three expectant fathers who are pacing the waiting room as their wives are in labor, when suddenly the nurse emerges and congratulates one of them, "Mazel tov Yankele, you're the new father of twins!"*
>
> *"Wow, how about that," Yankele replies, taken aback, "I work for the Doublemint Chewing Gum company."*
>
> *A few minutes later she's back, and approaches Elimelech with the news that his wife has just had triplets.*
>
> *"Wow, that's unbelievable," the stunned Elimelech says, "I work for the 3M Company."*
>
> *The next father then gets up, rushes to the door to leave, and blurts out to the nurse, "I need a breath of fresh air, I work for 7–11."*

This is surely *the* parsha of pathos, poignancy, passion.

Who cannot be moved by the plea of a lost son ("Is my father still alive?"); or by his father's struggle with depression; or by the tears of a son who invites his broken father into exile knowing it will turn into 400 years of brutal slavery.

This is a novella of forgiveness and reconciliation, of repressed feelings, painful memories, remorseful reminisces, all tinged with bittersweet emotions that sets the stage for a long exile in Egypt, *the* precursor to all future exiles.

The book of Genesis has now come full circle: the Torah pendulum swings from family fragmentation and furor to reconciliation and respect; opposites which the Maharal, Rabbi Yehuda Loew from Prague, the seminal Jewish thinker of the 16th century, compares to exile (*golus*) and redemption (*geula*), in that they differ by only one letter (an *aleph*). Kabbalists have traditionally viewed this first letter in the Hebrew alphabet as a symbol of "one," as in a mystic sense of indivisibility and unity, and blame internal division and discord as the paving stones for the road to exile.

After 22 years, the divisive brothers are about to redeem themselves by reuniting Jewish brotherhood into one force of harmony. In sharp contrast to last week's parsha when Yosef acts "like a stranger" with no emotion, he is now suddenly "unable to control himself."

In a stellar moment, Yosef, a son long presumed dead, turns the corner of his life by revealing himself to his brothers, "I am Yosef [*ani Yosef*]."

> *Two brothers rent a boat, catch a lot of fish and return to the shore.*
> *"I hope you remember the spot where we caught all those fish," Max asks his brother.*
> *"Oh sure, I made an 'X' on the side of the boat to mark the spot."*
> *"What!? You idiot! How do you know we'll get the same boat?"*

Yosef embraces his shocked and speechless siblings, and mentions God's name no less than four times, reminding both his brothers and God that the mitzvoh of reunion is at hand.

> *One morning Benny goes to shul to pray for the millions he needs to save his business. By chance he happens to stand next to another Jew who is praying for a hundred dollars to pay an urgent debt. So Benny takes out $100 from his wallet, presses it into the man's hand who, overjoyed, gets up and leaves the synagogue.*
> *Benny then closes his eyes, and begins to pray, "And now, God, that I have your undivided attention..."*

115

When Yosef forcefully injects a Divine presence into his stunning display of *ahavas yisroel* ("love among Jews"), the timing is appropriate: this is the first time in their lives that the brothers actually speak to one another.

The tension increases when Pharaoh inappropriately greets the father of his right-hand man, by asking him, "How old are you?"

The Egyptian ruler, notes the 12th century Rashbam, Rashi's grandson and famous Tosafos scholar, was taken aback by Yaacov's unusually aged appearance.

Judaism's usual approach is this: wine and wisdom improve with age (Solomon Nissim Algazi, 18th century Talmudist); however, reality is reality. Old age? It's a natural disease (Immanuel, 13th century Roman-Hebrew poet); a bad sickness (Joseph Zarfati, 18th century Turkish rabbinical scholar); a crown of willows (Dimi, 4th century Amora).

Yaacov's reply is painful and bitter; a snapshot summary of his life story: that his "aged" appearance stems from years of struggle and suffering, a theme the Midrash summarizes via a quote from Job: "I was not tranquil [because of Esav], neither was I at quiet [because of Lavan], nor did I have rest [because of Dina], but trouble came [because of Yosef]."

Mrs. Greenberg notices a little ol' man rocking in a chair on his front porch.

"Hello there! I couldn't help but notice how cheerful you look. Tell me, what's your secret for a long happy life?"

"Well, I smoke three packs of cigarettes a day, I drink a case of whiskey a week, I eat nothing but fast food, and I never exercise."

"Wow! How old are you?"

"Twenty-three."

Yaacov, interestingly, never once inquires about his son's "missing years," nor questions how he became viceroy of Egypt, convinced that it was all *anus al pi hadibur*, "compelled by Divine decree."

Yosef agrees and tells his brothers: "Do not be distressed or reproach yourselves because you sold me hither; it was to save life that God sent me ahead of you."

This parsha concludes with the announcement that Yaacov "stayed in the land of Goshen," a word that is linked to *vayigash* as in "drawing close" — yet Rabbi Shabtai Hakohen (*Shach*) writes that the patriarch never set foot in the country. How is that possible? Although he was (physically) in Egypt he was (spiritually) still in *Eretz Yisroel*, an explanation that Rabbi Yoel Teitelbaum, the formidable Satmar Rav, explains the possibility that pure souls, acting as their body's life-force, bind their bodies to a different plane.

Yaacov was initially afraid to go to the idolatrous land of Egypt but was assured by God that the holiness of the Holy Land would be "close to" him at all times.

This is the next-to-last parsha of family conflict resolution which began with Cain vs. Abel (resolved by Abel's murder); Lot vs. Avraham, Yitzchak vs. Ishmael and Yaacov vs. Esav (all resolved by separation); Lavan vs. Yaacov (resolved by treaty); Yosef vs. his brothers (starts with separation, concludes in reconciliation).

Since that day, rivalry and competition has been a standard commonality in the literature of siblings.

> *When his brother bought a Rolls-Royce one day, Harold felt a bit inadequate with his ol' Dodge. One day they both pull up at a traffic light, and Harold shouts to his brother in his Rolls, "Hey, you got a phone in your Rolls? I've got a phone in my Dodge!"*
>
> *"Of course," replies the brother snobbishly, "I have a phone."* ▶

"Cool! Hey, you also got a fridge in there, too? I've got one in the back seat of my Dodge!"

"Yes, I have a refrigerator."

"That's great, man! Hey, you got a TV in there? You know, I got a TV in the back seat of my Dodge!"

"Yes," replies the irritated brother, "of course, I have a television. Don't forget, the Rolls-Royce is the finest luxury car in the world!"

"Yeah, I know, but tell me, you got a bed in there? I got a bed in the back of my Dodge!"

The brother is now very upset because his car doesn't have a bed so, when the light changes, he speeds away, drives straight to the dealer and promptly has a bed installed in the back of his Rolls-Royce, complete with silk sheets and a brass-trimmed headboard. Early the next morning he drives around searching for his brother's car and sees it parked in the street, with all the windows strangely fogged up from the inside. He toots his horn and Harold rolls down the window, his head soaking wet.

"Hey, Harold, bro! Guess what! I've got a bed in the back of my Rolls-Royce."

"What's the matter with you!? You got me out of the shower just to tell me that?!"

VAYECHI
Live and Let Die

The aging father, approaching 100, gathers his sons around him to disburse final words of wisdom.

"You know," he smiles proudly, "your mother and I have been happily married for 58 years."

"Fifty eight years! Wow! Tell us dad, how'd ya manage that?"

"Well, it's like this. Always remember, it's up to the man to make all the big, tough decisions in life, and leave the little, trivial decisions to the woman."

"Really? Does that really work?"

"Oh, sure. In fact, after 58 years, so far, I've not had to make one single big, tough decision!"

At first glance the name of this week's parsha, *Vayechi*, is a misnomer. Although it means, "And he lived," the parsha's entire content focuses not on the life of Yaacov but on his death (at age 147).

Yet this fits neatly into the belief system of Judaism, as evidenced by the Torah's total absence of the word "death" in describing his demise ("Yaacov our father did not die"), unlike Avraham and Yitzchak (who both "expired and died") — a recognition, according to Prague Rabbi Yehuda Lowe (*Maharal*), that those who live a life of great spiritual accomplishments and vitality never disappear but continue to "live, eternally."

One day three rabbis are awaiting their turn to give eulogies, and start speculating on what they would like their own friends and families to say about them at their own funerals. ▶

119

> *"I would like to hear them say that I was a pious schol-ar, a role model of Torah," says the first rabbi.*
>
> *"I would like to hear them say that I was a great family man, good son, wonderful husband, and father," says the next rabbi.*
>
> *The third rabbi thinks, and says, "I'd just like to hear them say...'Look! He's moving'!!"*

This is the first parsha that reveals the number ("seventy souls") of Jews from Yaacov's family who originally go "down to Egypt," as guests under Yosef's protection.

The oldest is Serach, daughter of Asher, whose great longevity grants her the singular status of being *the* eyewitness to the entire Egyptian-Judeo experience. That a "great and populous nation" emerges from only "70" Jews is extraordinary; but was it exactly seventy, or is the Torah, as it does often, using this in a typological context, symbolizing simply a "large" number? In fact the Torah itself only lists 69, excluding daughters-in-law, but including one wife (Rachel; "proof" of her unique status in the family).

If 70 *is* a precise count, and our Sages agree that it is, then who was the seventieth "soul"?

No one knows; but the possibilities include Yaacov, or God Himself ("I will go down with you to Egypt"); or Yocheved, daughter of Levi (who, according to legend, was born "between the Egyptian entrance walls.")

Torah scholars are fascinated by the meaning and symbolism of numbers.

> *One day the cheder Rebbe asks his talmidim to think of a number, multiply it by three, add five, take away the number you first thought of, then add seven, subtract two, and then add back the first number.* ▶

"Now close your eyes," says the Rebbe, pausing before he says, "dark, isn't it?

All Torah portions are traditionally delineated either by a new paragraph (if printed), or an indentation in the text (in the case of a hand-written Torah scroll) — except this parsha which begins right in the middle of the previous parsha (*Vayigash*). This division is known as a "closed" parsha (*s'tuma*), in contrast to an "open" parsha (*p'sucha*) which has a recognizable beginning.

Rashi, the classic medieval commentator, declares this parsha a "Super Closure" one, intended to alert us that, with the passing of the "beauty and harmony" (*tiferes*) of Yaacov, son of a saint and grandson of a spiritual revolutionary, we have reached the end of a highly accomplished dynasty; the Midrash calls the expiration of this extraordinary era of Judaic activity a catastrophic closing of "the eyes and hearts of Israel," and yet, it is just the end of the beginning.

The adventures of the Jewish people are about to enter a new and exciting phase, the birth of a new generation.

One day Sammy decides to send some flowers to his friend who is moving his business, and is startled when his friend calls to say that he just received a card that read, "Rest in Peace."
Sammy angrily calls the florist to complain.
"I'm terribly sorry," she apologizes, "But you know, somewhere there is a funeral taking place right now, and they have flowers with a note saying, 'Congratulations on your new location!'"

Who will be the successor to Yaacov, the inheritor of the spiritual leadership of the people of Israel?

Yaacov, on his deathbed 17 years after arriving in Egypt, does what all those facing death do: takes life more seriously, cognizant of the post-death expression *zechrono l'vrocho* ("may his memory be for a blessing") appendix to his name; an activity that so sharpened his senses that he was able to accurately predict the future ("in the end of days," *b'acharis ha'yomim*) by analyzing the past; as articulated by the slogan, "He who does not learn from the lessons of history, is doomed to repeat them!"

Does this mean Yaacov was a patriarch *and* a prophet? No.

The Divine Presence, explains Rashi, had suddenly "departed," making Yaacov's clairvoyant glimpses merely pre-death observations intended, according to Don Isaac Abarbanel, the leading scholar-philosopher-statesman of Spanish Jewry during its grim demise, to match his children's personality traits (comparing Issachar to a "strong-boned donkey," Dan to "a viper") with specialized blessings (who will be strong, sneaky, prosperous, etc).

This is the first time that the Torah "personalizes" their identities, as Yaacov eyes the "bigger picture" by cleverly focusing on each individual, an early example of a strict Torah philosophy: in order to forge a single national identity each Jew must recognize that the strength of the collective body (*klal*) depends upon the peaceful interactiveness of different personalized characters (e.g.; Issachar's Torah scholarship must co-exist comfortably with Zevulun's business acumen, and so on).

Yaacov, as expected, reserves his most extensive blessing for Yosef, using the singular when referring to himself as "thy father." This choice of words raises scholarly eyebrows: is Yaacov hinting that his blessings are more valuable than those bestowed by Avraham and Yitzchak? No, explains Rashi, to whom "the blessings of thy father" simply meant "the blessings thy father has received."

Yaacov seeks to merge *all* the blessings: from Avraham (who was promised the land of Israel), to Yitzchak (who was promised a broader territory, "all these lands"), to his own ("You shall spread abroad to the west, east, north, and south;" i.e.: all four corners of the earth).

The Hebrew for "spread abroad" is *u'faratzta*, which was originally understood not just in geographic or demographic terms, but in spiritual and cultural modes, in that the Jew, as "the descendant of Yaacov," was expected to carry and convey a message (monotheism) wherever he found himself, and in whatever language he found himself.

> *Everyone knew that Cohen was the best lawyer in the firm Donovan, O'Murphy and Cohen, so one day his friend asks him, "Hey, how come your name is last? Donovan spends his days playing golf, O' Murphy spends his at the racetracks, and you're always in the office. Your name should be first!"*
>
> *"It is," smiles Cohen, "all my clients read from right to left!"*

This scene, of final blessings and sharing advice, is the foundation for the Judaic tradition of ethical wills, paralleled in this weeks Haftarah by Isaiah, affluent nephew of King Amaziah (known as "the Prophet of Peace"), who picks up the theme of a dying Yaacov lavishing advice and blessings to his sons by paralleling it with King David who, also on his deathbed, did the same with Solomon his son ("Keep faith, walk in God's ways, carry out the laws..."); the prophet had witnessed a turbulent war in Judah, twice, and the destruction of the northern kingdom, and stressed ethical behavior above all else.

> *A large family once assembled in their lawyer's office, anxiously awaiting the results of their late father's* ▶

> will. *After grave dancing for years they could hardly wait to get their hands on the enormous wealth he had accumulated. Clearing his throat, the attorney began to read, "Being of sound mine and body, I spent all my money..."*

The Talmudic sage Eleazer ben Hyrkanos does the same with his son ("Let your children sit at the knees of wise scholars"); as does the 13th century Ramban ("Speak in gentleness to all men, at all times"); and Rabbi Moshe Sofer ("If you can do only a little, then do that little with utmost devotion.")

The time has come: Yaacov must now choose leadership.

"As is the generation, so is the leader," observed the Talmudic Rabbi Yossi ben Maon.

"I wanted to be a leader, a role model," said Joe E. Lewis, "so I went on a diet, swore off drinking and heavy eating — and in fourteen days I had lost exactly two weeks!" George Burns was upset that "all the people who know how to lead this country are busy driving taxis or cutting hair!" Henny Youngman's ambition was to be an atheist leader but he gave up because "they have no holidays." Jules Farber is convinced that "the time is at hand in the United States when the wearing of a tallis and a yarmulke will not bar a man from leading the country, unless, of course, he's Jewish."

And the winner is..... in a surprise upset, Judah, charismatic fourth son of Leah!

What happened to Simeon and Levi? Disqualified, "their weapons being tools of lawlessness," after their mass revenge murder of Shechem. And Reuben? "Unstable as water," having besmirched his first-born (*bechora*) status by "lying with Bilhah, his father's concubine." And Yosef, the favorite front-runner? Rejected, despite a sterling character and proven leadership skills, because he is hated by his brothers; unity being paramount.

Judah (reasonable, rational and responsible) thus prevails as the vigorous progenitor of the royal House of David ("the scepter shall not depart from Judah"), as Rashi gushes with admiration for his brave public admission of guilt (he "elevated himself"). Judah's choice is solidified by familial democracy, as his brothers choose to identify themselves by his name (Judeans, or *Yehudim*), making him the Torah's first leader to be chosen according to the will of the people.

> *After his Shabbos d'var Torah, the rabbi suddenly announces that he has accepted a position at another shul, and that this would be his last week with the community.*
>
> *"Don't worry," he assures the congregants, "I'm told that my successor is a good man with a great personality, a good sense of humor, accessible, humble, and very learned."*
>
> *Several members suddenly burst into tears, and one shouts, "Rabbi, that's exactly what your predecessor promised us!"*

Before blessing his own sons the bed-ridden Yaacov singles out and blesses two grandchildren (Ephraim and Menashe, sons of Yosef), an honor that catches the attention of all Torah scholars, especially since so little is known about them. And more: by placing a hand on each child's head, the *zeida's* interaction has trickled down the centuries to become *the* traditional erev Shabbos parental model for *Birkas Habonim*, the poignant blessing that all Jewish sons "be like Ephraim and Menashe."

The obvious question is: Why? Why not strive for a son to be like Moshe or Avraham?

The answer is twofold: the unique quality of these two brothers was the fact that they never fought; thus they were the epitome of such sibling compatibility as to inspire the Davidic lyrics, "How good and pleasant is it for brothers to sit peacefully together."

Neither Avraham nor Yitzchak had such *nachas* or *mazel*, the lives of their children are summarized by disagreement; and the next generation of Yosef and his brothers was even worse.

> *After her husband's funeral, the widow started making arrangements for an appropriate gravestone and chose the inscription "May he rest in peace."*
>
> *A few days later, she was shocked to discover that her husband had been less than faithful during their marriage, and ordered the stonemason to change the inscription.*
>
> *"I'm sorry, ma'am," he says, "It's too late. I just finished chiseling it in the granite."*
>
> *"Well, then," she thinks, "Is there enough room to add a few more words?"*
>
> *"Yes, if they're short."*
>
> *The widow points to an inscription on one of the other stones and says, "Add that line over there!" — and leaves, satisfied with her ex's message: "May he rest in peace... until we meet again."*

Contentiousness seemed to be a tragic pattern, a Judaic Greek-style family tragedy, until Ephraim and Menashe broke the trend. But the brother's entry into the Torah's "Hall of Fame" is much more existential: they symbolize survival and continuity, eternal conservators of Jewish traditions and values.

If it was hard to raise "Jewish" children, imagine the challenge of "Jewish" grandchildren! The ability of Menashe ("strong and courageous") and Ephraim ("modest and studious"), Yaacov's only Egyptian-born grandchildren (from Osnas, his daughter-in-law) to grow up in the lap of Egyptian royalty yet withstand the temptations of exile, notes Rav Yaakov Kamenetzky, the respected 20th century American rosh yeshiva, makes them *the* premiere role models for all future "Second Generations."

Yaacov has touched on a sensitive subject that most Jews obsess about: mortality, or to be more blunt, how do I want to be remembered after I am dead?

> *Pinchas was a very successful marketing director. One day, sadly, his wife Simi dies. At the cemetery, Pinchas's friends and family are appalled to read the headstone:*
>
> *"Here lies Simi, wife of Pinchas Levy, MCIM, Post Graduate Diploma in Marketing and Senior Marketing Director of Quality Marketing Services Ltd."*
>
> *Suddenly, Pinchas bursts into tears. His father-in-law comes over to him, and says, "This is really distasteful. I'm shocked that you would pull a cheap stunt like this on our Simi's headstone."*
>
> *"You don't understand," Pinchas sobs through his tears, "They left out the phone number."*

With this parsha we dramatically end, literally and ideologically, the astonishing and complex first book of the Torah, having witnessed God's rule, influence, and power; all condensed into a twelve-week period that covers 2,309 years from creation to the infant stirrings of Israel.

Yaacov's last dying and modest wish, which he repeats twice, is to have his body returned "to the grave I prepared for myself;" the Torah uses the expression to "lie down with [his] fathers," as more than just a request for a specific real estate location, but as a desire to join the fate of his "ancestors," a legacy of a shared mission in death as in life; an alignment of unity that explains why the word "kin" ("I am about to be gathered to my kin") appears in the Hebrew singular form.

Initially, Yosef, his regal son and precocious dream interpreter, is reluctant: fulfilling a sworn oath was serious business, especially to ones own dying father, however, Yosef eventually, and ironically, with Pharaoh's permission, fulfills his father's last will and testament, an act of compassion that is "rewarded" by living long enough (to

110) to see his own great-grandchildren.

> *Yankele, from the Bronx, goes to vacation in Florida and decides to send his wife a quick e-mail. However, he can't find the scrap of paper on which he had written her e-mail address, so he types it from memory. Unfortunately, Yankele misses one letter and his message is inadvertently sent to an elderly rebbetzin whose husband had passed away only the day before.*
>
> *When the grieving rebbetzin checks her e-mail, she lets out a piercing scream, collapses, and is found dead by her shocked family — who sees this message on her computer screen...*
>
> *Dearest Wife,*
> *Just got checked in. Everything prepared for your arrival tomorrow.*
> *Your Loving Husband*
> *PS: Sure is hot down here.*

So, all's well that ends well? Not exactly.

The Midrash claims that Yosef is punished by dying before his brothers, for the Halachic crime of ordering Egyptian physicians to embalm not only his father's body, but his own as well. Embalming is quintessentially an Egyptian, not a Jewish, burial rite; one of a panoply of practices designed to obscure the reality of death. This very idea is anti-Genesis, which considers human life an extension of the earth: "For dust you are," God tells Adam, "and to dust you shall return" (which is why Jews in Israel are buried without a coffin).

> *One evening, the local priest calls one of his members to inform him that his mother-in-law has died, and asks whether he wants the body cremated, buried, or interred?*
> *"Hey Father," the son-in-law yells into the phone, "Take no chances, do all three!!"*

This ends the Book of Genesis, the first book of the Torah when everyone rises and says, *Chazak, chazak v'nitchazek*, "Be strong, be strong, and let us be strengthened!" — a roar of encouragement to continue on to Exodus, the next book of the Torah.

Why repeat the word *chazak* three times?

To symbolize the past, present, and future.

Shmos
(EXODUS)

It took fifty chapters in the first Book of Moshe to cover 2,000 years; in contrast, the book of Shmos covers less than 200 years in 40 chapters; and the majority of those chapters — from the Patriarchs to the Exodus — only cover a few years.

When the Behag ("*Ba'al Halachos Gedolos*") gave each of the Five Books of Moshe their own titles (Bereishis was called *Sefer Hayashar*, "Book of the Upright;" Vayikra was *Sefer Kohanim*, "Book of the Priests"); Bamidbar became *Chumash Hapekudim*, "The Book of Counting;" and Devarim was called *Mishneh Torah*, "The Review of the Torah"), he gave no special name to Shmos, simply referring to it as *Sefer Hasheini*, "The Second Book," seemingly unmoved by its unique character, theme or content.

This literary "discrimination" caught the intrigue of the great 19th-century Netziv (Naftali Zvi Yehuda Berlin), rosh yeshiva of the distinguished Lithuanian Yeshiva of Volozhin, who concluded that the Book of Shmos, with its evolving story of the chronicles of the House of Yaacov to a national history that explicitly, for the first time, enunciates the concept of Israel as a chosen people, is a direct continuation of Bereishis, and thus no more than a "second" chronicle.

This position is buttressed, according to the 13th-century Rabbi Moshe ben Nachman (*Ramban*), by the repetition of the list of names of those who descended to Egypt, ensuring the narrative flow and historical process from Bereishis through Shmos.

And so begins the genealogy of the House of Yaacov.

So, What's in a Name?

Mrs. Rosengarten tries to call the local record store but dials the wrong number and gets Mr. Greenbaum's house by mistake.

"Do you have 'Eyes of Blue' and 'A Love Supreme'?" asks Mrs. Rosengarten.

"Well, no," answers the puzzled Mr. Greenbaum, "but I do have a wife and twelve children."

"Is that a record?" she inquires.

"I don't think so, but it's as close as I want to get!"

The title to this weeks momentous parsha, ancient Israel's foundation epic, comes from its opening, V'eileh shmos, "And these are the names...," a genealogical introduction to the House of Yaacov and its twelve sons, "each with his household."

This mere small clan of 70 souls, in a brief span of prosperity, astonishingly bursts the demographic bubble ("the land was filled with them"); an explosion in population that causes apprehension in a new, but well-entrenched tyrant King ("who knew not Yosef"), to see the Jews as a threat to the nation of Egypt.

Why does the Torah use the present tense for "coming" (habo'im) to Egypt when Yaacov & family were already in Egypt for many years? Because this was the post-Yosef era, one with considerably less Judaic influence, in which the local Jews were viewed by a fresh generation of Egyptians as disloyal wannabee-citizens.

Pharaoh's first reaction?

To curtail the fertility and fecundity of the Jewish people, "lest they multiple" (pen yirbeh); and so he resorts to affliction, enslavement, oppression, forced labor. Does this work? No (the more they afflicted, *ken yirbeh*, "the more they multiplied.") His fallback position? Active depopulation: a direct genocidal decree; death sentence by drowning for all newborn Jewish boys.

> *A Mid-East speaker was denouncing the Jews for causing the problems in early Egypt, when a heckler interjects, "Yes, the Jews and the bicyclists."*
> *Thrown off course, the speaker asks, "Why the bicyclists?"*
> *The heckler replies, "Why the Jews?"*

It is against this backdrop, of a persecuted, suffering, anonymous mass, that the hero of this chapter is born, Moshe, *the* most influential Jew in Jewish history, second child of Yocheved and Amram, (leader of the Jewish community of Goshen in north-eastern Egypt — and one of the few Jews alive who still remembered Yaacov).

The question is apparent: why is this parsha, and the entire second Book of Moshe, called "Names?"

Doesn't its Greek-derived title, *Exodus*, have a much more compelling ring to it? And weren't these names already enumerated, in great detail, in the final verses in Genesis? Why repeat them?

By beginning with a word of continuity ("*And...*"), the Torah deliberately makes a linguistic link between *Bereishis* (the book of Creation) and *Shmos* (the book of actions and redemptions.) Why? Because Jewish history can only be grasped and appreciated by getting to know the actual individuals involved.

So what's in a name? Plenty; in fact God, in His very first act, orders Adam to name all the new animals.

> *When Shane Ferguson was asked how a Jew could have such an un-Jewish name, he replied, "Before I arrived in America 100 years ago I was warned to change my* ▶

133

> *Hebrew name — that it was not 'American' enough.*
> *So on the boat trip over I thought and thought for weeks and finally came up with a new, US-sounding name.*
> *But when the ship docked and the immigration official barked at me, 'Name?' my mind froze and I blurted out, 'shein fergossen! [I've forgotten it already!'].*"

The children of the Bible are given names that sum up their parents feelings and hopes; thus Yosef calls his first-born son Menashe ("to forget"), explaining, "God has made me forget my troubles," and his second son Ephraim ("to be fruitful"), saying, "God has made me fruitful in the land of my affliction."

For centuries, Jews chose names which identified themselves with distinctively Jewish traits: Katz was short for *Kohen Tzedek* ("priest of righteousness"), Sacks stood for *Zera Kodesh* ("holy seed"); and so on.

In the late 18th century the emperor of Austria-Hungary required Jews to have official surnames: that's how the son of David became David*son*; the rabbi became *Rabbi*nowitz; the tailor became Schneider; one Jew became Grossman because he was tall, another was Klein because he was short. Well-known cities produced names like Prager and Warshawsky. The wealthy Jews bribed their way into such pleasant names as Gold, Silver, or Diamant, the poor ones ended up being called Frosch (a frog) or Gans (a goose).

Sometimes, US immigration officials simply wrote down 'Cohen' when they could not understand the heavy Yiddish, assuming it was the universal Jewish surname; one non-Jewish arrival, searching desperately for a true McCoy Americanized name, looked up the New York phone directory, found more Cohens than anyone else, and assumed being an American required him to be called Cohen, too.

Rabbi Avraham Yashayahu Karelitz (*Chazon Ish*) urged parents not to choose an uncommon or strange name for their child, as this might prove embarrassing later on.

> *One day three yeshiva boys go to the Zoo and cause a commotion outside the elephant cage. A cop shows up and asks them for their names and what they were doing.*
> *"My name is Jeremy," the first boy replies innocently, "and I was just throwing peanuts into the elephant cage."*
> *"My name is Larry," the next boy says, "and all I was doing was throwing peanuts into the elephant cage."*
> *"My name is Pinchas," says the third, "but my friends call me Peanuts."*

Judaism views Jewish names not as mere arbitrary designations, but as names that determine destiny ("as is his name, so is he"), a dogma derived from this week's Haftarah.

The Haftarah consists of reading of the Prophets, and is intended to give words of comfort, encouragement, and assurances that all will end well via God's compassionate redemption. It always bears some implied or general reference to the sedra. Why? Because its presence, on an expanded all-year basis, was covertly initiated to dodge the Antiochus IV Epiphanes ban on traditional Torah reading.

In this week's Haftarah, God advises Hosea what to name his children; in fact the Prophet had already changed his own name (which means, "God delivers") to Joshua (which means "God is noble").

"The earned name," notes Phineas ben Hama, "is much more than the given name;" to which Koheles adds, "Every man has three names; one his father and mother gave him, one others call him, and one he acquires himself."

Rashi claims that the Hebrew midwives, Shifra and Puah, who were ordered to serve as proxies to infanticide and instead thwarted Pharaoh's evil intentions, were actually "second" names for Yocheved and Miriam (Moshe's mother and sister) to indicate how they helped Jewish infants both physically and emotionally: Shifra means to "make better," while Puah is akin to a mother's comforting sounds (*"poo, poo..."*) to calm crying babies.

Even the nameless are important.

What is the mighty King of Egypt's name? No one knows; Pharaoh is just a generic title. What is Moshe's real birth name? No one knows; the name Moshe (which means, "I drew him [*m'shesihu*] out of the water") was chosen *ad hoc* by a "rebellious" daughter of Pharaoh who finds the baby floating in a papyrus box-basket amongst the willowy reeds of the Nile.

And what was her name? It's not mentioned, either.

Yehuda Leibush ben Yechiel Michal (*Malbim*), the preeminent Russian Torah commentator of the 19th century, combines two Egyptian words *mo* (water) and *sheh* ("to exit," or "escape") to arrive at *Moshe*.

It is ironic, in light of a Midrash that credits not changing their Hebrew names as saving the Jews from perpetual servitude, that God continues to call Moshe only by his Egyptian name (even after liberation); in sharp contrast to his father who, according to Frankfurt Rabbi Shimon Hadarshan (Shimon the Biblical Orator) called him *Chaver*, his mother called him *Yekusiel*, his sister called him *Yered*, his brother called him *Avi Zanuach*, and his nurse called him *Avi Socho*.

These multiple names perplexed some scholars, who suggest that the diversity results from the non-conformity of *mo*, since water, with no identity of its own, always adjusts to any container into which it is poured.

And more: we don't even know God's preferred name, since His mysterious enigmatic introduction when asked to identify the ancestral God of the patriarchs ("Let me see Your Presence"), is *Ehyeh-Asher-Ehyeh*, "I am/shall be/become what I am/shall be/become," from the verb "be" (in short, "I Am Who I Am"); a reply of austere directness and pure ambiguity, a vague formulation of two verbs that encourages a variety of infinite theological interpretations, a theological recipe wherein God (a verb, not a noun) is not the same in each and every mix.

The Torah in fact allocates no less than 70 different "aspects" to God; but these are not names, merely reflections of many-faceted images within human experience. That is why there are no nouns to be found in the Siddur in reference to God (other than "King," or "Father"); but merely "descriptions" cast in the language of multiple action verbs: We praise God "who blesses the years," "who welcomes repentance," "who redeems the people," and so on.

The famed Rav Chaim, formidable rosh yeshiva of Volozhin and renowned student of the Vilna Gaon, declared that "a person's name is the very essence of his soul," knowing that "essence" is Greek for "being."

It is not a name as we know names to be but a declaration, an aggressive "essence of being," intended to refute and unshackle humankind's superstitious enslavement to all other gods-with-names.

How was it originally pronounced? No one knows. Why? Because its pronunciation has been forbidden for so long

So what's in a name?

Betty calls out to her husband as she is being rushed into labor, "Don't forget, our family's tradition is that the oldest living male, my brother, gets to name the children!"

"But, but..." sputters her husband, "I know your brother. He's a moron! We can't trust him!"

"Don't be silly, he'll be just fine."

A few hours later she delivers twins, a girl and a boy. At the naming ceremony, the husband is relieved when his brother-in-law names his daughter "Denise," but his smile quickly turns to shock when he discovers his son's name: "Denephew."

In this parsha we meet a Jew with a compassion for the afflicted and unfortunate; Moshe, an *onov mikol odom*, the "humblest of men," whose heroic saga after he confronts the hopeless horror of slavery, is a true paradox: his presence and influence, despite his extreme docility and demureness, looms large throughout the Torah.

And yet within the complexity of his fate, his birth, a major event in Jewish history, is described with no fanfare, no lengthy family lineage, just a simple sparse announcement, "The woman conceived and bore a son," accompanied by an understatement, *ki tov*, "this is good" (the same words used by God during Creation).

Consider his near invisibility: Moshe's life begins as an unnamed baby in a temporary wicker basket (*teivas gomeh*); the Pesach Haggadah ignores him totally in his own adventure; he becomes nationally homeless (poignantly expressed when naming his first son, Gershon, from *ger shom*, which means, "I am a stranger in a strange land"); the daughters of Ru'el and his future wife Tzippora simply describe him as "a man of Egypt" (in contrast to Yosef, who Potiphar's spurned wife contemptuously calls, "the Hebrew slave"); he spends the last 40 years of his life "hiding" behind a facial veil so that the Divine radiance does not frighten the folk; and finally, God ensures that the site of his grave remains unknown to history.

Moshe's biography would have to include "The Missing Years," because several decades of his life, from maturity until he returns as God's elected emissary, are squeezed into three short verses; the Torah is strangely silent about this 60-year gap, a disappearance literally in mid-narrative, leaving us clueless as to Moshe's character or spiritual development.

This parsha fast-forwards through the birth of Moshe, skips over the crucial moment when Moshe first discovers that he is Jewish, ignores his formative teenage years, devotes only 22 verses to his young adult life, and condenses eight of his remarkable decades into five terse, concise chapters.

Yes, the Torah also applies this policy of obscurity to Avraham ben Terach, the father of Judaism, who we meet only as a fully integrated adult already endowed with deep spiritually, however, in sharp contrast to Moshe, the Midrashim expound at length on Avraham's early life, helping us recreate a detailed profile.

Why such telegraphic brevity with Moshe?

By speeding through Moshe's early and middle years, the Torah is making the statement that beginnings are less important than endings; that judgment must be reserved for what one ultimately achieves in life.

Many redeemers of Israel enter the most significant chapter of their lives in adulthood; Moshe at 80, Aaron at 83, and the great Rabbi Akiva only began to study Torah at the age of forty.

> *Three little ol' Jewish women are sitting on their nursing home porch, discussing the travails of getting older.*
>
> *"Sometimes," says the first one, "I find myself standing in front of the fridge with a jar of mayonnaise and I can't remember whether I need to put it away, or start making a sandwich."*
>
> *"I have the same problem," sighs the second lady, "sometimes I find myself on the landing and I can't remember whether I was on my way up or down the stairs."*
>
> *"Baruch Hashem," chides in the third woman, "I don't have that problem, knock on wood," as she raps her knuckles on the table, and then suddenly stands up, "That must be the door, I'll get it!"*

Moshe's initial encounters with God at a burning thorn bush, one unconsumed by its own flames, "in the desert-like climate of Midian," helps him rediscover the legacy of Avraham, changing the course of human history.

The site of desolation is chosen for this paradigmatic revelatory experience, according to the Midrash, to teach that seeing-is-believing; that God can be both found and felt in the unexpected, that no place on earth is too humble or low to receive the spirit of Godliness, as long as the ingredients of idolatry are absent.

> *Ol' Mr. Frenkelberg had to spend time in a Catholic hospital. One day, the Sister and nurse are making their rounds and come into his room, and notice that the crucifix on the wall is missing.*
> *"Good morning, Mr. Frenkelberg," the Sister greets him good-naturedly, "Say, what did you do with the crucifix?"*
> *"Oh, sister," he replies, "I took it down. I assumed that one suffering Jew in this room was enough."*

The parsha devotes nearly 40 verses to Moshe's extraordinary dialogue with God's "still small voice," the longest Divine-human personal exchange in the entire Torah.

Why? Because in the silence and safety of Horeb, "the mountain of God" (the same Sinai site that hosts the future public revelation of Torah), He has Moshe's absolute undivided attention; it is from here that the Rambam claims that God can only be found by such *inner* consciousness experiences as the opening of mind or soul, so poignantly expressed by the 11th century poet, Isaac Ibn Ghiyath, "I sought You out and found You in my thoughts: My heart has eyes within that let me see."

Where others may have only seen a thorn bush: Moshe saw inspiration, vision, stimulus; causing Samson Raphael Hirsch to add that each human being is similarly capable of receiving the Divine message and inspiration.

> *An old man is sitting on a hotel porch holding a small piece of rope when a visitor asks him, "What's the rope for?"* ▸

> "It helps me tell the weather," he replies, "I was inspired to make my own weathervane."
>
> "Oh yeah! How can you tell weather with that thing, old man?" asks the incredulous traveler.
>
> "Because, when it goes from side to side, I know it's windy. And when it gets wet, it's raining."

It is from this episode that our Sages call God's word *eish daas*, "a law of fire," in that great ideas, dreams, and thoughts are ignited by inspiration, set aflame by exhilaration, and burn with enthusiasm — and are transmitted to others, never consumed.

That is why the Rambam grants to each human being, capable of being seized by great visions, the capacity of prophecy if the intellect is sufficiently refined; Yehuda Halevi, the Sweet singer of Zion, disagrees, and sees prophecy only as a gift that the Heavens give to select individuals.

> "Hey!" Yankel yells across the road when he spots Beinish, "When are ya gonna pay me back the money you owe me?
>
> "Yankele!" yells back Beinish, "What do you think I am! A prophet?

He may not have been a *born* leader, but Moshe is prolific in leadership, blessed with the ability to be *nosei b'ol im chaveiro*, to share his fellow's burden AND fate; to empathize with the suffering of his fellow Jews. A slew of events transforms him from a shepherd of flocks to the leading shepherd of the whole House of Israel; even as he reluctantly, with disarming honesty, demands of God, "Who am I, that I should bring the Israelites out of Egypt?"

This question 'Who am I?' is directed at himself, a senior citizen entering into the final trimester of his life, estranged from the

Jewish people for eight decades.

When ordered to return and rescue "his brothers" he instantly declines *shlichus* (from the Hebrew verb *shlach*, "to send"), to serve as God's agent ("Send someone else," he begs). Why? "I am not a man of words, but slow of speech and tongue."

Moshe's objections are to no avail; the Heavens are unswayed and assign to him a "spokesman," none other than his elder brother Aaron; the Midrash is however unconvinced: it sees no physical impediment in Moshe but a concern that he is no longer fluent in the language of his people, and thus lacks the capacity to move their hearts and minds.

This is true: as his life progresses we witness an articulate Moshe giving speeches, rulings, warnings — even arguing with God with not a trace of stammer nor stutter, as the ever-confident messenger expands his lexicon with ease.

> *Mendele is on his way home from work when he sees a sign in front of a house: "Talking Dog for Sale." Excited, he rings the bell and the owner tells him to check the dog out in the backyard. Mendele goes 'round the back, walks up to the dog, and asks, "Say, do you talk?"*
>
> *"Sure do," the black mutt replies.*
>
> *"So, what's your story?"*
>
> *"Well," answers the dog, "I discovered my gift of speech when I was still a puppy, and my dream was always to help out my country, so I volunteered for the CIA where I spent the last 20 years jetting around the world, going from country to country, sitting in rooms with spies and world leaders, because no one figured a dog would be eavesdropping. I was the CIA's most valuable spy, but the flying really tired me out, so I asked for a desk job closer to home and I've been doing undercover security work at JFK airport, mostly wandering near suspicious characters and listening in. I've prevented several hijackings and received a bunch of medals. Along the way, I married, had a* ▸

mess of puppies, and now I'm just retired."

Mendele is stunned, and quickly runs inside the house to the owner, "Hey! How much for the dog?"

"Ten dollars."

"Ten dollars! That's a metzia! The mutt's amazing. Why sell him so cheaply?"

"Oh," the owner replies, "He's such a liar. He didn't do any of that stuff."

It's About Time

The title of this parsha, in God's second appearance to Moshe, comes from the verse, "I appeared [*Va'eira*] to Avraham, Yitzchak, Yaacov," a dramatic emergence that contains a stunning admission, "I have remembered My covenant."

It has been 210 years, and the Heavens are moved to compassion by the sounds of Jewish children being brutalized, giving us a glimpse into God's, as opposed to man's, perception of time and unleashing a never-ending study by Torah philosophers on the subject.

"A thousand years in Thy sight are but as yesterday," sings the Psalmist; "No loss like the loss of time," sighs Samuel Uceda, Palestinian commentator; "Time," concludes Abraham Hasdai, a 13th century Hebrew translator from Barcelona, "will free the fly, and cage the eagle!"

When asked why the famous Tower of Pisa leaned, the teacher replied, "What's the point of having the Time if you ain't got the inclination?"

The Torah originally uses a different duration of the predetermined countdown to freedom in Covenantal conversation with

Avraham, "Your seed will be a stranger in a land not their own, and they shall afflict them for 400 years." So how is this number reconciled with this week's disclosure, "It came to pass at the end of [*miketz*] 430 years?"

Rashi sees punctuality in the expression, *b'etzem hayom hazzeh*, "on this very day," in that this *was* the predetermined end to the period of bondage, and bridges the 30-year gap by starting the prophecy three decades later, when Avraham bore Yitzchak; the 13th century Rabbi Moshe ben Nachman (*Ramban*) disagrees, and asserts that 400 years reflects an accurate duration, however the suffering was extended another 30 years as punishment for the sin of the Amorite.

> *Schwartzy, a convicted felon, manages to escape from prison two years into his 10-year sentence, becoming the lead story on the 6 o'clock evening news.*
>
> *Schwartzy takes every precaution as he slowly works his way home, carefully avoiding crowds, taking back alleys, little traveled routes, running across deserted fields — until he finally arrives home, tired, hungry and exhausted, and rings the front doorbell.*
>
> *His wife opens, and shouts, "You good-for-nothing!! Where've ya been!? You escaped over six hours ago!!"*

In their pre-development as a nation, God's initial inclination was that the children of Israel had to experience not only whips, shackles and taskmasters, but also the powerful form of subtle slavery, a bondage that chains the very soul, debases and demeans the body, and mires the whole in a morass of misery.

Persecution in foreign lands had defined the Jewish identity, causing a near-terminal constriction of spirit and self-image; it was time to open their eyes to a future expectation and vision of hope.

Why do the Heavens refer to the land of Israel as a *moroshoh*, "heritage," and not a *yerusha*, "inheritance?" Rabbeinu Bachya, the 14th century Torah commentator notes that the former is a "temporary" step towards final ownership, a causative bridge between generations, from (the ideal) heritage to (reality of) inheritance.

God does more than just renew His pledge in this week's parsha, He *expands* it — from four assurances of national redemption (this is the basis for the four Seder cups of wine) to seven, an appropriate number. Why? Because *shevah* ["seven"] is the Hebrew root for *sh'vuah* ["oath"]).

Did the Jews listen? No. Why not?

Because "their spirits were crushed (*mikotzer ruach*) by the cruel bondage," a descriptive expression that Rashi translates as "a shortness of breath" in a tormented folk collapsing under the weight of despotism.

> *A Frenchman, an Italian, and a little ol' Polish Jew are captured by terrorists and condemned to be executed, but, as is the custom, are given a choice of a final meal.*
>
> *"I want some good French wine, French pastry, French fries, and French bread," the Frenchman wails. His captors give it to him, and shoot him when he finishes.*
>
> *"Give me a big plate of pasta," cries the Italian, "Like me mama used to make me." His captors give him the pasta, and quickly shoot him when he is done.*
>
> *"I want a big bowl of fresh strawberries," says the little ol' Polish Jew.*
>
> *"Strawberries!" screams the executioner, "its September! Strawberries aren't in season for several more months!"*
>
> *"So...I'll wait!"*

God's emissary (Moshe) and the despotic, totalitarian regime of Pharaoh, the "wicked" one, continue to face-off in this parsha which highlights the King of Egypt as being the first person in the Torah to coin the term "Israelite people."

Ironically, the magicians of Egypt play a critical role in Jewish redemption, since it is their failure, prior to this cosmic contest between the God of the patriarchs and the gods of Egypt, to solve Pharaoh's dreams that results in the children of Israel finding themselves in Egypt.

The wizards reappear, no less than five times, in this parsha, turning their own rods into serpents and copy-catting the first few plagues.

> *An elderly Egyptian sorcerer is walking along the Nile when he sees a frog on the road.*
> *"If you pick me up and kiss me," says the frog, "I will turn into a beautiful young woman and grant your every desire."*
> *The Egyptian picks up the frog, puts it in his pocket, and continues walking.*
> *"Hey, hey!" yells the frog, "You didn't kiss me!"*
> *"Well, I thought it over and at my age, I'd rather have a talking frog."*

Nissim ben Reuben Gerondi (*Ran*) concludes that God chose the Empire of Egypt on purpose. Why? To display His Power in *the* recognized land of sorcery; a den of witchcraft wherein, says the Midrash, the populace could quickly distinguish the counterfeit from the real McCoy, but by the third plague (lice), the magician's luck runs out; they fail in their pseudo-plague imitation and are forced to recognize "the finger of God."

> *A magician was working on a cruise ship and every night his audience was different, which allowed him to do the same tricks over 'n over again.*
> *There was only one problem: the captain's parrot watched the shows and his sharp eye soon figured out how the tricks were being done. Having a mean streak, the parrot would interrupt each show, "Look, look! It's not* ▶

> the same hat!" or "Look, look! He's hiding the flowers un-
> der the table!," or "Look, look! All the cards are the same
> Ace of Spades!"
>
> The magician was furious but couldn't do anything be-
> cause it was his boss's parrot. Then, one day, the boat hits
> an iceberg and sinks; the magician and parrot find them-
> selves, ironically, clinging to the same piece of wood, in the
> middle of the ocean.
>
> They stare at each other for days and nights in hate,
> uttering not a single word, until, a week later, the parrot
> finally speaks up, "Okay, Okay! I give up! What'd you do
> with the boat?"

This parsha is the first to introduce seven of the ten terrifying images of multiple plagues, their character arranged in pairs: blood and frogs come from the Nile; vermin and beasts are troublesome creatures of dry land; pestilence and boils are diseases; hail and locusts are a blow to agriculture; and darkness, which signifies death, is appropriately paired with a plague of first-borns.

The first three (*dam, tzefardea, kinim*) have something in common: none were initiated by Moshe, but by Aaron instead. Why? A lesson: never to forget ones "friends."

Dam and *tzefardea* involved the River Nile (named after Nilus, an important Egyptian deity); *kinim* involved dust. Moshe remembered he has a debt of gratitude to the River (which carried him to safety in a floating basket) and the dust (that hid the corpse of the Egyptian that he killed).

> Just after she is fired, the maid takes $5 from her purse
> and throws it to Fido, the family dog.
>
> "Why'dya do that?" asks her former employer.
>
> "Well, ma'am," she replies, "I never forget a friend, so
> I just wanted to thank Fido for all the times he helped me
> clean the dishes!"

The popular slang, "don't bite the hand that feeds you," is a direct hand-me-down of the Talmud's, "Do not throw stones into the well that you drink from."

This tangible expression of appreciation is known as *hakoros hatov*, the purpose of which, according to Rav Eliyahu E. Dessler, rosh yeshiva of Gateshead, is not just for the benefactor, but also the recipient.

The Hebrew word for thanks (*toda*), notes Rav Yitzchak Hutner, the former rosh yeshiva of Chaim Berlin, also means "to confess," thus linking the expression of gratitude to making a confession that we are often ungrateful (*kafoi tov*) to those who assist us in life.

> *After his wealthy uncle advises him to always appreciate the good things in life, the nephew asks, "So how did you make so much money?"*
>
> *"Well, I remember like it was yesterday. It was 1932, the depth of the Great Depression. I was down to my last nickel, which I invested in an apple. I spent the entire day polishing the apple and, at the end of the day, I sold the apple for ten cents. The next morning, I invested those ten cents in two apples, and then I spent the entire day polishing them and sold them late in the evening for twenty cents. I continued this system every day 'n night for an entire month, by the end of which I'd accumulated the sum of $1.60 — and then, thankfully, my wife's uncle Bernie died and left us two million dollars."*

God's use of the number ten coincides with the flexing of Godly power and authority. It first appears in Genesis, when God creates the world with "ten utterances" (the word *vayomer*, "and He said," appearing ten times); the number next appears when God frees His people from Egyptian bondage via ten plagues; and again at Mt. Sinai when the Jews receive the Torah.

Were the Ten issued directly from God to Israel?

No one is sure: Ibn Ezra says "yes;" the Rambam says "no" (that only Moshe understood, whereas the Jewish people only "heard" without comprehending); the Ramban compromises, with a "yes, but;" in that the Jews only comprehended the first two (the existence of an infinite, invisible, incomprehensible God), requiring Moshe to repeat the final eight.

Why the confusion?

The tradition of "613" (*taryag*) is derived from the gematria (611) of the verse, *Torah tziva lanu Moshe* (that the Torah was given via Moshe) plus an additional two (to bring it up to 613) commandments issued directly by God (the first two, *Anochi Hashem*, "I am God," and *Lo yihyeh*, "You shall have no other gods.") This conclusion is not just based on gematria but on grammar: there is a switch from first person in the first two Commandments to third person form in the remaining eight.

Were there exactly "ten" plagues? It depends who's counting, and who's interpreting.

The Hebrew word for plague (*makkos*) appears only once, in the Book of Samuels, and is attributed not to a Jew but to a gentile Philistine, "He is the same God who struck the Egyptians with every kind of plague [*makkos*]."

Rashi, the prince of Torah commentators, who generally adheres to the most literal meaning, claims that the Philistine was specifically referring to God's strike against the Egyptian military at the Red Sea, and its subsequent parting of waters that led to the Jews' safe passage.

The Torah itself describes this as the greatest of all the Exodus marvels, yet, inexplicably, leaves it out of the ten traditional "plagues." In fact, Jewish tradition prefers the expression *osos u'mofesim*, "signs and marvels," with one exception: the last one, the first-born slayings, the only one characterized as "a true *nega* [plague]."

Some Torah scholars include Moshe's rod-into-a-serpent (*tanin*), an act ordered by God, making it eleven, not ten, "signs and marvels." And by adding the events at the Red Sea, the number goes up to twelve. And in order to maintain the purity of "ten" plagues, remembered through Rabbi Judah's mnemonic device, *detza"kh, ada"sh, baha"b*, the Book of Jubilees combines boils and pestilence into one plague.

These contradictions caused a headache for the rabbis who composed the Haggadah, and so they added a series of tannaitic homilies to God's final Red Sea "plague" in order to distance it from the previous "ten," thus multiplying this last strike to "50-250 blows."

The Vilna Gaon claims only three ways in which God manifests Himself; via *hanhagas nissim* ("overt miracles," an example being the Heaven-sent manna, and quenching thirst from a rock); *hanhagas nissim nistarim* ("hidden miracles," as in rain falling in Israel in proper times and amounts, health and wealth, etc), and *hester ponim* ("the hiding of God's Face," wherein man is left to his own devices, no longer relying on manna but on his own harvesting in order to eat).

But there is an obvious question: why not just one plague, one body blow, the last one?

Because the series of ever escalating "signs and marvels," a demonstration of Divine might and sovereignty within this cosmic battle, were intended to impress the Jews as much as frighten their enemies. It was important that this slave people, led by an old man with no army, weapons nor chariots, witness the slow, humiliating destruction of a mighty Pharaoh who in ancient Egypt was considered an earthbound regal god.

The series of grandiose miracles and the Exodus were thus pure PR; to acknowledge God's existence and power, and to recognize that there is a Godly dimension in the world whose intent it is to transform Israel into a harmonious holy nation.

151

To Italian Rabbi Ovadiah Sforno, 16th century commentator, the widely publicized exit was meant to impress on all future generations (of Jews *and* Egyptians) the recognition not just of *Vidatem ki ani Hashem*, "I am God," but that God intends to play an active role in the adventures of the Jewish people.

This is why the centrality of Judaic remembrance ("this day shall be to you one of remembrance") appears in this parsha; the gift of memory intended as an antidote to the curse of spiritual amnesia, an insight that bondage can also apply to forgetfulness 'n ignorance, the twin precursors to self-recognition of who and what we are.

Forgetfulness is the Torah's greatest challenge.

> "Nu, *Tommy*," Sophie asks her husband after a round of golf, "How vas your game, dear?"
>
> "Vell, I vas hitting pretty vell, but my eyesight's gotten so bad I couldn't see ver de ball went."
>
> "But Tommy, you're 75 already, vy not take my brother Sammy along?"
>
> "Vat, are you crazy! He's 85! He doesn't play golf anymore!"
>
> "Yes, Tommy, but he's got perfect eyesight, and vould vatch the ball for you."
>
> So the next day Tommy swings the ball as Sammy looks on as it disappears down the fairway.
>
> "Do you see it?" asks Tommy, peering off into the distance.
>
> "Yup, I sure do!"
>
> "Vell, ver is it?"
>
> "I forgot."

BO
Up Close and Personal

The galloping Egyptian chariots arrive at a fork in the road with the sign pointed both ways. Befuddled, the captain yells out to a little Jewish boy standing close by: "Hey, does it make any difference which road I take to Pithom? "Not to me," he yawns.

This weeks dramatic parsha chronicles the departure of the Jews from Egypt, yet its title *Bo,* despite many translations, does not mean "Go [*bo*] to Pharaoh" but "come," thus making the verse read, "Come to Pharaoh, I will be with you!" — a literary hint that the confrontation is about to become up close and intensely personal.

The 12th century French Rabbi Joseph ben-Isaac (*Bechor Shor*) sees the interplay of "I" in this context as a royal "we," as in Heaven's poignant attempt to lift Moshe's spirits and reassure him to carry on ("Come, let's join forces and go *together*") despite the failure of seven terrifying plagues.

The right term for "go" had already been established by God's *lech* ("go") directive to Avraham.

But wait: doesn't "Exodus" mean to go? No, it is an expression of a continuing process, one of coming and going.

Meanwhile, Jewish mystics note that the gematria of *Bo* (3) equals the number of plagues in this parsha, the final three that climax Egypt's doomed confrontation with Moshe. Gematria, where the numerical value of each Hebrew letter gives mystic meaning to the word, is often used to support various Torah interpretations.

> *"Rebbe, tell me," a chossid asks his mentor, "Why do we eat kugel on Shabbos?"*
> *"Because kugel and Shabbos have the same gematria," replies the wise rebbe.*
> *A few hours later, the chossid comes running back, "Rebbe, Rebbe! I added it up. You made a mistake! The gematria of Shabbos is greater than the gematria of kugel!!"*
> *"Okay! Okay! So just have another piece of kugel!!"*

In 1988, this parsha was used as 'Exhibit A' by an Egyptian law professor (Nabil Helmi) who filed a lawsuit against the State of Israel for a 3,400-year old debt. The plaintiff wanted to be reimbursed for everything his country had once "lent" the Jews. His evidence? A climactic verse from this week's parsha, "The Israelites drained Egypt of its wealth," which the plaintiff claimed "provides ample proof of the biggest robbery in history."

Helmi can even pinpoint the date of the crime (the 14th of Nisan), who's idea it was (God, having promised Avraham that his descendants would not leave Egypt empty-handed, but "with great substance"), the mastermind behind it (Moshe), the perpetrators ("Jewish women"), the victims ("their Egyptian neighbors"), a description of what went missing ("silver, jewels, gold, utensils, garments"), the losses (nine million tons of gold) — and even where the money went (to build a Golden Calf, and a Tabernacle).

> *A hold-up guy walks into a Chinese restaurant and says, "Give me all your money."*
> *The man behind the counter says, "To take out?"*

I agree with the Egyptian professor's mischievous lawsuit, on one condition: that the equitable concept of "quid pro quo" also be applied so that our destitute ancestors get a reparation offset for generations of backpay degradation, and workers comp for years of servitude.

Their stay in the "iron furnace" of Egypt left them *kotser ruach*, "broken in body and spirit," after building the "store-cities" of Pitom and Ramses;" a form of labor known as *corveire*, wherein no matter how much one receives in salary, it is taken away in the form of punitive.

The Mechilta, a 3rd century Midrashic work, claims that these were post-plague "gifts," a result of the deep remorse of the Egyptian populace as to their horrific treatment towards their next-door-neighbors.

"To harden the heart" is a figure of speech that suggests one is drained of such feelings as anguish or compassion for another; an image conjured up of the most human of organs turned to rock. Yet by "hardening" Pharaoh's heart, anti-Torah forces have an argumentative pretext that God did not allow Pharaoh to repent, depriving him of his free will, paralyzing his response to the plea of *Shalach es ami*, "Let My people go."

However, prior to five of the plagues Pharaoh was warned of the consequences and still refused, putting himself in a position described by Rabbi Shimon, "When God warns a person on three occasions and he does not turn from his (evil) ways, God closes the door of repentance."

The Torah blames it on his increasingly *kaved lev* nature, which means "a heart heavy-with-stubbornness," a self-generated and not Heaven-directed "hardening;" a necessary prerequisite, notes the 16th century kabbalist Eleazar ben Moshe Azikri, to gratuitous hatred.

Like all humans, Pharaoh had a God-given capacity to choose between good and evil, and deliberately chose cruelty over compassion, bringing absolute destruction upon his family and country. This is a "Pharaoh-mentality," with "Pharaoh" being spelled *peh-*

raish-ayin-heh, whose letters, when re-arranged, also spell *arufah,* which refers to the back of the neck, the Biblical symbol of stubbornness; hence the expression *kasheh oref,* "stiff-necked," a metaphorically-speaking description of stubbornness; a wise-cracking quality of obstinacy that seems to follow the Jews wherever they go.

> *"If there are any idiots in the room," the sarcastic lecturer addresses his new class, "will they please stand up."*
>
> *There is a long silence, until Morrie Rosenberg slowly rises to his feet.*
>
> *"So Morrie," says the lecturer with a sneer, "how come you think you're an idiot?"*
>
> *"Well sir, I don't, I just hate to see you standing up there all by yourself."*

It is the "hardening" not of Pharaoh's hands nor brains but of his heart that hints at his evil; which is why Jews pray to God not with all their might nor body but with all their "heart and soul." In fact there are no less than ten references to God "hardening" Pharaoh's heart, and ten more instances wherein a defiant Pharaoh hardens his own heart.

The Torah's term for heart (*lev, levav*) appears no less than 850 times, a recognition that it is *the* central discerning organ of emotion and intellect, character and morality; thus, when God judges an individual, He "probes the heart;" when He wishes to reform, He promises to "replace the heart of stone with a heart of flesh," as per the Psalmist's, "Create in me a clean heart, O God, and put a new and steadfast spirit within me."

This is not just a Jewish insight: Egyptian tomb paintings picture the weighing of dead hearts against feathers, the supposed hieroglyph for truth, to ensure they are empty of evil before rewarding the dead with eternal life (in the background hovers a demon who waits expectantly for the defendant's heart if a negative verdict is rendered).

This parsha confirms that a "hardened heart" is synonymous with moral atrophy, and a predisposition to cruelty; it was the heart, despite its tiny size, that our Yiddishists credited with containing the entire world (*di klainer hartz nemt arum di groisseh velt*); as the "Pharaoh Syndrome" entered the Judaic lexicon to describe a psychological self-inflicted illness of those who were so cold and callous ("a heart of stone") as to be immune from sharing the pain and feeling of others.

> Beryl goes running to Freddie, the local philanthropist, bangs on the door, and, with tears in his eyes, tells him what has happened to a poor family in the neighborhood.
> "Freddie, you gotta help out! The father is dead, the mother is too ill to work, and nine starving children are about to be thrown out into the cold, empty streets unless someone pays their back rent, which comes to $937."
> "Oy, that's terrible! But tell me, Beryl, how do you fit in?"
> "I'm the landlord."

At the ninth plague Pharaoh's stubborn streak shows cracks of further weakening. In fact, it is the earlier assault of hailstones (*barad*) that causes Pharaoh to blink first, blurting out an admission ("God is righteous") and a confession ("I and my nation are sinners") at the beginning of this parsha. The sight of the next, eighth plague (*arbeh*), was also surely horrifying: a disintegration of the country as Egypt's greenery is devoured by locusts that descend in such great numbers that "they cover the surface of the land."

Abarbanel views these last three plagues as a group with special significance: each sharing the element of darkness; however the 10th, final and most extreme plague is different from all other plagues. The plague of the firstborn dramatically staples the

Egyptian demise to the metaphoric and sudden rebirth of Israel.

This ultimate encounter, unleashed in the "middle of the night," slays the country's firstborn males (*makas b'choros*), including Pharaoh's son as he sits by the side of his father's throne. The Midrash and Ibn Ezra both claim that this mass killing ("there was no house where there was not someone dead") was the *only* real form of severe retribution, noting that none of the other plagues caused Egyptian fatalities, they were merely a reaction to Pharaoh's insolence; a requital in kind (*midoh k'neged midoh*) for the pains the Egyptians caused the Jews (the first plague of blood, for example, struck the Nile because the Egyptians "cast the Israelites' children into the sea").

Pharaoh himself had derived his power by birthright, being the firstborn of the firstborn of the firstborn. With neither first-born nor slaves, the entire Egyptian society would crumble, thus the final plague struck at the very epicenter of Pharaoh and his civilization, paving the way for the liberation of the Jews; and more: Egyptian culture, notes Rabbeinu Bachya, 14th century Torah commentator, deified both their sheep (the first of the Zodiac signs) and their firstborn, who ruled by primogeniture. the Divine assault had a twin goal, not so much retribution as eradication of false gods. And because lamb was a sacred deity, this became the only plague in which the Jews were required to put a mark of identification (lamb blood) on the doorposts and lintels of their homes, a special sign to divert the Angel of Death to "pass over" these bloody portals.

It is also from this parsha that the Haggadah "borrows" (*derech derush*) three of the four children's *Ma Nishtana* questions as an inspiring curriculum outline for the Pesach's *seder tisch* (the fourth, a reference to the Wise Child, appears later, in Deuteronomy).

Each of the three profound pedagogical verse-questions, despite seeming thematically repetitive, is different because each addresses a different type of child ("According to the son's intelligence, the father instructs him); a guide that education must be relevant, meaningful, effective: in other words, know your audience!

> *The Zookeeper is surprised to see an orangutan sitting under a tree absorbed in two books; the Torah, and Darwin's 'Origin of Species.'*
> *"Hey, monkey! How come you're reading those books?"*
> *"Well, I was just curious...am I my brother's keeper, or my keeper's brother?"*

The escalation of plagues is a hermeneutic device described by the Midrash as *kal vachomer,* from "minor to major," intended, according to the 13th century Spanish Rabbi Moshe ben Nachman (*Ramban*) to demonstrate God's power rather than punishment.

And it works: "Tell me exactly who is going?" Pharaoh asks Moshe, his tone obviously changing, in response to the request to let the Jews take a three-day leave of their serfdom to pray to God.

"Our young and our old," replies Moshe, a clear indication that prayer is not just restricted to adults; and the inspiration for the Psalmist's, "Lads and maidens, old men and youths," a daily hallelujah that, according to the famous Radak, clearly confirms the role of children in the service of God.

And so Moshe mentions Jewish children first; in order to emphasize priorities; that, in contrast to pagan Egyptian religions wherein the young were of no significance, Jews place their children on a spiritual pedestal, considering it incomprehensible not to have the young (symbolizing the future) stand together with the old (a holy link with the past).

> *The fifth grade rebbe gives his class an assignment: to ask their parents for real-life family stories that come with a moral attached.*   ▶

The next day, little Sophie tells her class, "My bubba lived on a farm in Poland and every week she would go to the market and sell eggs. One day, she tripped and the basket of eggs went flying through the air, breaking all over the road. The moral of her story is not to put all your eggs in one basket!"

"Excellent," says the rebbe, who then asks little Rivka to go next.

"My cousin also lived on a farm in Russia, and they raised chickens for the meat market. One day, a dozen eggs hatched, but only produced three live chickens. The moral is don't count your chickens before they hatch!"

"Very good," says the rebbe, who then points to little Toby.

"My Daddy told me about our aunt Basha who was a paratrooper in the Israeli Army and fought in the Six Day War. Well, one day her plane was hit so aunt Basha had to bail out over enemy territory, and all she had was a bottle of whiskey, a machine gun, and a machete. So aunt Basha drank the whiskey on the way down so it wouldn't break, and then she landed right in the middle of 100 enemy soldiers. She killed 70 of them with the machine gun and then, when she ran out of bullets, my aunt killed 20 more with the machete before the blade broke off, and then she killed the last ten with her bare hands."

The class was silent, until the rebbe gasps, "Good heavens, Toby! What's the moral of that story?"

"Stay away from auntie Basha when she's been drinking!"

Pharaoh knew that by keeping the youth in Egypt, he was causing a break in the chain of tradition in which fathers teach sons ("Remember the days of old, ask your father and he will tell you."). And so Pharaoh offers to only let the "adult men" leave.

The offer is rejected, and the ninth plague, a palpable, three-day deathlike eclipse of "total darkness" (*choshech*), is on its way. Ibn Ezra, an experienced maritime traveler, compared it to the heavy, thick fogs he encountered at sea in the middle of the day.

The names of the two surviving Houses of Israel (Judah, Levi) are legendary, and even the names of the ten "lost" Tribes (Reuven, Shimon, Ephraim, Naphtali, etc) have been passed down within Jewish families, yet there is an obvious absence: the names of women and wives are conspicuously unlisted.

Although Moshe is the obvious hero of the narrative it is impossible not to be touched by a litany of uncommissioned brave heroines whose acts and inspiration made liberation, and thus Jewish existence itself, possible; and so the Talmud credits the adorned and perfumed women of Israel for maintaining morale and keeping up the spirits of their despondent, despairing husbands; encouraging them to continue having children and raising families despite Pharaoh's death decrees.

In fact the Torah's first act of passive civil disobedience comes to us courtesy of Shifrah and Puah, two brave midwives (Yocheved and Miriam, according to the Midrash) who refuse to carry out Pharaoh's order of genocide-infanticide; Pharaoh's nameless daughter then defies her father's decree, draws the baby Moshe from the Nile, and raises him as her own; and then there is Moshe's mother, Yocheved (who bore a son at age 130 in courageous stealth and faith, defying her husband Amram's wish that wives cease bearing children in order to deprive Pharaoh of more Jewish victims), Moshe's sister, Miriam (whose watchful eye protects her baby brother bobbing in an ark in the waters), and wife, Zipporah (who saves her husband's life by circumcising their son after he fails to do so, attracting the wrath of God.)

> *That one should never underestimate the power of a woman became obvious one day when three Jews were walking in the woods and unexpectedly came upon a large raging, violent river. They needed to get to the other side, but had no idea of how to do so.* ▸

So Morris began to pray, "Dear God, please give me the strength to cross this river" — and pooof!, the Heavens granted his wish and gave him big arms and strong legs, enabling him to just make it to the other side in about two hours, nearly drowning a few times.

Seeing this, Itzi immediately turned his eyes upwards and prayed, "Oh Almighty One, please give me the strength, and just in case, also the tools to cross this river" — and pooof! God gave him a rowboat and he was able to row across the river in about an hour, after almost capsizing the boat a couple of times.

Simcha, the third Jew, was stunned. He had seen how the prayers of his two friends had worked so he also began to pray, "Oh Lord of the Universe, please give me the strength and tools, and also, just in case, the intelligence to cross this river" — and pooof! he is immediately turned into a woman who quickly looks at the map, walks a few dozen yards upstream and then simply walks across the bridge.

BESHALACH
Say a Little Prayer For Me...

The title of this week's parsha, *Beshalach*, comes from the verse, *Vay'hee beshalach meedor dor*, "And it was that [God] sent them [*beshalach*] from generation to generation."

Yet *Beshalach's* Hebrew root (*shaloch*) can also mean "to accompany," leading the Midrash to paint an imagery of Pharaoh himself "escorting" the Jewish people out of Egypt, a humble act of remorse which, according to Rav Elazar Menachem Schach, rosh yeshiva of Ponovitch, was deserving of a reward.

This parsha is packed with startling drama and rich dialogue; an escape from Egypt, a Red Sea parting, manna from heaven, Moshe's striking of a rock for water — and a subtle lesson in the pros and cons of prayer, and reliance of faith.

The Jews find themselves trapped in tumultuous terror at a place called Pi Hachiros; behind them are the thundering horse sounds of 600 well-armed, vengeful Egyptian chariots; ahead lies the pounding waves of the Red Sea. Their immediate reaction?

Hysterical desperation: first, a "cry out to God [*vayitzaku*]" in "panic and prayer," followed by a sarcastic assault against Moshe, blaming him for their predicament, accusing their liberator of perfidy in leading them to certain death at the swords of Egyptian horsemen ("We would rather serve the Egyptians than die in the desert!")

A stunned Moshe turns to God and also pleads for Divine intervention. God's response? Unexpected and uncharacteristic: stop wasting time in "lengthy" prayers (*Ma titzak eilai?* "Why do you cry out to Me?") and take matters into your own hand.

> *A Jew on a mountain-climbing expedition lost his footing and began to slide over a precipice. As he slipped over the edge, he managed to grab hold of a branch of a gnarled tree growing out of the side of the cliff. He held on for dear life, seeing a drop of hundreds of feet below him. Knowing that he would not be able to hold on forever and with no help in sight, he began to pray: "O God, please save me, do not let me lose my grasp and be smashed on the rocks below." Suddenly, there came a reply: "Do not worry. Just let go of the branch; I will catch you and gently guide you to safe ground." The desperate man thought for a moment and then asked: "Is there anyone else I can talk to?"*

"Go forward," advises God, in the Torah's premiere lesson of survival; a realization that action takes precedence over contemplation; that trust in God alone is insufficient if you lack the courage to trust in yourself.

Nachshon ben Aminadav gets the message: his spirit suddenly shifts from passive to active as he bravely steps into "the midst of the sea," causing the waters to split into "a fortress wall" (*choma*). This single act of faith and ennoblement energizes an entire nation to march forward through a dry seabed, an act that symbolizes the final and full transition of a folk from slavery to freedom.

The moral of Nachshon's small (physical) step yet giant (spiritual) leap is not lost on the 12th century Spanish Sage, Moshe ben Maimon (*Rambam*), who marries the themes of prayer and action into a "positive commandment."

It is the parting of these waters that motivated the rabbis of the Talmud to make a startling comparison: *Kashe l'zavgom k'kriyas yam suf*, "It is as difficult for God to pair couples as it was for Him to split the Red Sea."

The question is obvious: why should an All-powerful God have difficulty splitting some waters? And even if it *was* difficult for a Deity, how could it possibly be analogous to the pairing of couples?

The similarity lies in initiative: no pairing (*l'zavgom*) can occur unless a man and a woman take matters into their own hands, as Nachshon did, and actively seek, find, maintain, and enhance, a relationship. Only *after* this human effort will God help couples find each other; a concept known as *bashert*. What was difficult for God at *kriyas yam suf* was the discipline to refrain Himself from immediately helping His people under siege, awaiting human initiative.

This parsha is also known as *Shabbos Shira* because of its melodic highlight: the magnificent 18-verse *Shir Hashirim* ("Song at the Sea"), the greatest ode in the entire Torah that, as a source of collective memory, is a central part of our daily prayer's *Mi Chamochah* and "Blessing of Redemption (*geulah*)."

Shir Hashirim is an elated Psalm of praise and *niggun* (melody) of redemption, spontaneously sung by a rescued people who had just witnessed the dramatic drowning of the Egyptian cavalry.

It is here, among rich language, vivid metaphors, and lyrics of passion and appreciation, that Miriam, co-orchestrator of the chorus, is first identified by name, as a Prophetess.

That an exhilarated nation responds not in prose nor study but in poetry and tune, the most liberating and soul-uplifting of all activities, with such lyrics as *Zeh kayli v'anveihu* (This is my God and I will praise, beautify and exalt Him), becomes the Halachic source of *hiddur mitzvoh*, the search to perform a mitzva in the most beautiful way possible.

The prisoner lined up for death by firing squad is granted one last wish from the warden, "Would you like a special meal?"

"No."

"A cigarette and a blindfold."

"No."

"Perhaps, a final prayer," asks the Chaplain.

"No."

"Well, is there anything we can do for you before you go?"

"Yes," replies the condemned man, "music is my life and my passion, and there's just one favorite song I'd like to sing through to the end please, with no interruptions."

"Sure," the guard nods, "Go right ahead."

So the prisoner starts to sing, "One billion bottles of beer on the wall...."

The Rambam rules that one may reside anywhere in the world except Egypt, a prohibition that is repeated three times (the first in this parsha) by a Torah concerned about the influence of heretic beliefs and corrupted attitudes; described by the classic *Sefer Hachinuch*, a medieval work on the meanings of mitzvos, as "evil and sinful."

The implication of return to Egypt — renewed bondage and forfeiture of independence — is why the rabbis of the Talmud link the survival of Israel to its avoidance of Egypt, and even conclude that the large Jewish community of Alexandria, despite their fidelity to Torah, was destroyed for transgressing this one prohibition of living in Egypt from the time of Alexander the Great (c. 333 BCE) until the period of the Roman emperors Trojan and Harden.

This is why our Jewish mystics were excited to pair 'Pharaoh' as the third word in the verse (*Vayehi beshalach paroh es ho'om*, "Now when Pharaoh let the people go") to 'Amalek,' the third-from-last word in this parsha.

The back-to-back lesson?

The Heavens may have parted the sea, turned bitter water to sweet, rained down quail and manna, and guided the Jews with pillars of cloud and fire, but it wasn't until the Jews finally fought their Amalekite-nemesis that their painful evolution and growth as a nation was complete.

In fact, ancient Israel even had a special *kohen mashu'ach lamilchomoh*, "Priest anointed for battle" whose role was morale: to address the folk and urge them not to be afraid, because God was with them.

The "war kohen" is the precursor to today's military chaplain; a position that George Washington brought into law in 1775 with a short *dvar Torah*: "The blessing and protection of Heaven are at all times necessary, but especially so in times of public distress and danger" (the term 'chaplain' is un-Jewish: it comes from the French *chapelains* which itself is derived from *cappellanus*, men who carry the *cappa*, Latin for cloak, into battle, which legend traces to the tunic of Martin of Tours, a Roman soldier who converted to Christianity in the 4th century, and was later canonized).

> *The Israeli General inspecting a military graduating class asks the officer-in-charge about his men's bravery.*
>
> *"My men, sir, are Baruch Hashem, the bravest in the country! Watch this."*
>
> *The officer points to a man in front, and snaps, "Hey you! Private Mendele! See that tank headin' this way. I want you to stop it with your body!"*
>
> *"What! Are you crazy?" Mendele screams back, "It'll kill me, you idiot! I'm out of here!"*
>
> *"You see," the officer says to the bewildered General watching Mendele run away, "You gotta be pretty brave to talk like that to an officer and a general."*

Amalek appears immediately after the Jews' voice their doubts, linking the gematria of Amalek (240) to the Hebrew word for doubt (*sofeik*).

Moshe had obviously learned his Nachshon lesson well: in response to the Amalekite assault at Rephidim, the leader of the Jews does *not* turn to the Heavens but immediately deputizes Joshua and orders his future charismatic successor to counterattack.

Only then, *after* placing the people's destiny into the hands of one of their own, does Moshe, standing on a hill with upraised hand (*Yareem Mosheh yado*) invite God to join the physical fray.

And it works: for the first time in this saga the argumentative, bickering and fractious Jews do not groan, growl nor grumble, but respond with bravery and action, emerging victorious from their first military challenge as a free people.

> *After a long day's battle, the Company Commander and his First Sergeant, a Torah scholar, hit the sack for the night. The Commander asks his companion, "Look Reb Tzvi, up into the sky, tell me what you see?"*
>
> *The pious soldier looks up, sighs, and says in awe, "I see millions of stars."* ▸

"And what does that tell you, Reb Tzvi?"

"Astronomically, it tells me there are millions of galaxies and potentially billions of planets. Theologically, it tells me God is great and we are small and insignificant. Meteorologically, it tells me we will have a beautiful day tomorrow. What does it tell you, Sir?"

"It tells me somebody stole our darn tent!"

YISRO
Go with the Goy

Yankele Ostrovolitch decides to join the Hancock Country Club but he knows they don't accept Jews, so he changes his name to Sir Howard Madigan Trafalgar the Third, retains a plastic surgeon to change his Jewish appearance to an Anglo-Saxon one, and takes tutoring lessons to alter his lower East Side Yiddish accent to the honeyed upper-class linguistics of Martha's Vineyard.

The big day comes and he shows up for his interview in front of the membership committee.

"Please state your name," asks the distinguished WASPY chairman.

"Sir Howard Madigan Trafalgar the Third," he replies in a smug British accent.

"And where were you educated, Mr. Trafalgar?"

"Oh, the usual places: Eton, Oxford, Yale..."

"And your religion?"

Yankele hesitates, then answers confidentially, "Goy."

This momentous parsha is named after a gentile, Yisro (Jethro), who may have been Moshe's father-in-law, but he was also a pagan high priest from Midian, an ally of the ruthless Amalek, and a leader of several sects of idolatry.

The question is obvious: Why?

Perhaps because he was the first to offer Moshe, fleeing after killing an Egyptian task master, hospitality, safety, comfort, friendship — and even a wife (his daughter Zipporah). Rabbi Hayyim Ben Alter, the 18th century mystic, has an interesting theory: Yisro is chosen to demonstrate the need for including the wisdom of other peoples into Jewish life.

He is not the first gentile to mix with Jews...

170

> *Two guys have been learning together for 20 years. One of them is going to make a bar mitzva so he invites his friend to come.*
>
> *"I'm sorry, I can't."*
>
> *"But I really want you to come."*
>
> *"You don't understand. I just can't come."*
>
> *"But why can't you come?"*
>
> *"I'm not Jewish."*
>
> *"What do you mean? We have been learning together for 20 years!"*
>
> *"I enjoy the intellectual stimulation."*
>
> *"But we learned that a goy that keeps Shabbos is 'chay-av misoh'" (must be punished with the death penalty).*
>
> *"I never kept Shabbos. Every time I was ready to leave my house, I put a key in my pocket."*
>
> *"But we have an Eruv (an enclosure permitting carry-ing on Shabbos) here."*
>
> *"Oh, that Eruv! I don't hold by that Eruv."*

The main clue to Yisro achieving Judaism's eternal recognition appears right in the opening salvo, *Vayishma Yisro*, "and Yisro heard"... heard what?

No one knows exactly what he heard, nor which wonder and miracle impressed him the most. But Rashi, the indispensable commentator of commentators, narrows it down to two: the miracles of sea splitting (which the Haggadah claims were five times greater than the plagues), and the victories against Amalek.

The master 18th century ethicist from Italy, Rabbi Moshe Chaim Luzzatto, and Levi Ben Gershon (*Ralbag*, also known as Gersonides), agree: the reason Yisro suddenly decides to visit his kin in the wilderness is to check out the rumors, a lesson that one should go out of his way to see the perfection of God's power.

Yisro is the perfect paradigm to promote God's seven international Noachide laws of morality, and is the inspiration behind the great respect and esteem that the 12th century Spanish Moshe ben

Maimon (*Rambam*) displayed for converts, as evidenced by his remarkable letter to Ovadia the Ger ("Regarding proselytes, our obligation is a great, heart-bound love.")

> *Moshe was fed up with the life in Brooklyn so he moves to a small mid-western town that has no Jews, but he misses the weekly drasha he used to hear from the rav so he starts going to the local church every Sunday just to hear the sermons. He has no interest in conversion but seeks intellectual stimulation. Soon word gets out that there is a Jew in their midst and the locals complain to the priest. The next Sunday, Moshe is sitting in the front row of the church near the pulpit waiting to listen to the sermon. The priest gets up, and, looking straight at Moshe announces, "I must insist that all Jews leave this church!"*
>
> *Moshe stays seated. The priest, raising his voice, repeats, "All Jews are to leave this church, immediately!"*
>
> *A stunned Moshe gets the message, stands up, goes over to the cross, takes Jesus off the wall and says, "Come on, let's go. We're not wanted here!"*

So paralyzed is Yisro by the charm and elegance of Sinai, witnessing a peoplehood (*ga'alta*) being infused with a religious purpose (*kanisa*), that he immediately offers a sacrifice, and publicly confirms that "God is greater than all gods" — in fact, neither Moshe nor Aaron had thought to offer such a blessing until the ex-sheik of Midian arrives.

Yisro is thus *the* epitome of a righteous proselyte (a *ger tzedeck*), entering Jewish history as the first person to mutter the now popular expression, *Boruch Hashem* ("Blessed be God"), a potent gentile display of spiritual recognition and incredible allegiance that earns him his own-named parsha.

Irving is lost in a Russian forest when he suddenly stumbles across a synagogue. Tired and weak, he collapses at the entrance where the rabbi finds him and nurses him back to health. A few days later Irving is up 'n about and asks the rav if he could borrow his horse, ride home and return it later.

"Sure," the rabbi replies, "but this is a special horse. We call him Yisro. You have to say Boruch Hashem to make him go — and Amen to make him stop."

So Irving jumps up in the saddle, says, "Boruch Hashem," and the horse starts walking. He then yells, "Boruch Hashem, Boruch Hashem," and the horse begins to trot. He then shouts, "Boruch Hashem, Boruch Hashem, Boruch Hashem" — and the horse really takes off.

A few miles later Irving suddenly sees a huge cliff approaching and frantically shouts to the horse to stop, "Whoa, stop, hold on!!!!"...but nothing happens, and the horse continues at a fast pace straight to the cliff.

The terrified Irving then remembers the rabbi's instructions, and screams, "Amen!!" — and, to his relief, it works. The horse comes to a screeching halt, just a few inches from the edge of the abyss. Irving leans back in the saddle, lets out a deep sigh, wipes his forehead, and says, "Boruch Hashem."

The Jews, three months out of Egypt, nearly 2,500 years after creation, are about to encounter the monumental Ten Commandments, or more accurately, the "Ten Utterances (*aseres hadibros*)," given by God, *kol gadol v'lo yasaf*, with "a great voice [to] My special people;" all accompanied by dramatic imagery and a Heavenly promise that the Jewish people will be a *mamleches kohanim v'goy kodosh*, a "kingdom of priests and a holy nation."

Baruch, editor of a Jewish weekly, was sick 'n tired of all the abusive letters-to-the-editors he received following his editorials, so he decided to run the Ten Commandments ▶

> *one week in lieu of his usual commentary.*
> *A few days later came a letter: "Cancel my subscrip-*
> *tion. You're getting too personal."*

And yet there is a paradox: some sages say the Jews accepted the Torah willingly, with a *na'aseh v'nishma* promise ("We will obey, we will hearken"); but others dispute that interpretation, claiming the folk were reluctant.

One version has God hovering a mountain over their heads with an ominous warning, "If you accept the Torah, all will be well, but if you refuse, *sham t'heh kvuraschem*, there your graves will be;" another has God threatening, "If you accept the Torah, you will survive, but if not, I will turn the world back to chaos, *tohu vavohu*."

Which theory is correct? Were the masses eager — or reluctant?

With human nature being what it is, probably "both" are correct. It is normal to have a dose of ambivalence; the same contradictory nature the liberated Jews display later with their backs at the Red Sea: some boldly advocating moving forward, others wavering in hesitation.

Although the exact sequence of events has challenged many Torah scholars, all agree that this Divine revelation at Sinai was *the* most supernatural event of history, *the* apex of a people's spiritual experience, a time when the Jews "trembled" below a "thick cloud upon the Mount" to the loud sounds of thunder, lightning, shofar.

> *When a student was once asked to list the Ten*
> *Commandments in any order, he replies, "3, 6, 1, 8, 4, 5,*
> *9, 2, 10, 7."*

Before he leaves, Yisro, wise and seasoned (having honed his administrative skills by serving in Pharaoh's inner court), notices that his son-in-law, serving as Israel's only sitting judge (from "morning to evening") looks tired, and offers three words of constructive advice on the responsibility of leadership: delegate, delegate, delegate.

Yisro (who the Ramban claims is really Chorev, a "father-surrogate" whose name stems from the root "to love") even delineates the resume of the legal delegates of a nascent nation: they must be trustworthy and accomplished, despise money, and fear God (*anshei chayil yirei Elokim.*)

God agrees, leading the Abarbanel, famed Spanish Torah commentator, to ask the obvious: why didn't Moshe, the master prophet, think of this himself? He did, however, having received the Torah personally, he felt personally obligated to be its judge.

Yisro was less concerned with making the judiciary more efficient ("the task is too heavy; you cannot do it alone"), than with Jewish continuity — for if only the one who receives Torah can transmit Torah, then future generations would be lost the moment Moshe dies.

Did Jewish history prove Yisro right?

Yes, and no: Moshe eventually appoints a charismatic successor (Joshua), but the moment Joshua dies, everything falls apart, and Yisro's designated system of judges splinters into two unstable, rival Israelite kingdoms.

> When the new rabbi-judge gets up in shul to give his first sermon, he's nervous and hesitant. Suddenly a voice from the back booms, "Tell us everything you know. It'll only take a minute."
>
> "Why don't I tell the shul everything we both know," the rav replies, "it won't take any longer."

One of the great mysteries in the Torah is the near total anonymity of Gershon and Eliezer, Moshe's two sons. There is no hint of their relationship with their father, nor, an even more ominous omen, do we hear anything about their descendants.

Some scholars link the fact that Moshe's two boys were absent at Sinai, and thus deprived of the first-hand experience of God's thunder and lightning, as a cause of their estrangement.

That the sons of Moshe do not assume any mantle of leadership is unusual in a religion which regards public office as a form of "property," an inheritance from father to son, unless the son is either incapable or unsuitable.

Does the Torah give any hint as to any shortcomings?

No, but the Midrash does: "Your sons sat around and did not engage in Torah," hinting that, unlike Joshua, the boys never helped out in holy matters; all parents know: raising kids is oft-times *mazel*.

> One day Mrs. Schwartz hears about a rav in town that specializes in disciplining children so she sends her boys to him. The rav takes Moishie into his study, alone, and asks him sternly, "Where is God?"
>
> Moishie does not respond, so the rav raises his voice and asks again, "Moishie, where is God?"
>
> No response. So the rabbi leans over closer, shakes his finger in the scared boy's face, and explodes, "Tell me! Where is God!"
>
> The terrified 8-year-old jumps out of his chair, runs home as fast as he can, races up the stairs to his bedroom and slams the door. His younger brother chases him home and finds him quivering under the bed, "Moishie! What happened?"
>
> "Yankie, we're in big trouble this time. God's missing — and they think we did it!"

It seems that the ultimate teacher of all teachers, Moshe, responsible for bringing Torah to the entire nation, had no *nachas* with his own sons; a family tragedy that plagues many families, when leaders are unable to balance their communal and personal obligations, a challenging juggling act recognized in this weeks commandment to honor (*kabed*) one's parents, a central feature of Yiddishkeit (it's no coincidence that *kabed* is derived from the Hebrew words for "heavy" and "burdensome.")

> *One morning over breakfast Harvey turns to his wife,*
> *"Gaby, listen, I've been thinking. I don't want to sound cruel, but*
> *your mother has been living with us for 20 years now. Don't*
> *you think it's about time she got a place of her own?"*
> *"My mother?" replies Gaby, dropping her spoon in*
> *shock, "I thought she was your mother!"*

At this pivotal moment in a nation's formation, it is Yisro, and not Moshe, who decides that his grandchildren should be reunited with their father; and when he sends notice, "I am bringing your wife and her two sons," he uses the term *her* sons, not *yours*; a subtle grandfatherly rebuke that serving the people is great, but it's time to also pay some attention to the wife 'n kids.

Our Jewish mystics consider grandparents so important that they derive the Hebrew word for Terach, the non-Jewish father of Avraham, from *ruach* ("spirit"). Despite his idol-worshipping, he is still the foundation from which the house of Yaacov was conceived, raised, nurtured.

This grandparent-grandchild relationship is unique in the human world, it does not exist in the animal kingdom where there is no perpetuation beyond a single generation.

So important is "family" in Jewish life that the cherub figures adorning the Torah ark-cover are the faces of children: a gentle sign that what supports Torah is family.

> *It's his granddaughter's birthday, and Zaida promised*
> *her a doll for her birthday. So they both stroll hand-in-*
> *hand to the local toyshop, and asks the salesman behind*
> *the counter, "How much is a Barbie doll?"* ▶

"It depends."

"On what?"

"Well, you can get a Shabbas Mummy Barbie doll for $19.99, or a Cinderella Barbie doll for $19.99, or a High School Barbie doll for $19.99, or a Mother Barbie doll for $19.99, or a Divorced Barbie doll for $399.99, or a ......"

"Hey! Wait a minute!," Zaida interrupts, "how come the divorced Barbie doll is so expensive!?"

"Because it comes with Ken's house, Ken's car, Ken's business, Ken's furniture, Ken's cat, Ken's boat...."

MISHPATIM
And Justice for All

> *Judge Morrie is trying to be fair to both sides so he strikes his gavel, and announces, "Before I begin this trial, I want everybody to be aware of this fact. The lawyer for the defense has paid me $15,000 to swing the case his way. The lawyer for the plaintiff has paid me $10,000 to swing the case her way. In order to make this a fair trial, I am returning $5,000 to the defense."*

After a 400-year reign of perverted institutionalized slavery, it is in this parsha, *Mishpatim* ("civil laws") that the Heavens give the Jews parameters to live by, in order to structure their lives and realize their potential.

The parsha opens in mid-story with the conjunction "and" ("And these are the laws that you shall place before them") intended, according to Rashi, the grand educator from France, to link this parsha's "mundane and minute" civil laws, which by definition mankind would have followed anyway, to last week's Godly Ten Commandments (*Aseres Hadibros*).

And more: in order to remind the Judaic judiciary to judge with the purity of Sinai, the Torah juxtaposes *mishpatim* to the mitzva of the altar (*mizbe'ach*) where the glory of God hovered.

In their attempt to dilute the import and unprecedented thrust of Sinaitic laws, many non-Jewish scholars have tried to pin the charge of "copy cat" on the Jews. In particular, that the Laws of Moshe are based on the ancient Near East legal practices of the Sumerians, Babylonians, Assyrians, Hittites (the most famous being Hammurabi's Code of Babylonia).

This is nonsense: and the proof is obvious.

The Torah's formal presentation of law ("These are the rules...") begins immediately with the laws of slavery; a widely accepted and popular practice in those times and places. Thus, an anti-slavery thrust was unique (and unpopular, for obvious reasons) among the non-Jewish codes of antiquity.

Why place slavery laws in such a primary position? This is Judaism 101: Israel's entire national experience at that point, carved into its very psyche and consciousness, had been one of slavery. The Heavens purposefully placed their diverse "rules" (*mishpatim*) in perspective.

A basic principle of democracy is to follow the majority. Yes, say our sages, majority rule *is* a good principle but it still depends on what the majority is up to; for not only can a "multitude lie," warns Ibn Ezra, but the adage, "tyranny of the majority" is no empty slogan (consider Germany in the 30's, when Adolf got the popular, and yet, immoral vote, which gave him the authority to conceive and construct an Auschwitz).

In this parsha we find the phrase, *"lo sihyeh acharei rabbim l'hattos."* Torah linguists render this as "do not follow the mighty [multitudes]." *Rabbim* is akin to *rav*, also meaning "powerful." In this light, Rav Hertz reads the verse, "as a warning not to follow a majority blindly for evil purposes, especially to pervert justice."

And so the first verse ends with, *asher tasim lifneychem,* "you [Moshe] should put before them," an order for reasoning and common sense (*seichel*) rather than blind obedience. Why? Because mitzvos backed by understanding are the most potent.

Rabbi Shmuel Eliezer Halevi Edels (*Maharsha*), the brilliant 17th century commentator claims that these first laws of Moshe are intended to sensitize the Jew to a value system of respect for others. The 13th century *Yod Rama* notes that Hillel uses a variation of this parsha's general prohibition of damaging others. When challenged by a gentile to be taught the entire Torah "on one leg,"

Hillel responds with *V'ahavta l're'acha kamocha* ("love your fellow as yourself") and continues with: "What is hated when done to you, do not do to your fellow; all the rest is commentary."

Included in its litany of rights and wrongs, this week's parsha contains the famous "eye for an eye, tooth for a tooth" passage, probably one of the most misquoted of all Torah verses.

Anti-Semites, in their desire to denigrate the Old Testament, often point to this dictate as "proof" that the Jews, and their God, were barbarous, stern, primitive seekers of blind vengeance and vigilantism. Nothing could be further from the truth. Yes, the phrase is dramatic. No, it does not require the gauging of an eye for an eye — but simply establishes a principle of justness and fairness: the punishment must fit the crime; not too harsh, nor too lenient.

> *"Where do you work?" asks the judge of a man accused of drinking 'n fighting at a bar.*
> *"Here and there."*
> *"And what do you do for a living?"*
> *"This and that."*
> *"Take him away!" the judge orders.*
> *"Wait, wait! When do I get out!?"*
> *"Sooner or later."*

The communal response of 600,000 Jews, as if in rehearsed symphony, to Moshe's list of 613 civil and ritual legislative commands, statutes, ordinances, thou shalts and thou shalt nots, is simple and direct: "We shall do and obey" (*na'aseh v'nishmah*), a voluntary ratification of this Covenant of God, a promise of adherence uttered not on national terms but as a religious commitment.

Commenting on this seemingly odd order ("do-first, understand-second"), Rabbi Ovadia Sforno, 16th century Italian scholar, sees a healthy Judaic respect for authority and recognition that Judaism is an acquired taste requiring practice before passion.

Like everything else in Jewish life this acceptance concludes in celebrations, as the folk "ate and drank," an activity that they never seem to get enough of.

> *The Rosenbergs are out celebrating when the wife no-tices a familiar face at the bar.*
> *"Honey," she says to her husband, "See that guy over there at the bar. He's been drinking like that ever since I left him seven years ago."*
> *"Don't be silly," he replies, "No one celebrates that much!"*

This parsha warns the Jew, once again, to be concerned for the disadvantaged, especially the "widow and orphan," causing the great neo-German 19th century Rabbi Samson Raphael Hirsch to highlight why these two categories are singled out by the Torah for special protection. In Hebrew, both *almonoh* (widow) and *yosom* (orphan) are derived from the verb "to mutilate," or "cut off." In the case of the widow it is the loss of the companionship and support of a husband and in the case of the orphan it is the deprivation of parents to hold hands with, to lean and depend on.

Therefore, the Halacha in both cases is *lo se'annun*, "not to op-press" those who have no-one to rely upon; a dictate that carries with it, according to Rashi's grandson, Rabbi Shmuel ben Meir (*Rashbam*), the severe punishment of *midda k'neged midda*, "like for like."

In fact, this parsha's very first mitzva comes with an explicit reason ("because you were strangers in the land of Egypt"), the or-der not to make a stranger suffer.

The characteristic factor in all these statutes is empathy; and that, as God's firstborn and as part of a people ordered to be "a holy nation," the Jew must infuse his life with religiously significant events designed to make the world a better place.

A man looking for sympathy walks into a dentist's office and says, "Can you help me?"

"What's the problem?"

"I think I'm a moth."

"A moth!? You don't need a dentist, you need a psychiatrist!"

"I know."

"Then why did you come in here?"

"Because your lights were on!"

TERUMAH
Giving is Receiving

*The crumbling old shul in Poland needed some desper-
ate renovations so the rabbi asks the shammes to bring by
the local gvir so he can see for himself.*

*After the rav makes an impassioned appeal, the rich
man agrees to donate 500 rubles when, all of a sudden, a
piece of plaster falls off the damp ceiling and lands on his
shoulder.*

*"Rabbi," he says, brushing himself down, "It's worse
than I thought. I'm going to increase my donation to 5,000
rubles."*

*Before the rabbi can even thank him, some more plas-
ter lands on the gvir, causing him to scream out, "I'll double my pledge."*

*As he turns to leave, all shaken, an even larger chunk
of plaster falls, this time hitting him on the head, causing
him to holler, "Okay, okay. I'll give 20,000 rubles!"*

*The shammes quickly jumps up and shouts, "Hit him
again, Lord! Hit him again!"*

The title of week's parsha, *Terumah*, means "contribution" (as in
tithe) within the context of the Jews being ordered (*V'yikchu li
trumoh*) to take a "*trumoh*" of produce (about 1/50th). The term
appears no less than three times; perhaps defining three types of
givers, from the highest level of *li trumoh* (the Jew who gives because God orders so), to *asher yidvenu libo* (the Jew who gives for
selfish reasons, in that it makes him feel better to help others), to
the lowest level of *tikchu es trumosi* (the Jew who gives against his
will, motivated by shame).

Rav Mordechai Gifter of Telz notes the order: first the Torah
asks for money, and only afterwards explains why this absence of
purpose exemplifies the essence of the Mishkan, in that the volun-

tary act of giving raises materialism to a level of holiness.

The Pupa Rav would often wonder why even the most committed, observant Jew often hesitated to do a mitzva that required a financial commitment, and resorted to linguistics for the answer. The Rav cleverly transformed the word *b'tzedek*, a shortening of the term *b'tzedek echezah panecha* ("with righteousness I will gaze upon Your countenance") into a Yiddish acronym for *biz tzu di kesheneh* ("until it comes to the wallet"), to help explain why God asks the Jews to open their wallets immediately after they declare their unequivocal acceptance of the Torah.

"Charity" itself comes from Latin and conveys the idea of loving benevolence to the needy. An alternative word is "philanthropy," from a Greek term, which indicates love of mankind. In contrast the Hebrew *tzedokoh* means "righteousness" or "justice," and represents the building blocks in the *Jewish* road towards building a righteous and just society.

> The local yeshiva is having a charity auction so Sid goes and decides to bid on a parrot. But his every bid is briskly bid up by a voice in the crowd. A determined Sid keeps upping his bids until he is finally the winner.
> "By the way," he asks the auctioneer as he goes to pay, "Can this parrot speak?"
> "Yep, sure can. Guess who was bidding against you!"

Jews are urged to give anonymously, so that donor and beneficiary are unaware of each other's identity. The Temple had a *lishkas chasho'im*, a "secret charity chamber" where clandestine donations were dropped off so that the poor 'n needy could take in similar secrecy.

Tzedokoh even regulates attitude: "If one gives his fellow all the good things in the world but with a sullen face," writes Avos d'Rabbi

Nosson, "it is as if he has given nothing; but he who receives his fellow man with a pleasant countenance, even if he gives him nothing, it is as if he has given him all the good things in the world."

"If your God loves the poor so much," the wicked Turnus Rufus once taunted Rabbi Akiva, "why then doesn't He provide for them?" Akiva's reply explains the concept of the merit of giving *tzedokoh* is that it's a mitzva that supports the supporter.

Rabbi Avraham Yitzchak Neviezer supported his son-in-law and founder of the Telshe Yeshiva, Rabbi Eliezer Gordon, for many years, despite the enormous financial burden. He refused to be relieved of this obligation, telling his wife, "Who knows who is supporting whom?" Reb Eliezer eventually accepted a prestigious rabbinical position in Eisheshok and his father-in-law could no longer detain him. The day after he left, Reb Avraham Yitzchak died, and it then became clear who had been supporting whom.

To give is to receive; an opportunity, says the Midrash, for meritorious self-development, a chance to be "God-like" to another.

Thus the Rambam, based on Pirkei Avos', "All is judged according to the number of deeds," concludes that it is better to give $1 to charity 100 times, than $100 one time. That is why the Chofetz Chaim politely turned down a donation large enough to cover his yeshiva's entire operating expenses, explaining, "I cannot allow any one Jew to monopolize the mitzva of tzedokoh and thus deprive others of the opportunity as well."

> *The rosh yeshiva makes an appointment to see Irving, the town's most successful, yet stingy businessman.*
>
> *"You know Irv," the rabbi begins, "You're very successful. You make over a million a year but never give a dime to charity. Maybe it's time to change, and perhaps donate to our yeshiva?"*
>
> *"Rabbi," Irv replies, "Are you aware that my mother* ▶

> *is dying after a long, painful illness and has huge medical bills far beyond her ability to pay?"*
>
> *"Uh, no," mumbled the embarrassed rosh yeshiva.*
>
> *"And are you aware that my brother, a disabled veteran, is blind and confined to a wheelchair and is unable to support his wife and six children? And what about my sister's husband? Did you know that he died in a dreadful traffic accident, leaving her penniless, with a mortgage and three children?"*
>
> *"I'm sorry," the rabbi stammers, "I had no idea."*
>
> *"And if I don't give any money to them, why would I give to you?"*

This parsha, through its Haftarah text, implies that there can be no peace without wisdom. Its magnificent opening ("And the Lord gave Solomon the gift of wisdom") is immediately linked to, "and there was peace between Solomon and Hiram [his powerful neighbor, the King of Tyre]."

Statesmanship requires *seichel*; and the lack of it (wisdom) inevitably deteriorates into dogma. And so the sages answer their own question ("Who is wise?") with "He who learns from all men."

This is why, at the end of the *Amidah* and *Kaddish*, the custom is to take three steps back upon saying *oseh sholom bim'romov*, "He who makes peace in His high places, may He make peace for us and for all Israel" — because the pursuit of peace sometimes requires taking a step backwards and respectfully recognizing the presence of others.

The lesson: learning from others is the unselfish acknowledgment that there exist other points of view; that no one is infallible, that mistakes occur.

This week's parsha also introduces several "firsts" — the Jews first involvement in the arts 'n crafts, and the first communal religious institution in Jewish history, the *Mikdosh*, which Rashi translates as "a House of Holiness."

This command is a Godly request, "Let them make Me [li] a Sanctuary [mikdosh] that I may dwell among them;" however Rashi prefers to interpret the Hebrew word li not as "for Me," but "for My name's sake."

And God is specific: for when it comes to His house there is no room for the Torah's usual parsimonious use of words; and thus no less than four Torah portions (Terumah, Tetzaveh, Vayakel, Pekudei) are turned into a meticulous construction guide seeking precision in fulfillment.

Why the obsession with detail?

The clues lie in God's last few words, "I will dwell among you (v'shachanti b'sochom)," a royal self-invitation that requires a physical perfection, down to the last nail 'n lumber size, in order to ensure that the Holy of Holies (encompassing the Ark of the Testimony) matches the perfection of its future occupant, the Shechina (God's presence.)

It is the first Shabbos in the newly constructed shul and the president proudly introduces their new, highly prized chazzan.

"Two years ago," the cantor boasts to the congregants just before he begins, "I insured my voice with Lloyds of London for $750,000."

A few minutes into the services, a voice yells out from the back of the shul, "So what did you do with the money?"

After the creation of a physical universe (stars, planets, trees, mountains, etc) it was left to the children of Israel, challenged with the tikkun (mending) of the world, to passionately create a social universe of warm, sensitive, caring community sanctuaries (schools, synagogues, mikvas, cheders, etc), as meaningful environments, a magnet for Jews.

"Once mikvas were cold but Jews were warm," cried the Gerer Rebbe, "now, alas, it's the other way around."

Our ancestor's great desire to feel a closeness to God motivated them to build a beautiful Divine sanctuary, to work towards injecting holiness into their lives; aware of the fact that one must work to feel holiness, that it doesn't just come naturally.

"Even Adam," writes Shimon ben Eleazar, "tasted nothing before he worked, tilled and tended [and only then] did God allow him to eat "of every tree."

The Torah's use of grammar here is instructive: God's orders to build are given to "you" (*ve'asisoh*), in the second-person singular, with one exception: the instruction for the Holy Ark (which housed the Torah, the foundation of Israel as a people) which is directed to "they" (*ve'asu*), in the third-person plural. Is this intended for the then-nation of Israel? No, but for the "they" of the future, on whose shoulders lie the task of constructing an eternal Torah in their own generation's midst.

This daunting job to build the great Tabernacle work of art was entrusted to the highly talented Betzalel, great-nephew of Moshe, whose theophoric name means, "In the Shadow of God," as in, "under Divine protection."

Since the era of Betzalel there has been an enormous Judaic artistic ingenuity in illustrative scriptures, ranging from Haggadas to Megillas, respectful of the Torah's adage, "This is my God and I will adorn Him" — by way of an attractive Succa, an exquisite Lulav, a handsome menorah, etc.

The question is obvious: what's the purpose of constructing a physical, man-made "earthy" space to contain a non-earthly Omnipresent God?

Isaiah was also puzzled by this: the impossibility of limiting God to one physical space, "The Heaven is My throne/And the earth is My footstool/Where could you build a house for Me,/What place could (possibly) serve as My abode?" Even Solomon, the wisest of them all, questioned the value of constructing an earthy home, "Even the Heavens to their uttermost reaches cannot contain You, how much less this House [on earth] that I have built."

The clue lies in the title of the parsha: the root letters of *terumah*, usually translated as "gifts," mean "exalted, uplifted, fortified, encouraged" — the feelings that Jews get from being in an ennobled sacred space (such as a shul) where the atmosphere is conducive to a closer relationship to God.

And more: community breeds unity; Jews assembling, especially for a shared sacred purpose, develop stronger and closer bonds to each other (as that observation goes: If I could rewrite the alphabet, U and I would be a lot closer together!)

"I shall dwell in their midst" thus means not "in the Sanctuary" but "in the midst of the people" — in other words, amidst the builders, not the building. Remember: a home only becomes a house when it has occupants.

Thus the most architectural magnificent and most impressively decorative *shul* of them all is still nothing but an empty shell, lifeless without the presence of a vibrant, devout, loyal assembly. This is why certain prayers "of sanctification, *d'varim sh'bikdushoh*" (e.g.; *Kaddish, Kedushah, Barchu*, etc) are invalid if only a handful of Jews are present, since Sinai decreed that a *minyan* of ten (the Torah's basic social unit) constituted the minimum cohesiveness of a "community."

> *Separated from his community in the wildnerness, a Levite stumbles on a nomad and begs him for some water. "Sorry," the nomad replies, "I have no water but I do have a great selection of ties for sale."*
> *"Ties!" screams the Levite, "I'm dying of thirst. I need a drink!" He stumbles over to another nomad, and gasps, "Water, water! I need water!"* ▸

"I have no water, but I also have some handsome ties for sale."

"What! Is everybody crazy here!" the Levite yells as he stumbles back into the desert. A few hours later, dehydrated, he sees a magnificent hotel ahead. He barely makes it to the front door, crawls out of the sand and into the lobby, croaking, "Please, can I have a drink of water?"

"I'm sorry Sir," the doorman politely replies, "We don't let anyone in without a tie!"

TETZAVEH
From Rabbis to Robes

> *A well-dressed, immaculately groomed lawyer opens the door of his BMW, when suddenly a car swings by and pulls the door totally off its hinges.*
>
> *The police arrive as the lawyer is bitterly shouting, whining, raving and ranting about the damage to his precious car.*
>
> *"You know, you lawyers are all the same," says the officer, "So materialistic! Look at ya! So worried about your BMW that you haven't even noticed that your left arm is totally ripped off!"*
>
> *"Oh no!" screams the lawyer, noticing a bloody left shoulder where his arm once was, "Where's my Rolex?!"*

Since clothes maketh the man, this Purim-time parsha of *Tetzaveh* discusses the precise attire (*bigdei Kehuna*) to be worn by the priesthood when performing Temple or Tabernacle services (*avoda*).

Chassidism loves this parsha: the desert sanctuary comes alive as a metaphor for a Jews' personal inner sanctity; the building instructions are a blueprint on how to conduct oneself; the "eternal light" (a *ner tamid*) an inspiring symbol on how to illuminate one's life and drive away, as Reb Levi Yitzhak of Berditchev says, *machshavos zaros*, "alien (improper) thoughts."

> *"You know," Miriam says to her best friend, "whenever I'm down in the dumps I buy myself a dress."*
>
> *"Well, now I know where you get them from!"*

This wardrobe parsha is filled with drama: a special hat, pants, belt, shirt; all entirely white to symbolize purity.

The High Priest had four more elaborate garments, made of gold and specifically designed, in order, writes the Ramban, to express the "honor and splendor" of royalty. According to Ibn Ezra it is in order to stand out from the rest of the community while aspiring to loftier goals.

The parsha suddenly comes alive with textiles and color, tassel-like pomegranate-shaped fringes on the hems of long robes, tiny golden bells (beneath the *ephod,* a tunic-like garment), and such precious stones as carnelian, emerald, sapphire and amethyst. Jewish mystics paired each garment as atonement for a different sin. The turban atoned for haughtiness; the cloak for *loshon hora;* the trousers for adultery; the tunic for murder; the belt for improper thoughts; the breastplate (*choshen*) for miscarriage of justice; and the apron (*ephod*) for idolatry. Because these sins resulted from the lack of certain character traits (*middos,* which in Hebrew also means "measure"), the priests' appearance had to be a perfect (spiritual) fit; made to measure, *mido vad.*

What is the Torah lesson of clothing?

That it takes more than a casual, informal approach to perform God's service, an activity that requires an extra sense of concentration, awe, reverence. And more: a noble appearance gives rise to awe and respect; qualities which in turn create a more potent willingness to look and learn, absorb and follow.

This fashion consciousness was serious business: the Torah even implies death for those who conduct the service in the absence of a regal appearance.

"Judge not a man by his dress; not garments but character stress," were the poetic thoughts of Russian-Hebrew poet Gabriel Rosenzweig; but Ben Sira was adamant, "praise none for his beauty; abhor none for his appearance."

Is fashion more important than food? Surely not: and yet a Talmud proverb advises, "If need be, spare from your stomach, and spend on your back;" although to the Yiddishists of central Europe, it would not have helped: "Beautiful clothes do not hide the hump!"

Dressing for the occasion is deeply ingrained in society: how one feels depends on how one looks. If you wanted to look good in the *shtetl* and were dirt poor, there was plenty of Yiddish advice: "Pinch your cheeks and keep their color rosy."

> After Sadie's husband dies, she tells her closest friend Ruth that after paying all the expenses she has no money left to buy clothes.
>
> "How can that be? You had $25,000 just before he died. Where did all the money go?"
>
> "Well, the funeral cost me $5,000, the hospital bill was $3,000, I made a donation to the Chevra Kadisha of $1,000, and then I spent all the rest on the memorial stone."
>
> "Wait a minute," Ruth says, doing some silent math, $16,000 for a memorial stone? My God, Sadie, how big was it, what was it made of?"
>
> Sadie extends her left hand, and replies, "Three and a half carats."

The Rambam goes one step further: he takes the Torah's focus on priestly clothing and extends it as Jewish law to rabbinic dress: it must not "drag along the ground," and it must be "suitable and clean, with no stains or grease-marks." Why? In order that clothes not "bring disrespect to the wearer." And a *tallis koton*? It should "not be worn conspicuously long." Why not? "Because it appears like haughtiness."

How about patched shoes? Never in summer, but okay in winter (but only if he "is a poor man.") How about perfume (usually not), scented garments (definitely no). Why? "To avoid suspicion."

Dressing differently has acted as a weapon against assimilation ever since the Jews used their distinguishing attire to prevent wholesale integration into Egyptian society.

The importance of appearance in this parsha is an extension of last weeks parsha which describes Moshe's facial skin as being "radiant" after his (second) *mysterium tremendum* brush with God at Sinai. Other linguists interpret the Hebrew as "beams of splendor," or "divine rays of glory."

Some, incorrectly, translated it as "horns," which is why Michelangelo's Moshe is displayed with horns rather than rays.

Simeon ben Lakish had a unique explanation: the early Talmudist traces Moshe's unusual appearance to left-over ink on Moshe's pen that, when passed through his hair, caused beams of splendor to appear.

The Tosefos school of study respectfully disagreed, claiming that these "rays of light" were a purposeful "gift" from God to alert the folks, in the aftermath of a sinful calf of gold, that no one would ever again have the Divine spark of Moshe.

Moshe's new semblance, a result of his face-to-face (*ponim el ponim*) ethereal and exalted encounter with God, was so frightening that Aaron and a recalcitrant, fearful nation of Israel "were afraid to come near him," causing God's foremost disciple to cover his own face with a mask.

This "invisibility" is contagious: by the time we get to this week's parsha Moshe himself, although obviously present, is not explicitly mentioned by name but only by the pronoun "you."

In fact this is the only parsha (other than *Sefer Devarim*, mostly narrated by Moshe) that erases his name. Why? The Torah is alluding to Moshe's earlier defense plea to have his name "blotted from the book" when the nation was in danger of being destroyed.

The Jews were spared, but their leader's wish was partially fulfilled with his name conspicuously absent in this parsha.

Masks conceal, notes that great Chassidic sage Menachem

Mendel of Kotzk, "and the truth is not necessarily as things appear."

Appearances can express strength or weakness, both symbols of status and separation, walls of distinction. Note how close the Hebrew word for clothing (*b'godim*) is to betrayal (*b'gidoh*).

The Hebrew word for wearing a costume, *l'hischapes*, comes from the root *lechapes*, which means "to look for," because costumes hide the truth, allowing what the ancient Greeks cruelly called "pretend play at the theater," intended as a cathartic sublimation of drives, when slaves and prisoners were allowed to masquerade at being free.

> *Sidney answers a help wanted ad at the local zoo and the interviewee tells him it's a highly unusual job, that their only gorilla has died unexpectedly, and until they can get a new one, Sidney must pretend to be a gorilla, and put on a gorilla suit for a few days.*
>
> *The pay is good, so Sidney takes the job, puts on the suit and is led to a cage. After a few hours of sitting and doing nothing, he gets bored, so he begins to jump up 'n down and make gorilla noises. The children outside the cage start clapping 'n cheering. To entertain them even more, Sidney then climbs the tree in the cage, grabs a vine and starts swinging higher 'n higher 'n higher — until suddenly, the vine breaks and he goes flying through the air, landing in the lion's cage next door. The Jew is in great panic as the huge, hungry-looking beast approaches him.*
>
> *"Help, help!" he screams, "Get me out of here! I'm not really a gorilla! My name's Sidney! I'm a man in a gorilla suit! Heeelp!"*
>
> *The lion quickly pounces on him, holds him down, and whispers, "Hey, za shtil! Vill ya shut up, already! Ya gonna get us both fired!!!"*

It is no coincidence that the mask of Moshe and the clothing of the *kohanim* occur near Purim, *the* Yom Tov of parody, of masks 'n masquerades, illusions 'n delusions, false impressions 'n exaggerated expressions.

On Purim, everything is upside down, topsy-turvy, against the norm. Even the rosh yeshiva of Slobodka would dress up like a horse on Purim (no, disguises are not Halachically mandated); and even the mitzva to fast and eat is reversed: on Purim one fasts, then eats; on Yom Kippur one eats, then fasts.

> *It is just before Yom Tov so Herbie tries on a new suit in Goldie's tailor shop — only to discover that the arms are too long.*
>
> *"No problem," says Goldie, "just bend them at the elbow and hold them out in front of you. See, now it's fine!"*
>
> *"But the collar's up around my ears."*
>
> *"No problem, 'tis nothing…here, just hunch your back up a little…no, a little more…there, that's perfect."*
>
> *"But I'm stepping on my cuffs!"*
>
> *"Okay, Okay…just bend your knees a little to take up the slack…now look in the mirror, the suit fits fully!"*
>
> *Herbie, twisted like a double pretzel, leaves the store and shuffles by two little ol' Jewish ladies.*
>
> *"Look," says one, "at that poor man."*
>
> *"Yes," replies the other, "but what a beautiful suit."*

All That's Gold, Does Not Glitter

A son calls his elderly Yiddish mama and asks, "Ma, how are you?"
"Not too good, I'm feeling very weak."
"Why ma?"
"Because I haven't eaten in 23 days."
"That's terrible. Why haven't you eaten in 23 days?"
"Because, I didn't want to have my mouth full just in case you called!"

Our sages relate to this parsha, *Ki Sisa*, which contains the Torah's most infamous incident of idolatry, the "original sin" of the Jewish people known as the *cheit ha'eigel* ("sin of the calf"), as a watershed in the evolution of Jewish spiritual history; and link it to the later spy debacle as two of the most disastrous events of their 40-year sojourn in the wilderness.

The wide desert, a mundane and unhallowed environment, is the backdrop to a catastrophic debacle and a spectacular series of events; welcome to the first national tragedy of the impatient Jewish people, one that proves that not all that is gold, glitters.

"The generation of the wilderness," commented Chassidic sage Rabbi Yitzchak of Slonim, centuries later, "enthusiastically gave up their silver and gold to make a god; our generation gives up God to make silver and gold!"

Under the watchful eyes of Aaron and Hur, the people dance and sing around a calf of gold, a god they could "see."

Who is Hur?

He is the son of Miriam; and vanishes immediately after this incident. Tradition has him killed off by the orgy of people because of his non-cooperation; and rewarded by the Heavens with two famous descendants that make their mark in construction: Betzalel, his grandson and architect of the Tabernacle, and King Solomon, builder of the Temple.

At the pathetic sight of wild debauchery in idolatrous worship, Moshe smashes the sacred stone tablets, written "with the finger of God," an act attributed to "anger." Or is it?

The Rashbam, a member of the 12th century Tosefos school, disagrees, claiming that, at the unholy sight, the "faithful shepherd of Israel" lost his strength, causing him to drop the tablets, unable to bear their heavy burden; not so much out of anger but because of disappointment, disillusionment, and "despairing" of his ability "to correct this egregious sin."

One Midrash claims Moshe's goal was to deflect God's anger onto himself; another suggests that he purposefully caused *sh'vurei luchos*, the "broken tablets," for sheer educational "shock value," in order to publicly emphasize his attitude towards apostasy.

Ibn Ezra takes a mystical approach: by smashing the tablets ("a contract of testimony"), Moshe was actually defending his (adulterous) folk by destroying the "marriage contract between the groom (God) and his bride (Israel)," thus declaring the sin null and void.

In ancient times the breaking of tablets was a figurative act, a custom of the old East that symbolized a contract's annulment; that is why Halacha uses the verb *shavar* ("to break"), in reference to promissory notes, as in *shoveres kesubosoh*, a woman who "breaks" her marriage contract.

Sid and Sarah are considering a trip to Alaska, a trip that Sid had long dreamed of taking. ▶

> *"Wouldn't it be great," he says, "to stay in a log cabin without electricity, to hunt moose, bath in the river, and drive a dog team instead of a car. Say honey, if we decide to live there permanently, away from civilization, what would you miss the most?"*
>
> *"You," she replies.*

True, Moshe was delayed in coming back from the mount. However being late seems to be a Jewish addiction, an annoying practice resulting in no Jewish function beginning when it should.

It seems that "Jewish" time always clashes with real time — but even God has been accused of lateness: "How long, O Lord?" asks the Psalmist, surely aware that God is "outside time," yet nevertheless perturbed that the Heavens have not intervened in Jewish history sooner.

> *Rebecca goes into the local animal store seeking a pet that can do everything. The owner suggests a faithful puppy.*
>
> *"No, no dog."*
>
> *"How about a cat?"*
>
> *"No, a cat certainly can't do everything. I want a pet that can do everything!"*
>
> *The shop owner thinks for a minute, then says, "I've got it! A centipede!"*
>
> *"A centipede? I can't imagine a centipede doing everything, but okay, I'll try a centipede."*
>
> *Rebecca takes the centipede home, puts it down in the kitchen, and says, "Clean it!"*
>
> *Thirty minutes later, she is stunned: the kitchen is immaculate! All the dishes and silverware are washed, dried, and put away; the counter-tops are clean; the appliances sparkle; the floor waxed. An elated Rebecca takes the centipede into the living room, and orders it, "Go clean!"*
>
> *Twenty minutes later, the carpet is vacuumed; the furniture clean and dusted; the sofa pillows are plumped; the plants watered.* ▶

> "Unbelievable," Rebecca mumbles, then turns to the centipede, "Do me a favor, run down to the corner and get me a newspaper."
>
> The centipede walks out the door. Ten minutes go by, twenty, thirty minutes…and no centipede.
>
> A worried Rebecca goes to the front door, opens it, and finds the centipede sitting outside.
>
> "Hey! It's been nearly 45 minutes! What's the matter?!"
>
> "I'm goin'! I'm goin'! I'm just putting on my shoes!"

This week's parsha is a reminder of the consequences of delay: the impatient folk make a calf of gold only when "Moshe is slowed [*boshesh*]" on the mount. How late is he? Six hours. How do we know? From a Midrash that reads *boshesh* as *ba shesh*, "He arrived (at) six."

If Moshe was delayed, the people have a point: after all, the Torah is usually insistent on promptness and punctuality (especially in the pursuit of a mitzva).

The question is obvious: How could they?

Incredibly, the same folks who had just responded, six weeks earlier, to the awe of the Revelation and receipt of Torah with a resounding battle cry of *na'aseh v'nishma*," were now groveling at the feet of an "idol," described by the Psalmist as "the work of men's hands. They have mouths, but cannot speak; eyes, but cannot see; ears, but cannot hear."

The Ramban leniently blames the presence of fear; the absence of Moshe created a vacuum that the Jews tried to fill, not with a God *per se* but with the search for a legitimate intermediary (*shaliach*) between themselves and God; Rav Yerucham Levovitz, the famed Mashgiach of Mir, agrees, and sees fear behind a frightened nation's need for a "physical" presence to fulfill their desire for *avodas Hashem* (Divine service.)

But this sympathetic logic can only go so far, for the cure for loneliness is not usually idolatry.

This parsha also introduces a fascinating image: the sight of a solitary and slightly presumptuous Jew arguing, even gently threatening, a precipitous God.

The Heavens react to Israel's cardinal and corruptive sin of gross apostasy with a declaration of destruction ("Allow me and I will annihilate [va'achalem] them!") causing Moshe, the human protagonist who has patience for fools and tolerance for sinners, to immediately rise for the defense.

> *Rosenbloom is a brilliant lawyer with a tough case, all the evidence points to his client being guilty of murder — except there is no corpse.*
>
> *So he devises a dazzling closing statement, "Ladies and gentlemen of the jury, I have a surprise for you all. In the next sixty seconds the person my client is charged with killing will walk into this courtroom."*
>
> *Stunned, the whole room turns to the door....but nothing happens. Rosenbloom, a satisfied look on his face, quickly admits that he made it all up however, he argues, "You all looked with anticipation, thus proving that some reasonable doubt must exist in your minds as to whether anyone is dead. I therefore insist that you return a verdict of not guilty against my client!"*
>
> *A few minutes later, the verdict is pronounced, Guilty!*
>
> *"But how?" sputters the flabbergasted lawyer, "you must have had some doubt, all of you stared at the door."*
>
> *"Oh, we looked," replies the jury foreman, "but your client didn't."*

Moshe powerfully presents his case in three encounters with God, or in the words of the Torah, "pleads (*vayechal*)" for a second chance; a scene that is reminiscent of Avraham arguing against God's intent to destroy Sodom and Gomorrah.

But his tactics differ.

Moshe's strategy is to "humanize" God, and thus appeals to His common sense, compassion, love — and vanity: "What will the Egyptians say if You destroy the Israelites You rescued? And remember the Patriarchs...is this how You fulfill Your promise to make their seed as numerous as the stars?"

This returns us to the opening words of the parsha, *ki sisa es rosh*, which traditionally means "when you lift up the head" (an idiom for, "to take a census, a head-count"), but our linguists see in it a brilliant Hebrew pun; the same expression also means, "to forgive, to pardon," in the context of Moshe's struggle to "ransom" (a form of atoning) his sinful folk away from a Divine wrath "so that no plague [literally, 'blow'] may come upon them."

His choice of words, notes the 16th century Rabbi Shlomo Ephraim Lucintz (*Kli Yakar*), reveals a daring and defiant leader who identifies completely with his people, "If you are going to forgive them [*im tissa*], then do so; if not, then wipe me also from Your book."

Book? What book? The Torah?

No: there has only been one reference to a book so far, and that is the *sefer habris,* written *after* Sinai to document the terms of the partnership between God and Israel.

This is why our sages call this Moshe's finest hour, an intimate portrait of a leader under stress, challenged with a *Mission Impossible*, maintaining a collective *bris* (covenant) between God and a corrupted people. And he succeeds. Not only does God forgive Israel its ingratitude and betrayal but promises them another covenant: "I will do tremendous, awesome and terrifying wonders [for you]."

This is not to say there was no national atonement; there was.

In the aftermath of shame and salvation, the Jews construct a portable Temple (*mishkan*) for God's "residence," using the same gold and silver utensils, proving that no object is in itself evil but only its purpose. Both the new tablets and the original, broken ones, are placed together in the Ark that travels with the Tabernacle, and later transferred to the Temple as a permanent reminder of the earlier atrocious Golden Calf abomination.

Considering the national trauma, it is not surprising that Moshe never again meets God out-of-sight, but in the midst of the populace, in an *ohel mo'ed* ("Tent of Meeting") where his encounters take place for all to see — as a symbol of stability intended to reduce anxiety, destroy doubt, minimize fear.

> *Little Baruch is playing outdoors, using his mother's broom as a horse. When it starts to get dark he goes inside, leaving the broom on the back porch.*
>
> *When his mother can't find it, he tells her, "It's outside, mum."*
>
> *"Please go get it."*
>
> *"But ma, I'm afraid of the dark."*
>
> *"Don't worry, my son, God is out there too, so there's no need to be scared."*
>
> *Little Baruch opens the back door slightly, and whispers, "Psst, God, if you're out there, please hand me the broom."*

From Golden Calf to Golden Opportunity

> *After building the worlds most secure zoo, the architect and contractor are astonished to discover that the kangaroo is able to get out of his enclosure every night. To stop the kangaroo from hopping out they redesign and build a new 19-foot fence.*
>
> *However, the next morning they still find him hopping about the grounds.*
>
> *And so a 20-foot fence is put up, followed by a 30, and even a 40-foot fence, all to no avail.*
>
> *A bystander camel in the next enclosure turns to the kangaroo, and asks, "Hey Joey, how high do you think they'll go?"*
>
> *"Uh, I'd guess about 1,000 feet...or until they remember to lock the gate at night!"*

Vayakhel-Pekudei, opens with, *Vayakhel Moshe*, "Moshe then gathered," a reference to a new public assembly whose aim is to nullify a previous "gathering," less than a week before, in which the same Jewish community (*kehilla*) had assembled in rebellion to venerate a calf of gold.

The noun *kehilla* is derived from the verb, "to gather," and appears in this context with a more pure intent: Moshe instructs his people in art and furniture, architecture and construction, in order to begin worshipping God in a new Temple, the first-of-its-kind, made out of the same (gold) material.

This important continuum, from Golden Calf to golden opportunity, thus has a redeeming correlative: the Torah is obviously pleased as it describes its own architectural sonnet of a sanctuary in highly poetic prose, with its "sky-blue, purple and scarlet wool, rams skins dyed red, spicy incense."

The second parsha, *Pekudei*, is derived from the opening words, "These are the records (*pekudei*)" of the Tabernacle.

The question is obvious: why should Moshe have to account for all the construction materials? Wasn't he trusted? Yes, but the Torah is warning those who seek public office: that to manage community money is not only serious business but open business; that counting and accounting go hand-in-hand.

And so Moshe, according to Rabbi Moshe Schreiber (*Chasam Sofer*), acting in the spirit of priestly honesty, publicly counts, weighs, and numbers the silver and gold, not just to preserve his own sterling reputation but to set an example of integrity for future leaders as to how to avoid suspicion and appearance of wrongdoing.

> *After the rav finishes his Shabbos sermon, little Freddy pulls at his coat, "Rabbi, when I grow up and start making money, I'm going to give you some."*
> *"Why Freddy, that's very sweet of you...but why?"*
> *"Because my daddy says you're one of the poorest preachers we've ever had."*

This Shabbos is called *Shabbos Shekalim* because the parsha is focused on contributions ("Everyone whose heart so moves him shall bring gifts to God"), rotating around every adult male's obligation to give a half-shekel toward the building of the sanctuary-Tabernacle (*mishkan*).

Why only the men? According to Rashi, the fundamental commentator on the Torah, this "guilt money" was not applicable to Jewish women who had nobly refused to participate in the shameful Golden Calf incident.

The power of the opposite sex is related in a Midrashic tale:

Pesikta d'Rav Kahane describes how Alexander the Great, who has "left no place unconquered," arrives at Cartinga, a country populated entirely by women. "If you engage in battle with us and are victorious," a delegation of the city of women tell him, "your name will go out into the world as one who has destroyed by the sword a country of women. And if we engage you in battle and defeat you — then you will be too ashamed to show your face before kings.

So Alexander departs, and writes on the gate: "I, Alexander of Macedonia, behaved like a foolish king until I came to the state of Cartinga and learned wisdom from the women."

> *Yankele, a married man, squanders his paycheck by staying out all night gambling and partying with the boys.*
>
> *When he tries to sneak into his house in the wee hours of the morning, his furious wife attacks him with a barrage of epithets, nagging, berating, screaming, "How would you like it if you didn't see me for a couple of days!!"*
>
> *"That would suit me just fine!!"*
>
> *So the next day Yankele doesn't see his wife. Several more days go by, and he still doesn't see her. Finally, a week later the swelling is down a bit and he sees a little — out of the corner of his left eye.*

The venerated leader of the Jewish people has a twin philanthropic request: Moshe asks for volunteers (tradesmen) and donations (of building materials).

The response? A generous outpouring of gifts, ranging from gold earrings, silver bracelets, and brilliant jewels; as emphasized by the Torah's multi-use (nine times) of the verb *heiviu* ("they brought"), and suggestive of the lingering guilt over the calf incident ("With earrings the Israelites sinned and with earrings they were redeemed.")

Moshe ben Nachman (*Ramban*) and Isaac Abarbanel (15th century Portuguese exegetic) disagree: they attribute the generosity of the Jews to their joy at being able to give to God.

But they agree on the lesson: in order to do God's work *everyone* needs to chip in, *kol n'div libo,* "according to his or her generosity."

When the Torah describes the contribution of gemstones from the tribal princes (*nesiim*) it leaves out one of the Hebrew letters (*yud*), purposefully penning the word defectively. Why? Because this group hesitated, and waited until they saw what everyone else had donated, restricting their contribution to complete the task.

> *The frustrated foreman decides to trick his ten lazy employees into doing some work for a change, and announces, "Today, I've got a really easy job for the laziest one among you. So, will the laziest man please put his hand up."*
>
> *Nine hands go up.*
>
> *"Why didn't you put your hand up?" he asks the tenth man.*
>
> *"Too much trouble."*

Remarkably, this group of princes, notes Rashi, quoting the Midrash of Sifrei, underestimates the nation's generosity and enthusiasm, and are reduced to donating only the precious gems for the High Priest's breastplate and garments (items unavailable to the "common" folk).

There is a paradox in this parsha: why does the Torah feel the need to repeat the highly detailed instructions from a previous parsha (*Terumah-Tetzaveh*), an architectural epic "to-do" list prepared by God for Betzalel?

The answer lies in relationships: to God the calf of gold was akin to marital infidelity, a tangible symbol of betrayal. Now was a time for reconciliation, when the "skilled laborers" of wisdom (*chochmei lev*) returned to finish the job and complete *the* nuptial home between God and the Jews.

Our Jewish mystics see in this rapprochement the reason why Betzalel, which means, "to rest in God's shadow," was chosen, at the tender age of 14, together with his architect "partners" (Oholiav ben Achisomoch, from Dan, the lowliest of the tribes), to become master craftsman for this yeoman's task.

Betzalel, son of Uri, grandson of Chur, and a descendant from a powerful tribe that symbolized monarchy and dignity (Judah), had all the necessary components; he was endowed with a wisdom (*chochmoh*) learned from others; an insight (*binah*) acquired from life's experience; and an understanding (*daas*) that sprung forth from his mystical intuition (our sages even credit him with having a quicker grasp than Moshe in understanding the Divine plans for the sanctuary).

As such, the "newlyweds," like an excited young couple opening their wedding gifts, retrace their original design and decoration ideas of their Sanctuary (one bride's idea of housework? To sweep the room with a glance).

But how to celebrate?

Moshe takes his cue from God: since creation was crowned with a mandated Shabbos, Moshe concludes the construction of the portable Tabernacle (the embodiment of holy space) with a reminder of the spiritual importance of Shabbos. The result? The merging, for the first time in the Torah, of holy space with holy time, an event so significant that the Torah describes it in more verses than it initially devoted to the entire creation of the universe.

So intertwined are the concepts of Shabbos and Mishkan that, to this day, the legal "work" boundaries of Shabbos (39 laws) are a direct derivation of the labor involved in the Tabernacle's construction.

"Nisht auf Shabbos geret, *not to talk about it on Shabbos,*" says Gerry, "*but I'm thinking of selling my car.*"

"*Really,*" replies an interested Gideon, "*not to talk about it on Shabbos...but how much are you asking for it?*"

"*Not to talk about it on Shabbos...but $3,000.*"

"*Not to talk about it on Shabbos...but I'll give you $2,000 for it.*"

"*Let me think on it.*"

Later on they return to shul for Mincha, and Gideon leans over to Gerry, "Not to talk about it on Shabbos...but did you think about my offer?

"*Yeah, but not to talk about it on Shabbos...I already sold it after* shlishi *during* layning."

The portable Sinai that Betzalel builds provides the children of Israel, as they begin to physically distance themselves from the original Mount of Revelation, with a continued avenue of Godly communication. The same "cloud by day, and fire by night" that hovered over Sinai now reappears over the *Mishkan* and the Tent of Meeting (*Ohel Moed*), a visible immediacy of God's Presence.

The Book of Exodus, which started with the Jews enslaved, now ends with God's Presence a constant feature in their lives.

With construction complete, the client (God) is satisfied and moves in ("God's glory filled the Tabernacle") — thus allowing the second Book of the Torah (*Shmos*) to end on a satisfying 'n stimulating note.

After explaining the laws of Pesach, the cheder Rebbe asks his young class to use the word matza *in a sentence.*

"Matzas are eaten at the Seder," says 7-year-old Yaakov.

"Very good," the Rebbe smiles. "How about you, David?" ◗

"Matzas are made without salt," says young 8-year-old David.

"Excellent," replies the Rebbe when suddenly 6-year-old Izzy, who had only been in the country a few months, raises his hand and triumphantly declares, "Time matzas on!"

This ends the Book of Shmos, the second book of the Torah when everyone rises and says, *Chazak, chazak v'nitchazek*, "Be strong, be strong, and let us be strengthened!" — a roar of encouragement to continue on to Leviticus, the next book of the Torah.

Why repeat the word *chazak* three times?

To symbolize the past, present and future.

Vayikra

(LEVITICUS)

Leviticus primarily deals with "offerings" and "sacrifices" (*rayach nicho'ach l'Hashem*, "a satisfying aroma to God.") What's the difference between them? A "sacrifice," notes Rabbi Samson Raphael Hirsch, implies giving up something that is of value to oneself for the benefit of another; an "offering" implies a gift that satisfies the receiver.

This third, and central book of the Torah, is known as the "Book of Holiness," and the first parsha, *Vayikra*, is also known as *Toras Kohanim*, "The Law of the Priests."

Welcome to holy practices (*korbonos*), holy places (the Temple), holy people (priests), holy dates (Jewish festivals) — and holy experiences, beginning with the parsha's very first words, the "call [*Vayikra*] of God."

Big Aleph, Little Aleph

> *Uncle Miltie walks into a hearing aid store, and asks the sales girl, "How much do they cost?"*
>
> *"That depends," she replies, "we have from $2 to $2,000."*
>
> *"Let's see the $2 one."*
>
> *The sales girl puts the device around Miltie's neck and says, "See this button? Just stick it in your ear. See this little string? Just run it down to your pocket."*
>
> *"How does it work?"*
>
> *"Well, to tell you the truth, for $2 it doesn't work, but when people see it on you, they'll talk louder!"*

The title to this week's parsha comes from the opening words, *Vayikra el Moshe*, "God called to Moshe and God spoke."

Isn't this redundant? Why "call" before "speaking?"

Nachum of Chernobyl, a Chassidic master, explains that one must first experience the call and only then responding to the words themselves.

To the 18th century Baal Shem Tov from Podolia, founder of Chassidism, "Everything created, contains a spark of holiness;" Rav Abraham Isaac Kook, writing in his mystical *Orot Hakodesh*, agreed: "There is nothing in the universe that is absolutely secular;" and the poet Emily Dickinson was inspired to write, "We never know how high we are/Till we are asked to rise/And then if we are true to plan/Our statures touch the skies."

The idea of *kadosh*, which is associated with holiness but in fact means, literally, separateness, underlines God's previous charge of discipline to Israel, *V'atem tih'u li mamleches kohanim v'goy kadosh*, "And you shall be for Me a Kingdom of Priests and a Holy Nation."

To live as a Jew is to be addressed as a Jew; to be told one's personal destiny (a sense of calling, a vocation in itself) requires a disciplined hearing of the call first. German philosopher-psychologist Moritz Lazarus, in his 19th century classic *Ethics*, claims the expression "I am sanctified!" to be "the noblest word framed by the human tongue!"

"Vocation" comes from the Latin *vocare*, "to call;" and rabbinic texts are full of ordinary Jews who become extraordinary Jews (from Moshe to Jonah) after hearing such a call, a call to action (a reminder to the messenger not to forget the message.)

But what exactly is God "calling" out to Moshe? A lesson in sacrifices.

It is a common myth that these offerings were brought as bribes or gifts to God; they were not. They were a way of worship, tokens of gratitude, a mark of festive occasions, or a method to expiate sins.

> *A Jew, suddenly gripped with remorse, goes running to his rav with an admission, "Rebbe, Rebbe, I have sinned in my profession."*
> *"What is it that you do?"*
> *"I'm a house painter. I've done sloppy jobs, I've used inferior quality paints, and I've diluted my paints with turpentine. I've cut corners and, worse of all," the man sobs, "I lied about it to my customers. Rebbe, tell me, how can I make amends?"*
> *The rav looks at him and says, "Repaint, Repaint, and thin no more."*

Thus, as a willing vehicle of spirituality to help one articulate his thoughts, emotions, and needs, sacrifices were for the Jews' benefit, not God's. The word *korban*, however, does not mean "sacrifice" (which implies a loss); it comes from the root *karov* (near), as in "being brought closer [to God]."

The Heavens identify five categories: the burnt offering (*olah*, "that which goes up"); the meal offering (*mincha*); the sacrifice of well being (*zevach shelamim*, from *shalom* which not only means peace but also "wholeness"); the sin (*chatas*), and guilt offering (*asham*) — there is an interesting omission: the Torah does not permit atonement for any willfully committed sin.

Specific sacrifices demonstrated the need to express specific feelings, ranging from belief in God, giving thanks, or simply apologizing for having done wrong, a practice which incensed such great prophets of Israel as Isaiah ("What use to Me are your many sacrifices? I am sated with the burnt offerings of rams!") and Amos ("Though you offer Me burnt offerings and your meal offerings, I will not accept them"). They felt these Jews sinned knowingly and then simply went to the Temple to superficially express regret — and then continued to misbehave.

Samuel was blunt ("To obey is better than sacrifice") after calling the disobedient Saul a hypocrite. But don't be confused: The Heavens are not depicted as rejecting sacrifices in principle, only those brought in the wrong spirit.

> It is Rosh Hashanah morning and the rabbi notices that Sophie Rosenbaum has been crying hysterically throughout the davening, so he goes over to comfort her, "Sophie, zug mir, is everything okay?"
>
> "No, rabbi," she wails, "my husband passed away last night."
>
> "Baruch dayan emes! That's terrible news. I'm truly sorry to hear that. Where did it happen?"
>
> "In our kitchen," she sobs.
>
> "In the kitchen? Were you with him? Do you remember his last words?"
>
> "Yes, rabbi."
>
> "What did he say?"
>
> "He said, 'Sophie, Sophie….please…please put down the gun…'"

The Hebrew word *im* ("if") appears three times in this section ("if the offering is an *olah*, if a *mincha*, if a *shehlamim*"), yet the term *asher* ("when") is only used once, in reference to a leader.

This attracted the attention of Ovadiah ben Jacob Sforno, 16th century Italian talmudist, who saw the "when" as implying that inevitably even the most powerful and wealthy leaders are sure to sin ("It's better to eat oysters openly than to open oysters secretly," was how the skeptical English author Israel Zangwill said his farewells to Dr. Schechter).

Meir Yehuda Leibush ben Yehiel Michal (*Malbim*), 19th century Russian scholar, agrees, and ties this thought into the parsha's conclusionary words ("realizes his guilt"), in that even the powerful have a responsibility for self-criticism and remorse.

Rashi, quoting a Midrash, links *asher* to the word *ashrei*, which means "fortunate," as in, fortunate is the generation whose leader is "manly enough" to admit his sins.

> It is late on Yom Kippur afternoon, just before mincha, when the trainee associate rabbi suddenly enters the shul, and walks shakily towards the rav. His face is gray, his eyes look tired, and he is panting, out of breath.
>
> "Rabbi," he rasps, "I've got to drink some water. I'm thirsty and dry."
>
> "What! You're a rabbi! A role model! Today is Yom Kippur, and you want to drink?"
>
> "Please, just a small drink, I can't take it anymore!"
>
> The rav, momentarily moved by his colleague's suffering, gives him a glass of water to quench his terrible thirst. He gulps down the entire glass, wipes his brow, turns to the rav, and sighs, "Thank you, thank you. I promise, I'll never eat schmaltz herring on Yom Kippur morning ever again!"

The sacrificial slaughter of animals was *the* deeply personal form of ancient Jewish worship, a highly focused activity that allowed one to recalibrate their outlook on life.

The Mishna, the foundational manuscript of Judaism, has Shimon the Righteous including *avoda* (worship, via the rituals of sacrifice) as one of three things sustaining the entire world.

This sacrificial activity ended in 70 CE when the Second Temple was destroyed, and was replaced by prayer (*tefilla*), study (*talmud Torah*), and the doing of good deeds (*gemillas chassadim*) — although both the Ramban and the Rambam, despite their famous dispute as to the meaning of animal sacrifices, state unequivocally that in the time of the Messiah, animal sacrifices will be restored.

In Biblical days, these sacrifices were only validated if offered in Jerusalem's Temple by ordained priests.

The question is obvious: what about the Jews of Judea who were scattered across the holy land? Surely a trek to Jerusalem was a great difficulty, given the primitive means of travel?

And so the rabbis divided the country into 24 districts (*ma'amados*), and assigned a special week to each district wherein local delegations would go up to Jerusalem. Once there, these emissaries timed their morning and evening sacrifices to when their back-home constituents gathered to pray in their synagogues (a model for the future practice of daily shul prayers.)

And to ensure that there were no second-class Israelites, offerings were "equalized" (*each* being "a satisfying aroma to God") by way of sliding-scale dues: the Jew who could not afford the choicest of a sheep or goat, could use a pigeon; and if one was too indigent to even afford a pigeon, then a tenth (*ephah*) of plain ground-wheat would do just fine.

> *Sammy the bachelor receives a cookbook as a birthday gift from his older sister.*
> *"Nu," she asks a few weeks later, "are you using my gift?"*

"Uh uh, nope. Ain't nothing I can do with it."
"Too much fancy cooking in it, eh?"
"Yep! Every one of the recipes begins the same way —
'Take a clean dish and...'"

Humility, modesty, and demureness ripple through this parsha, causing Torah scholars to pay close attention to the small *alef* at the end of the opening word, *Vayikra* (the only place in the Torah in which an *alef* is found in this form.)

Moshe, writes the 13th century scholar, Jacob ben Asher (the *Baal Ha-Turim*) would have preferred *Vayikar*, without the *alef*, a term of chaos and randomness that God uses in the context of Bil'am, the evil prophet of Midian. The miniature *alef*, suggests Rav Kook, the towering first chief rabbi of Palestine, symbolizes not just personal humility, but Moshe's burning zeal.

Its size, suggests ben Asher, shows willingness to compromise. Not so, argues *The Rosh* (Rabbeinu Asher), who sees the letter's reduced size as reflecting the humility of Moshe — especially in a parsha wherein Aaron's name does not appear even once.

This omission is puzzling. Why?

Because Vayikra deals with the sacrifices in which the priesthood led by Aaron play a major role. Moshe, concerned that a *Vayikra* directed to him would belittle his brother's dignity, minimized his own role with a small *alef*.

On his first day at cheder, the boy who would grow to become the saintly Tzemach Tzedek asked his grandfather about Moshe being denoted by a small *alef*.

His grandfather (the *Alter Rebbe*) then showed him how, in the Books of Chronicles, Adam is written with a large alef. The contrast was simple, he explained, and can be summarized thus: "A little humility goes a long way." Moshe, despite all his qualities of greatness, was humble, modest, self-effacing, and reduced his ego when writing about himself (hence, a small *alef*); Adam, on the other hand, knew he was the first human being, the progenitor of the future, and felt proud and smug about himself, increasing his ego by writing an ostentatious *alef* to ensure his proper recognition from history.

Meanwhile, the homiletic Midrash, compiled between the 3rd and 10th centuries, has a poignant epilogue: because Moshe has used a less-than-regular size letter God remains with some leftover Divine ink.

What to do?

God takes the surplus and smears Moshe's forehead with it, creating the glowing "rays [*keren*] of splendor" that frighten the children of Israel when he descends from Sinai.

> *The cheder teacher is explaining the importance of the Ten Commandments, humility and honoring parents, and asks a room full of 5 and 6-year-olds, "Is there a commandment that teaches us how to treat our brothers and sisters?"*
>
> *"Yes," says little Yossele, without missing a beat, "Thou shall not kill!"*

The Talmud lists four things that require *chizzuk* (strengthening): Torah, good deeds, prayer, and *derech eretz*; the latter defined by Rashi, the teacher *par excellence* of the Jewish people, as courtesy, good manners and respect, as evidenced by how God opens this parsha by addressing Moshe not in such aggressive terms as *daber, amar,* or *tzav* ("speak, say, or command") but by a soft, gentle and loving "call (*vayikra*)."

This is why the second century rabbis chose this parsha, despite its stern legislation, as the first introductory chapter of Torah

to teach Jewish children the "proper way" (*derech eretz*), declaring that, "Small children are pure, the sacrifices are pure, let those who are pure come and occupy themselves with things that are pure!"

As *the* educational parsha, the written structure differs from other Torah readings: instead of the standard paragraph breaks there are several blank spaces. Why?

These spaces, explains Rashi, are intended to make the study of Torah a positive experience for children, a chance to pause, review, absorb. Furthermore, they simultaneously act as a reminder to parents and teachers that *chinuch* (education) requires patience, forbearance and composure.

> *The rosh yeshiva goes into a computer store and asks the salesgirl for the latest model.*
> *"This little computer," she proudly points out, "will do half of your job for you."*
> *"Great! I'll take two."*

The Midrash ties the end of this parsha, "If a person sins and deals deceitfully with his fellow in the matter of a deposit or pledge, or through robbery, then he shall restore that which he has taken," to the beginning of the next one, which begins, "Command Aaron and his sons: This is the law of the burnt offering..."

What's the connection?

That only the Jew who has observed the first law (conducting himself morally in business) can carry out the second (and serve God).

This concept is behind the radical idea that one must *earn* the right to pray found in some Siddurim that begin with twin verses, *V'ahavta l're'acho kamocho*, "Love your neighbor as yourself," and *V'ahavta es Hashem Elokecho*, "Love the Lord your God" — in other words, only by fulfilling the first can one even begin to fulfill the second.

After being accused of assault and battery, Sonny calls his lawyer, "Mr. Greenberger, I've got a half-million bucks. Can you get me off?"

"You have my word," replies Greenberger, "you will never go to jail with that much money."

Leviticus at Its Most Levitical

"Bist meshuge! You're crazy!" the rabbi screams at one of his congregants who had taken up parachute jumping in a sky-divers club."
"But rabbi, I'm so close to Heaven up there."
"Yes, that's true. But you're going the wrong way!"

The title to this week's parsha, *Tzav*, means "to order." Its instructions speak directly to the Aaron dynasty of Jewish priesthood (*kohanim, levi'im*) who are obligated to offer sacrifices as proxies for the whole nation of Israel.

The ritual minutiae are highly detailed: how to dispose of burnt ashes, distribute blood, pour oil, etc.

Fire, metaphorically, is an integral component of Temple worship ("The fire on the altar shall be kept burning; it shall not go out"), and many an aspiring rabbi-preacher has been told, "If you can't put fire in your sermon, put your sermon in the fire!" Ben Sira was blunt: "According to its fuel, so will the fire be."

This is what Chassidus calls *hislahavus* ("fiery enthusiasm"), the carrying out of a religious activity not with routine but with a fire-in-the-belly; with zeal and enthusiasm, energy and excitement

The parents were impressed: their little Moishie loved music, so they bought him a violin, which he practiced day and night with zeal. But the family dog would howl loudly when he heard the screeching sounds.
The father, trying to read in the den, listens to the dog and the violin until he could take it no longer: finally ▸

> *he jumps up, slamming his paper to the floor, and yells above the noise, "Moishie, for crying out loud! Can't you play something the dog doesn't know?"*

In modern Hebrew, the word *tzav* has a serious, harsh military-governmental connotation, yet in ancient context its root forms the noun *mitzva* which evokes the opposite emotion of joy, elation, simcha.

And herein lies Judaism's great paradox: in this weeks Haftarah, Jeremiah cautions the Jews that even the most meticulous of all their offerings carries less weight with God than their personal conduct; a stunning acknowledgment that the Heavens judge not by the letter of the law but by its spirit ("A handful of flour brought by a poor man voluntarily is, according to Isaac Nappaha, declared more precious than two handfuls of incense brought by the High Priest!")

On what does Jeremiah base this supremacy-of-ethics?

On the fact that God's appearance at Sinai was accompanied not by any specific mention of sacrifices but by the morality of Ten Commandments.

Yet although Jeremiah's prophecies of doom come true, and he personally witnesses Jerusalem's destruction, he is still known as the "Prophet of Hope" because he never lost faith.

There is an element of sadness in this parsha as Moshe performs his final act as High Priest, a loss not of his choosing but of Divine displeasure at his earlier stubborn rejection to lead the Jewish folk out of Egypt.

Moshe begins the eight-day inauguration of the Priests (*miluim*) on a high, but on the seventh day is suddenly informed to step aside for his brother, continuing only in the reduced status of a plain Levi.

Is Moshe troubled, anguished? All humility aside, yes, he is.

There is a give-away clue, the *shalsheles* note in the text's cantillation (*te'amim*), a symbol that resembles a ladder and is tradition-ally sung in an up-and-down, rise-and-fall manner, suggestive, say our sages, of internal struggle. Whenever this note appears in the Torah it does so in the context of someone's inner conflict (it ap-pears three more times; between Avraham and Lot, Yosef and his brothers; Eliezer, servant of Avraham, in his quest to find Yitzchak a wife).

To his credit Aaron introduces "a new phenomenon" (*chiddush*): he reacts to his brother's leadership not with animosity or envy, but with "joy in his heart," to which Moshe reciprocates, "Just as you rejoiced in my greatness, so I rejoice in your greatness."

It is also from this parsha that we get a lesson in wardrobe sensitivity: the *kohanim* are ordered to change out of their finest linen priestly robes into ordinary, non-ceremonial garments before disposing of altar ashes. Why?

The Midrash tells us: "Clothes are man's glory;" leading Johanan ben Nappaha, early Palestinian *Amora*, to proudly declare, "My gar-ments are my honorees." "Dress," writes the 19th century German author A. Brull, "mirrors a nation's pain and sorrow, its pleasures and joys;" and Rashi then adds the obvious, "It is unseemly to wear the same clothing in the kitchen as when pouring wine for a master."

> One day little Shmuly is flipping through a very old Chumash when suddenly an old tree leaf that had been pressed between the pages falls out.
> "Mamma, mamma, look what I found!"
> "What is it, dear?"
> "I think it's Adam's suit!"

"If you're dressed up on the outside," goes the old adage, "then you're dressed up on the inside;" a slogan that the Jewish mystics use spiritually, as a strengthening of inner convictions. But Moshe

Hayyim Luzzatto, Italian kabbalist, scholar, poet and mystic of the 18th century warns, in his *Mesillas Yesharim*: "Gorgeous headgear and embroidered apparel give rise to pride and border on lust."

This parsha's focus on wardrobe is why Jews change from weekday into better clothes erev Shabbos and why garments must be new or cleaned before each Jewish holiday. All religious ritual, according to the 13th century Spanish Rabbeinu Bachya ben Asher, must be conducted in a respectful, decorous manner.

> *One year, just before Rosh Hashanah, Abie decides to get his Tallis cleaned and asks his friend to suggest a reliable dry cleaner.*
>
> *"I always take my Tallis to Moishie, the Jewish dry cleaner downtown, he knows what to do and only charges $4 bucks."*
>
> *So Abie goes down to Moishie's only to discover that it has changed hands to Jones & Sons. He approaches the new owner and asks if he still meets the old prices. Mr. Jones assures him that he does, so Abie leaves his Tallis and returns the next day, only to be handed a bill for twenty four dollars.*
>
> *"I thought you met Moishe's prices!?" he yells at Mr. Jones.*
>
> *"I did. I charged $4 for the Tallis, and $20 bucks to get all the knots out of the fringes!"*

This parsha represents our first introduction to *kashrus*, the Jewish dietary laws.

So, does adherence to kashrus automatically endow holiness?

No, argues Rabbi Ovadiah Sforno, the formidable 16th century Italian commentator: it only *prepares* the Jew for holiness. The order to "be holy," he writes, is a summation intended to identify the end goal, the massaging of an entire community into a holy nation (*goy kadosh*) whose battlecry is repeated in the *Kedusha* prayer: *nekadesh es shimcho ba'olom*, "We will make Your name holy in the world."

> *For several weeks before Shavuos, Betsy decides to shed some excess weight, and takes her new diet so seriously that every erev Shabbos she changes her route so as not to drive past her favorite bakery. But erev Yom Tov the temptation is getting to her so she makes a vow, to drive by the bakery but only stop if there is a parking spot right outside the busy store. When she comes home later she is schlepping bags and bags of cakes and cookies.*
>
> *"So," comments her husband wryly, "I guess there was a parking spot in front of the cake shop."*
>
> *"Sure enough," his wife replies, beaming, "the eighth time around the block, there it was!"*

The basic rules are these. A kosher animal is one that its cud (ruminant) and has split hooves. A kosher fish is one that has both fins and scales. A kosher bird is more difficult to determine, since the Torah only lists non-kosher birds, one then deduces that all the other birds are kosher.

Kashrus laws, like the *mezuzah*, or the "red cow without blemish" (*para adumoh*), an incomprehensible and intractable ritual, fall under the category of "*chok*," in that they defy any rational human explanation.

It is unfounded that kashrus has to do with health considerations, or that some animals have a level of "uncleanliness," or that we should avoid predatory creatures lest we prey on others, or that we must avoid those creatures that were once worshipped as gods.

None of these reasons matter.

The only correct approach to non-kosher animals, advises Rashi, the classic medieval Torah commentator of commentators, is that they are to be avoided simply because God has said so. The Rambam in his *Guide for the Perplexed*, on the dietary laws says, "They train us to master our appetites and not consider eating and drinking the end of man's existence."

Suzie joins a health club and yet still puts on weight and doesn't understand why. Pressed by her friends to think, she describes how she had made her husband's favorite cake for Shabbos and that he had only eaten half of it. So the next day she kept staring at the other half, until unable to resist, she cuts a thin slice for herself.

But one slice leads to another, and another… until she has eaten the rest of the cake.

Was her husband upset, ask her friends.

"Oh, he never found out. I made another cake and ate half!"

Kashrus restriction is only one of many ways the Laws of Moshe disciplines Jewish lives into a *goy kadosh* (a "holy nation"); from how we speak to how we dress, from what we say to what we eat — a pattern of restraint designed and prescribed by a master physician intended to prevent the clogging of ones spiritual arteries.

"The reason you're so fat," the psychiatrist tells Morrie, his patient, "is because your whole life is oriented toward food. You like parties for the hors d'oeuvres; a ball game to you means hot dogs, peanuts and beer; watching TV is a long succession of snacks; and…"

"Wait a minute," interrupts Morrie, "Don't you serve anything during psychoanalysis?"

The discipline of kashrus helps the Jew attain a certain spirituality; an armor, so to speak, of self-control against the daily temptations of a "non-kosher" lifestyle. That is why Jews, in order to structure the act of eating into a powerful vehicle of sanctification, reenact the procedures of the Temple priests: they wash hands, bless meals, "break" challah, sprinkle salt (because the sacrifices, the "food of God," were once sprinkled with salt).

Our sages call our home table a *mizbe'ach* (an "altar"), an appropriate place for "kosher" food, eaten only after a blessing is recited in order to raise the awareness of God's presence at the family table. Our rabbis decided that to complete a meal without thanking the Heavens for the earth's life-sustaining produce was forbidden.

> *A dietitian was once addressing a large audience: "The material we put into our stomachs is enough to have killed most of us sitting here, years ago. Red meat is awful. Soft drinks erode your stomach lining. Chinese food is loaded with MSG. Vegetables can be disastrous, and none of us realizes the long-term harm caused by the germs in our drinking water. But there is one thing that is the most dangerous of all and we all have, or will, eat it. Can anyone here tell me what food it is that causes the most grief and suffering for years after eating it?"*
>
> *A little ol' Jewish man sitting in the corner raises his hand, and shouts back, "Wedding cake!"*

The Agony and the Ecstasy

> Walking home from shul one Shabbos morning with her husband, the rebbetzin asks, "Nu, how do you think your d'var Torah went today?"
>
> "Excellent," the rabbi replies with obvious glee, "this time I think my sermon really got off the ground."
>
> "Well," the rebbetzin mumbles, "it sure did taxi long enough!"

This week's parsha, *Shemini*, continues the tale of Aaron's investiture as High Priest, with the enigmatic beginning, "On the eighth day;" the first day after a week (*yemei milu'im*) of collective purification that involved bringing atonement offerings (*kappara*) for the sin of a Golden Calf.

This week of unity is followed by *the* day, a "Welcoming Ceremony" formed to greet the arrival of God's presence (*Shechina*) as He prepares to "dwell" among the folk....but tragedy looms ahead.

> One year during the family's summer vacation, little Danny is running on the beach when he suddenly comes across a dead sea gull laying on the sand.
>
> "Mummy, mummy," he yells, "what happened to him?"
>
> "It was a tragedy, he died and went to Heaven."
>
> "And God threw him back down?"

One of the most climactic moments in Israel's experience as a newly formed nation, occurs exactly one year after the Exodus, in the "first month" of Nisan (*hachodesh harishon*); a time of new beginnings and fresh creations, when the end of the rainy season means the fig tree is in bud, grain begins to ripe, wheat stalks harden, wild springtime flowers carpet the fields, and fruit trees start their blossom.

Menachem Mendel, the energetic Rebbe of Koznitz, took the Hebrew term *aviv* (for Spring) and broke it in two: *av*, meaning "father," and *y'v*, whose numerical value is 12, in order to emphasize Nisan's role as the "father of the twelve months," a gematria that also mystically tied the Jewish calendar to the function of the 12 Hebrew tribes.

Obviously, if Nisan was important then its first Rosh Chodesh in history was especially so.

God's temporary desert Temple (*Mishkan*) was inaugurated on this day by the *Kohanim* as the Jews made vows, gave donations, arranged their tithes, brought the first-born of their flocks, delivered offerings, and listened to Moshe's eight-part *parshiyos d'var Torah*, in recognition of the eight days it took to prepare for this gala.

This day may be the "eighth" in human time, however, by being God's "first day" among His people, our Jewish mystics see this as the "eighth anniversary day" of creation.

In *Jewish* time, the previous centuries are "incomplete;" God "resting" on the seventh day only because there was nothing more to create.

This changed on the "eighth" day, the day His joint venture with the Jews was about to begin, a day delegated for the human to improve (*tikkun*) what had been created; the first day the Jew finally invites God not just to visit on occasion, but to "move in," permanently, in order that the circle of Creation is finally closed.

Rabbi Samson Raphael Hirsch saw the number "8" as a symbol of the spiritual, akin to the mandatory eighth-day covenantal event of circumcision being the spiritual birth of an infant boy. That is why our rabbis answer the Haggadah song, "Who Knows Eight?" with "Eight Days of Miloh."

The question is obvious: why precisely on the eighth day?

Three top sages suggest three different reasons: it is the first day after a woman's seven unclean days (Simeon bar Yohai); it is the first day of vigor and strength for the newborn (*Rambam*); it means having lived through one Shabbos (Midrash).

Yet an "eighth" day event seems unusual; a cycle of "sevens" being more the norm in the building block of Jewish time.

This observation convinced Judah Loew of Prague (*Maharal*) and Shlomo Ephraim Lunschitz (*Kli Yakar*), both great 16th century talmudists, that everything natural in the world is related to the number "seven" (the days it took for creation) while everything spiritual rotates around the number eight; and so the Mishkan, *the bastion of spirituality that transcended the realm of normal time,* came in "eights;" the High Priest had eight articles of clothing; there were eight spices of incense; eight carrying poles, and so on.

This is why the "8th" day of Sukkot (*Shmini Atzeres*) is greeted as a "Special Day" of unity between God and Jews; and why Chanukka, an eight-day Yom Tov, focuses on a *nes nigleh* ("open miracle") intended to celebrate the continuing presence of God.

> *A distraught patient calls her doctor and asks, "Is it true, this medication you gave me is for the rest of my life?"*
> *"Yes."*
> *"Oh, no! She begins to wail.*
> *"What happened? What's the problem?"*
> *"My condition must be very serious, this prescription is marked and no refills' after seven days."*

It is during the waning hours of the day's festivity, when agony suddenly interrupts the ecstasy.

Two righteous heroes of Israel (Nadab and Abihu, the eldest of Aaron's four sons), die in "the blink of an eye," devoured by God's destructive fire. The father's response? Weeping, wailing, shouting, anger, despair? No.

Incredibly, "Aaron was silent" (*Vayiddom Aharon*), an astonishing acceptance of a devastating celestial judgment; a silence that Philo, first-century Alexandrian philosopher and exegete who interpreted the Greek version of the Torah (*Septuagint*), claims "spoke more clearly than speech."

Aaron, *the* indefatigable activist and Jew of initiative, suddenly withdraws into himself, hushed and soundless, with not a word of anger towards God. At that single moment, the sounds of silence enters Judaism as having moral and religious values (and a contemporary slogan is born: "Silence is Golden!")

"The one who curbs the tongue shows sense," voiced Solomon's Proverbs, adding, "Even fools, if they keep silent, are deemed wise!" Rabbi Joshua ben Levi doubled its worth: "One word is worth a *sela* [a small coin], but silence is worth two [*sela'im*]."

"The prudent keeps silence in such a time," whispers the Hebrew prophets (Amos.) Silence to the Talmud's Judah of Kfar Neburya, a third-century *Amora*, "was the highest form of praise, the best of all medicines;" to his contemporary, Abba Arika Rab, it was "a mark of nobility," to Rabbi Akiva, a "fence of wisdom."

> As he was walking to shul one Shabbos morning, the rabbi, who was notorious for his long sermons, bumps into a member who asks him, "Nu rabbi? What are you going to talk about today?"
> "I'm going to discuss how to praise God with the milk of human kindness."
> "Condensed, I hope," replies the congregant.

But why are the brothers punished?

Some rabbis point to acts of unauthorized ritual; others that the sons lacked faith in God's ability to send fire from Heaven (although the 18th century commentator *Or Hachayim* cannot accept that Nadab and Abihu did anything wrong at all; even Moshe credits them with being holier than he and Aaron).

Rabbi Yishmael has a theory: it was carelessness in the presence of holiness, specifically, an attempt to serve as inebriated *kohanim* ("They gazed upon God, and drank.")

Since the priests and Levites were Halachic decision-makers, the fate of Aaron's sons was a warning that intoxicating beverages have no place amongst those who deal in such holy matters as teaching (*lehoros*). Rabbi Menachem Mendel Schneersohn, the seventh Lubavitcher Rebbe, would often use this episode to warn that dangers lurk within an over-focused zealousness, that even tzaddikim must be careful in their pursuit of a mitzva.

This parsha thus highlights the evils of drinking and leadership: an activity that dulls the senses of distinguishing (*lehavdil*) between right and wrong.

> One evening Izzie, drunk from a Purim party, stumbles to his car, opens the door and sits down. "Oh, my God!," he cries, "I've been robbed!"
>
> He calls the police and tells the operator, "Thieves have been in my car! They've stolen my dashboard, my steering wheel, my brake pedal, even my accelerator!"
>
> "We'll be right over," the operator replies.
>
> A few minutes later, Izzie calls back. "Never mind," he says with a hiccup, "I got in the back seat by mistake."

But why should the God of the universe care what we eat?

Because the Torah seeks to integrate every aspect of life, including such a basic daily activity as eating, with purity. It frowns on any monk-like withdrawal and demands that the Jew not only participate fully in the activities of the world, but enrich these acts by sanctifying every moment of existence.

A healthy mind and healthy body absent a healthy soul was considered insufficient.

Since what, and how we eat, affects character and soul, attention to food was present right from the start: God's positive and negative commands to the first couple of Eden involved eating ("eat from all the trees of the garden; do not eat from the Tree of Knowledge"); and later, during their flight from Egypt, God sent manna to feed His folk and then, at Sinai, He first introduces the notion of national sanctity around food: eat, be satisfied, say a blessing.

> *An industrious kosher chicken farmer was always experimenting with breeding to perfect his product, especially trying to satisfy his family who were very fond of the leg portion — but there were never enough legs at dinner for everyone.*
>
> *Then one day he comes running into the living room, "I did it! I finally did it! I bred a chicken that has six legs!"*
>
> *"Wow, dad, that's great," shout his excited kids, "tell us, how does it taste?"*
>
> *"Don't know," he replies glumly, "I can't catch the son of a gun!"*

Death as Part of Life

> A Levite priest informs three Jews that they have a terminal disease and only four weeks left to live, and then asks how they intend to prepare themselves for their inevitable end.
>
> "I'm going to go out," cries the first Jew, "and teach Torah to the masses."
>
> "I'm going to dedicate all of my remaining time," sobs the next Jew, "to serving God, my family, and my fellow Jews."
>
> "I'm gonna go right over to my mother-in-law's house!" says the third Jew.
>
> "Why?" they all ask.
>
> "Because, at least it'll be the longest four weeks of my life!"

Jackie Mason, that great Jewish humorist, traces the Jewish fixation with health and sickness to this parsha, *Tazria,* and its frequent companion *Metzora*; a double portion and an unusually lengthy text, unique in all of Leviticus, that can be subtitled, How-To-Deal-With-Mysterious-Disease.

This parsha is confronting a natural human fear: the dreaded risk of a contamination from various infections spreading person-to-person, house-to-house.

The Hebrew term, *tzara'as,* comes from the Aramaic *segiruta* ("isolation"), and is a collective term for eruptive skin diseases (akin to eczema, vitiligo, psoriasis) that manifest themselves physically on skin, clothing, and even in walls. Tzara'as is also a source of *tumoh,* a "spiritual defilement" that requires certain purification procedures (*tahara*), such as seven days of isolation, an "exile" of the ritually impure (*tamei*) intended not to protect public health, but to prevent the spread of *ritual* contamination.

> *"The priest sent me to find you," a messenger tells Hershy one day, "He's examined your disease and has good news and bad news."*
> *"What's the good news?" asks a stunned Hershel.*
> *"You have twenty-four hours to live."*
> *"Oh no!…but if that's the good news, what's the bad news?"*
> *"I've been trying to reach you since yesterday!"*

The parsha begins with the laws of purification for the Jewess (*yoledes*) who, by giving birth brings children ("a heritage from the Lord") into the world, and the distinct mitzva of ritual circumcision (*bris miloh*) as the *sine qua non* of Jewish covenantal identity.

The question is obvious: Why is the woman who has given birth ritually impure? Why the need for an offering? After all, if procreation is the very first of all commandments, isn't a mother fulfilling a God-given purpose?

Don Isaac Abravanel, the Torah statesman of Spanish Jewry, claims that her offering is not sin-related but one of thanksgiving (for herself and child) for surviving the pain and danger of childbirth; an echo of the Midrash's Rabbi Abba bar Kahana, "The embryo dwells in its mother's womb and the Holy One, blessed be He, watches over it that it does not fall and die. Does this not warrant praise?"

When does life begin? For a boy, *Jewish* life begins "on the eighth day," a time frame that matches what was needed for creation itself, including at least one Shabbos. Yet the mother's ritual impurity is 14 days for a daughter (vs. 7 for a boy), leading some commentators to suggest that it takes longer to recover from the birth of a girl (a position not yet medically proven). Samson Raphael Hirsch sees it in terms of a "female covenant," where the second seven days takes the place of a boy's bris miloh.

After delineating five kinds of "impurity" (lumped together by Halacha as *tumos hayotzos migufo*), the parsha then reminds the folk, priests and Prophets what they must do in order to become a "priestly nation (*mamleches kohanim*)."

The priest? He is to act as a combined ritual diagnostician, quarantine officer and residential "pest" controller. The Prophet? His duty is to be a spiritual medic: "Follow his prescription!" advises the Haftarah, referring to Elisha's medical counsel.

> A man phones a mental hospital and asks the receptionist if there is anybody in room number 27. She goes and checks, and tells him, "No, Sir, the room is empty."
> "Great! That means I must have really escaped."

Medicine's modern-day concept of isolation wards derives from this parsha, "He [the leper] shall dwell alone: outside the camp shall his habitation be." However, Jewish mystics were quick to point out that the Torah's idea of *isolation* was not restricted to physical disorders. There are times, says Sinai, to be alone ("A person who does not have an hour to him or herself every day," goes the Chassidic adage, "is not a person.")

And so Avraham isolated himself from his idolatrous environment; Moshe isolated himself on Mt. Sinai; Bilam isolated himself (*vayelech shefi*, "he went to be alone") to help him make decisions; and Elijah isolated himself from Ahab in a wilderness where there was only *kol demamah dakkah*, "the sound of infinitesimal silence."

> For their annual holidays Morrie and Estie decide to get away from it all, but end up totally lost on a safari, isolated in the dark jungles of Africa.
> "Don't worry," Morrie soothes his terrified wife, "We have nothing to worry about. I didn't pay our pledge ▶

> *to the Yeshiva this year."*
> *"So?" she wails in fear.*
> *"They'll find us!!"*

This parsha teaches that in order for spiritual leaders to achieve real community influence they could not restrict themselves to the *beis sefer*, a "House of the Book" (for beginners), the *beis talmud*, "House of Learning" (for older children), or the *beis midrash* (for advanced students), a term derived from the verb *darasa* or *darash*, "to study," or "to seek" (in Arabic, *madraseh* also denotes a Muslim religious seminar; and *Taliban* comes from *talaba*, "to seek."). Today it is known simply as *the yeshiva*, literally, "a sitting" (in later years, the *beis midrash* also referred to a "House of Gathering," a *shul*, where *seforim* were available).

The root of *tumoh* (spiritual impurity) is *amour propre*, conceit, a negative character trait that separates one from God: "He and I," says God of the haughty, "cannot exist in the same place!"

Pride? "The root of all evil," cautions Hayyim Vital, a 16th century kabbalist from the Galilee. Arrogance? The "equivalent to all the other sins," notes the Palestinian Sage Rab. "If ever man becomes proud," warns the Targum Onkelos, an authoritative Aramaic translation on the Torah, "Let him remember that a mosquito preceded him in the order of Creation!"

Our Jewish mystics pick up this theme by equating the numerical value (65) of the Hebrew word for "I" (*ani*) with the Hebrew word *tumoh*; a gematria that credits self-arrogance as the root cause of *bitul*, the spiritual defilement and nullification of belief in God.

When the priest takes the obligatory "string of scarlet and hyssop" to purify a leper's affliction, our rabbis connect disease to pride, in that both the hyssop (a lowly plant) and the scarlet thread are both symbols of humbleness, lowliness, subjugation of egoism.

> *The Freedbergs, touring from the States, go to an Israel Philharmonic concert in the Tel Aviv Mann Auditorium and are impressed by its unique, stunning architecture.*
>
> *"Tell me," Mr. Freedberg asks his guide, "is this auditorium named after Thomas Mann, the world-famous author?"*
>
> *"No, it's named for Fredrick Mann from Philadelphia."*
>
> *"Really? I've never heard of him. He must be very modest. What did he write?"*
>
> *"A check."*

The Torah's elaborate procedural system is both compassionate and aggressive; the former because the Torah makes it a communal, and not an individual, health problem. Why? Because "*all* Israel is responsible one for the other."

The problem of *tzara'as* or a lesion is approached in a highly combative manner: if the disease has infected the entire house, the remedy is total evacuation and complete demolition, stone-by-stone, and a total rebuild.

What if the afflicted refuse to leave?

The 12th century Rambam, author of the magnum opus *Mishneh Torah*, gives a famous answer: it is the innate personality of every Jewish soul to do the right thing. And if not? Jewish law steps in with a controversial concept known as *kofin oso ad sheyomar rotzeh ani*, an approved coercion that compels abeyance via "force" (lashes, prison, etc.)

> *At the yeshiva's annual picnic, the rebbe, although convinced his students would do the right thing, nevertheless writes a sign above a tray of apples saying, "Take only one apple. Remember: God is watching."*
>
> *He returns a few hours later to discover another* ▶

sign over a large basket of chocolate cookies, saying, "Take all the cookies you want. Remember: God is watching the apples."

In a play on words, *metzora* is seen by Reish Lakish as an abbreviation (*notarikon*) of *motzi ra,* "one who brings forth evil," reinforcing an ancient Jewish tradition that makes its first appearance in the Tannaitic Midrash, when a kohen admonishes a Jew, "My son, plagues come only as a result of slander."

Rabbi Shimon ben Elazar traces the linkage back even further to the early Prophets, when "leprosy clung to Gehazi (Elisha's servant) after he spoke "slanderously of his master." Such punishment-affliction was considered *negah*, of being struck with such Divine displeasure that brings, in the immortal words of Shakespeare's Romeo and Juliet, "A plague o' both your houses!"

Yisroel Meir Kagan (*Chofetz Chaim*), the early 20th century saintly scholar, elaborated on this theme: that Heaven is aroused by the injurious presence of "evil speech" (*loshon horoh*), defined as gossip and slander, lies and defamation.

Proverbs labeled the Jew who spoke slander "a fool," deserving, according to Mar Ukba, 3rd century sage, to "be stoned!"

Israel Salanter Lipkin, master Lithuanian mussar moralist, asked his followers to discipline themselves by avoiding slander "at least one hour a day;" the Talmud's Raba ben Joseph traced Isaiah's demise and martyrdom to his loose lips (calling his folk, "people of unclean lips"); while the ultimate sin of Moshe was his calling his people "rebels."

The Torah's most famous victim? Miriam the prophetess who publicly chastises her brother Moshe over his relationship with his "dark-skinned" Midianite-Kushite wife Zipporah.

God sternly rebukes the siblings for displaying prejudice and

Miriam is quickly "stricken with leprosy, white as snow."

Our sages thus defined *loshon horoh* as a spiritually infectious and contagious disease, identical to the spilling of blood ("Life and death are in the power of the tongue!"), an epidemic akin to a plague that, if not contained, could destroy an entire community.

> *"Hey Yankel, did ya hear about Mandelbaum and Rosenstein..."*
>
> *"No, no, no," Yankel interrupts his friend, "You're always gossiping! Give it a rest will ya! Why do you always have to talk about other yidden! Look, if you feel the need, just change the names to another ethnic group for once!"*
>
> *"Oh, okay. That makes sense. Well, Hashimoto and Suzuki were talking one day at their nephew's bar mitzvah..."*

This parsha on health frowns on carelessness with ones safety, and focuses on such medical issues as euthanasia ("assisted suicide") and the sanctity of life, its preservation both a religious and moral duty, greater even, declares the 4th century sage Eleazar ben Azariah, than the keeping of the holy Shabbos ("Regulations concerning danger to life are more stringent than ritual prohibitions!")

Since the body is "on loan" from God, our sages saw mankind not as owners but as custodians, and declared that the Torah prohibition of assault and battery (*havala*) applies to oneself as well as to others. This is why such activities as drug taking infringe on the basic Halachic directive, to "diligently guard ones life."

Judaism not only opposes anything which would injure, mar or mutilate the human body, as an affront to human dignity by compromising the integrity of God's property, it also extends this belief to after death by opposing routine and indiscriminate autopsies.

The Torah's directive of *v'nishmartem me'od l'nafshoseichem*, prohibits self-mutation, in contrast to the Chinese who bind the feet of infants, ancient Greeks who bound female breasts for shrinkage (known as *atresia*), African tribes who extend the neck with graded rings, and other cultures who used body mutilation (nose and genital piercing) to "improve" their beauty.

Why then is ear piercing, a mark of servitude in Biblical times and a common practice today amongst Orthodox Jewish women, permitted? Perhaps it is because it is not permanent.

The rabbis of the Talmud went a step further: "Too much sitting," they concluded, "aggravates hemorrhoids; too much standing injures the heart; too much walking hurts the eyes." The conclusion? "Divide your time between the three!"

> *After graduating medical school Rabinowitch and Greenblatt decide to open an office in a heavily Jewish neighborhood, and proudly put up a sign that says, "Dr. Rabinowitch and Dr. Greenblatt, Psychiatry and Proctology."*
>
> *The local rabbinate is not too happy, so the two doctors change it to, "Hysteria and Posteriors."*
>
> *This didn't go across well either, so they try, "Schizoids and Hemorrhoids," then "Catatonics and High Colonics." All are rejected, until finally they settle on, "Dr. Smith and Dr. Jones, Odds and Ends."*

ACHAREI MOS/KEDOSHIM
Hermits and Holiness

> *"Shmuly, what's happened to your car?" asks Sylvia who sees it all smashed and covered with leaves, grass, branches, dirt, and blood.*
>
> *"Oh, I ran into a lawyer."*
>
> *"Well that explains the blood...but what about the leaves, grass, branches, dirt?"*
>
> *"Oh that, well, I had to chase him all the way through the park."*

There are two reasons why Torah portions are joined together: either to fit the weekly schedules into the annual cycle, or because their subject matters are complimentary.

At first glance the themes of this week's double portion, a merger of *Acharei Mos* with *Kedoshim*, seem out of sync; the former opening with the Torah's fullest description of Yom Kippur; the latter, despite a hallowed title of "holiness," concerns itself with such unholy business crimes as theft and cheating.

"To be a successful businessman you need extraordinary talents," notes Israel Salanter, mussar master, "and if you have such talents, why waste them on business?" Nachman of Kasovier, 18th century rabbi from Galicia, writing in his *Toldos Yaakov Yosef*, adds, "Some people think of business when they are at the synagogue. Is it too much to ask them to think of God when they are at business?"

The connection between holiness and commerce is obvious: a desire to infuse meaning into the mundane — and to level the business playing field with honest, fair play.

> *"You know Boris," the art gallery owner tells one of his exhibiting artists who is in hospital, "one guy came by the showroom yesterday and showed a lot of interest in your paintings."*
> *"Really? What did he want to know?"*
> *"Well, he asked me if your work would appreciate in value after you die."*
> *"What did you tell him?"*
> *"I said, 'yes, of course it would,' so he immediately bought all your paintings."*
> *"Wow! That's great news. Who was he?"*
> *"Your doctor."*

Jews are encouraged, immediately after the annual passing of the holiest day of the year, to continue that day's sanctity and spirituality into every aspect of living, in order to transform life itself into an extraordinary purposeful experience.

That is why a section of this parsha is read on Yom Kippur, a warning (that commences, "I am the Lord your God…") not to follow the immoral codes of certain ancient nations.

Which nations is God referring to?

According to Yehudah Hanasi, they existed during the period of Ezra; men who, according to the last of the Hebrew prophets (Malachi), "acted treacherously" against their wives (which is why Ezra felt the need to re-establish the integrity of Jewish marriage).

> *A Brooklyn rabbi and an Irish priest get into a car accident after the priest, speeding, suddenly smashes into the back of the rabbi's car. Standing in front of an Irish judge a few weeks later, the court turns to the priest, "Tell me Father, how fast was the rabbi backing up when he hit you?"*
> *As he nears the end of his criminal trial, Sammy suddenly stands up and declares to the court, "Your Honor,* ▶

I would like to change my plea from 'innocent' to 'guilty.'"

"Sit down!" the angry judge shouts, "If you're guilty, why didn't you say so in the first place and save this court a lot of time and inconvenience?"

"Well, your Honor, when the trial started I thought I was innocent, but that was before I heard all the evidence against me."

Rabbi Hiyya compared and then crowned this double parsha, with its detailed rules for interpersonal human behavior, as being equal to the Ten Commandments, in that from them "the essential laws of Torah can be derived" (*rov gufei Torah teluim bo*).

Our sages call the first command of *Kedoshim*, "You shall be holy for I your God am holy," an eternal decree (*lechukas olam*), the *mysterium tremendum* calling card of a folk chosen to aspire to the loftiest of lofty goals, *imatatio dei*, the imitation of God (*ki kadosh Ani Hashem Eelokeichem*.)

The question is obvious: how does one become holy?

The little Hebrew word *ki* is key; it can be read either as a suggestion that Jewish holiness depends on God's holiness; or in reverse, as an "if-then" structure, wherein the Jews "shall be holy, if/when I your God am holy."

This intimately staples God's holiness directly to the Jews' state of sanctity; a sacred symbiosis in reverse (i.e.: God is holy only when Jews are holy).

The clue to holiness can be narrowed down to two words, *vehalachta bidrachav*, "You shall walk in His ways;" in other words, via earthly emulation of God's traits — if God is merciful, patient, respectful and kind, the Jew must be merciful, patient, respectful and kind.

It is in this parsha that we discover the most famous of all ethical mitzvot, surely one of the Torah's most quoted passage, *V'ahavta l're'acha kamocho*, "Love your neighbor as yourself," a five-word directive embraced by Rabbi Akiva, the 2nd century Talmudic giant, who crowns it the "fundamental principle of the Torah (*zeh klal gadol batorah*)."

At first glance, this Golden Jewish Rule sounds selfish; "as yourself" seems egotistical.

"It represents a sort of equation," writes Rabbi Apple. "Love of neighbor equals love of self. Love of self equals love of neighbor. I have a duty to love others; I have a duty to love myself. If I only love others without loving myself, I have become too small. But if I only love myself without loving others I have become too big."

The danger is this, as articulated by Chassidus, which uses the same words in *l'cha pesel* (from, "Do not make for yourself a graven image") and *p'sol l'cha* (from, "Hew for yourself two tablets of stone") to conclude that if the Jew puts *l'cha* (himself) first, on a pedestal, it approaches idolatry (an I-doll!).

The Ramban, noting the concern, points out that the text does not say *v'ahavta et re'acha*, but *l're'acha* — not *et* which implies that I and my neighbor are on a par but "I" — which denotes "for" (i.e.: my duty is not necessarily to love my neighbor as myself but to love "for" him that which I love for myself; in pragmatic terms, as I wish to be done to me, so must I do to others).

The poet W. H. Auden, aware of the problems posed by this mitzva, was cynical, "You shall love your crooked neighbor/With your crooked heart."

The author of the *Or Hachayyim Hakodosh* is more mystical: he emphasizes the term "*kamocho*" to suggest that, because each is made in the Divine image, only by loving another (neighbor) does one become complete (and vice versa: one's identity is defective and diminished in the absence of such attitude).

But what exactly does Akiva's so-called 'Golden Rule' mean?

Hillel's answer was in reverse: "What is hateful to you, do *not* do to your fellow."

The Ramban, a 13th century Spanish commentator, explains the Torah's wish: to reinforce, once again, that an assault on a fellow Man, created in God's image (*demus deyukano*) is an assault on God, a mutilation of the Divine image; therefore the Torah is "concerned with love in its qualitative and not quantitative sense" (i.e.: no one expects the same intensity of love to be extended to ones animal or possessions as to ones wife, child, or parent).

Linguists point out that the Hebrew verb for love (*ahav*) does not only describe an emotion but an action since it requires the preposition *le*, which means "to," or "for." What then does *kamocho*, "as yourself," really mean?

This term is not used adverbially but adjectivally; in that it means love your neighbor "similar to you" [i.e.: as yourself] since all are created in the image of God (*b'tzelem Elokim*), as summarized by the Midrashic Sifrei, "In your love for your neighbor you shall find God."

Some take this parsha as permission to be God's policemen: one may "rebuke your fellow" — but only if there is "no hate in your heart;" a standard which led Rabbi Elazar ben Ezariah to note that, "there are none in this generation who know how to reprove." Many Chassidic masters opposed all hellfire-and-brimstone sermons (noting that the *Tochecha* curses are only read twice a year), on the theory that rabbis should teach, not admonish (the better the teacher, the less need to rebuke!)

To love another was to literally love Torah, a conclusion reached from the daily *u'va l'tzion* prayer that equates the 248 *mitzvos asei* (positive commandments) to the 248 limbs of the human body.

> *When Sarah finds out her gentile neighbor is not feeling well, she immediately rises to perform the mitzva of* bikkur cholim, *picks up the phone, dials her neighbor's* ▸

> *house, and asks her how she feels.*
>
> *"Not so good," comes the reply, "I have a terrible head-ache, I'm nauseous, every bone in my body hurts, I must be coming down with the flu."*
>
> *"Listen, I'll come right over. I can clean up a bit, make you a nice hot bath, cook dinner and help out with the kids."*
>
> *"Oh, that's so sweet of you."*
>
> *"I'll stop off at the market first. Tell me, what does Rick like to eat?"*
>
> *"Rick?"*
>
> *"Rick, your husband?"*
>
> *"Oh, my husband's name is Carl."*
>
> *"Carl? Oh no, I must have the wrong number."*
>
> *"Does that mean you're not coming over?"*

Before it focuses on the nature of holiness, this parsha defines its own audience, speaking not to "the Children of Israel" but to "*all* the congregation [*b'hakhel*] of the Children of Israel." Is there a difference? Absolutely: one cannot become holy in a vacuum.

The great Rav Yehezkel Abramsky attributed the word "all" to mean a triple-holiness of nation, religion and community. Perhaps that is why the land of Israel (*Eretz Yisroel*) makes a prominent appearance in this double parsha; a land unique with such inherent holiness that it itself rejects (*taki*) the Jew who defiles it by indulging in the "abominations" (idolatry and incest) of previous nations. The Hebrew verb *taki* literally means "to regurgitate," a vomiting up of any immoral inhabitants in order to maintain its purity.

Rabbi Yehudah Leib Alter of Ger (the *Sfas Emes*), emphasizes that no one Jew can attain holiness without merging and identifying publicly with "*all* of them [the whole of Israel]."

To be a Jew at home and not outside, in "full assembly," in society, was not sanctity but chagrin.

To Rabbi Moshe Schreiber (*Chasam Sofer*) the message is clear:

hermits and holiness do not mix. To withdraw from society, and become cocooned in ones own solitude, makes it impossible to perform interactive mitzvos that require honesty, morality, charity, reverence, and consideration for others, in the category of *dinim sh'bein odom l'-chaveiro...*

This is why the Hebrew root for *kadosh* is a derivative of "to separate," a reminder that, when mingling within a community, one should try to distance oneself (*perushim*) from self-indulgence, evil influences and immoral failings; in other words, *kadesh atzm'cha b'muttar lach*, "sanctify yourself [only with people and ideas] that are permitted to you."

The concluding verse, "I am the Lord Your God" (or its abbreviated "I am the Lord"), appears 14 times; a multiple reminder that the basis for an orderly society is not defined by human ethics but from a religious code (*mitzvos*).

That is why the words "who brought you out of Egypt" is tacked on to the very last mitzva, the one on "fair weights and measures in commerce," in order to emphasize that one of the conditions of freedom and liberty is to always behave honestly.

> *One morning Beryl prays to the Heavens, "Dear God, so far today I've done all right. I haven't gossiped and I haven't lost my temper. I haven't stolen anything or cheated anybody. I haven't been grumpy, nasty or selfish, but Dear God, in a few minutes I'm going to be getting out of bed and from then on, I'm probably going to need a lot of help. Amen."*

Being Holy or Looking Holy?

> Ol' Mr. Cohen arrives at Ellis Island from Poland and has to pass an English test to get his citizenship papers.
>
> "Please use the word 'cultivate' in a sentence," the examiner asks.
>
> "Dat's easy," says Cohen, "Last vinter on a very cold day, I vas vaiting for de bus, but it vas too cultivate, so I took the subvay home."

The title to this week's parsha, *Emor*, means "speak," as in, "God said [*emor*] to Moshe, speak to the sons of Aaron."

A unique syntax occurs in the opening verse with a double command: "And say [*ve'amarta*] to them," implying not an imperial relationship between a ruler and his elite priesthood, the *noblesse oblige* of the Jews, but a feeling of closeness.

This order, to guard their sanctity in the context of defilement from the dead, is couched in a softer, gentler and less demanding style than in the more imperative, emphatic form of *daber* ("to speak").

> "Hey," Sammy the defendant whispers to his lawyer in court, "would it help if I send the judge a box of cigars?"
>
> "What! Are you crazy! This judge is a stickler on ethics. We have to approach him gently, respectfully, a stunt like that would seriously prejudice him against you!"
>
> A few days later Sammy is acquitted, and turns to his attorney, "Thanks for the tip about the cigars, it worked!"
>
> "Don't mention it. I'm positive we would have lost the case if you'd sent them."
>
> "But I did send them." ◗

> "What?"
> "Yep, and good thing I remembered to enclose the plaintiff's business card."

This parsha continues the theme of Leviticus, an attempt to define the boundaries of holiness, delving into the difference between appearance and reality, and laying down the dictum: clothes don't always make the man — or in popular slang, you can't judge a book by its cover; nor, in the cynical wit of the Yiddishists, a holy man by the length of his beard.

Only the holy may use holy things, the Zohar concluded. Attitude and intention are paramount, says Rashi, as evidenced by Moshe's choice of words to Aaron that the sacrifices must be "acceptable for you" (*lirtzonchem*) instead of "acceptable for God."

This required an obligation by Jewish leaders (in this case, the priest) to spurn vain offerings in order to accrue goodwill and promote righteous conduct.

Commenting on the parsha's opening words ("They shall be holy to their God"), Naftali Zvi Yehuda Berlin (*Netziv*), the great 19th century Lithuanian commentator, pondered whether the holiness of a priest was conditional or non-conditional. His conclusion? A kohen was not automatically holy, but was obligated to attain holiness via conduct — and clothing.

Ezekiel then clarifies this in this week's Haftarah: after "the priests return from the sacrificial service, they must take off the clothes they wear and put on other [everyday] clothes." Why? In order that "they not imply holiness by their clothes."

> Mollie Spiegel, an elderly Jewish lady, is always being invited by her neighbor Maria Hernandez to her Sunday Mass. Not wanting to upset her neighbor she finally ▶

agrees and, one fine Sunday morning, the two women, dressed in their finest, go to Church.

Mollie watches as the Bishop, vested in a very ornate suplice and cassock, walks down the aisle swinging an incense pot with smoke rising from it. As he passes her, Mollie gently leans over, tugs at his coat, and whispers, "Pssst, I love your outfit, but your purse is on fire!"

This parsha is labeled by our sages as *Seder Mo'adim*, the sequence of holidays (including Shabbos), because it opens with the "festivals of God [*mikro'ei kodesh*]" which are to be "celebrated each at its appointed time."

In contrast to the other two parshas (*Shmos, Pinchos*) which only list the three pilgrimage festivals (Pesach, Shavuos, Sukkos), this Torah portion produces a much more comprehensive list, enumerating and describing the nature of *all* the Jewish festivals sequentially, even Chanukka.

How is that possible? Isn't Chanukka a *post*-Torah Yom Tov?

Yes, but our Jewish mystics find it in the immediate contiguous order that the Jew maintain an "eternal light" in the Sanctuary; a proximity that is not "coincidental" but anticipative of an annual kindling day in the future (i.e.: Chanukka).

The Ramban, a leading Torah scholar of the Middle Ages, translates the term *mikro'ei kodesh* as a "sacred gathering," but Rashi, the grand educator, and his Tosefos grandson, Shemuel ben Meir (*Rashbam*), disagree on the syntax and insist on the plain sense (*peshat*). They interpret *mikra kodesh* as an "announcement," or "proclamation," in that each of these set, sacred times of God must be "called" (*tikra'u osom*) at its appropriate time.

The arrival of a Yom Tov was considered a public notice of the imminence of holiness, a warning to the Jews to cease and desist in certain "forbidden" activities (*melacha*).

When the parsha writes, "You must declare them [the set times as sacred holidays]," it uses the redundant word *otam* for "them," a word that is normally written with a *vav*, but not here, which makes it read as *atem* ["you"]. This order, in contrast to the rest of Leviticus which is addressed to the priests, is directed to the Sanhedrin sages who are now given permission to declare the timing of God's Calendar *vis a vis* the Jewish festivals.

The Hebrew word for festival (*chag*) has the same root as *chug*, "a circle," perhaps a reminder that no matter how the wheel of life turns, from joy to sorry, from tragedy to triumph, it is business as usual for the circle and cycle of the Jewish calendar.

"Time, like a scale, raises the light and lowers the heavy," was a favorite saying of the Vilna Gaon who, like many other Torah scholars, saw life-and-death in circular terms. "The world is like a fountain-wheel," mused the Midrash, "the buckets ascend full and descend empty, [in other words], who's rich today may not be so tomorrow."

> When the cheder teacher asks little Miri to summarize Jewish holidays, she replies, "They tried to kill us, we won, let's eat."

The festivals are a roller coaster of feasting and fasting, which, in the end, balances itself out.

Consider: Rosh Hashanah (feast), Tzom Gedalia (fast), Yom Kippur (more fasting); Sukkot (feast); Hoshana Rabbah (more feasting); Simchas Torah (keep feasting); Month of Heshvan (no feasts or fasts for a whole month, get a grip on yourself!); Chanukka (eat potato pancakes); Tenth of Tevet (do not eat potato pancakes); Tu B'Shevat (feast); Taanis Esther (fast); Purim (eat and drink); Passover (eat and drink, but carefully); Shavuot (dairy feast, cheesecake, blintzes, etc); 17th of Tammuz (fast); Tisha B'av (very strict fast, don't even think about cheesecake or blintzes); month of Elul (end of feast-fast cycle, enroll in Center for Eating Disorders before High Holidays arrive again).

No wonder food and festivals seem synonymous with the need to diet...

In order to meet the Divine challenge to invest the world with various manifestations of holiness, this parsha adds time, as expressed by Jewish festivals (*hamo'ados*), as a motif of sanctity (*kedushas hazman*).

> *"Say son," asks Itzie's father, visiting his yeshiva dorm room for the first time, "What's the big brass gong and hammer for?"*
> *"Oh that? It's my talking clock."*
> *"A talking clock? How's it work?"*
> *"Watch this," says Itzie, who takes out a hammer and gives the gong an ear shattering sound. Suddenly there's a scream from the other side of the wall, "Hey! Knock it off, will ya! It's ten o'clock at night!!"*

Judaism is a religion of time, and scorns not only the scientific notion that the arrow of time is homogeneous, but rails against the "Two-Times-a-Year-Judaism" (those who attend shul only on Rosh Hashanah and Yom Kippur), the "Cardiac Judaism" (in my heart I'm a Jew), "Gastronomic Judaism" (eating Jewish foods), "Pocketbook Judaism" (giving charity only), and "Drop-off Judaism" (dropping the kids off at Sunday school).

God's time begins with the end in mind; a cosmic master arrow that hurtles through the generations towards a utopian climax (Messiah), defined as *the* harmonious integration of all, when "the wolf will lie with the sheep, the lion will eat straw with the cattle, and the suckling will frolic on the viper's hole." The steering wheel of this spiritual time machine is in the hands of mankind, charged with transporting itself from the past, where it was once "placed" in a Garden of Eden, to a future "planting" on "God's mount."

This Judaic belief, less concerned with yesterday's takeoff than with tomorrow's landing, stands in conflict with general philosophy wherein the past is real in a way the future is not.

That is why the concept of now (i.e.; "the present") simply does not exist in a classical Hebrew where *zman*, the word for time, is related to *hazmonoh*, which means "preparation." In other words, the value of counting months lies in the time used in preparation of reaching an identifiable end, a Godly destination called *mokom* in Hebrew, which, coincidentally, is God's Name for Space.

This suggests that between past and future is nothing, time having no reality of its own, like the circus, always packing up and moving away from us. The Jews were expected to be *lema'alah min hazman*, a folk uniquely transcending its shackles, secure in the knowledge that God had tithed time into holy segments; a belief that inspired Rabbi Joseph B. Soloveitchik to declare that absolutely nothing in life is sacred unless, and until, man made it so.

"Time by itself is nil," mused the 19th century Rabbi Meir Leibush ben Yechiel Michal (*Malbim*), dispelling any notion that the Heavens' concept of "time" matches that of man's since one "yesterday" in our terminology equaled a "thousand years" of God's time.

The first spoken words of God to man are, "Where are you?" — an attempt to focus Adam not to his physical state, but to his spiritual one.

> *A hiker, lost and confused, goes over to a little ol' Jewish man sitting beside a barn milking a cow. "Excuse me, could you tell me the time?"*
>
> *"Sure," replies the little ol' Jewish man as he raises the cows udder, "It's 3:45."* ▶

> *"Are you sure?"*
> *The little ol' Jewish man again raises the cows udder and says, "Yep, it's 3:45."*
> *"How in the world can you tell the time by raising a cow's udder?"*
> *"Well, when I raise her udder I can see the town hall clock over there across the way."*

The popular saying, "There is a time and a place for everything" is derived from *Kohelet*: "There is not a man but has his hour; not a thing without his place."

Since man travels *odom nosai'ah b'soch hazman* "through the highways of time," the Lubavitcher Rebbe (Menachem Mendel Schneersohn) would often emphasize the import of living "with the times," meaning one could extrapolate the lessons of life for tomorrow only by being in sync with the clues found in that week's Torah reading. The Rebbe believed that man acted as a hinge in history, allowing the pages of time to be turned over in accordance with God's wishes. This dependency has always been an integral part of Judaism; the notion that we don't merely fill our days and nights, months and years – but that we fill them with substance.

In other words: if you rest, you rust, to which our Yiddishists add, "Before you decide about your aim in life, check your ammunition. A Jew's cartridges are the *taryag mitzvos*, "taryag" being the vocalization of *taf-resh-yod-gimel* which adds up, and denotes, the 613 commandments.

This helps explain God's first instruction to the worlds first Jew: the instant Avraham shakes free of his idolatrous chains, he is ordered to "Go!" (*lech*), to get moving, hurry up, go show the world the beauties of monotheism, and encourage them to hop onboard.

The lesson is clear.

Time stands still for no one; or in the no-nonsense language of Sholom Jacob (*Mendele*) Abramowitz, the popular 19th century Russian-Hebrew-Yiddishist, "A Jew never has time; he is always on the run."

> *Shlomo is lying on his hammock peacefully, pondering life, gazing in awe at the sky, and feeling so close to God that he whispers, "God, are you listening?"*
>
> *"Yes," God replies.*
>
> *Shlomo sits up, and sees an opening, "God, what is a million years to you?"*
>
> *"My dear Shlomo. A second to me is like a million years to you."*
>
> *"God, what's a million dollars to you?"*
>
> *"My dear Shlomo. A penny to me is like a million dollars to you. It means almost nothing to me."*
>
> *Shlomo suddenly goes into deep thought, and asks, "God, can I have a million dollars?"*
>
> *"Sure," God replies, "In a second!"*

B'HAR/B'CHUKOSAI
Love at First Fright

> When a water pipe bursts in a lawyer's house, he calls a plumber who runs right over, fixes it in a few minutes and hands the customer a bill for $600.
> "What, $600!?" he screams in shock, "That's ridiculous! I don't even make that much as an attorney!"
> "Neither did I," the plumber replies, "when I was a lawyer."

The first part of this week's double portion, *B'har-B'chukosai*, means "on the mountain," a reference to Sinai; and contains, twice, the order "not to wrong one another," either in the context of business-monetary matters, or via speech.

Our sages agree that the latter, slander (since character restoration is near impossible) is much more "hurtful" than the former (which only affects money).

The order, "do not defraud," is immediately followed by the counsel to "fear God" (described by Moshe Ibn Ezra, 11th century Spanish poet and philosopher, in his *Shiras Yisrael*, as "the noblest quality;" one which Proverbs describes as "the beginning of wisdom."

This parsha also sets forth important laws related to the ownership of real estate in *Eretz Yisrael*; in that God owns the land and that the Jews are, at best, simply tenants ("Mine is the land; for you are merely residents with Me"); the validity of the lease being contingent upon the morality of the Jews' behavior — or as Frank Lloyd Wright put it: "A lot of homes have been spoiled by inferior desecrators."

The fixation on land finds its way into the Haftarah, where Jeremiah, a lonely and sad prophet who lived during the great crises of Babylonian destruction, pays his cousin, despite sitting in a prison in a city under siege, 17 shekels of silver for property "in the territory of Benjamin." Jeremiah acts in accordance with the Torah's "duty of property redemption," a first right-of-refusal that obligates relatives to retain ancestral holdings within the family or tribe.

This is why Naboth refuses to sell his inherited vineyard to King Ahab, even at a substantial profit; why Boaz exercises his right of redemption in the Book of Ruth; and why Jewish women who inherit family property in the absence of male heirs, marry men of their own tribe in order to keep the assets "in the family."

This parsha also reveals the principles of Torah time in the context of holy real estate: just as days were divided into weeks, Judaism divides the years as well.

If every seventh day was holy, so was every seventh year a year of special solemnity, known as *Sh'mitta*, the "Sabbatical year of rest," when the land lay fallow, untended, unexploited.

This "Sabbath to the Lord," a powerful reminder that He created this world ex nehillo (*yeish me'ayin*) in six days and rested on the seventh, was devoted to three rather difficult standards in a mixed agrarian/urban society: cessation of agriculture (when the land was to remain uncultivated and the soil "rested"); the reversion of land to its original owner (the assumption being that it was sold because of financial pressures); and the freeing or manumission of Jewish slaves and their children (whose status came about either through poverty or other acts).

Slaves were also "free" not to become free; but if they freely chose this direction they were expected to have their ears bored to show their voluntary consent to become, basically, slaves forever.

> *An enterprising convict spends several years digging his way out of prison. Finally, he emerges in the middle* ▶

> of a preschool yeshiva playground.
> "I'm free, I'm free!" he shouts, "Thank God, I'm free!"
> "Big deal," yawns little Surie standing nearby, "I'm four."

This Sabbatical year, based on the "land is the Lord's," was then extended to the 50th year (after 7-times-7 cycles), and called *Yovel* ("jubilee"), a practice that ceased sometime between the First and Second Temples.

The Hebrew root of *jubilee* is "to emit," or "to liberate" (in Latin *jubilo* means "to shout"), and is derived from a word (*jobel*) whose original etymological meaning was a "ram," a reference to the blowing of "a ram's horn" (*shofar*) that joyfully heralded in the start of the fiftieth year.

The Book of Jubilees (*ta lobelaia*) is an anonymous apocryphal Hebrew treatise penned during the rule of John Hyrcanus (135–105 BC) and before the destruction of the Jerusalem Temple. It contains a wealth of popular legends based on the number 'seven' in the context of time (i.e.: 7 days in a week; 4 x 7 days in a month; 52 x 7 days in a year, etc).

This *sh'mitta-yovel* ideology was a unique revolutionary social-economic contribution to mankind, described by Isaiah as *the* calendar symbol of messianism.

The canon that neither people nor land could be sold forever made it impossible for a select few to accumulate wealth (via large portions of land) to the detriment of the overall community (klal). And more: its multiple moral guidelines acted as an encouraging How-To-Guide for employer-employee relations, labor law, industrial disputes. The jubilee order to "proclaim freedom in the land" is directed not just to all its workers but "to *all* inhabitants," employees *and* employers.

> *"Hey boss," Sammy asks his supervisor, "Tomorrow we're doing some heavy house-cleaning for Pesach, and my wife wants me home to help her with cleanin', movin', haulin,' and other stuff."*
> *"Sorry Sam, I'm short-handed. I just can't give you the day off."*
> *"Thanks, boss," Sammy smiles, "I knew I could count on you!"*

Rav Avraham Pam, 20th century yeshiva dean of *Torah Va'daas*, noted that the only quality that differentiated a slave from a free human being was the ability to control one's free time. Italian Rabbi Ovadiah Sforno, a major commentator of the Middle Ages, went one step further: the significance of the "day," as a unit of *Jewish* time, was meaningless until after the Exodus. Why? Because a day meant nothing to a slave who was deprived of any power to shape it.

When Ludwig Boerne cried out, "Because I was born a slave, I love liberty more than you," he was confirming that only the liberated, emancipated from tyranny, could appreciate time as a precious gift; a Divine boon to be used wisely, judiciously, meaningfully.

The noble 18th century words on the Liberty Bell in Philadelphia, "Proclaim liberty in the land to all its inhabitants" (a universal theme expressed by the French national slogan, *liberty, equality, fraternity*), is first found in Leviticus…but found its way into speeches (Martin Luther King Jr. used the word "freedom" nineteen times in his "I Have a Dream" speech); rock songs (from Paul McCartney to the Grateful Dead to Bobby McGee's, "freedom's just another name for nothing left to lose"); and wars (US Presidents have fought for freedom and liberty, with Abraham Lincoln, in his Gettysburg address, addressing a new nation "conceived in liberty," considered by the Declaration of Independence as *the* defining fundamental value of democracy, an echo of John Locke's, "life, liberty, and the pursuit of happiness;" supported by Franklin Roosevelt's "Four Freedoms" — of speech, of religion, from want, and from fear. The P'nai Yehoshua saw the Torah's use of *yosh'veha* ("its inhabitants") instead of *avadeha* ("its servants") in the context that *everyone* — not only servants, need freedom. This is a startling concept, expanded upon by the rabbis of the Talmud who warned that, "He who acquires a servant acquires a master over himself." This is not meant cynically but as reality: that a good employer must be concerned not just with himself, but with workers' (and their) families' well-being.

> *The owner of a large manufacturing business walks through his factory, and greets one of his workers, "Hey you, how long ya been working here?"*
> *"Ever since I heard you coming down the stairs!"*

The second parsha, *B'chukosai*, means "My laws," and is known as the *Tochacha* ("warning," or "reproof") portion, because it is one of only two times in the Torah where this admonition is recited.

It is a reminder: the recognition that there are limits to human reason (i.e.: there is Reason, and Above Reason), as articulated by the psalm of David, "I do not exercise myself in things too great or things too wondrous for me."

It is not true, as the Yiddish phrase claims, that *m'tor nisht fregen*, "one mustn't ask;" one can, but not every answer will come easily or quickly — especially in the face of this parsha, a vivid Catalogue of Calamity that addresses issues of reward and punishment.

It begins on a high with 13 short blessings, then quickly plunges into a 28-verse litany of 30 *Sturm un Drang*-type curses, a scenario of worsening consequences that suggests a vengeful and punishing God. No wonder it is read with a sense of dread and shuddering: "I will decree upon you panic, disease, fever, making your eyes weaken and your souls suffer; you shall sow your seed in vain, for your enemies shall eat it; your strength shall be spent in vain, and I will punish you seven times for your sins."

In long and excoriating detail, God warns Israel that the consequence of non-compliance is a condition unworthy of *siyata d'shamaya* (Divine assistance), resulting in severe punishments and terrible calamities.

> *George, seeing that his rabbi is getting on in years, asks him if he can remove a curse that has plagued him for 50 years.*
>
> *"Maybe," replies the rabbi, "You must think hard, and tell me exactly, what were the last words you heard before this terrible curse fell upon you."*
>
> *"Oh, I remember the words exactly. They were, 'I now pronounce you man and wife.'"*

The question is this: if the troubles of Israel are neither random nor chaotic but escalate in direct proportion to her dereliction of the Laws of Moshe, which particular law is the parsha referring to? All 613 of them? Some of them?

Rav Yaakov Kamenetsky, the popular 20th century American rosh yeshiva, narrows it down to the sin (*aveira*) of *bittul Torah* ("neglecting to learn Torah"); Rashi, the fundamental Torah commentator, links it to the seven-year cycle laws of *sh'mitta*.

Rabbi Eleazer ben Simeon disagrees: the Torah is a "package deal," he declares, any part of which may not be transgressed.

But this is not Love at First Fright; for it ends with a blessing of consolation, "Yet, even then, I will not reject nor spurn them," and a sigh of collective relief that no matter how wayward the House of Israel strays, the promises in the covenant, invoked in this parsha no less than five times, will never be abrogated.

A reminder of God's forgiving and unconditionally loving side thus ends the Book of Leviticus, stapled to a cosmic disclosure that the Heavens continue to influence the health, tranquility, and livelihood of the people of Israel.

What is startling is that all the rewards in this parsha are materialistic, selfish, this-worldly ("I will grant rains in their season; you shall eat your fill of bread," etc). What happened to the spiritual dividends?

Ibn Ezra, a Jewish scholar of the 12th century, concluded from this that human nature is only motivated by physical wishes. Not so, argues the more optimistic 13th century Ramban, convinced that since it's obvious God grants spiritual favors, only material wants and needs are stated.

In a very visceral sort of way, many Torah students have been concerned and confused by the obvious sight of disparity: the wicked prospering, the righteous suffering; a blatant contradiction to the Psalmist's assertion, "I have been young and am now old, but I have never seen a righteous man abandoned."

Some claim that this parsha's cause and effect dogma applies not to the here-and-now but only to the hereafter; others suggest that these rewards and punishments refer not to individuals but to the Jewish nation as a whole.

> *On his annual holiday, Yankie returns home from College, and sits down with his parents, "Ma, I had the toughest time of my life. You wouldn't believe it, dad. First, I got angina pectoris and then arteriosclerosis. Just as I was recovering from these, I got tuberculosis, double pneumonia and phthisis. Then they gave me hypodermics. Appendicitis was followed by tonsillectomy. These gave way to aphasia and hypertrophic cirrhosis. I completely lost my memory for a while. I know I had diabetes and acute ingestion, besides gastritis, rheumatism, lumbago and neuritis. I don't know how I pulled through it.... It was the hardest spelling test I've ever had!"*

The final chapter of this week's parsha contains the Torah's most explicit method of how to properly assess a person's worth in money (shekolim); by recounting an oath, which Judaism takes very seriously, to donate the value of ones own life to the Temple.

But how is this "worth" determined? The parsha, way ahead of modern personal-injury claims, uses a formula that analyzes age, gender, and the capacity for future labor (i.e.: contribution to society).

> One day Bobby, who worked at the local Tel Aviv brewing company, lost his balance, fell and drowned in a vat of kosher wine. The Chevra Kadisha calls his wife and breaks the sad news to her.
> "Hopefully," the widow sighs, "his death was mercifully quick?"
> "We don't know," replies the undertaker, "but he did climb out twice to go to the bathroom."

This ends the Book of Leviticus, the third book of the Torah when everyone rises and says, Chazak, chazak v'nitchazek, "Be strong, be strong, and let us be strengthened!" — a roar of encouragement to continue on to Numbers, the next book of the Torah.

Why repeat the word chazak three times?

To symbolize the past, present, and future.

Bamidbar

(NUMBERS)

This fourth Book of the Torah consists of a geographic chronology of the adventures of the Jewish people that can be divided into three phases, each varying in content, style, duration. This travelogue with destiny begins in *midbar Sinai*, "the wilderness of Sinai," a term the Torah uses seven times. Why seven? Because this traditionally mystical number suggests "completeness."

The first occupies only about nineteen stagnant days, containing no "stories" *per se* as it deals with the structure and movement of the camps. The contrast in the next phase, in Kadesh-Barnea, is dramatic: the undated narrative pauses for the passing of the generation that left Egypt, symbolized by the tragic deaths of the leadership (Miriam, Aaron, Moshe). Finally, there is a confident regrouping on the plains of Moab, just prior to entering the western part of the land of Israel, where a vivid recount reaffirms that the legacy of Sinai now rests firmly in the hands of the younger generation.

There is nothing sinister in the fact that 38 years in the wilderness is unaccounted for: the Torah's purpose is very focused, concerning itself only with progressive milestones that are directly relevant to the realization of God's promises to the Patriarchs.

How One Counts Also Counts

> *How to count the working population of the USA:*
> We start with 237 million, out of which 104 million are retired. That leaves 133 million to do the work, but 85 million of these are school kids, which leaves 48 million, from which we deduct the 29 million federal government employees who don't work.
>
> Thus, we are left with 19 million, out of which 4 million serve in the Armed Forces, leaving us a working population of only 15 million.
>
> But wait!
>
> We must deduct the 14.8 million people who work for state and city governments, which leaves us with only 200,000 — minus the 188,000 sick in hospitals and the 11,998 felons in prisons, which leaves just two out of 237 million people to do all the work!
>
> That leaves ….. you and me: and you're just sitting there reading Torah jokes all day!

The title to this week's parsha, *Bamidbar,* is a generic expression describing the austere pallet of being "in the desert."

Isaiah, as usual, is more poetic: the desert is "the highway for God;" a remote place without landmarks, described by Arthur Koestler, Hungarian novelist, as the "waterless land and the arid past of the nation."

The Jews find themselves in a vast world of nature's uncertainty, where time has no rules and where the only consistency is the lack of trees and water, a fiery sun, and lots of sand, sand, and sand.

"I envy you your deserts," Ben Gurion once told the Jews of California, "not just because they are deserts, but because you can afford to keep them deserts!"

And yet, because this parsha is primarily involved in a numerical exercise it is not known by its desert character but as "Numbers," from the Latin *Numeri* and the Greek, *Arithmoi*.

God obviously wants the Jews counted, yet again (earlier counts occurred after the Golden Calf, and after the Tabernacle was dedicated), implying what all accountants know: counting is a progressive act that creates order and balance out of disarray, distraction, disorientation.

The parsha counting produces 603,550 males over the age of 20; in essence, a tally of military troops that shows the Jewish folk have remained a static population despite the passing of 40 years. Is this a surprise? No. Remember: the Heavens were explicit right from the start: "I have not chosen you because of your great numbers."

This is an ancillary lesson of Jewish history — that it does *not* take large numbers to achieve great spiritual influence.

The perfect example?

Avraham and Sarah, only *one* lonely couple, and yet they built a humanized world by sheer example and education, proof positive that civilizations can be preserved by the few and righteous.

Then why bother counting? Didn't God know how many Jews there were?

Yes, but He counted, says Rashi, the great medieval commentator, in appreciation, akin to the love and concern that motivates a shepherd to continuously count his precious flock.

> One day Rivke is walking past an insane asylum when she hears all the residents chanting, "Thirteen, thirteen, thirteen!"
> Curious, she finds a hole in the fence and looks in — only to be poked in the eye, and hear everyone start chanting, "Fourteen, fourteen, fourteen!"

Commenting on the "numbers game," Philologos, from the New York *Forward*, writes how in Naples of Italy, buyers of *lotteria* tickets still rely on Neapolitan *cabbala* (a left-over of 16th-century Italian kabbalism) to "reveal" the secrets of numerical values.

The same obsession with "numbers" is why the University of Wisconsin moved their foreign language department out of their 13th floor and replaced it with their Hebrew Studies department (assuming, that Jews are not superstitious over the number "13.")

From King David through to the return from Babylonian exile, the Jews repeatedly conducted a national "head-by-head" census, however the rabbis of the Talmud made their apprehension official: "Israel must not be counted, not even for religious purposes."

Why not?

The reasons range from the metaphysical (people are individuals, not numbers); the mystical (Moshe was not leading one group, but a group of ones); the rebellious ("Thanks-God-But-We-Just-Want-To-Be-Sure" approach, an affront to God's repeated assurances of Heavenly protection), the privacy factor (in Judaism the slogan, "I've got your number," is knowing a person's intimate essence); to plain good manners (counting trivializes the spirit of a person); to the superstitious (in antiquity, victims of calamities were "counted," so it was considered bad luck to count the healthy).

But if counting was *verboten*, how then did the Jews count?

Through such surrogates as a half-shekel coin which was originally introduced as a "poll tax" for the upkeep of the Temple. Remember: the shekel was a weight before it was a coin, and literally means that every Jew is required to "weigh in" as an equal contributor.

Interestingly, the Hebrew term for "counting their number," *ki sisa* (the name of another parsha), and "lifting their heads" is the same. Both signal the spiritual elevation of those involved in the act of giving.

To Torah linguists the word *sapar* (to count) is similar to *si-payr* (to tell a story) in that the tale itself affirms that each Jew is incomplete until he joins his brother's other "half" donation, rendering them both complete, and therefore united; the whole being not only the sum of its parts, but *greater* than its parts.

> *Ol' Mrs. Greenblatt is patiently answering the census taker's questions — except one, her age.*
> *"But everyone tells their age to the census taker," he complains.*
> *"Oh yeah! Did my neighbor Mrs. Itti Bloomberg tell you her age!?"*
> *"Certainly."*
> *"Well, I'm the same age," she snaps.*
> *"As old as Mrs. Bloomberg," he writes on his form.*

How then does one count a minyan?

By saying Torah verses that contain exactly ten Hebrew words: for example, *magdil yeshu'os malko v'oseh chesed lim'shicho l'Dovid ul'zaro ad olam*, "He is a tower of strength to His king; He shows mercy to His anointed, to David and his descendants for ever;" or *hoshi'ah es amecha u'varech es nachalasecha ur'em v'nas'em ad ha'olam*, "Save Your people and bless Your inheritance, sustain them and tend them for ever."

Note that in both these examples the tenth word is *olam*, which means "forever," or "world," implying that if an *olam* (minyan) is present, it is as if everybody in "the whole world" is there (by the way, what do you call steaks ordered by ten Jews? a fillet minyan!).

The Yiddishists of Eastern Europe would "count" a minyan negatively, *nisht einzt, nisht tzvei*, etc, "Not one, not two, not three," and so on...

Whenever the Torah uses the term *lochem* (or *lecho*) it is in the context of our own benefit, as in *usefartem lochem*, "count for your own sakes." Thus it is no coincidence that this week's parsha is read on the Shabbos preceding Shavuos when the time of counting "seven complete, whole [temimos] weeks" is near the end.

The Sefira count is a very carefully worded one: instead of saying this is the eighth day, we say, "Today is one week *and* one day of the omer," a methodology that the Rambam calls a *mitzvas aseh*, a positive commandment, one that creates a greater anticipation and motivates us to not just count the omer but to make the omer count.

Yet "counting" is a misnomer.

Why? Because we do not actually count (*lispor*) the omer but keep track of the days (49) as well as the number of weeks (7) between the first and final "wave" of the omer (a signal of the harvest's start and the crop's conclusion). Jewish mystics then use the art of numerology (*gematria*) to conclude that the countdown was essential for Jewish unity. How? Because the number of letters in the Twelve Tribes of Israel is ...forty-nine!

And the 50th day, that of Shavuos?

This was the day of the receipt of Torah, the day that tied it all together — which explains why Jewish law requires that the sefira "count" be done not individually but communally (*k'ish echod b'lev echod*), in conscious unison as a nation.

> *After Kaplan wins the lottery by choosing number 49, his fiend Uri asks, "Hey, what made you pick that number?"*
> *"I saw it in a dream, just like Yosef! Six sevens appeared and danced before my very eyes; since 6 x 7 is 49, I chose forty-nine."*
> *"Hey, wait a minute! Six times seven is 42 you idiot! Not forty-nine!"*
> *"It is? Okay, Uri...next time, you be the mathematician!"*

The center of this parsha deals with the four-directive layout of the camp of Israel wherein the Twelve Tribes, now coalesced into a community, are positioned around the living quarters of their Levite leadership.

This encampment is in the form of a Star of David whose twelve focal points are formidably linked in order to safeguard the "13th" spot, the holy inner Sanctuary where the Presence of God dwells; a nation's heart known as the *Ohel Moed*, "Tent of Assembly."

The *Ramban*, the first to introduce Kabbalah into Torah commentary, places this vigilance around God's "home" on a Halachic parallel with all the other laws of Sinai; while Don Isaac Abarbanel, the classical 14th century exegete of Torah, was puzzled by the fact that this positioning and marching formation did not follow the traditional tribal chronology that rotated around the wives of Yaacov (wherein Leah's five sons always came first, followed by Rachel's three boys, and then the four sons of the handmaids).

A Midrash comes to Abarbanel's help: the layout is orchestrated to forge multi-faceted partnerships, each installed in the place befitting *him*; thus the large *avant garde* tribe of Judah, being destined for the monarchy, led the others; the leadership of Yissachar-Zevulun, camped to the east from where the sun rises, provided "light;" Dan accompanied Naftali-Asher in order to benefit from their special blessings, and so on.

"Cling to a good neighbor, shun an evil one," wrote the rabbis of the Mishna; or, as Pirkei Avos put it, "Woe to the wicked man and his neighbor; fortunate is the righteous and his neighbor."

> *Freddy sees his neighbor coming home upset, and his first instinct is to help, "Hey, Buddy, what's the problem?"*
> *"My car won't start. There's water in the carburetor."*
> *"Water in the carburetor?" Freddy laughs, "Buddy, you don't know a carburetor from an accelerator!"*
> *"No, there's definitely water in the carburetor."*
> *"Okay, okay, I'll have a look. Where is it?"*
> *"In the lake!"*

NASSO
Hair and There

The title to this week's parsha, *Nasso*, means to "lift up," as in "to take a count," for by lifting an object, one is able to single it out and identify it.

This is the longest parsha in the Torah cycle, rich in texture and content, as it tackles the collective destiny and historical mission of the people of Israel. Why is it so long? Because of the repetitive wording of the sacrifices of the 12 tribal leaders (*nesi'im*), despite the fact that each chieftain presents the same offering.

Not only does the Torah use more than 70 verses to describe identical ingredients, it then insists on laboriously summarizing the totals one-by-one (12 silver bowls, 12 silver basins, 12 gold ladles, and so on).

This is not the only place where the Torah uses a "long-hand" style of accounting; the Ramban and Sifre, an early Midrashic compilation, link this literary style to the Tanach's listing of the 31 kings that Joshua defeats (wherein the number "one" is repeated 31 times, after each king).

Why?

The Torah desires to focus on the singular, to emphasize that a nation's significance ultimately rests on the individual whose neglect of the mitzvos can quickly lead to a communal "breaking of faith" (*limol ma'al b'Adonai*).

The Torah was given "in the sight of *all*," professed the prestigious *tanna*, Simeon bar Yohai, convinced that "if one Jew was absent, God would have withheld the Revelation." Philo, first-century Alexandrian philosopher, notes that the Ten Commandments were addressed in the *singular*, convinced that their abeyance was "equal in worth to a whole nation, even the world."

Rabbi Moshe Leib of Sassov, commenting on the blessing of a *whole* people being in the singular, sees its structure as a guide, that the greatest blessing of them all is that of unity, motivated by Hillel's formidable challenge: "If I am not for myself, who will be for me? And if I am for myself, what am I? And if not now, when?"

The ancient Sifra disagrees: the most important blessing is not unity, but "peace [*sholom*] in the land," Ezekiel's everlasting covenant ("seek it, pursue it"), which the Midrash elevates above all else.

Sammy goes on a safari one year with Sylvia, his wife, who insists on taking her mother with them. For the sake of peace and sholom bayis, Sammy agrees.

One evening, deep in the jungle, Sylvia awakes to find her mother gone. She quickly wakes up her husband and they both go looking for her, only to come upon a chilling sight.

Sammy's mother-in-law is backed up against a thick, impenetrable bush, with two large lions facing her.

"Oh, my God!" cries Sylvia, "What are we going to do?"

"Nothing," says Sammy, "The lions got themselves into this mess, let 'em get themselves out of it!"

The second century sages were in consensus: Eleazar Hakappar crowned peace "the climax of all blessings;" his contemporary Eleazar ben Shammua made it the "essence of all prophecies." It was "the name of God" (Zohar); the prerequisite to rebuilding Jerusalem (Nahman of Bratzlav, in his *Sefer Hamiddos*) — and the only goal that tolerated telling lies to preserve it (Eleazar Bar Kappara).

But how to achieve such peace?

There is a general consensus among our sages that it can only be attained by avoiding the evil of *loshon horo*, a practice that covers a broad spectrum of slanderous gossip, careless speech, or just nasty words. This artless art can ruin relationships, demolish partnerships, discredit God, damage the innocent — in short, destroy lives, making it a matter of life *and breath*.

The real art of conversation?

Not only to say the right thing in the right place, but also to leave unsaid the wrong thing at the tempting moment.

> *When Ellen sits next to Mrs. Goldstein at a Yeshiva dinner one year, she notices her extraordinarily enormous diamond ring, "Wow! I've never seen anything like it. It's the mother of all diamonds, it is gigantic, flawless, glittering...My, that's some diamond you've got there."*
>
> *"I know," Mrs. Goldstein sighs, "but this is no ordinary diamond, it's the famous Goldstein diamond."*
>
> *"So what's wrong with that?"*
>
> *Lowering her voice, Mrs. Goldstein whispers, "It comes with a terrible curse."*
>
> *"It does?" Ellen replies, moving to the edge of her seat, expecting to hear some juicy gossip, "So tell me, what's the curse?"*
>
> *"Mister Goldstein!"*

This parsha reaches a crescendo in the Torah's symphony of greetings and blessings by introducing the art of the priestly blessing (*Birkas Kohanim*), a benediction of love that consists of the 3 best known verses and 15 words in the entire Torah ("May the Lord bless you and keep you; May the Lord cause His face to shine upon you and be gracious unto you; May the Lord lift His face upon you and grant you peace.")

Why 15 words?

Gematria lovers point to Isaiah's, "With the name Yah, God fashioned the worlds," and note that the *yud-hai* letters of 'Yah' equals 15; indicating that upon creation, the Heavens already had this blessing for Israel in Mind.

The simplicity of this blessing of eloquence, whose words glide rhythmically through promises of Divine providence and hope, are said at life's most sacred junctions (at a *bris*, beneath the wedding *chuppa*, during the *yomim tovim.*)

Is it a coincidence?

A version of these blessings, inscribed in silver, is the oldest Biblical text so far discovered. Non-kohen rabbis are prohibited from giving the priestly blessings or raising hands in the kohanic way ("Thus shall you [the *kohanim*] bless the Children of Israel"), so, in order to avoid misunderstanding, they use introductory words ("May God bestow upon you the threefold Scriptural blessing..."), although Rabbi Yose, a non-kohen, said that if his Talmudic colleagues invited him he would not hesitate to participate.

The parsha also introduces us to the idea of the holy ascetic (*Nazir*), those who are recognizable by their long hair, who take a vow of abstinence from wine and are forbidden to come in contact with the dead.

> *Judge to defendant: "You've been brought here for drinking."*
> *"Okay," he replies, "Let's get started."*

The Hebrew root of *Nazir* means "to make separate," much like the root of *kodosh,* which means "to make holy," but it has the same connotation of separateness (in that something is considered holy when it is separated from the profane); and thus the Nazir is akin to the tribe of Levi who are separated from worldly activities in order to better focus on serving God.

The most famous Nazirite of them all was Samson, a classic hero-prophet, last of the judges, a Judaic Hercules with legendary superhuman strength (and whose birth is only one of two in the Torah foretold by an angel; the other being Yitzchak). Samson kills a lion with his bare hands, throws flaming foxes into Philistine vineyards, plunges into battle armed only with revenge and an ass's jawbone, assassinates Agag, his enemy's king — and still finds the time to wed a non-Jewish girl (Delilah).

Jewish mystics link his Hebrew name (Shimshon) to the sun (*shemesh*) which denotes "daylight," compare it to his wife's name, which means "of the night," to prove that this Jewish-Gentile match could never be successful. Since these are obviously not the ascetic or monastic acts of a typical self-restrained Nazirite, many Torah scholars (Rabbi Yehuda, Rambam) throw doubt on his Nazirite status. This is Samson Nazirite — unlike a regular Nazirite.

The Nazir believed that his acts resulted in self-sanctification, and humility.

Extremely long disheveled hair was a humbling admission that, in the service of God, appearance mattered little.

"Absalom gloried in his hair, so he was hanged by his hair," warn the rabbis of the Mishna — although Simeon ben Mensasya seems to disagree: before introducing Eve to Adam, the *tanna* describes how God "plaits her hair."

Rabbi Y. Y. Kanievsky (the *Steipler*) understood the concern of the Nazir to be a weapon against becoming conceited, a severe sin known as *ga'ava* ("haughtiness") which Mishlei describes as, "an abomination" that drives away the presence of God ("I and him [a *ba'al ga'ava*] cannot live in the world together").

The 11th century Bachya ben Joseph ibn Pakuda might have praised Nazirite discipline as a role model (arguing that it was necessary to combat daily temptations), but such other major Torah scholars as Aharon Halevi (author, *Sefer Hachinuch*), the sage Samuel, Rabbi Eleazar Hakappar, and King Solomon all thought the life of the Nazirite was extreme, self-destructive — and thus sinful.

The Rambam, the great philosopher and commentator who cautions for "middle-of-the-road" moderate behavior, severely criticizes ascetics ("sinners," he calls them) who do without the physical comforts that the Torah allows. Why? Because their acts and beliefs imply that "God is the enemy of the body."

Vows and oaths are considered serious business in Judaism, and were to be utilized only sparsely, and in serious circumstances.

The Torah then introduces us to the *Sotah*, a wife whose husband suspects her of infidelity, and a special procedure which determines her innocence or guilt.

In short: she first brings a sacrifice (in front of God, *v'he'emidoh lifnei Hashem*) and then drinks "bitter waters" in which the name of God has been dissolved.

> *Summoned in front of the* beis din *a Sotah asks the rabbis if she can take the potion intravenously.* "No," *they reply.*
> "Why not?"
> "Because you can't take God's name in vein!"

If the wife is guilty, her internal organs fail and she dies. If innocent, and falsely accused, she is blessed with children (if she has none) or all subsequent pregnancies and labors are significantly easier.

The act of "drinking" God's name is the only approved case of erasing *the* "Name" which is normally prohibited; and why many Jews write 'G-d' with a dash instead of an "o".

Why this exception to erasing God's name?

In recognition of the concept known as *sholom bayis* ("For the sake of peace between husband and wife"); a dogma the Torah considers so important that even God is willing to allow His name to be erased in its support.

The concept of the *Sotah* has its counterpart in the relationship between Jews and God, which our rabbis often depict as a "marriage."

The same term for human marriage, *kiddushin* (from *kadosh*, which means "sacred," or "consecrated") also describes this bond, just as the words spoken under the chuppah, *harei at m'kudeshes li* ("behold, you are consecrated to me") are similar to those used when performing a mitzva, *asher kidshanu b'mitzvosav* ("He has consecrated us with His commandments.")

The Kabbalists consider Mt. Sinai the solemn canopy of Israel's union with God, as commemorated by Shavuos whose proximity falls near this week's parsha, wherein the story of Ruth is read, a tale that, from beginning to end, speaks of love.

The Torah pauses the Jews' march towards their national goals and aspirations just long enough to introduce such internal matters as family fidelity (*Sotah*); a proper relationship to the materialistic world (*Nazirism*); and *gemilus chasadim* (acts of compassion) for the stranger (*ger*) — all part of an Isaiah tapestry to "unlock the shackles of injustice, undo the fetters of bondage, let the oppressed go free, break every cruel chain, share your bread with the hungry, bring the homeless poor into your house, and when you see the naked, clothe them."

But why does the Torah concern itself with the ascetic and the unfaithful woman in the same parsha? Is there a relationship between *Sotah* and *Nazir*?

The laws of Sotah begin with the word *ma'al*, which means "trespass" (or "embezzlement"), in order to emphasize that the vows of marriage are sacred, and that spousal unfaithfulness is akin to the guilt of trespass.

The Torah's first trespass occurs in the Garden of Eden, when Adam eats from the forbidden Tree of Knowledge, which the Midrash describes as a vine with fruit grapes. This grape vine is the ingredient of wine, which the Nazir vows not to drink in order to avoid temptations. The moral? Excess wine can lead to immorality.

Sometimes it is the women who are overly suspicious of their husbands...

After Adam stays out late for a few nights, Eve becomes upset and accuses him of running around with other women.

"That's ridiculous," replies Adam, "Remember, you're the only woman on earth!"

Later that evening Adam is awakened by Eve poking him in the chest.

"Hey, what are you doing?"

"Counting your ribs!"

The Kvetching Sedra

Manny is pleased with himself and calls his neighbor over, "Hey, watch this. I taught my dog some new tricks."

He picks up a tree branch, throws it, turns to his dog, and says, "Fetch!"

The dog immediately lies down, and starts complaining, "I'm tired and hungry, I didn't sleep last night, my girlfriend left me, I can't run as fast as I used to, I'm...",

"Hey," asks the neighbor, "What's he doing?"

"He thought I said kvetch!"

The opening word of God's instruction manual on How-To-Light the seven-branched gold candelabrum of the Tabernacle are the words *B'ha'aloscha es haneros*, which do not only mean, "when you kindle the lights," but are also based on the verb derived from *alah*, which means "to go up" (as in: "when you make the lights ascend").

It also contains the laws of *challa*, the designated portion of kneaded dough that is set aside for a Kohen, in the same status as tithing (*aseir t'aseir*), a law that applied only to bread: and the mitzva of *pidyon haben*, held 30 days after a firstborn son is "bought back" (redeemed) from the *Kohanim*, the priestly class, who are legally entitled to keep the firstborn for service to God ("For every firstborn among the Israelites, man as well as beast, is Mine [God's]."

The cost of the pidyon? Five silver *shekalim*. Why five? Rashi traces the amount to the 20 pieces of silver, which equates to five silver shekalim, that was paid to acquire Rachel's firstborn son (Yosef). This set the minimum cash criteria, according to Reb Yitzchak Bunim, for the value of a servant of God ("Pay for My servant, at least what the heathen paid for a Jewish boy — not one penny less!")

But this Torah portion, one of protests and criticism, surely qualifies as the *Sefer Kvetch,* the Book of Complaints, as everybody seems to jump on the protest wagon, grumbling and griping "in the ears of God."

> *The burly immigrant from Moscow steps off the plane at Ben Gurion Airport to be asked by a reporter, "Tell me, what was life like back in Russia?"*
> *"I couldn't complain."*
> *"And how were your living quarters there?"*
> *"I couldn't complain."*
> *"And your standard of living?"*
> *"I couldn't complain."*
> *"Well, if everything was so good back in 'ol Russia, why did you bother to come here?"*
> *"Oh," replies the new* oleh, *"Here I can complain!"*

What a tragedy.

Despite their brush with the Divine, and despite a miraculous leap from abject servitude to miraculous freedom, the cantankerous, querulous Jews fail in their newly-found liberty, unable to seize their history and destiny. Not only is the dream of *Eretz Yisroel* delayed, but an entire "generation of the desert" (*dor hamidbar*) is doomed.

Rabbi Samson Raphael Hirsch singles out this parsha wherein confusion reigns as *the* dividing line in Biblical Jewish history, while Volozhin's formidable rosh yeshiva Naftali Zvi Yehuda Berlin (*Netziv*), weeps at the thought of an "aimless wandering" that causes an entire nation to suddenly and inexplicably lose its spiritual compass and sense of purpose.

The Torah paints these disgruntled, dissatisfied and despairing

Jews with an unflattering character brush, calling them "murmurers, riffraff," and nagging whiners of discontent, chronic complainers who publicly *kvetch* about boredom and the lack of choice in their culinary pickings (the term *kvetch* comes from the German *quetschen*, which means, "to squeeze," as in the reflexive Yiddish *kvetshn zakh*, or *gebn a kvetsh, which means* "to exert yourself;" in colloquial Hebrew, the verb *l'kavtshetsh*, means "to squeeze," or "to crumple.")

Their "gluttonous craving" creates an offensive nostalgia for such delicacies as Egyptian "cucumbers, melons, leeks, onions, garlic" conveniently forgetting that for dessert they and their families were given lashes and oppression served up on trays of humiliation.

> *When the fish in the Red Sea hear that the Jews were thirsty they approach Moshe with an idea. The liberator of the Jews listens intently as the fish describe how they can provide drinking water through their own gills…however there is one problem: it is salt water.*
>
> *After the fish graciously offer to remove the salt with their mouths, a grateful Moshe gives them the name by which they are still known by all Jews today by ordering them to, "Go Filter Fish!"*

Eldad and Medad refuse to go with the elders. R. Simeon said: "On their own, Eldad and Medad chose to remain in the camp. For when the Holy One ordered Moshe, 'Gather unto Me seventy of the elders of Israel,' Eldad and Medad said to themselves: We are not worthy of such distinction." When they themselves began to prophecize, an enraged Joshua demanded that they be *kla'em*, which can mean either "imprison" or "destroy."

Moshe does neither; instead he wishes that "all God's people were prophets!"

This response led such Jewish sages as the Rambam ("all have the moral and intellectual potential to become prophets"), Yehudah Halevi ("prophecy does not depend on rank, lineage or material endowment"), and Rav Shimson Raphael Hirsch to conclude that no particular socio-economic class is automatically entitled to spiritual status, and thus there can never be a monopoly on spiritual leadership ("The lowliest of the nation shares with the highest the opportunity of being granted Divine inspiration.")

This parsha is not the first time that the Heavens have to man the Complaints Department.

After His unruly folk loudly accuse Him of "bringing us out into this wilderness to starve to death," God responds with a shower of manna; when they whine about thirst, God responds with water issuing from a rock; when they complain that the water is bitter and undrinkable, God makes it sweet and potable.

The question is blaring: with such a history of whining and wailing, why does God lose His patience only in this week's parsha and respond with an anger of fire plagues?

The clue lies in the text, *Vayehi ho'om k'misonanim*, "The people took to complaining bitterly," suggesting that the grumblings were no longer about immediate and legitimate needs (such as hunger and thirst) but had become unreasonable, a way of "letting off steam" just for the sake of fomenting unrest, rebellion, dissatisfaction.

Even Moshe, overwhelmed and demoralized, catches the complaint virus; "I cannot carry all this by myself, it is too much for me." God's solution? To share the burden among "seventy of Israel's elders."

Is this advice original?

No: remember, Yisro, Moshe's father-in-law, had already urged just such a solution ("seek out trustworthy men, and let them share the burden with you.") These co-leaders of the nation, a distinguished group the Mishna calls the Sanhedrin, were chosen not for their nobility, but for their sensitivity and empathy to their fellow man...

> *"Doctor, my leg hurts. What can I do?"*
> *"Limp!"*
> *"But I also have a ringing in my ears."*
> *"Don't answer!"*

This curse of complaints spreads to Moshe's own immediate family, as Miriam and Aaron disturb their brother's domestic tranquility by accusing him of arrogance, challenge his morality, and gossip about Tzippora, their sister-in-law. Why? Because she is different ("He married a Cushite woman!")

Were Aaron and Miriam racist?

No: there is no word for race in the Torah, nor in any of the early rabbinic texts; "others" are never described by the color of their skin but by their fidelity to God (they are called "idolaters," or "eaters of treif.")

The punishment is speedy and severe: the Heavens strike and disfigure Miriam, the instigator, with "snow-white scales" of *tzora'as*, causing her to be removed from the camp for seven days. Moshe pleads with God (successfully) for a cure for their "sin of folly," the shortest prayer in the entire Torah: *El na refah na la*, "O God, pray heal her."

Although the complaining overwhelms everything else, this Torah portion also contains God's instruction manual on how-to-light the seven-branched gold candelabrum of the Tabernacle. Indeed, the opening words *beha'alotecha et hanerot* ("when you kindle the lights") give this Torah portion its name.

Literally, *beha'alotecha et hanerot* means "when you make the lights rise," which can be interpreted poetically or practically.

The Midrashic Sifre claims this refers to the fact that the priest had to stand up on a step to kindle the menorah lights; however Jewish mystics, seeking not a scientific answer but a spiritual explanation, questioned why flames rise upwards in the first place.

The charismatic Rav Abraham Isaac Kook, first chief rabbi of Palestine, mystically saw the Divinely-allocated task of a flame like everything else in nature, striving to rise to God, and pointed to the "flame of God" expression in *Shir Hashirim* (the only time God is mentioned in the "Song of Songs.")

Many a rabbi searching for a good bar mitzva theme has turned to a Rashi from this parsha: why does the Torah use the term *laha'alos* ("to ascend") instead of *lehadlik* ("to kindle") the lights?

The rabbinic homily is tempting: that up until his bar mitzva a boy's "flame" is directly linked to his parent's educational "kindling," but the moment he is Halachically responsible for his own acts he "ascends" independently — and yet the original source of his continuing flame, his nurturing parents and *rebbeim*, if properly ignited, never leaves him, akin to a candle still burning even after the match is removed.

Thus, not only can this tradition (*mesorah*) be transmitted generationally (*dor v'dor*), but so can its brightness of hope, its luster of optimism and its glistening desire.

The candle flame solidifies the quiet role of light, dancing noiselessly and shining as a challenge, a dare to recall the *yid* as the *ner tamid*, a human eternal light charged with couriering truth and morality to the world, centuries after the flame was kindled at Sinai.

The vignette of Aaron kindling the flame in this week's parsha thus symbolizes the passing of the torch from one generation to another, the combined wicks generating one common light.

> *One Chanukka the rabbi arrives in shul and is surprised to see only one person, an elderly Jewish farmer.* ▶

"Should I proceed?" asks the rabbi.

"Sure, why not?"

"Well, is it worth having a service for such a small congregation?"

"Let me tell ya, rabbi," replies the little ol' Jewish farmer, "when I take a bucket of food to the hens, and only one turns up I don't send it away hungry."

The rabbi, moved by this simple analogy, then goes to the bima and proceeds to lead the single Jew through the entire morning service, including a long and very forceful sermon on Chanukka, its history and tradition, and on the laws of lighting the menorah.

When he finally finishes he turns to the farmer, "Was that all right?"

"You know rabbi," the farmer replies tersely, "When I take the bucket to the hens, and only one turns up, I don't give it the whole bucket!"

SH'LACH L'CHO
I Spy With My Little Eye

Three spies are caught and sentenced to death. As the first spy is blindfolded and lined up against the wall, he whispers to the others, "Pssst, don't worry. I've got a great idea. Just follow my lead."

"Do you have any last words?" asks the officer in charge.

"No."

"Okay, then...Ready...set....aim...."

Suddenly, the spy yells out, "Tornado, tornado!" and when the gunmen all turn around, he escapes.

"I get it," the next spy whispers to himself, and when asked, "Do you have any last words?" he replies, "No."

"Okay, then...We're ready...set...aim...."

"Flood, flood!" he shouts, and, predictably, when all the executioners turn around to see, he also escapes.

Morrie, the third spy, now understands the plan and feels so relieved that he even helps put on his own blindfold, calmly leans against the wall, and when asked, "Do you have any last words?" yawns back, "No."

"Okay, then...Ready...set...aim...." — when suddenly Morrie yells out, "Fire, fire!"

The title to this weeks parsha, *Sh'lach L'cho*, means "send for yourself," a reluctant and angry response from Heaven to a request for espionage that ends in a decree from God that *that* generation must die out in the wilderness, destined to 40 years of wandering; one year for each of the days they spied in infamy, its climax of tears still reverberating via the Tisha B'Av's of the Jewish calendar.

Isn't this an unfair collective punishment? Just because of the malevolence and lack of integrity of ten Jews, the Israelites as a whole sinned? Weren't they simply obeying their leaders?

Rabbi Meir Yehuda Leibush ben Yehiel Michal (*Malbim*), a 19th century Russian rabbi famed for his focus on Torah linguistics, blames not the reconnaissance spies but the folks back home who, using their God-given right of free will, exerted enormous pressure on Moshe to send them.

Since Moshe and God knew that the results would be far from objective, the Midrash interprets God's words, *Sh'lach-l'cho anashim* ("Send men for yourself") not in the context of a direct command, but as a frustrated response to go ahead, send spies "if you want to!"

> *One day Beryl decides to apply for a job as a spy and during his interview is asked to take an envelope up to the fourth floor of CIA headquarters.*
>
> *As soon as he is alone, the curious Beryl steps into an empty hallway, opens the packet and reads, "Mazel tov! You're our kind of guy! Report to the fifth floor."*

The insecure Jews camp at Paran and decide to send out an advance party, a reconnaissance group of 12 Jews known as the *meraglim*, one for each Tribe.

These spies were not your every day gofers; each being a distinguished and pious prince of Israel, men of the highest caliber. Their job? To spy out the people, land, cities, and natural resources that the nation had been ordered to conquer.

In fact, this parsha does not call them spies, but "men" on a mission; their spy status is only introduced later, in Deuteronomy, when Moshe reminisces back on Jewish history.

> *The rabbi bumps into one of his congregant's sons and asks him why he doesn't come to shul more often, and join the Army of Hashem.*
>
> *"But I'm already in the Army of God," the boy replies.*▶

> "Well then, how come I only see you in shul *twice a year?*"
> "Because..." the boy thinks quickly, "I'm in the Secret Service!"

The Jews certainly remembered God's earlier twin promise to Avraham, that the holy land, the climax and entire *raison d'être* of their destiny as a holy nation, was good ("flowing with milk and honey"), and that their opponents faced certain defeat...but, they just wanted to be sure.

This hesitancy reflects an incredible lack of faith and trust, especially for a generation that had personally witnessed plagues (*makkos*) in Egypt, seas split, and daily miracles (*manna*).

The question then is obvious: why didn't Moshe simply talk them out of it?

Rav Levi Ben Gershon (*Ralbag*, also known as Gersonides), traces Moshe's vacillation to his original demurrer to God at the burning bush, a candid admission that he is "heavy of mouth and speech" (*k'vad peh, k'vad lashon*), a dysfunction not just in pronunciation but, as revealed here, an inability at times to communicate.

> One morning Hershel notices an ad from the Mossad for "ruthless spies," so he applies for a job and finds himself in a waiting room with two other applicants. A Mossad officer invites the first man into a room and asks him, "Do you love your wife Shoshana?"
> "Yes I do, sir."
> "Do you love your country?"
> "Yes I do, sir."
> "Which do you love more, your wife or your country?"
> "My country, sir."
> "We need to know for sure so we brought in Shoshana and she's in that room over there. Take this gun, and go kill her!" ♦

The man hesitatingly goes into the room, and after a few seconds comes out with his arm around his wife, his tie loosened, sweat pouring down his face. "She's my wife. I can't do this!" as he puts down the gun and leaves.

The next guy comes in, sits down and is asked the same questions, and gives the same responses. He is handed the gun, and told to go kill his wife Suri. But after a few minutes, he comes out hand-in-hand with Suri, "I can't do it! She's my wife, the mother of my children..." as he puts down the gun and leaves.

Finally it's Hershel's turn, and it's the same scenario. The interviewer gives him a gun, and tells him that they have his wife Ruthie in another room and order him to kill her.

Hershel picks up the weapon, goes into the room, and there is a sudden bang! bang! bang! followed by lots of screaming, punching, and crashing sounds. Fifteen minutes later, all is quiet.

Hershel stumbles out of the room, totally bloodied from head-to-toe, turns to the interviewer and complains, "Some idiot put blanks in the gun! I had to kill her with my own bare hands!"

Ten of the twelve spies return as prophets of doom, with the proverbial good and bad news scenario: the land is great, but "we looked like grasshoppers" and felt "powerless" against the indigenous residents of Canaan (Anakites, Hittites, Jebusites, Amorites), "men of great measure [*anshei midos*]."

Rashi interprets *midos* not as "measure" or "merit," but from the Hebrew word *madon* (or *madim*), as militarily experienced, bellicose "men of arguments and struggle."

In contrast, the other two idealistic Jewish spies (Joshua and Caleb) see the same enemies yet return with a confident and calm demeanor, courageous in their convictions, determined to inspire their folk with their romantic visionary battle cry: "Let us by all means go up, for we shall surely overcome them" — a brave precursor to the later signature rally cry of the Civil Rights Movement, "We Shall Overcome."

The name of Moshe's brother-in-law, Caleb ben Yephunneh, is a play on words, from the root *panah*, to "turn away" from the negativism of the other ten fault-finding fellow spies.

Joshua is also a name-change: originally he was called Hoshea son of Nun, Prince of Efraim, but Moshe changes it to Yehoshua, by adding the prefix of God [*Yah*] to form the new appellation, "God saves."

These two Jews, in the face of potential mutiny against Moshe, become the sole resolute characters in this week's parsha who are rewarded with a future: they become the only members of that generation to survive, and enter Canaan.

Not only are they described as being taller in stature than their peers because of their faith in Jewish destiny, but also because of their belief in themselves; a stunning display of the power of optimism.

A true optimist? One who goes through life knowing where there's smoke, there's smoked salmon; and that a bad matza ball makes for a good paperweight.

> "Tell me," the dean of admissions of the School of Agriculture asks Shaya, a prospective student, "Why have you chosen this career?"
> "Because I dream of making $1,000,000 in farming, just like my father."
> "Your father made $1,000,000 in farming?"
> "No, but he always dreamed of it."

Perception and persistence have always overcome pessimism.

Water wears out stones, observes Job; one only needs to keep knocking, advises Moshe Ibn Ezra, to succeed in entering; when Isaiah saw that the bricks had fallen, he declared, "We will rebuild with hewn stones;" when he noticed the sycamores cut down, the prophet was unmoved, "Cedars will be put in their place!" — an attitude that neatly comes together in the witty lyrics of Arthur Guiterman, "Talent made a poor appearance, until he married Perseverance."

> *A man walks into a doctor's office with a cucumber up his nose, a carrot in his left ear and a banana in his right ear.*
> *"What's the matter with me?" he asks the doctor.*
> *"Well," the doc replies, "You're not eating properly."*

The contrary spies cross one major red-line in their ill-fated mission: they slander the Holy Land itself, disparaging and degrading Israel as a place "which devours its inhabitants," implying that those who dare live there are doomed to die.

The Torah doesn't elaborate on what caused such maligning paranoia and skewered reality but Rabbi Ovadia Sforno, the formidable 16th century Italian Torah commentator, suggests that they saw an air polluted, and crops infested with insidious bacteria. But this flies in the face of the fact that the spies return with a luscious cluster of grapes cut from a vine in the Valley of Eshkol; proof, says Moshe ben Nachman (*Ramban*), 13th century Spanish Torah giant, of a holy land climate responsive to healthy produce, rich nutrition, clean water.

So what was the crime of the spies? Interpretation.

The spies turn the positive into a negative, a result of not being able to shake off an inbred slave mentality; nor, according to the Lithuanian sage Yisroel Ordman of Telshe, of possessing the humble ability to seek out virtues rather than faults ("We were given two eyes," goes the Chassidic adage: "One very powerful for introspection, so we should find our smallest faults; the other very weak, for viewing others'. Only too often we switch their functions.")

> *"Next week," the rav announces one Shabbos morning, "my dvar Torah will be about the sin of being untruthful. To help you prepare, I want you all to read the 51st chapter of the Book of Genesis."*
>
> *The following Shabbos, the rabbi gets up and asks for a show of hands on how many had read the 51st chapter of the Book of Genesis.*
>
> *After nearly every hand goes up, the rav says, "Genesis has only fifty chapters. I will now proceed with my dvar Torah on the sin of lying."*

The Torah uses the word *dibas* in explaining the spy's speech, a term with nefarious connotations, akin to evil speech (*loshon horo*). The result?

The Jews plunge into a state of high anxiety, panic, fear. They begin to weep and moan, grumble and snivel ("Better for us to go back to Egypt") — and the same generation that was forgiven the sin of the Golden Calf is now unforgiven, doomed to die in the wilderness, permanently etching the egregious reconnaissance episode and the sin of self-belittlement as the worst of all sins in the entire Torah.

The lesson?

Never give up; all peoples face adversity at some time in their life, and those of faith simply refuse to be defeated by it (remember: Beethoven was totally deaf when he wrote five of his greatest symphonies).

> *A duck walks into a bar and asks the bartender, "Hey, you got any crackers?"*
>
> *"No."*
>
> *The duck leaves, returns the next day and asks, "Hey, you got any crackers?"*
>
> *Again, the answer is "No."*
>
> *The duck walks out, returns the next day and asks,* ▶

> "Hey, you got any crackers?"
> "Listen," replies the annoyed bartender, "I told ya yes-terday and the day before, No! And if ya ask me one more time I'm gonna nail your beak shut!"
> The duck leaves, returns the next day and asks, "Hey, you got any nails?"
> "No, no, no!"
> "Great, so, you got any crackers?"

Some of Moshe's admonition is by reference: *di zahav* for exam-ple, refers to the sin of the Golden Calf, with *di* meaning "enough" and *zahav* implying gold; suggesting that an inability to deal with excessive wealth brought the Jews to this sin.

> "You know, people are always coming to us with their guilt and fears," one psychiatrist is telling two of his peers at a convention, "but we have no one to go to with our problems. Since we're all professionals, why don't we hear each other out right-now?"
> The others agree that this is a good idea.
> "I'm a compulsive shopper and deeply in debt, so I over bill patients all the time," one psychiatrist confesses.
> "I have a drug problem that's out of control," the sec-ond one admits, "and I frequently pressure my patients into buying illegal drugs for me."
> "I know it's wrong," confesses the first psychiatrist, "but no matter how hard I try, I just can't keep a secret!"

This parsha also introduces the mitzva of the four-cornered garment and its requisite fringes (*tzitzis*), the only article of clothing that all Jews are commanded to wear (other than the *kippa*, "head covering," mandatory for the priests in the Temple), which occu-pies the entire third paragraph of the *Shema*. This command is rare. Why? It is one of the few that the Torah explains with a rationale:

to teach Jews to be constantly aware, "Look at it and be reminded of all the commandments," in that ones daily experience is always infused by the Divine.

> *Faivie is driving on Purim, more than a bit drunk, his car weaving all over the road when a cop pulls him over.*
> *"So, where've you been?"*
> *"A Purim party," slurs Faivie with smile.*
> *"Well, it looks like you've had quite a few; by the way, did you notice, a few intersections back, that your wife fell out of your car?"*
> *"Oh, thank God," sighs Faivie, "for a minute there, I thought I'd gone deaf."*

The Ramban adds the numerical value (*gematria*) of the *tzitzit* strings (8) to their knots (5) to arrive at *ehad* (13), the last word in the *Shema* which means "One," implying that tzitzit fringes are akin to the unity of God. The Torah also equates *tzitzis* with the "signs" of a rainbow, bris, Shabbos, and tefillin which are also reminders to "remember and observe" (mitzvos).

"Seeing," say our sages, "leads to remembering and remembering brings to action."

> *As she approaches her wedding day, an excited Chanale asks her mother if she remembers what she did to make her marriage so successful.*
> *"Yes," her mother answers, "Two times a week we would go to a nice restaurant, have a little wine, some good food, and friendly companionship. I would go on Mondays, your father went on Thursdays."*

KORACH
Rebel, Without a Cause

Baruch suddenly feels a man's hand in his pocket as he strolls through a Jerusalem alley, "Hey! What do you want?"
"A match."
"Why didn't you ask me?"
"I don't talk to strangers."

This parsha can be subtitled: Jews don't hate, or do they?

The Torah wastes no time: by aggressively opening with *Vayikach Korach*, "And Korach took," it immediately sets the stage for division and disaster.

This is *the* parsha of *machlokes* (strife) — and it begins with a linguistic cliffhanger: we are boldly told that Korach "took" but not "what he took," reversing the traditional sequence when objects usually follow verbs.

Rabbi Shlomo Yitzchaki (*Rashi*), the classic medieval Torah commentator of commentators, quickly comes to the rescue: Korach's heart, lacking the humility of refinement and restraint, took him "off to one side," the side of hubris, conceit, insolence; a disconnect that withdraws him into a zealous island unto himself.

The rabbis of the Talmud point to this parsha's manipulative rebellion and dirty politics as the most perilous moment for Israel during its sojourn in the wilderness. Rav Moshe Feinstein, the leading top 20th century Halachist, calls the sly, devious Korach "the father of controversy," *the* exemplar of contentiousness, the Torah's professional troublemaker, and most famous rabble-rousing Jew of all time.

> *George thinks he's George Washington. During one of his sessions with a psychiatrist, he lowers his voice and confides to the doctor, "Tomorrow, we'll cross the Delaware and surprise them when they least expect it."*
> *As soon as he leaves, the psychiatrist rushes to the phone, dials and whispers, "Psst, King George? This is Benedict Arnold. I have the plans!"*

Korach is the spiritual forerunner of a later Middle Ages sect, the Karaites, who also tore asunder the Jewish people with their attack on the authority of the rabbinate.

But wait: isn't Judaism open to debate and dissent; and isn't the Talmud replete with opposing viewpoints and differences amongst the sages themselves?

Yes, but Korach v. Moshe falls under a category known as *shelo l'shem shomayim* ("not for the sake of Heaven"), in sharp contrast to the genuine *l'shem shomayim* ("for the sake of Heaven") and constructive differences of Halachic interpretation between two authentic religious models, Hillel, the "humble" *nasi*, and Shammai, the "short-tempered" *av beis din*.

Rabbi Eliyahu, the 18th century Gaon of Vilna (*Gra*), adds another component that delegitimates the Korachites as an authentic expression of conscience and controversy: they were also bitterly divided amongst themselves.

Jewish history thus labels Korach not as the populist democrat he pretends to be but as an "evil demagogue" of disunity; a peddler of hate, rancor, malevolence — the basis of that rabbinic adage: *al tischaber im rasha*, "don't befriend evil people."

> *Bernie and his wife are having a family argument and, in a desperate attempt to make amends, he offers his wife* ▶

> *a two-week vacation in France. She declines. He then offers her a brand new car. She declines. He then offers to renovate her kitchen.*
>
> *"No!" she screams, "That's not what I want!"*
>
> *"So, what do you want!?"*
>
> *"A divorce!"*
>
> *"Oh," Bernie says, "I hadn't planned on spending that much!"*

This parsha is a perfect example of the *leitwort* literary style, a "lead word" that the Torah uses repetitively, over and over and over, emphasizing a point via alliteration.

The key word in Korach reflects movement.

Instead of using the more obvious verb "to come" (*bo*) when Moshe calls for them, the Torah has the two dissenters (Datan, Aviram) using the unexpected *lo na'aleh*, "we will not go up," and then records their cynical complaint, "You brought us up [*he'elisanu*] from Egypt to have us die in the wilderness."

When God's patience runs out He uses the same Hebrew verbal root (*alah*) to demand that Moshe "get up [*he'alu*]" and punish the rebels.

These expressions ("go up...bring up...get up," etc) seem to have a literary life of their own, humming merrily along until, in a sudden vocabulary reversal in line with the concept *middoh keneged middoh*, "measure for measure," the Torah announces the swift and severe punishment, that they "will go down [*yarad*] alive to Sheol [the underworld];" in other words, the Jews who refused to "go up" to negotiate peace with Moshe end up "going down" to their deaths.

> *An irate Mr. Goldenberg calls his local Jewish newspaper to complain that his name is in the obituary column.*
>
> *"Really?" replies the editor calmly, "Say, Mr. Goldenberg, where are you calling from?"*

Unfortunately Jewish unity has remained an unreachable goal, a pipe dream, music to the ears of a long line of enemies from Titus to Arafat who were the undeserved beneficiaries of the disgraceful Jew vs. Jew pattern; proof incarnate that a house divided against itself is a ghastly self-destructive travesty.

In a tantalizing preview of the future, the Torah describes how Moshe, after killing an Egyptian, bumps into two Hebrews fighting each *other*. His bewildered question, "Why are you hitting your fellow Hebrew?" and the argumentative response, "Who made *you* ruler and judge over us?" is a sad glimpse of the internal fighting that is about to burst onto the stage of Jewish history as its most potent Achilles heel.

"We have met the enemy and he is us!" cries out this anguished parsha.

God was aware of this challenge, and held back giving the Torah until all the Jews camped "as one" (*attoh echod v'shimcha ehod*) — an unambiguous Heavenly cry for the *sine qua non* of Judaism: unity.

When the early Kabbalists compared the Jewish folk to a Sefer Torah they understood that a Sefer Torah had no holiness unless all of its letters were complete and whole. Similar was their attitude towards a Jewish people: it maintained its strength only when it was complete and whole, otherwise it was prone to suffocation from within.

And more: as a reminder that at the heart of the Jewish nation lies a singular Jewish soul, the first time the Hebrew word for "nation" appears it does so as *Am*, in first person singular (consider: in classical Hebrew neither the verb *Shema* nor the noun *Israel* have plural terms; and the first recorded question that man says to God is:, "Am I my brother's keeper?")

In an attempt to cement Judaic harmony, the Rambam transforms the famous Torah dogma ("do not do to others....") into a positive command — only to see Jewish unity deteriorate into a cruel running joke about ten Jews and eleven opinions.

The term *korach* is derived from *korcha*, which means "split", indicating a break-up among the Jews which caused the ground to "split" and swallow the troublemakers in a swift and severe devastation by fire. In Hebrew it can also mean "bald, barren," in that by the time he was finished Korach was "balded and barren" of everything, including his own life.

A rose, writes William Shakespeare, by any other name smells just as sweet: not so in Judaism that gives great significance to each name as defining one's persona, a concept known as *k'shmo ken hu.*

Korach is an uncommon name, appearing only once in the entire Torah, and is derived from two basic root-letters that spell out *kar*, the Hebrew word for cold; implying that by separating himself from the community Korach was an aloof, coldly detached and chillingly distant Jew (in modern Hebrew, a *Karchon* is an ice pop!)

That is why the Torah is in a hurry to reveal his character flaw as a "taker," not a giver, an *oisnitzer* as they say in the mother-tongue, one who wants more than he offers. Putting sugar in your mouth won't help if you are bitter in your heart, our Yiddishists would grumble, even as Solomon ibn Gabriol was musing how an eye of a needle is not too narrow for two lovers, but the entire world was not wide enough for two enemies.

Moshe responds in an uncharacteristic manner: the titan of self-effacement resorts to a rare self-defense display of self, and respectfully points out his own honesty and altruism, in line with Proverbs, "A soft-spoken answer can repel anger."

He seeks not confrontation but harmony, not a showdown but peace...

> *...similar to the rabbi who is confronted by three gentiles who ridicule him.*
> *"Good morning father Avraham!"*
> *"Good morning father Yitzchak!"*
> *"Good morning father Yaacov!'*
> *"I am neither," the rabbi replies gently, "I am, however, Saul, the son of Kish, who was on a three-day search for the lost donkeys, and I'm glad I've finally found them!"*

Korach's résumé was impressive: wealthy, intelligent, illustrious; a scholar, leader and, according to the Midrash, a prophet imbued with so much *ruach hakodesh* (Divine inspiration) as to become one of the privileged carriers of the Holy Ark. And more: he had impeccable *yichus* (genes), boasting Yaacov as his great-grandfather, making him not just any descendant of a distinguished lineage but, according to Rabbi Isaac Luria (*Ari*), the brilliant 16th century Safed kabbalist, Korach was *the* Levite with the greatest potential.

And yet by picking a fight with a Jew (Moshe) who clearly has God on his side, Korach reveals his slip of stupidity.

What ignites him to lead a mutiny?

Jealousy and resentment: he is personally *baleidicked* when Moshe, acting on God's order, bypasses him and gives his cousin (Elizaphon ben Uziel) the specific position of *kehunah gedolah*, chief prince of the House of Kehat.

Seemingly determined to prove a *Pirkei Avos* thought; that "Jealousy, desire, and honor remove a person from the world," Korach, now more viciously emotional than rational, hurls his self-serving "monopoly of power and prestige" accusative missiles at Moshe and Aaron ("You have gone too far!"), assaults and ridicules two of the most fundamental symbols of Judaism (*tzitzit, mezuzah*); and then rides the tide of religious antagonism by instigating a mass nihilistic rebellion, seeking not unity but factionalism.

His provocation convinces "250 scholars (*nesee'ay edah*)," including such serial detractors as Datan and Aviram, to join him in his destructive disturbance, unconcerned that the penalty of promoting a fire of contention, strife and argumentation "in the midst of all Israel" has the capacity to tear apart the very fabric that unites the Jewish people.

Korach & friends were obviously absent that day in cheder when they taught, "How good and pleasant, when brethren dwell in unity together," preferring to embrace that great philosopher Milton Berle's line, "The trouble with having friends is the upkeep!"

The new rabbi was startled to see a fight erupt in shul on his first morning. During the Shema, *half of the congregants stood up out of respect, the other half stayed seated, the decorum being destroyed by shouts of "stand up!" or "sit down!"*

The new rabbi doesn't know what to do so he goes to see the oldest founding member of the shul, a 98-year-old rabbi in a nursing home.

"Tell me," the rav asks, "What's the tradition in our synagogue? To stand for the Shema?"

"Oh no," the old rav replies as he strains to remember.

"Oh, then the tradition is to sit for the Shema?"

"No, no, no...that wasn't the tradition either."

"Well, please try to remember. You can't imagine what goes on every morning. Those who stand shout at those who sit, and those who sit yell at those who stand."

"Ah ha!" he cries out, "Now I remember! That was the tradition!!"

The longest perennial puzzle of community life is this: why is there so much disrespect, discord and friction among Jews who share so much history and heritage?

When Titus's Roman warriors destroyed Jerusalem they found no less than 24 different Jewish factional groups fighting amongst themselves; each convinced that he, and *only* he, had the right path to ensure the "survival of the Jewish people (*kiyem ha'uma*)."

"They fought with each other," records the historian Josephus, "doing everything their besiegers could have desired."

The result?

"Roman horses waded in Jewish blood up to their noses, the blood flowing in streams to the Mediterranean [a mile away] uprooting heavy rocks in its course;" only one surviving faction, Rabbi Yohanan Ben Zakkai's group, was left standing in this unnecessary civil war, the others were never heard from again in Jewish history, nor was the "sound of laughter from God," causing a saddened Rabbi Elazar Hakappar to conclude that "a quarrel-ridden house is doomed to destruction."

> One day a big city lawyer goes duck hunting in the rural countryside, and shoots a bird that falls into a farmer's field. As the lawyer climbs over the fence to retrieve the bird, an elderly farmer sitting on his tractor yells out, "Hey! This is my property! You can't come in here!"
>
> "Listen ol' man," the arrogant young attorney shouts back, "I'm the best trial lawyer in the entire country. If you don't let me get that duck, I'll sue you and take everything you own."
>
> "Sorry sir," the ol' farmer begs off, "but apparently, you don't know our custom on how to settle disagreements out here in the country. It's called the Three Kick Rule."
>
> "What's the Three Kick Rule?"
>
> "Well, first I kick you three times and then you kick me three times, and so on, back and forth, until one of us gives up."
>
> The young, fit attorney decides that he can easily take on the ol' codger so he smugly agrees. The ol' farmer slowly climbs down from his tractor, goes over to the city fella, and delivers a kick from his heavy work boot into the lawyer's groin. The attorney drops to his knees. The next kick nearly breaks the attorney's nose. The third kick to ▶

the kidney pulverizes him.

Slowly, the attorney gets up from the ground, summoning his last ounce of strength and staggers over to the farmer, "Okay...now...it's my turn!"

"Naw, I give up," the farmer yawns, "You can keep the duck!"

CHUKAS
The Mother of all
Mystery Mitzvos

> A Swiss tourist lost in Brooklyn decides to ask for directions, and approaches two yeshiva boys.
>
> "Entschuldigung," he says, "Koennen Sie Deutsch sprechen?"
>
> The two boys stare at him.
>
> "Excusez-moi," he tries, "Parlez vous Francais?"
>
> The two continue to stare.
>
> "Parlare Italiano?... Hablan ustedes Espanol?"
>
> With no response, he drives off, and one boy turns to the other, "Y'know, maybe we should learn a foreign language?"
>
> "Why? That guy knew four languages, and it didn't do him any good!"

There is a long line of scholars and students who are engaged in the endeavor of *ta'amei hamitzvos*, reasons for the Divine commandments. And if they fail to find a rationale for a given commandment, does this exempt them from the specific mitzva? No.

"The components of the Torah remain the law," writes Samson Raphael Hirsch, "even if we have not discovered the cause and connection of a single one!" — and yet "tis better thrice to ask your way," Guiterman's poetry advises, "Than even once to go astray."

Man's finest quality? According to Ibn Gabriol's *Mibhar Hapeninim*, is "to inquire, probe, query;" and Moshe Ibn Ezra agrees: "Who is ashamed to ask, diminishes in wisdom" — or in the wit of our Yiddishists: Each wherefore has a therefore!

The art of questioning is at the heart of the Jewish religion, even *klotz kashers*, Yiddish for the most ridiculous queries.

307

> *Max takes Ruthie out for a deluxe dinner on their 50th wedding anniversary in the most fancy high-priced kosher restaurant in elegant London.*
>
> *"Max," she asks, after the waiter serves her finger-bowls, "What's in this little paper cup inside the silver dish?"*
>
> *"I don't know, honey, but everything else was delicious so go ahead, eat it."*
>
> *"Max, you know me, I can't eat it if I don't know what it is! Please ask the waiter."*
>
> *"Ruthie, don't embarrass us by showing your ignorance! Just eat it, it'll be good."*
>
> *Instead she calls over the waiter, "Sir, what's in here, in this little silver bowl?"*
>
> *"Oh, that? It's a fingerbowl, Madam. When you finish eating, you dip your fingers in it to cleanse them, and then wipe them on your napkin."*
>
> *"You see!" Max sneers at his wife, "You ask a foolish question, you get a foolish answer!"*

Mendele Moker Seforim reminds us, "not all questions may be asked, nor is there an answer for every question;" an observation that lies at the heart of this parsha.

The spectrum of Torah mitzvos is divided into three categories: testimonial (*edus*), logical (*mishpotim*), obscure (*chukim*).

The first refers to those that prevent the Jewish people from forgetting what God has done for them (such as remembering the Exodus from Egypt twice each day or *bris miloh*); the next are those that logically form the basis of civilized law, even in the absence of Torah law (murder, robbery); and finally, *Chukas*, this parsha's title, which means "statutes," or "edicts," a reference to mitzvos that defy reason.

An example of mitzvos that defy logic would include the prohibition of meat and milk (*basar b'chalav*), marrying a brother's widow (*yibum*), not mixing wool and linen (*sha'atnez*), the Yom

Kippur scapegoat (*se'ir l'Azazel*) — and, the Mother of all Mystery Mitzvas, the ritual slaughter of a red heifer (*parah adumoh*), which opens this parsha.

This last law, abandoned with the destruction of the Temple in Jerusalem, is probably the most impenetrable mitzva in the entire Torah; a seemingly illogical concept that ashes can both purify the impure yet make the pure impure. Neither its reason nor origin has ever been clearly understood, causing all scholars to simply return to its Torah source, "I have decreed it, and you do not have permission to question it." Even the wisest of them all, King Solomon, admits it's purpose "is far from me".

That God's law is inviolate rests on the philosophy that human thinking is relative; that if allowed to succumb to one's subjective notions then what might be unethical to one may be ethical to another.

> *A Zen Master from Tibet, visiting Manhattan on a hot summer day, orders a drink from Hymie, a little 'ol Jewish vendor.*
> *Hymie hands over a nice cold soda can and the Zen Master gives him a $100 bill which the little 'ol Jewish guy puts in his pocket. After several minutes go by, the Zen Master asks politely, "Oh, Sir, where's my change?"*
> *"Change?" Hymie replies, "Change must come from within."*

The 14th century commentator, Rabbeinu Bachya, translates *chok* (singular for *chukim*) as a border, as in "the sand is a border to the sea." Rabbi Shlomo Ephraim Lunschitz (the *Kli Yakar*), a 17th century Polish Torah commentator states that the more enigmatic chukim are only undecipherable to us, but not to the Creator.

The Talmud's Rabbi Yitzhak had a straightforward answer why Jews should not seek answers: reasons are not given because some may assume they are not applicable at this point in time, and proceed to negate the law itself (or as Groucho Marx, that great philosopher would put it, "These are my principles. If you don't like them I have others!")

Apparently that's what happened to our wise King Solomon whose harem expanded in contradiction to a Biblical order that a king not take many wives. A self-assured Solomon looked at the Torah's reasoning ("Lest his heart be swayed [from following My ways])" and decided his heart would never sway, and simply continued his hobby of collecting spouses, thus breaking a direct Torah command.

Rashi, commenting on Brachot, advised his students "not to investigate laws, but simply say it is a decree from Above;" a stance that made many Torah scholars uncomfortable, ranging from Ibn Ezra who saw reason as "God's emissary," Raphael Norzi, the 16th century Italian moralist, writing in *Se'ah Soleth* ("Without reason there is no perfection of soul"); Shneur Zalman, of *Tanya* fame ("Virtue arising from reason is higher than virtue which is not founded on it"); and the formidable philosopher Saadia Gaon, in his *Emunos V'Deos* ("Wherein shall a man find complete repose, save in reason?")

Levi Yitzhak of Berdichev, the 18th century Chassidic giant, hedged his bets: yes, there are reasons but they are only known to the spiritual soul, not the physical intellect. The Gerer Rebbe (*Sfas Emes*) was convinced that understanding of mitzvos would come in due course, but only *after* their repeated performance.

The Rambam ("Reason is more to be trusted than the eye") disagreed: *mishpotim* were rational, he argued, from a human perspective; *chukkim* were rational from God's perspective; and in his *Guide to the Perplexed* elaborates that the lack of reasoning would drive many Jews into assuming that "God's actions are purposeless."

So what were the "reasons" for obscure commandments?

"These precepts have a cause," the Rambam responds, "but it

is not known to us." Why not? Because of "the deficiency of our knowledge or the weakness of our intellect."

The lesson? Assume nothing.

> *"I must be speeding," Rivkin says to himself when he sees a police car in his rear view mirror with its blinking red lights, "And hey, I can outrun this guy" — so he floors it.*
>
> *The two cars are racing down the highway, 60, 70, 80, 90 miles an hour...but when the speedometer passes 100, he gives up and pulls over to the curb.*
>
> *"Listen mister," the policeman barks at Rivkin, "If you can give me a good reason for your speeding, I'll let you go."*
>
> *"Well," says a quick-thinking Rivkin, "Three weeks ago my wife ran off with a police officer, so when I saw your flashing lights in my rear view mirror I thought you were that officer trying to give her back!"*

In fact, all mitzvos are ultimately "unfathomable decrees" designed to test the obedience of the Jews.

The reward "for a mitzva is a mitzva," was the tradition, despite an extensive literature known as *Ta'amei Mitzvos* (literally, "the tastes of the mitzvos") that attempts to "explain" the orders of Sinai. That is why this commandment is not called *Chukas Haparah*, the law of the red heifer, but is known as *Chukas Hatorah*, a law of the Torah, in order to demonstrate that the Torah's entire structure of heteronomous law (*halacha*, from the root *halach*, "to go"), is based on a higher understanding, one beyond man's ability to fathom.

When the Torah itself admits, "This commandment is not too wonderful [*nifles*] for you," it uses a Hebrew word (*nifles*) that is derived from the root *peleh*, a "miracle;" implying that some mitzvos are not rationale on the surface and their fidelity by rational, logical-thinking Jews is, miraculously, based purely on faith.

Does this suggest that Judaism disapproves of rational under-standing, or is anti-intellectual? No; in fact the Torah frowns on a belief system that requires leaving one's mind behind before entering.

The 12th century Spanish poet, Yehudah Halevi, known as the "Sweet Singer of Zion," and other great rabbinic philosophers be-lieved that if reason contradicts Torah, then the textual interpreta-tion is incorrect.

And since illiteracy was the enemy of Torah, its teachers ("your elders"), were responsible for the burden of *Torah le'am* in a joint venture with the father ("Ask your father, he will inform you.")

Originally those who explained the *edus*, *mishpot*, or *chok* through the generations were respected, unsalaried rabbis ("Just as I gave you the Torah *gratis*, so must you give the Torah without charge"), earning their livelihood from regular jobs (such as car-penters, shoemakers, blacksmiths).

> *The rabbi's Shabbos topic was the evils of television:*
> *"TV is an intrusion on the family, it's a waste, it steals away precious time that is best spent on other things, and it fills the mind with unkosher thoughts! I advise you to do what my family has done! We put ours away in the closet."*
> *"That's right," mumbles the rebbetzin, "And it gets aw-fully crowded in there."*

Who said, "I love work, but hate the rabbinate?"

None other than a first century rabbi of the Mishna (Shemaya). His was not an isolated voice.

"I have chosen the way of modesty [for] I hate the rabbinate," confided the 19th century scholar, Emden, in his *Megillas Sefer*. His German namesake, the formidable talmudist Yaakov Emden, writ-ing in his own *Edus B'yaakov* a century earlier, echoed his frustra-tion: "Blessed is He who has not made me a rabbi."

> *Rabbi Mittleman, a trainee slightly absent-minded rabbi, goes to a conference for the Humor Impaired, hoping to learn how to tell jokes to assist his Torah sermons. He sits transfixed as a cleric gets up and gives a dynamic opening, "My friends, I want you to know...the best years of my life were spent in the arms of a woman that wasn't my wife!"*
>
> *The room was shocked! Then the speaker added, with a smile, "And that woman was my mother!" — and the crowd burst into laughter as he went on to deliver the rest of his talk.*
>
> *Rabbi Mittleman is duly impressed, rehearses the joke for weeks and when he gets offered a pulpit position, is determined to open with the same effect.*
>
> *On his first Shabbos, he gets up, clears his throat, and begins..."The greatest years of my life were spent in the arms of another woman that was not my wife!"*
>
> *The kehilla sits up shocked, stunned into silence...having achieved his opening effect, Rabbi Mittleman desperately tries to remember the punch line, and finally blurts out, "...and I can't remember who she was!"*

In eastern Europe anti-rabbinic scorn was indiscriminate, poring forth from Chassidic masters (Nahman of Bratzlav, "It was hard for Satan alone to mislead the whole world, so he appointed prominent rabbis in different localities!"), to Misnagdishe giants (Israel Salanter, "A rabbi who they don't want to drive out of town isn't a rabbi; and a rabbi whom they actually drive out of town isn't a man!")

This is how the Chassidic rebbe from Ropcyce, Galicia (Naphtali Zevi Horowitz) came to the rabbinate: "At first I did not want to be a rabbi, for a rabbi has to flatter his flock, and I thought of being a tailor. Then I saw that a tailor has to flatter his customers, and so has a shoemaker, and a mikva-attendant; and I said to myself, "Where, then, is a rabbi worse off? And so I became a rabbi."

The rabbis of yore were known for their intellect, piety, personal qualities. But the times they were a'changing: in 1951 *Time Magazine* quotes the advice one rabbi (Schechter) gives another (Finkelstein): "Unless you can play baseball, you'll never get to be a rabbi in America!"

> "My d'var Torah at the dinner last night was a smash hit," bragged the notoriously egocentric young rabbi, "I had the audience glued in their seats."
> "Wonderful, wonderful," rejoined the older rav, "Clever of you to think of it."

This parsha is a continuation of the desolate theme of numbers, of dreams turned into nightmares, a focus on the darker side, on a seemingly endless capacity for evil and dark impulses, trapped in the shadows of the wastelands and desert wilderness.

The Torah tales are suddenly not so heroic but full of fear, envy, despair, jealousy, infidelity; of rage tinged with failure, dissension, conflict. In short: *We're On the Road Again!* as the American pop folkists would sing.

This is a tough time for the Jews: 38 years have gone by since the return of the scouts and the ominous shadow of the Angel of Death is again on the loose, slaughtering (the Bashanites) and stalking Moshe, Aaron, and Miriam.

The three siblings all die in the same year, ceasing as "middleman" to God; Miriam being the first to die (on Nisan 10th), followed by Aaron (four months later on *Rosh Chodesh Av*), with Moshe dying on the following 7th Adar.

Which of the three siblings does the "stiff-necked nation" (*am k'shei oref*) mourn the most?

The clue lies in the previous parsha, wherein the Torah juxtaposes Korach and Aaron as the exemplars of contentiousness and peacefulness, respectively.

Aaron is the one singled out for mass mourning, by all the "men and women" of the community. Why? The folk have a special affinity and strong bond for this Jewish leader who represented the entire nation in his service in the Sanctuary, praying constantly for their spiritual and physical well being; and, more pragmatically, because he pursued peace among them, fighting animosity, and restoring domestic harmony (*sholom bayis*) between spouses — even "legitimizing" the use of untruths and half-truths if it results in peace, harmony, unity (*achdus*).

Miriam, the Torah's only woman-Prophetess, dies suddenly in a vast, nondescript desert. Her death is immediate, unsuspecting, and so sparsely recorded that it takes up only half a verse ("Miriam died there and was buried there.")

There is no account of wailing, nor mourning: yet with her death dies a mystical spring, "Miriam's Well," a perpetual traveling source of water that sustained the people due to her merit.

> *A man is struck by a bus one day on a busy Manhattan street and as he lies dying on the sidewalk, he gasps, "A priest, please, will somebody get me a priest!"*
>
> *A cop checks the crowd, but there is no priest, no minister, no man of God of any kind but a little ol' Jewish man steps forward, and says, "Mr. Policeman, I'm not a priest, I'm not even a Catholic. But for fifty years now I'm living behind St. Elizabeth's Catholic Church on First Avenue, and every night I'm listening to the Catholic litany. So maybe I can be of some comfort to this poor dying man."*
>
> *The policeman agrees and brings the octogenarian Jew over to the dying man, hoping he can bring him some last-minute spiritual sustenance.*
>
> *The little ol' Jewish man kneels down, leans over the injured man, and begins in a solemn voice, "B-4. I-19. N-38. G-54. O-72...."*

The sudden absence of Miriam's well causes the irritable folk, whining for water in this "wretched place," to start a devastating chain-reaction of events that leads to Moshe's transgression and the death of his life's goal.

His anger is a sign that he is clearly fed up with the children of Israel, a band of ex-slaves who consistently seem blinded to their good fortunes. And this is precisely the point: Moshe can no longer lead them because he has now combined temper with contempt and disrespect; by substituting force for faith he can give them water but not dignity.

Obedience is thus a major theme of this parsha; the "service of God," is, according to the late iconoclast Yeshayahu Leibowitz, Israel's "modern prophet of fury," the *only* guiding law in Judaism, "irrespective of all human needs."

The Heavens sternly inform Moshe at the waters of Merivoh (the "waters of strife") the result of his insubordination: "therefore [*lochein*] you will not bring this congregation to the land."

> Two thieves break into a lawyer's office to rob his safe, but are interrupted when the attorney walks in unexpectedly.
> After a long scuffle, the two finally flee and run out the door.
> "It ain't so bad," one says to the other, "We got $25 between us."
> "Whatdoya mean! We had $100 before we broke in!"

Welcome to the perils of leadership!

Judah ben Ezekiel was right: "Leadership shortens life."

The dedicated Moshe's attack on a rock (*sela*) results from sheer rage, impatience, exasperation and frustration; a momentary lapse in the sanctity of his own mission. Both the Rambam, the great 12th century scholar, and the Ramban, a leading Torah scholar of the

Middle Ages, link Moshe's sudden misfortune to his angry use of ill-advised language. Moshe has just signed his own death warrant; a stunning punishment that our sages say proves how the power of the tongue can be abused. His slandering of the people as *hamordim* ("rebels"), a term that one Midrash links to the Greek word for "fools," while another Midrashic wordplay links *mordim* with *morim*, which means "teachers," implies a significant deficiency in the leadership of Moshe, the "teacher of teachers."

Torah scholars note the similarity between the Hebrew word for leader (*dabar*), its root verb (*dbr*) which means "to speak," and *midbar* which, although usually translated as "desert" actually means "place of the word."

> *A guy picks up the phone in a lawyer's office, and answers, "Schwartz, Schwartz, Schwartz and Schwartz."*
> *The caller asks, "Can I speak to Mr. Schwartz."*
> *"I'm sorry, he's on vacation."*
> *"Then let me talk to Mr. Schwartz."*
> *"He's on a big case, not available until next week."*
> *"Then let me talk to Mr. Schwartz."*
> *"He's playing golf today."*
> *"Okay, then, let me talk to Mr. Schwartz."*
> *"Speaking."*

The Prophet Motivated by Profit

An archaeologist was digging in the Negev Desert in Israel and came upon a casket containing a mummy. After examining it, he called the curator of a prestigious natural-history museum.

"I've just discovered a 3,000 year-old mummy of a man who died of heart failure!" the excited scientist exclaimed.

To which the curator replied, "Bring him in. We'll check it out."

A week later, the amazed curator called the archaeologist. "You were right about the mummy's age and cause of death. How in the world did you know?"

"Easy. There was a piece of paper in his hand that said, '10,000 Shekels on Goliath'."

This week's parsha, *Balak*, contains a fascinating psychological exchange between a king (after whom the parsha is named), and a well-known pagan prophet, Bilam ben Beor, "the magician," and must surely rank as one of the great interactions in the Torah.

The art of negotiation might have begun with Avraham and the Hittites but it reaches a new high when this parsha's intriguing gentile prophet plays hard to get.

What are they haggling over?

Balak, king of Moab and son of Zippor, together with his "elders" versed in "occult arts," have decided that it's too risky to fight the Jews who have just won stunning victories over their own mighty enemies (Sichon and Og.) So they adopt an unconventional military defense strategy and hire a mercenary, Bilam, a crooked and sly sorcerer and verbal "hit-man" to hex their enemies.

How does Bilam's powers actually work? We are not told.

> "Hey, mister!" ol' Mr. Tuttlebaum screams out to the magician from the back of the theater, "How'd you do that trick?"
>
> "My magic is secret," the magician yells back into the crowd, "If I tell you, I'd have to kill you."
>
> "Okay then," ol' Mr. Tuttlebaum replies, "Just tell my wife!"

The moment Bilam takes on the job to curse the Jews, he enters Jewish history as "Bilam the wicked (*Bilam Harasha*)," motivated more by profit than the prophet motive.

Jewish mystics homiletically link his name to *b'lo am*, which means "without people," suggesting that he has deprived himself of a place amongst the community in Heaven (*olom habo*). And yet his supernatural prowess is legendary, and even the Midrash compares his extraordinary level of clarity of prophecy to Moshe himself.

But unlike Moshe, Bilam's unique ability lies in causing the downfall of nations via a missile barrage of verbal curses.

This time the trick falls short: the unrefined and arrogant one stupidly ignores an explicit order from God ("Do not curse the nation, for they are a blessed nation"), and ends up in a foiled plot that causes him, *thrice*, to involuntarily bless, rather than curse, his client's foe.

The tremendously haughty (*gayva*) guy simply cannot help himself. Convinced that he is a *yodea daas elyon* (one who knows the mind of God), Bilam recklessly lets loose with the words that will desert him; after the Torah ridicules his sublime poetry by juxtaposing it with the image of a talking donkey.

A dog sees a sign in a store window: "HELP WANTED. Must be able to type, use a computer, and be bilingual." He goes inside, wags his tail at the receptionist, and points to the sign. The office manager laughs, "I can't hire you. You have to be able to type."

So the dog jumps up on the chair, leans over the type-writer and punches out a perfect letter.

The manager is stunned, and stutters, "Sorry, you also have to be good with a computer." So the dog turns around to the computer, and executes a perfect program.

"Look," the dumb-founded manager mumbles, "You're obviously a very intelligent dog but I need someone bilingual."

The determined dog looks up at the manager, and goes, "Meow."

"Who practices magic will be harassed by magic," warns Levi, a 3rd century Palestinian *Amora*; *Sefer Hasidim* agrees, "His end will come to no good."

Nahman ben Isaac was sarcastic, "Sure the magician mumbles, but knows not what he mumbles;" and the Rambam was outright hostile to amulet-writers, calling them "authors of nonsense" and dismissing Jews who do such things as put a "Torah or tefillin in a cradle to induce a baby to sleep."

Judaism is adamantly against false prophets, which is why the parsha ends succinctly and specifically: "There is no sorcery for Yaacov nor magic for Israel!"

Yankie is an amateur astrologer who once prophesies to his king that his favorite concubine would soon die.... and sure enough, the woman dies.

The king is outraged, certain that the prophecy was responsible for her death, so he commands him, "Tell me Yankie! When will you die!"

The quick thinking Yankie realizes that the king is ◗

> *planning to kill him immediately, no matter what answer he gives, so he replies, "I do not know when I will die, but I do know that whenever I die, the king will die three days later."*

The era of prophecy is long gone (the last prophet being Malachi, after the return of the exiles from Babylonia), which is why our sages warn against Bilam-type attempts that even when proved correct are not automatically true prophecy.

Yet the Torah is keenly aware of human nature, and the desire to believe in mans ability to control the supernatural as a psychological need to comprehend the incomprehensible.

> *"Milty," Mrs. Pitzel nags her husband to go with her to a séance parlor, "Madame Freda is great! A real gypsy who brings the voices of the dead from the other world. Last week I talked with my mother, may she rest in peace. Milty, for $20 you can talk to your zayde who you miss so much!"*
>
> *Milton soon finds himself sitting at a green table under a bright colored light, holding hands with the persons on either side of him. Madame Freda, her eyes lost in trance, starts moving her hands over a crystal ball, mumbling, "Come, come…I hear you, I hear you…who is that?…Mr. Pitzel! Milton Pitzel's zayde!?"*
>
> *"Grampa?" Milty whispers, "Zayde? Is that you?"*
>
> *"Ah, Milteleh," a thin voice quavers.*
>
> *"Yes! Yes!" cries an emotional Milty, "This is your Milty! Zayde, are you happy in the other world?"*
>
> *"Milteleh, I am in bliss. With your bubba together, we laugh, we sing, we gaze upon the shining face of the Lord!"*
>
> *A dozen more questions did Milty ask of his zayde, and each question did his zayde answer, until, "Milteleh, I have to go now, the angels are a'calling me."*
>
> *"Just one more question, please."*
>
> *"Ask, ask, my grandson."*
>
> *"Zayde, when did you learn to speak English?"*

How ironic: Bilam's greatest blessing (*Ma tovu ohalecha Yaakov*, "How goodly are your tents, Yaakov!") turns out to be a direct negation of his own sordid will.

And more: his words powerfully echo throughout Jewish history and deep into our liturgy, becoming the very first words recited when entering a synagogue, "How goodly are your tents, Yaakov, your dwellings, Israel;" an acknowledgment from a gentile that the tents ("Houses of Torah study") reflect the powerhouse of the Jewish spirit, prior to the dwellings ("House of Prayer.")

Yet even in defeat, incredibly, Bilam's power for prophecy remains flawless and undiminished, as the parsha ends with his uncanny accurate description of what to expect from the Jews in the future; a blueprint that no other *navi* (except for Moshe in parsha *Ha'azinu*) has declared.

Bilam has failed, but still, in the hopes of getting paid, he gives Balak some advice: the way to break the spirit of the Jewish folk is to entice the men with Moabite women and tell the women not to submit until the men bow down to an idol. Balak does exactly that: and the result is another catastrophe for the children of Israel.

Ancient digs have found Hebrew inscriptions from that era verifying the pagan attraction; that in the custom of Jews tacking on God's name (*Yah*) to their own names, some imitated the gentiles (eg: the latter half of Hannibal's name is a nod to the false Canaanite god of Baal). And so we are startled to discover Saul naming his son *Ishba'al*, "Man of Baal," and his grandson *Merivbaa'al*, "Champion of Ba'al." Samuel was not pleased: and switched their names to *Ishboshes* and *Mefiboshes*, "Men of Shame."

> *After watching the Jew marrying a forbidden Moabite woman, one little girl turns to another, "Say, how come the bride is all dressed in white?"* ▶

> "Because white is the color of happiness, and today is
> the happiest day of her life."
> "Oh," she thinks as she stares at the couple, "Then how
> come the groom's all dressed in black?"

The saintly Rabbi Israel Meir Kagan (*Chofetz Chaim*) was intrigued by the fact that this parsha omits the traditional breaks in the Torah text, some at the end (*p'sucha*) and some in the middle (*s'tumah*) of a line. Yet here there are none from the time Balak commissions Bilam until the end of the prophet's prophesy. The absence of such breaks, which symbolize moments of reflection and promote a moral character that the Midrash claims helped broaden the vision of the Hebrew prophets, indicate that the humble "think-before-one-speaks" approach was something Bilam lacked. This ties into the legend that Bilam, one of seven non-Israelite prophets, had only one eye, a defect that robs a person of the perspective necessary to assess a situation properly.

Excessive negativity is referred to as the "evil eye," not the evil eyes; and it is from here that the Yiddishists retrieve the expression, *Kein einahora,* the wish that no "evil eye" should curse nor affect them.

The belief that looks can kill was widespread in the Talmud ("He cast his eye on him and he died"), and after visiting a cemetery Rav concluded that "ninety-nine die through an evil eye for each one who dies from natural causes."

The rabbis of Pirkei Avos then took this advice, and reversed it, "Don't be wicked (even in your) own eyes;" i.e. — too much self criticism is unhealthy.

The Mishna's Rabbi Joshua saw the "evil eye" not as an evil force but as a metaphor for human selfishness or envy, and promoted its opposite, *ayin tovah,* a "good eye," which he interpreted as good will, generosity, or simply, as always, seeing the best, not the worst, in other Jews....

> Moe and Lenny are strolling home from shul one Shabbos morning when suddenly a cab speeds past, and they see their friend Irving running frantically behind it, flailing his arms wildly.
>
> "Look at that!" cries out Lenny, "Irving is a Shabbos violator! I can't believe it! Look at him running for that taxi."
>
> "Wait a minute," Moe replies, "remember what the Rebbe taught us, the need to judge others favorably? I'll bet there are hundreds of reasons for Irving's behavior."
>
> "Oh yeah, like what?"
>
> "Well, maybe he's sick and needs to go to the hospital?"
>
> "Come on! He was running 60 miles an hour after that cab — he's healthier than Arnold Schwarzenegger."
>
> "Well, maybe his wife's having a baby?"
>
> "She had one last week!"
>
> "Well, maybe he needs to visit her in the hospital?"
>
> "She's home already!"
>
> "Well, maybe he's running to the hospital to get a doctor?"
>
> "He's a doctor!"
>
> "Well, maybe he needs supplies from the hospital?"
>
> "The hospital is a three minute walk, and in the opposite direction!"
>
> "Well, maybe he simply forgot that it's Shabbos!"
>
> "Forgotten Shabbos! That's impossible! Did you see his tie? It was his expensive paisley beige 100% silk Giovani one from Italy! He never wears it during the week!"
>
> "Wow, you're really observant! I didn't even notice he was wearing a tie."
>
> "How could you not notice? Didn't you see it caught in the back fender of the taxi?"

PINCHOS
Where There's a Will, There's a Relative

There are a slew of contradictory Midrashim telling us to act, or not to act, after the namesake of this week's parsha, *Pinchos*, a feisty Jew whose attitude was one of *b'ruach hakodesh*, fearless self-sacrifice.

The embarrassment surrounding Pinchos extends to his genealogy: his lineage is traced to his grandfather (Aaron) at a time when the general rule was to mention only the father's name. Why? Because Pinchos' first appearance in the Torah is tainted, named as the son of a daughter of Putiel, a descendent of Yisro, a righteous convert yet one who began his career "fattening calves to offer to idols (*shepitem agalim l'avoda zara*)."

This caused Pinchos' primary lineage to be derided; thus the Torah skips over this gene pool and takes him straight back to the father of all yichus, Aaron the High Priest, suggesting that this was Pinchos' true ethical inheritance.

> *"Well, well," says the local lawman, who has a reputation of being hostile to Jews, "So you have a dead mule on your hands. I thought you rabbis take care of the dead?"*
> *"Of course we do," relies the rav, "but it is customary to first get in touch with their relatives."*

Pinchos appears at the end of last week's parsha as a reluctant zealot and "upright" spear-throwing assassin of Zimri, a "brazen" blue-blooded son of Salu, chief of a Simeonite tribe and Moshe's great-nephew. Zimri's crime? Not just that he cohorts with Cozbi, his Midianite mistress, but that he does so with no *charpa un busha* (shame), "in the sight of the whole community."

Pinchos' spear does more than commit double homicide: it brings an end to the tragedy of Baal Pe'or, a staggering and decimating plague of punishment that destroys 20,000 sexual immoral Jews for tarnishing their lineage in their reckless pursuit of Moabite and Midianite women, accompanied by their unforgivable and calamitous flirtation with false gods.

> *One Israelite complains that it's not working out between him and his Midianite girlfriend, so the doctor advises him, "You want to improve your affair? Be fit! Get some exercise! Run ten miles a day!"*
> *Two weeks later, he calls for an update, "Say, how's your relationship going since you started running?"*
> *"Great! I'm 140 miles away already!"*

Not surprisingly, the theme in this week's Haftarah is more of the same: zealotry and zeal, but this time with Elijah, who Rashi, the preeminent medieval Torah commentator, compares to Pinchos.

Zealots is a Greek term (*zelotes*), itself a translation of the Hebrew *kana'im* which is derived from the verb *kanei*, "to be jealous." In God's vocabulary, being "zealous for My sake" (*b'kano es kin'asi*) was a badge of honor.

The Torah uses near-identical words (*b'kano, kinasi, b'kinasi*) to describe the circumstances surrounding Elijah and Pinchos, terms suggestive of an "impassioned jealousy," fueled by an obsessive anger at those who trample over a God who ascribes the same intense emotions (jealousy, envy, passion, rage) to Himself.

Yet this is one of the few characteristics of God that Jews are not encouraged to emulate. The mysterious Elijah, our annual Pesach guest and the herald of the Messiah, acts in a similar Pinchos-style burst of genuine ardor, fervently killing hundreds of idolatrous prophets, a bloodshed that forces him to run for his life from an angry Queen Jezebel.

The contrast is startling: Pinchos, despite the fact that zealotry was not a positive trait, is exonerated and even *rewarded* for homicide with a covenant of peace and everlasting priesthood; whereas the enigmatic prophet is forced to hide in wilderness caves for his multiple manslaughters.

This parsha also discusses the final and mandatory all-male census at the border of Moab near Jericho, but this time, it is not a census for war but a count of ancestral tribes by family. Why? To divide the estates in the holy land in accordance to birthright.

We are introduced to the laws of inheritance (in Hebrew *yerusha*, akin to *morasha*, "heritage," God's term that describes both the Torah and the land of Israel), and discover that this is much more than a method of asset redistribution.

In a clever play on words, the Mishna's Gamliel III advised his colleagues, "Make His will yours, so that He make your will His" — a metaphysical power that even the fictional *Mendele*, in *Biyemei Haraash*, respects: "When God wills it; even a broom can shoot!" (to which the Yiddish cynics warn: "Who comes for the inheritance is often made to pay for the funeral!")

"Hey, what's up?" Danny asks his friend Sammy who's almost on the verge of tears.

"Don't ask! Three weeks ago, a distant uncle died and left me $49,000 dollars."

"So? That's not bad."

"Wait, there's more! Two weeks ago, a cousin I never knew kicked the bucket and left me $85,000 dollars."

"Wow, sounds like you should be grateful."

"No, no!," Sammy chokes up, "and last week my great aunt passed away, and I inherited nearly a quarter of a million."

"So how come you look so glum!?"

"This week? Nothing!"

Last wills are always unpredictable to the relatives: "And to my wife who loved my cheery smile, I leave my dentures;" or the wealthy guy whose will began, "Being of sound mind and body I spent all my money."

The first Jew to establish an ethical will is Yaacov, who is also the first Jew in the Torah who is ill before dying and who, according to a startling Midrash, is so at his own request. Why? In order to set his affairs in order by giving testament to his sons.

Yaacov's example sets the tone for the last wills of future Torah personalities: they leave not riches nor wealth, but the philosophy of ethics, morality, the ways of the world.

When Spanish-born Moshe ben Nachman (*Ramban*), a classic Medieval commentator on the Torah, died, he advises his children how to pray ("Put all worldly matters from your mind, think before you utter the prayer"); when Yehudah ibn Tibbon died he passed on to his children his view on *seforim* ("Make bookshelves your pleasure gardens; gather their fruit, pluck their roses and take their spices and myrrh"); when the Vilna Gaon faced death, he stressed education ("teach your children pleasantly so they will become anxious to learn").

> *Eddie is getting on in years and develops a serious hearing problem, so his doctor gives him a set of hearing aids, which allow him to hear perfectly. A few months later Eddie returns for a routine check, and thanks the doctor.*
>
> *"You're welcome, I'm sure your wife and daughters are happy you can hear again."*
>
> *"Oh, I haven't told them yet. I just sit around and listen to the conversations I used to miss. I've now changed my will three times!"*

Five determined daughters of Tzelafchad (who had no sons) "justly" protest that they are as deserving as the men to receive their father's inheritance (*achuza*) in the land of Israel.

Poor Tzelafchad: this Biblical character is famous only because of the tenacity of his daughters; and so the texts try to put a human face to him. Moshe is assured that Tzelafchad was a respectable guy who took no part in Korach's revolt; the Talmud gives him credit for not being one of those who "murmured" about the hardships of the wilderness, and for not heeding the pessimistic report of the spies.

And yet Ibn Ezra suggests that Tzelafchad's failure to have any sons was a result of sin. Rabbi Akiva posits that he was the man seen gathering wood on Shabbos. Rabbi Yehudah ben B'seira links his name with *tzel pachad*, "in the shadow of fear," in that he was terrified that all his daughters would remain unwed spinsters (they were all over 40 when the inheritance question was settled and they eventually married their cousins).

The daughters' presentation is resolute, emotional, historic: they recall the disappointment of Rachel and Leah who were exploited ("Have we still a share [*chelek v'nachala*] in the inheritance of our father's house?") and disinherited by their vengeful father (Lavan) when they left his homestead for Canaan.

Moshe is impressed and swayed by their determination to

match their will with the will of God, and the parsha mentions them by name (Machlah, Noa, Choglah, Milkah, Tirtzah) no less than four times, in a Torah that often leaves women nameless.

The result?

The Forceful Female Five become the only women named in the new census, winning not just the right to an inheritance, but to the official recorded tribal and familial lineage. And more: they solidify the power of Jewish women, causing Rabbi Nathan to pen in his Sifre writings, "Better the might of women than the might of men" — especially evident in debate and dissent.

> *In the midst of a bitter family squabble, the wife turns to her husband, and yells, "You know, I'm the only woman alive who would put up with you."*
> *"I'll have you know," he shouts back, "that hundreds of women went out with me in my bachelor days."*
> *"Yes, I can understand why the large turn-over!"*

It is here in this parsha that the human tragedy of Moshe occurs: in a scene where the tension is palpable, God orders the man who had just spent 38 frustrating years as the liberator of the Jews to go up "the heights of Mt. Abarim" from where he can view the land promised to his people, a land so close but yet so far, the land across the Jordan that he will never set foot on.

And worse: he is told that his death is pending, and given a last peek at an anonymous grave in the mountain ranges of Pisgah, a solitary place (*hamakom*) where he dies alone, in God's presence.

How does Moshe respond?

In typical deeply heroic fashion: with dignity and concern about others, asking God not to leave the folk leaderless ("Let God appoint a man for the community, lest it be like sheep with no shepherd"); a plea that singles out Joshua as the next leader of the

Jews, and a special blessing from his predecessor, *Chazak ve'amatz*, "Be strong and courageous;" another example of humility when passing the torch of leadership.

Yet there are dozens of Midrashim that describe a totally opposite Moshe, a profoundly human man, still fully vigorous at 120 and overwhelmingly eager to enter *Eretz Yisroel*; a man who does not solemnly accept his own mortality but who cries out in his vulnerable despair.

He demands justice ("Where is my payment for the 40 years during which I labored for the sake of Your children?"), makes demands ("I will not budge from here until You void that decree"), and pleads ("Consider how much I had to bear for the sake of Israel, I suffered with them, shall I not then take part in their rejoicing?") — all to no avail.

> *A devoted wife of 50 years is sitting day and night by her husband's hospital bed, as he slips in and out of a coma. In a rare moment, he opens his eyes, and beckons her to come closer.*
>
> *"You know, Sizelle," he whispers, "I've been thinking. You've been with me through all the bad times. When I got fired, you were there to support me. When my business failed, you were there. When I got mugged, you were by my side. When we lost the house in foreclosure, you gave me support. When my health started to fail, you were still there, by my side. Sizelle, you know what?"*
>
> *"What, my dear?"*
>
> *"I think you bring me bad luck."*

MATTOS/MAASEH
Green Belts and Open Spaces

> *"Raise your right hand, please," the clerk asks ol' Mrs. Guttesman applying for a passport, "You must take the loyalty oath first."*
>
> *So the little ol' Jewish woman raises her shaking right hand, and the man begins, "Do you swear and make an oath to defend the constitution of the United States against all its enemies, domestic or foreign?"*
>
> *"Uhhh," she stutters, her face paling and her voice trembling, "All by myself?"*

We approach the end reeling from a pendulum of mood swings; a dizzying array of unbecoming conduct, mutinous minds, countless complaints, rebelliousness rumbles.

The word *Mattos* describes the heads of the twelve tribes to whom Moshe addresses the topic of vows and obligations. What's the difference between them? The first is a promise to do something, the latter a promise not to do something.

What about a vow (*neder*) and an oath (*shevuah*); are they the same? No: the former changes the status of an object (eg: if one "vows" not to watch TV, it has made TV a forbidden object), the latter places an obligation on the person (eg: if one "vows" to lose weight, this is an obligation on the person, and leaves the status of food unchanged).

All Torah sages are unanimous on this issue: Rabbi Yehuda Liwa ben Betzalel (*Maharal*), one of Europe's most seminal figures of Jewish thought, would explain the significance of vows and oaths by elucidating the famous verse against *loshon horo* (slander), "Life and death are in the power of the tongue."

The Chofetz Chaim, the saintly 20th century leader of world Jewry, noted that four Torah personalities (Avraham's servant Eliezer, Caleb, Saul and Jephthah) begin their careers with an oath, implying how vital it was for the Jew to properly direct his speech; while Rabbi Samson Raphael Hirsch, the great 19th century leader of German Jewry, says that God specifically directs the mitzvot of vows to the tribal heads (*rashei hamatos*), for only via the moral vehicle of befitting speech could they become creative "partners of God."

> The plaintiff's lawyer calls up ol' Mrs. Winkler to the stand, swears her in and asks, "Miss, could you please repeat the slanderous statements you heard, exactly as you heard them."
>
> "Oh dear no, they are unfit for any respectable, honorable, decent person to hear."
>
> "Okay, then," says the attorney, "just whisper them to the judge."

Since there are more Torah portions than Sabbaths, some parshas are combined into a "double portion," in order that the entire Torah can be completed annually. This week is one of those times.

The second title, *Maaseh*, means "journeys," a generic term for the entire travelogue sequence of Israel's exit from Egypt ("God desired that the journeys of Israel be recorded to tell of the merit of Israel.")

Out of this detailed account of borders comes an ethical gem with amazing modern relevance: the origin of a green belt, a mandatory "open land round the cities." Rashi describes its purpose: "to beautify" the cities, to provide air and space, greenery and foliage, flowers and playgrounds.

A Midrash takes it even further; motivated by Koheles ("Consider the work of God") and returns to the beginning when God leads

Adam around the garden, warning him, "See how beautiful and praiseworthy are My works. They have all been created for your sake; be careful that you do not spoil or destroy My world."

"You know tata," little Joey asks his father after a few weeks at cheder, "there's somethin' I just can't figure out."

"What's that, Joey?"

"Well, I learned in the Torah that the children of Israel escaped from them 'gyptians, and the children of Israel crossed the Red Sea, right?"

"Right."

"An' the children of Israel beat up the Philistines, right?"

"Er, right."

"An' the children of Israel built the Temple, right?"

"Yes, my son."

"An' then later, the children of Israel fought the Romans an' the children of Israel wuz always doin' somethin' important, right?"

"That's right, so what's your question?"

"Well, what I wanna know is this. What wuz the grown-ups doin' all that time?"

This parsha wishes to sear ancestral "places" into our collective memory, starting from a mountain of covenant (Sinai), through a myriad of middle places where an ungrateful folk quarrel, protest, and wish they had never left Egypt ("where life was so wonderful") — settling down in a place they finally call home, the long-promised holy land.

The question is obvious: Why?

What's the purpose of chronicling, in precise diary-style detail, a desert itinerary of 42 place names, many of whom (Rithmah, Rimmon-perez, etc) are not only now buried in historic obscurity, but never reappear in the Torah until now.

Is there any religious relevance? Yes.

The clue lies in the interpretive device known as *notarikon*, where Torah words are read as acronyms.

Our ancestors, sharing history and destiny, obviously knew what these places represented, and the Torah assumed that their names alone would be sufficient for future generations to also know what took place there. Or as Julius Gordon puts it: "Traveling is either an experience we shall always remember; or an experience which, alas, we shall never forget!"

But memory fades, and names become just that, names, leaving us in the dark as to what happened to our folk when they stopped off at these places. And more: the cataloguing itself is repetitive (each place is mentioned twice) and seems so inconsequential, dull, tedious, awkward ("from Rameses to Sukkot, from Sukkot to Etam, back to Pi Hachirot, then to Marah and eventually to the east of the Jordan...")

The encampments vary from a stay of less than 24 hours to days, months and even years (the most common being a two-year stop); 14 occur within the first year after the Exodus; another 8 take place after the death of Aaron on Mount Hor, in the final year before entering the promised land; 20 "journeys" fall within the intervening 38 years.

Jewish history may be, as Johann Gottfried Herder, 18th century German author describes, "the greatest poem of all time;" but it is also a history of movement, with forced migrations tragically being *the* fundamental Jewish experience along the long and winding road towards redemption. French publicist Bloy, in his admiring *Le Salut par les Juifs*, writes that Jewish history "obstructs the history of mankind as a dam obstructs a river." Why? "In order to raise its level." This is the underlying theme behind the parsha: whether a Jew on the move is moving not like Yonah, who is trying to escape from God, but as a real Jew, equipped with all the customs associated with the armory of *tefillas haderech* (blessings for the road.)

On this road to redemption, the Jew cries out three times daily in the prayerful *Shemonei Esrei*, "Redeem us speedily!"...but *whoa*, not too fast, warns a Midrash: "Israel's redemption is like a harvest — if a field is reaped too early, even its straw is no good. It is like a vineyard — if the grapes are picked at the right time, even the vinegar is good. It is like a woman with child — if born prematurely, a baby is not even viable." That is why this double parsha always coincides with the Three Weeks, the Jewish calendar's slow pace of the history of Jewish suffering, anchored by the exiles from destroyed Temples.

Jeremiah picks up the theme of this parsha of choice and consequence, reward and punishment in the Haftarahs of *Mattos-Maaseh,* which Rabbi J. H. Hertz calls the "Haftarahs of Rebuke," the first of three that precede the ninth of Av (Tisha B'Av). In these Haftarahs, the young 20-year-old prophet Jeremiah witnesses the reigns of the last three kings of Judah (Yoshiah, Yehoyakim, Tzedkiahu), only to end up leading the Jews into Babylonian exile.

Why does the Torah delineate that the Jews go from "here to there" and "there to here," but never mentions any arrival?

Some scholars claim its purpose is to show that the Jews were in it for the long haul.

As usual the Midrash minces no words, "Travel is hard on the clothes, person, and purse;" to Benjamin Disraeli, 19th century English prime minister and novelist, "Travel taught toleration."

Rabbi S. R. Hirsch sees not one long physical sojourn but many smaller spiritual ones, each stop recorded because it represented progression of destiny, not destination; Rashi leans heavily on a Midrashic parable wherein each physical-emotional-spiritual stop of a difficult journey that ends in success contains valuable lessons; Italian Rabbi Ovadia Seforno saw the detailed chronology as a show of the strength of Jewish faith in that they followed day clouds and night pillars, with no place ever to call home, never questioning, even when it made no sense to get up and leave.

The Ramban's humility allows him to admit that he simply doesn't know, that God's reasoning is "[an] esoteric secret." And the Rambam? The Spanish sage frowns on the term "wanderings" (which implies being lost), and prefers the Torah's stop and start terminology of "travels and journeys." Why? Because it implies a sojourn that is not disorientated nor rambling, but has specific meaning and direction.

Others claim that the purpose of naming each way station is to show future generations the level of God's compassion in His multi-year exercise of providing manna and water.

Simi the cat dies and goes to Heaven, and is greeted by God Himself, "Say, you've been a good cat all these years. Anything you desire is yours, all you have to do is ask!"

"Well, you know, I lived my whole life with a poor family and had to sleep on hardwood floors."

"Say no more," interjects God, and instantly, a fluffy pillow appears.

A few days later, six mice arrive in Heaven, and are also personally greeted by God who makes them the same offer.

"Well, you know, all our lives we've had to run from place to place. We've been chased by cats and dogs, and even women with brooms. If we could only have a pair of roller skates, we wouldn't have to run anymore."

"Say no more," interjects God, and instantly, each mouse is fitted with a beautiful pair of tiny roller skates.

About a week later, God checks in on the cat and finds him happily stretched out on his new pillow, "Hey Simi, are you happy here?"

"Oh God yes," the cat yawns and stretches, "I've never been happier in my life...and those Meals-on-Wheels you've been sending over are the best!"

This ends the Book of Numbers, the fourth book of the Torah when everyone rises and says, *Chazak, chazak, v'nitchazek*, "Be strong, be strong, and let us be strengthened!" — a roar of encouragement to continue on to Deuteronomy, the next book of the Torah.

Why repeat the word *chazak* three times?

To symbolize the past, present and future.

D'varim

(DEUTERONOMY)

Welcome to *déjà vu* time. In its original Hebrew, Deuteronomy, a Greek word which means "second law," was *Devarim* ("words"), lifted from *Eleh hadevarim* [words] *asher diber Moshe*, "These are the words that Moshe addressed to all Israel."

Midrashically known as *Mishneh Torah*, it means the Second (as in "repeated") Torah, because it is a recapitulation of the previous four Books of Torah — but not exactly: a few new mitzva innovations wind their way throughout its eleven chapters divided into three parts (rebuke, *mitzvot*, covenant). Rabbi Eliyahu, the 18th-century Vilna Gaon whose Torah hobby was structure-by-numerology, paired these three sections to the three central Books of the Torah, excluding *Bereishis* and *D'varim* as the "introductory" and "summary" sections.

The linkage was easy: not only do the opening words of Deuteronomy, *Eleh hadevarim* ("These are the things") correspond to Exodus' opening, *Ve'eleh shemos* ("These are the names"), but its second and third sections begin with the words *vayikra* and *va'yedaber*; the former an obvious match to *Sefer Vayikra* (Leviticus) and the latter coterminous to *Bamidbar* (Numbers), "in the desert."

Déjà Vu

"Honey," says Mona to her husband, "Where would you like to be buried."
"I don't know, dear," he replies, "Why don't you just surprise me?"

The rabbis of the Talmud generally frown upon seeking explanations (*semichut*) for Torah juxtapositions (or as Yogi Berry would put it, "The future ain't what it used to be!"), but they made an exception for Deuteronomy's complex order in search of new Halachic insights.

This may seem like God's *Book of Second Chances*, but it is far from being a carbon copy. It is a farewell message; a summing up of 40 years of leadership and teaching that begins with a grand introduction, "These are the words [*devarim*] which Moshe spoke to all Israel," and then switches to a monologue delivered by Moshe in the first person.

The Midrash includes Moshe himself in *all* Israel; directing his criticism not just to the folk, but to himself first, before rebuking others. But the question is obvious: Who's speaking? God or Moshe?

The Zohar, the magnum opus of Torah mysticism, has a neat answer: the Heavens are communicating via the mouth of Moshe, a type of Divine ventriloquism.

Moshe's mood is positive *and* negative; a recipe of encouragement and scolding from a leader who is about to step down from office. His is a fascinatingly long strand of rhetoric from *the* leader on leadership: *Eicha esa levadi*, "How can I alone carry your contentiousness, burdens and quarrels?"

The choice of *levadi*, "alone," is directly linked to the Tisha B'av cry of *Eicha esa levadi*, "How can I alone carry?"

To lead is a burden too great for one man to bear, Moshe warns, in his demand for judicial teamwork and team players endowed with the right stuff: wisdom, understanding, and being "full of knowledge."

Yet in his search to "appoint" (*havu lachem*) qualified successors, Moshe falls incredibly short: within the entire camp of Israel he can only find Jews with two (wisdom and knowledge) of the three necessary qualifications, "understanding" is thus the hardest character trait of them all.

What's the difference between being wise and being understanding?

The former requires wisdom and deep knowledge of *all* things; the latter requires wisdom and deep knowledge of only *one* thing: other people.

Torah linguists, trying to explain why the whole locution and tone of this final book of Torah is different, point to the etymology of the Hebrew noun *devir*, which is derived from the verb *daber* ("to speak").

The saintly Rabbi Michoel Ber Weissmandel, in an attempt to "prove" that Moshe's rebukes and God's deuteronomic curses were in fact blessings in disguise, once counted 613 letters from the letter *beis* in the word *devarim* to arrive at the letter *reish*. He then counted the same interval again to arrive at *chof*, then again to the letter *hei*, finally spelling out the word *brocho* (blessing).

In other words: those who accept these "words" (*devarim*) of admonition by showing fidelity to the 613 mitzvos would receive a blessing (*brocho*) rather than a curse.

In front of Moshe stands a mixed multitude, the sons and daughters of a generation of wilderness wanderers who, as an emerging *am segulah* ("treasured people"), are finally about to enter the promised land. Segulah is derived from the Latin *seligere* whose root meaning is "choice;" in Aramaic it means, "that which is pre-ferred." And for 4,000 years, Jews have upheld this belief: that they are God's elect, the "apple of His eye."

Rashi links the word to royalty, as in *segulas melachim*, "trea-sures of kings;" while Abraham Ibn Ezra, a Jew who exerted great influence on both the Rambam and Ramban, interprets *segulah* as a "desired, honored" *a priori* object that can never be duplicated.

And yet the Rambam instinctively didn't like the term Chosen People. Why not? The 12th century sage from Spain thought "cho-sen" smacked too much of a religious chauvinism that hinted at inherited biological differences between Jews and gentiles (*goyim*); divisions which didn't exist.

The parents are worried. Martin, their 10-year-old son is failing in math. Like all good Jewish parents, they try everything from tutors to hypnosis; but to no avail. Finally, at their wit's end, they take him out of yeshiva and put him in a private Catholic school.

At the end of his first day, Martin comes running home straight to his room, takes out his text books, and crams away at his homework for several hours, emerging only for a quick snack. This feverish behavior goes on for a few weeks until one day he comes home with his first report card and a large 'A' for math.

"Tell me son," his amazed father asks, "was it the nuns that did it?"

"No."

"Was it the one-on-one tutoring? The peer-mentoring?"

"No."

"The textbooks? The teachers? The curriculum?"

"No."

"What then?"

"Well dad, on that first day, when I walked in and saw that guy nailed up on the wall to a plus sign, I knew they meant business!"

Moshe delivers his farewell elocution *b'eiver ha'yarden,* from "the other [Israelite] side of the Jordan," an obvious geographic complication (since Moshe *never* crosses the Jordan) that caused great theological headaches for Abraham Ibn Ezra, the 12th century Spanish scholar whose Torah authority at the time was second only to that of Rashi.

His conclusion? That this verse contains such a colossal "secret" as to turn "the wise to silence."

> Izzie is planning a vacation and calls a seaside hotel to ask its location.
> "We're only a stone's throw away from the beach," says the cheery operator.
> "But how will I recognize it?"
> "Easy. We're the one with all the broken windows."

The "words" of Moshe are crystal clear and extra-sensitive, expressive and moving, being the dramatic opening salvo of a touching pre-death farewell speech, a resolute discourse intended to prepare the nascent Jewish nation for a new beginning in a soon-to-be conquered Eretz Yisroel.

The Deuteronomic irony is apparent: not once is there even a hint of any speech defect from the same man whose first response to God's free-the-slaves order was, "I am not a man of words."

The makeover of Moshe is startling: a stuttering "slow of speech" Jew from the book of Exodus now appears 40 years later as a master orator, the people's eloquent *poet laureate.* Perhaps the act of passing the scepter of leadership to Joshua is medicinally therapeutic? The leader of Israel can now stand on a stress-free platform, relieved from the pressured burdens of future responsibility.

Poised at the end of his career, Moshe speaks freely, gracefully, comfortably, turning words of personal wisdom, nostalgia and prophecy into a full mosaic of reflective sentences, paragraphs and chapters.

> *Shmuli the livestock vendor decides to name one of his prize bulls Caesar at a time when Caesar's name was being popularized everywhere.*
>
> *When the time came to ship the bull to a buyer, Shmuli instructed his wife Itti to take the animal, and put it on a boat over the river to the caravan station.*
>
> *But when Itti got to the river, she was distracted and let the bull loose to feed on the lush waterside grass; which attracted her husband's irate warning, "We came to ferry Caesar, not to graze him!"*

And the children of Israel listen attentively, mesmerized by the climactic tension, driven to reflection, concern, contrition. This is not surprising: in fact, it's common knowledge that people tend to give more attention to one who is dying, as though the grasping of the lessons of life are at their peak when the Angel of Death is hovering. Thus Moshe refuses to die without reinforcing, by way of repetition, what is expected of his folk and flock. The very temperament of Moshe's last verbal will-and-testament, as with any one approaching death, accelerates, in a compelling desire to achieve "closure" with ones life.

> *"I'm afraid I have some very bad news. You're dying, and you don't have much time left."*
>
> *"Oh no, that's terrible!," cries a distraught Sammy, "How long have I got?"*
>
> *"Ten...," the doctor says sadly.*
>
> *"Ten?" a crying Sammy screams. "Ten what? Months? Weeks? What?!"*
>
> *"Nine, eight..."*

With the hover of certain death (*maves*) in the air, the message of Moshe reiterates a timeless truth: that when Jews die they leave behind all they have and take with them all they are.

> *Freddie is accidentally hit by a car one morning and as he lies in the road, a priest suddenly appears and begins preparing him for the worse, demanding firmly, "Now's the time! Denounce the Devil and his evil!"*
> *Freddie says nothing.*
> *The priest, raising his voice, repeats the order — but Freddie remains mute, causing the puzzled priest to ask, "Why do you refuse to denounce the Devil and his evil?"*
> *"'Cause," replies Freddie, "until I know where I'm headin', I ain't gonna aggravate no one!"*

The concept of death has attracted rabbis (Norman Lamm: "Without death, life has no future"); novelists (Patrick Moore: "At my age I do what Mark Twain did. I get my daily paper, look at the obituaries page and if I'm not there I carry on as usual"); pseudo-philosophers (Woody Allen: "It's not that I'm afraid to die, I just don't want to be there when it happens"); comedians (Groucho Marx: "Either he's dead or my watch has stopped"); and social commentators (Yogi Berra: "Always go to other people's funerals, otherwise they won't come to yours.")

Judaism has a unique view to death and dying, one often based on humor and wit.

"There's only one death per customer so it must be a real bargain," cracked that famous Jewish philosopher Milton Berle.

Death is Mother Nature's way of telling one to slow down; and by its very definition, it is what happens to somebody else.

Rabbi Yisrael Meir Kagen (*Chofetz Chaim*), the pious Torah leader at the turn of the 20th century, would describe attendees at a funeral as either "live-ers" or "die-ers," noting that all present thought they belonged only to the former category, unwilling to face the reality that all "live-ers" are soon-to-be "die-ers" who will eventually be unable to plead atheism as a defense.

> One day a rabbi is waiting in a long line at his local service station to have his car filled with gas just before a long holiday weekend.
>
> The attendant notices the clergy waiting, and apologizes, "Sorry about the delay, rabbi. It seems as if everyone waits until the last minute to get ready for a long trip."
>
> "I know what you mean," the rav replies, "it's the same in my business."

V'ESCHANAN
Back to the Future

> *"Please God," a panicked Hershel prays after his foot is stuck in the railroad tracks with a train approaching, "please help me get out of these tracks. If you help me I'll stop drinking!"*
>
> *But nothing happens, his foot remains stuck, so Hershel tries again, "Lord, please, please get my foot out. I'll stop drinking...and swearing!"*
>
> *Still nothing and the train is just seconds away!*
>
> *He tries one more time, "Please God, please Lord, if you help me I'll quit drinking, swearing, smoking, cheating and lying."*
>
> *Suddenly his foot struggles free from the tracks and he dives out of the way just as the train passes.*
>
> *A shaken Hershel stands up, dusts himself down, looks up to Heaven and says, "Thanks anyway Lord, I got it out myself."*

In a passionate last-ditch effort to convince God to let him "cross over and enter the good land," Moshe begins his opening plea with *V'eschanan*, one of ten different Torah expressions for prayer.

Rabbi Shlomo Yitzchaki (*Rashi*), the classic medieval father of all Torah commentators, sees this as a prayer of the already righteous, those who approach God not in arrogant ego ("I deserve!") but in a soft anti-narcissistic eloquence of humility.

To the 10th century Josippon, prayer was "a conversation with God;" to the Ba'al Shem Tov, it was "a window to Heaven;" in Joseph Caspi's 13th century *Sefer Hamusar*, it is "a bridle to desire."

"Let others rely on their hands!" roars the Midrash, "Israel's weapon is prayer!"

> *A priest, mullah, and rabbi debate which is the best position for prayer.*
>
> *"Kneeling before the cross," says the priest, "is definitely the best!"*
>
> *"No," interrupts the mullah, "lying prostate, face down on the floor, towards Mecca is the most effective prayer position!"*
>
> *"I get my best results," says the rabbi, "standing in front of the bima with my hands outstretched to Heaven."*
>
> *A nearby telephone repairman has been quietly listening, and objects, "Hey, fellas, the best prayin' I ever did was the day I found myself hangin' upside down danglin' from a telephone pole."*

This power-packed parsha, that could be subtitled *Back to the Future*, is one of repetition, repetition, repetition as Moshe relays, to a distinctively patient audience, their history and commandments with an eye on a future that proves to be remarkably prophetic.

The Torah's use of reiteration is a highly effective tool of communication, a hammering home of a message in order that it not be erased by the passing of time, nor the aging of the audience (have you noticed?...people seem to read the Bible a lot more as they get older...why?...because they're cramming for their finals).

> *"You know Irving," Yankele, an elderly Jew confides in his ol' friend, "I think I'm losing my memory."*
>
> *"Hey, that happened to me," replies Irv, "but I did something about it."*
>
> *"What?"*
>
> *"I went to this great memory clinic and they cured me."*
>
> *"How?"*
>
> *"By using the latest psychological technique of association."*
>
> *"Wow, maybe I should go there. What's the name of the clinic?"* ▶

> *Irving's face suddenly freezes. He can't remember. He thinks and thinks, and then suddenly smiles, "Yankele, what do you call a red flower that has a long stem and sharp thorns?"*
> *"You mean a rose?"*
> *"Yes, by golly, that's it!" Irving then turns to his wife, "Hey Rose, what's the name of that clinic?"*

In sharp contrast comes this weeks parsha of optimism and joy, simcha, and good tidings, known as *Shabbos Nachamu,* the uplifting "Sabbath that comforts you," which derives its name from Isaiah's eponymous *nachamu nachamu ami* ("Comfort ye, comfort ye My people"), a reaffirmation that the last note in the symphony of the history of Israel would end in the composition of triumph.

Isaiah, the Jerusalem-born son of Amoz, was a brilliant and boundlessly gifted poet blessed with an exhilarating melodic style, tinged in grandiose themes of hope and cheerfulness; inspirational prophecies and enriching lyrics that directly inspired the Zohar's lofty battlecry, "Men fall only in order to rise."

This Haftarah inspired Handel to compose some of his best music, especially his setting for Isaiah's messianic prophecy about "exalted valleys."

This parsha also includes the two most foundational texts of Judaism: the Ten Commandments and the *Shema*, the exalted Watchword-of-our-Faith prayer, the linchpin of being a Jew, a symbol of the ultimate manifestation of faith and a quintessential statement of Jewish monotheism.

In fact, it is *the* most familiar passage in the entire Torah.

Jews recite the Shema twice a day, during morning and evening prayers, in an unambiguous assertion of man's acceptance of one Deity. That is why the Torah letters (*ayin,* and *daled*) of the first verse are enlarged, encoded to spell *aid*, which means "witness," for when we say the Shema, we are testifying to the oneness of God.

It is thus *the* most frequently performed of all Jewish mitzvos, accompanying us from childhood, with our first hesitant Hebrew words, to our final pre-death affirmation of Judaism; a journey whose backpack possessions include the Shema's famous *ahavas Hashem* directive, *V'ahavta eis Hashem Elokecha*, "To love God with all your heart, soul and possessions."

This explains why Moshe, in his last attempt to instill a deep profound faith, awe and fear of God in his people, spends the majority of this parsha dealing with the problems of idolatry and the value of belief. He chooses as his spiritual weapon of choice the cry of Shema, *the* center of life's reflections, a pledge of allegiance to one God, to ponder the everyday puzzles of life, existence, who we are — and where we're heading.

> *An American Jew, a Russian Christian, and an Arab Muslim are cruising along in a hot-air balloon when the Russian dips his hand into the clouds and says, "Ah! We're right over my homeland."*
>
> *"How can you tell?" ask the others.*
> *"Because I can feel the cold air."*
> *The Muslim does the same, and exclaims, "Ah! We're right over my homeland."*
> *"How do you know?" ask the others.*
> *"Because I can feel the heat of the desert."*
> *"Ah!" says the American after putting his hand down through the clouds, "We're right over New York."*
> *"How do you know that?" ask the amazed Muslim and Christian.*
> *"Because," the Jew replies, pulling up his hand, "my watch is missing!"*

But wait: doesn't, "Do not have any other gods [*al panai*] before Me" imply that other gods exist, albeit on a "lower" scale? In fact, why mention other gods at all?

The answers vary: from the reference being to "the 'gods' that others worship," or "the 'gods' that are 'other' (i.e.: ineffectual)," or simply generically, false gods for gullible people (i.e.: "nothing gods," a phrase from *elil*, "an idol," derived from the Hebrew *al*, "not.")

The Targum Onkelos, an authoritative Aramaic translation on the Torah, interprets *al panai* not as, "ahead of" but "besides God" (i.e.: "There are to be no other gods apart from Me"); the Ramban and Ibn Ezra, 13th and 12th century sages, read the phrase as meaning, "in God's Presence" (i.e.: "Since you have Me, no other gods should be countenanced"). Rashi, quoting a Midrash, suggests that God is saying, "As long as I exist you must have no other gods;" but the final word goes to a stern Rambam: "Do not even harbor the thought that there is any other God beside Hashem."

> *The congregants are excited when their new rabbi, an elderly man chosen because of his reputation of humility, gets up to give his first speech on the oneness of God.*
> *Some decide to count how long he spoke.*
> *On the first Shabbos his sermon lasts less than 2 minutes; the following week it goes on for nearly 3 hours, and then the next Shabbos it is down to a crisp 8 minutes, which causes the bewildered president to ask the humble rabbi to explain the logic behind the length of his sermons.*
> *"Well," the rav replies, "On the first Shabbos, I had just had my teeth pulled and my mouth was still terribly sore. But last Shabbos I had my new dentures put in and I felt fine."*
> *"But rabbi, what happened during the middle Shabbos, when you spoke for hours?"*
> *"Oh, then? That's when I picked up my wife's set of teeth by mistake!"*

Over the centuries Torah scholars have focused pensive and profound questions on the Shema itself: especially its famous first sentence whose conventional translation has been, "Hear, O Israel!

The Lord our God, the Lord is one [*ehad*]." However a more literal, and accurate, translation is, "Take heed, O Israel! The Lord, our God, alone is God."

This emphasizes Jewish monotheism's contrast to polytheism, in that the God of Israel is not "one," as opposed to two or more gods, but rather is the *only* one and unique God.

Does this mean that the Shema represents an exclusive Judaic possessiveness to a universal deity? No, but it indicates a responsibility that rests solely on the Jews, known as *kiddush Hashem*, to behave appropriately in order to spread, via association, the sanctity of God's Name.

But wait! If the Shema is a personal, internal declaration of faith, why does it begin with an order to a third party, "Hear O Israel?"

This translation is incorrect: the word *Shema* does not mean "to hear" but "to listen," a prerequisite of this final farewell by Moshe, of first grasping, and only then accepting God's existence. "O Israel" is thus a declaration of group identity; that the individual can only flourish in personal faith if the entire folk do so as well.

This requires communal cohesiveness, a United-We-Stand dogma.

> *Yitzchak's rosh yeshiva confesses his concern that the yeshiva's rowing team is consistently losing despite practicing for hours every day.*
>
> *"What do you suggest?" Yitzchak asks.*
>
> *"Go hide in the bushes," says his mentor, "and watch the opposing team during their trial runs. Maybe you can find out why we're not doing so well."*
>
> *Yitzchak spends the next few weeks spying on his competition, and then suddenly one late afternoon he jumps up, runs back to the yeshiva, bursts into the rav's office and yells in excitement, "I figured it out! I know how they do it! I've discovered their secret!"*
>
> *"What!? What is it!?"*
>
> *"They have eight guys rowing and only one guy shouting!"*

EIKEV
Not By Chance Alone

This week's parsha derives its name from its second word, *Eikev*, which literally means "on the heels of," as in "the result of," or "in consequence of."

Of what? Of what God requires. And that is? To keep the mitzvos and laws "for your good [*l'tov l'cha*]."

The words *eikev* and *Yaakov* are derived from the same Hebrew root; the latter because Yaacov was holding "on to the heel" of his twin brother (Esav) as they emerged from their mother's womb.

In this parsha Moshe continues the dialogue with an audience that is both attentive and respectful.

The Jews watch in awe as their leader struggles with the meaning of his life just days before dying, striving to teach an unsettling truth: that acts have consequences, that nothing happens by random nor by chance, that everything in life occurs "on the heel of" (*eikev*) something else.

But not to panic: whenever the Torah begins an admonition with the Hebrew term *v'atah*, "and now," as it does in this parsha ("And now, O Israel, what does God demand of you?"), it reminds one that no action is unredeemable, there is an acceptable Halachic exit strategy: it is called repent-forgiveness, known as *t'shuvah*, a near magic word in the Torah thesaurus and one of the great truisms of Judaism.

The belief in the power of *t'shuva* as an amnesty, a neat clearing of the slate, is so strong that our rabbis claim it can reduce yesterdays "deliberate sins" into mere "errors," even turning yesterday's sinners into tomorrow's saints.

T'shuva however is not a right but a privilege, an act of Divine mercy which defies natural law.

But from where does the concept that one-who-sins-has-the-inalienable-right-to-repent-and-be-absolved come from?

Certainly not from this week's parsha wherein God refuses to absolve the people for the intentional sin of a golden calf. On the contrary: the Heavens "refrain" — but only from *total* destruction. Nor was it present at the infamous episode of the defaming spies, which Torah scholars point to as the Biblical seed for *t'shuva* ("I will grant forgiveness"), that led to an entire generation being punished, *twice*, with 40 more years of desert wanderings and denial of entry into the land of Israel.

The only place where God grants *absolute* forgiveness for *intentional* wickedness, is found not in the Torah but in the book of Jonah, where the compassionate Heavens grant a total pardon to the gentile repentant nation of Ninveh.

In a famous exchange between Rav Elchanan Wasserman and the Chofetz Chaim the latter differentiates between God's mercy (a *teshuva me'ahava*), which is an act of heartfelt regret vs. God's justice (a *teshuva miyir'a*) which is repentance out of fear.

This parsha also includes the mitzvot of tefillin ("bind them as a sign on your hand, and let them serve as a symbol on your fore-head"); mezuzah ("inscribe them on the doorposts of your house and upon your gates"); the advice to "hearken My commandments *today*" (an exhortation to enthusiastically approach mitzvos with a fresh daily regeneration); the power of silence accompanied by the need for *shmias ha'ozen,* being "a careful listener" and the impor-tance of Jewish education.

> *"Nu, mein kindt," the mother asks little Eliezer after his first day at cheder, "What did you learn today?"*
> *"Obviously not enough, I have to go back tomorrow."*

The second paragraph of the *Shema* makes an appearance here-in, "You are to teach them to your children; when you sit at home, journey on the road, go to sleep, and when you rise."

And yet the inconsistencies are immediately apparent: the verse begins in the plural ("teach *them*") and suddenly takes a turn for the singular tense, revealing a Torah priority of responsibilities: the wider Jewish community is obligated to provide the educational infrastruc-ture so that the other irreplaceable partner in Jewish education, the individual parent, can teach not by knowledge but by example.

> *A math teacher who asks little Yankele, "If you had $1 and you ask your father for another $1, how many dollars would you have?*
> *"Still only $1," the boy replies.*
> *"Oh Yankele," the teacher sighs sadly, "You don't know your arithmetic"...to which Yankele sighs in return, "Oh teacher, you don't know my father!"*

The duty to finish ones task is also derived from this parsha. Rashi, the fundamental Torah commentator, focuses on the word *kol* in the verse, "Every commandment [*kol hamitzvo*] shall you observe," and prefers to pass over its plain meaning (*p'shat*) in favor of a translation not as "every" but as "all," reinforcing a Midrash that the expression means "to complete," in that the commencement of a good deed must be carried through to the very end, by others if not the originator.

The perfect example? Moshe carries "the bones of Yosef from Egypt" for years and years — but the final task of burial falls upon the people themselves who receive the credit.

Finally, this parsha contains the foundation for the *Birkas Hamazon*, known in Yiddish as *bensching*, the traditional blessing after meals ("When you have eaten your fill give thanks to God for the good land"); an invitation to "eat and be satisfied" (*v'achalta, v'savata, u'verachta*), to take the mundane physical act of eating and transform it into a spiritual moment of joy and gratitude.

So "thankful" were our rabbis that they devoted an entire chapter of Talmud on this format, fully cognizant of its psychological benefits: that in a fast-paced world, a moment of reflection, designed to heighten our awareness of a higher power, adds a certain sense of humility to our lives and sensitivity to others who go hungry.

We do not however bless food itself but, in ecstatic and inspiring poetic lyrics, praise the Manufacturer of its delivery service as evidenced by a "land flowing with milk and honey, gushing with streams and underground springs."

The Torah calls the special fruits and nuts of the holy land *zimras ha'aretz*, "the song of the land," and so we literally sing the paradigm of thanksgiving and appreciation after each meal.

The *bensching*, which can be recited in any language, consists of four blessings: a confirmation that God feeds everybody; a prayer for the land off Israel and food; a prayer for a rebuilt Jerusalem (which was added after its destruction); and an affirmation of *b'tuvo hagadol* (that God acts "for the best.")

To enjoy food in the absence of gratitude to *the Source* of nourishment was considered a theft against God, a failure to remember that "a loaf of bread on the table is a greater miracle than the parting of the Red Sea." The Torah was concerned that in the promised land of plenty and prosperity the Jews would forget the past and lose their moorings, causing blessings of affluence to turn into curses of haughtiness.

There is a Yiddish saying that the Heavens rejoice when the Jews rejoice, an adjunct to Rabbi Elazar ben Azarya's commonsense declaration, *im ein kemach, ein Torah,* "if there is no flour then there is no Torah."

This helps explain why the completion of Torah study is followed by a *seudas mitzva,* a "happy meal;" and why the great sage Huna advises aspiring Torah scholars not to live in a town "where you cannot get vegetables," why the first Torah benediction is on food (manna); why the only explicit blessing in the entire Torah (*Birkas Hamazon*), as revealed in this weeks parsha, is related to… *food!* — a substance which has attracted the world's greatest philosophers:

> • *"Nouvelle Cuisine, roughly translated, means: I can't believe I paid $96 and I'm still hungry"* (Mike Karlin):
> • *"I will not eat herring. I want my food dead. Not sick, not wounded, dead"* (Woody Allen);
> • *"I went to a restaurant that serves 'breakfast at any time,' so I ordered French Toast during the Renaissance"* (Steven Wright).

Thus it is no accident that every Jewish festival seems to come with a specific Yom Tov delicacy and a cornucopia of symbolic foods that borders on a Halachically mandated Culinary Gastronomic Judaism. Try and imagine Jewish holidays without apples-*lekach*-

honey-cake-carrot *tsimes* on Rosh Hashanah; fresh fruits of Israel on Tu B'Shvat; *hamantaschen* on Purim; blintzes-cheese cakes on Shavuos; stuffed cabbage- *kreplach-kibbeh* on Succos; jelly dough-nuts-or potato latkes on Chanukah — and what is a Shabbos without challa, gefilte fish, cholent, and kugel?

And no, the quintessential Jewish food, bagels and lox, is not linked to any Jewish festival; and yes, the philosophers are right — the bagel hole *is* the essence and the dough is only there for emphasis.

> *One day a gruff traveling Jew from Brooklyn enters a posh gourmet food store on London's fancy Regent Street and is asked by a polite salesman dressed in a morning coat with tails, "May I be of help to you, sir?"*
>
> *"Sure, give me a pound of lox."*
>
> *"No, no," responds the dignified salesman, "You mean 'smoked salmon.'"*
>
> *"Okay, okay, make it a pound of 'smoked salmon.'"*
>
> *"Anything else?"*
>
> *"Yep, a dozen blintzes."*
>
> *"No, no, no. You mean 'crepes.'"*
>
> *"Okay, okay. Have it your way. Make it an even dozen 'crepes.'"*
>
> *"Anything else?"*
>
> *"Yeah, a pound of chopped liver."*
>
> *"No, no. You mean 'pate.'"*
>
> *"Fine, a pound of 'pate', and I'd like you to deliver this to my hotel room on Saturday."*
>
> *"Sir," says the indignant salesman, "We don't schlep chazzerai on Shabbos!"*

RE'EH
Tithes and Taxes

The title of this week's parsha is *Re'eh*, which means: "to see." This word forms the beginning of an oddly formed sentence; "See, this day I set before you blessings and curses," a question that lacks a question mark.

This parsha makes it clear: the Jews' future well-being is not predicated on an ability to feel, smell nor hear but to "see," as in "to grasp" and "comprehend" that the long and winding road ahead is paved with behavioral choices that have consequences.

To see or to listen is the philosophical precursor to that age-old debate about religion — do you have to believe *before* you observe, or can you observe without yet believing?

The Sifre, an important early midrashic work, was blunt: "If you observe a little, you will end up hearing much."

These two verbs ("observe and hear") sum up a Judaism that grows on you; that through beginning to observe, you come to believe; this parsha thus challenges us to choose life by "finding our-selves," a formidable task, one that requires an ability not just to look ahead physically but "to see" the spiritual possibilities, a reality attained only through a prism strengthened by knowing the right way to think, behave, feel...

The ability "to see" is in itself a blessing, because life is not so obvious, which is why the Torah urges the Jew to use "this day" (i.e.: *today*, not tomorrow) to act appropriately because each and every day opens new possibilities of choosing, or changing, directions.

Freedom of choice is why this parsha is always read at the be-ginning of the month that precedes the Rosh Hashanah-Yom Kippur cycle, Elul, a time when, traditionally, Jews become introspective; the word *Elul* being derived from an Aramaic word meaning "to contemplate, examine, analyze," in order to strengthen the highway of *t'shuvah* (repentance) which draws Jews closer to God and to each other, *haba alenu letovah*, for the permanent good.

But what exactly does Moshe want the Jews to "see?" The be-havioral codes of holiness.

> "Where's the self-help section?" George Carlin asks the salesman in a bookstore.
> "Can't tell ya," he says.
> "Why not?"
> "If I told ya, it would defeat the purpose!"

The parsha begins by elaborating on the laws of kashrus (blood must not be consumed, "for blood is life"), *shechitah*, and defining which animals, birds and fish may be eaten.

> *Two minks in a slaughtering house see the slaughterer approach and one becomes highly agitated, anxious, and scared.*
> *"Zorg zacht nisht, Don't worry," consoles the other, "mer vet treffen on simchas, We'll meet at simchas."*

In the utopian Garden of Eden the original Divine plan was vegetarianism, based on the order right out of the gate that mankind should only eat plants and fruit, which were obviously in great supply. Meat eating became permitted after the flood as a concession to human weakness.

"Only in meat is there joy," says the Talmud; to which the great Yiddishist Shalom Aleichem cynically adds, "The best of milk dishes is a slice of beef," a contradiction of sorts which found its true expression (only in America) where kosher creativity has produced "kosher crab," processed "fin fish," and certified "kosher bacon bits."

This parsha gives us the *only* rational for kashrus, "You are a people consecrated," thus creating a folk that is identified not only by what they eat, but where, how, when and why they eat as well (in order "to master appetites and restrain desires," per the Rambam).

The act of eating impelled the Jew to act with the Godly (from the expression "goodly"), an essential mechanism to maintain separatism from other cultures, this helps fight the cancer of assimilation and help guarantee the survival and continuity of the Jewish people.

"A physician restricts the diet of only those patients whom he expects to recover," notes a Midrash, "so God prescribed the dietary laws for those who have hope of a future life" (what's a balanced diet? A cookie in each hand!")

> *After inviting Yehudi Menuhin over for dinner, his friend reminds him, "Don't forget to bring your violin."*
> *"My violin," Yehudi replies, "doesn't eat."*

Moshe is aware that the road to holiness requires leadership and so this parsha also issues a *Be Aware* warning for the layman: a challenge to recognize a rascal rabbi, a phony prophet, a miscreant messenger of God, a sham of a leader.

> *A man on crutches limps into a Church and goes over to a fount of holy water where the priest sprinkles some on his legs. Suddenly the man throws away his crutches.*
> *A young boy excitedly runs home to tell his mother what he'd just seen.*
> *"My son," she says proudly, "You have just witnessed a miracle! Tell me, where is this man now?"*
> *"He's over by the holy water on the floor, trying to get up."*

The Torah recognizes the harm and chaos that can result from the seductive ambiguity of "scoundrels and unbelievers" who deliver up deceiving prophecy, and of corruptive leadership masquerading under a cloak of righteousness.

Commenting on the verse "You shall seek out [*tidreshu*] His Presence and come there [*u'basa*]," our rabbis note that "to seek out" is written in the plural whereas, "to come," is in the singular tense; a suggestion that the *klal* (the group) must, while living in a mixed multitude, root out the roguish guides of Torah before individually approaching God.

But what is the criterion for determining a prophet's authenticity? Is it successful prognostication? The ability to predict the future? The power to employ miraculous signs?

Yes, and not necessarily: for even a broken clock is correct twice a day.

The true *navi* is recognizable by advocating strict adherence to Divine principles, and in the context of this week's parsha, involves fighting against the instability and threat of discontinuity from alien cultures, specifically the "sons of Beli'al" (*benei Beli'al*) who are trying to beguile the emerging Judaism of a holy people.

Thus the clue to genuineness lies through the consistency of purity and perfection, in observing an *overall* lifestyle; a conclusion that Torah linguists reach by combining the *b'li* to *ol* of the family of Beli'al to arrive at those who are "without value, worthless," having *shepar'ku ollo shel Makom,* "thrown off the yoke of God."

This is a warning that in the absence of religious restraints no morality is reliable.

That Jews are exceptionally charitable can be traced back to this parsha which introduces us to such unprecedented notions of communal compassion as debt remission and "tithing," an essential part of Torah legislation which involves a tax for the needy.

This comes as no surprise: the entire substructure of Torah is the protracted theme of *ahavas chesed*: beginning with God providing clothing (for Adam and Eve), and ending with arranging a burial (for Moshe).

Tithing (*ma'aser sheni,* the "second tithe," as expounded in this week's parsha) is an essential Torah legislation. Rabbi Akiva considered the act of giving "a fence for wealth" (as per a proverbial rabbinic saying, *asser bish'vil shetitasher,* "Give tithes so that you will be wealthy.")

Yes, it may cost you, but it does not make you poorer; for "the more we give," writes Rabbi Emanuel Feldman, "the more we receive, materialistically and emotionally."

Although the traditional answer to the *Who is a Jew?* question is one born to a Jewish mother, or converted according to the laws of Moshe, it is the "kindness" component of this week's parsha that gives an intriguing insight into what *makes* a Jew.

In a stunning conclusion, the rabbis of the Talmud declare that hardheartedness is a Judaic anomaly, "Whoever does not have compassion and mercy [is] not of the seed of Avraham;" in other words, a *sine qua non* of being a "spiritual" Jew is an instinctive ability not only to be sensitive and caring towards others, but to sense their hurts and respond unselfishly to their needs.

Thus, to be a "disciple" of Avraham and his religion is to be at peace with oneself. It wasn't sufficient to be a Jew in name only but in deed as well; to have, according to Pirkei Avos, the three characteristics of a "good eye" (a generous sense of benevolence); a "humble temperament" (contentment with ones own lot); and a "lowly spirit" (a rejection of extravagance, luxurious excess, materialistic overkill).

In short: manners and midos are mandatory.

> *A young Jewish girl turns to her grandmother,* "Bubba, *I'm really proud of you.*"
> "Vat's to be proud of?"
> "Your impeccable manners and social etiquette. I notice that whenever you sneeze, you always cover your mouth with a hand."
> "Have to," *the little ol' Bubba replies,* "how else can I catch my teeth?"

Yet it is a misnomer to say that the term *tzeddaka* means "charity." The word comes from *tzedek*, which means "righteousness" or "justice." In other words Judaism requires the Jew to do what is right, just and fair — and thus places more intellectual, moral, and spiritual emphasis on the heart rather than the mind.

The Torah was the first to lay down the rule that charity begins at home, not only for the purposes of teaching our children to be generous but a recognition of the human condition: that only those who are happy and content within have the right moral stamina to extend a helping hand to others.

The 12th century Moshe ben Maimon (*Rambam*), in his *Laws of Charity*, affirms this by instructing the Jew to "give with a friendly and joyful countenance," basing his insight on the terminology of a Torah that does not state bluntly to "do kindness," but to "love kindness."

This parsha thus answers the chicken-and-egg question of *tzeddaka*: Who comes first? The overseas yeshiva in Israel or the cheder next door? The long-distance poverty-stricken relative or the unknown beggar down the street?

Such tugs of war are common: yet the Torah lays down an order of priorities, "If there be among you a needy person, one of your brethren, within any of your gates, in the land which God gives you, you shall not harden your heart."

Rashi, the "prince" of Torah commentators, deduces from this that the need of "one of your brethren" (i.e.: a close relative) is greater; and one "within your gates" (i.e.: from your own city) must be helped before "the land which God gives you" (i.e.: Israel).

> *Goldstein answers a knock at his door and sees the usual* shnorrer *looking for his monthly handout.*
>
> *"What's the matter?" the beggar asks when he sees the disheveled and worried Goldstein.*
>
> *"I've gone bankrupt, haven't you heard?"*
>
> *"Of course I've heard."*
>
> *"Then what do you want from me?"*
>
> *"Ten cents on the dollar."*

Justice by Just Means

> Chaim is unable to decide on a career so his worried parents devise a plan to test him. They put $10, a Chumash, and a bottle of whiskey on the kitchen table, and then hide in the cupboard.
>
> "If he takes the cash he'll be a businessman," the father whispers to his wife, "and if he takes the Chumash he'll be a rabbi."
>
> "What if he takes the bottle of whiskey?"
>
> "Then, I'm afraid our son will be a drunkard."
>
> Chaim comes home, walks into the kitchen, and first flips through the Chumash, then immediately slips the $10 and whiskey bottle into his pockets and leaves.
>
> "Oy, oy!" the father says as he slaps his forehead, "It's even worse than I ever imagined."
>
> "What do you mean?" his scared wife asks.
>
> "Our son's gonna be a politician!"

"It's good to be the king," said Jewish comedian Mel Brooks, unaware of the serious demands that *Shoftim*, which means "Judges," places on the monarchy of Israel.

This parsha introduces the Jews to a new stage of urban civilization.

For the first time, we encounter the administrative pair of words: magistrate (*shofet*) and official (*shoter*), two categories that become the Torah's first hint at the concept of separation of power, something akin to a judicial and a legislative branch of government, as well as a decentralized government.

> The court of Chelm were sitting in a dispute over the amount of waste between a builder and his employee.
> "What's the issue?" asks the first rabbi. ▶

> *"My carpenter," replies the boss, "is fixing the roof, but as he works, he throws away about half the nails."*
> *"I this true?" asks the second rabbi.*
> *"Yes," replies the carpenter. "I take a nail out of the bag, and if it's facing the roof, I use it, and if it's facing away, I know it's defective, and I throw it away."*
> *"You fool!" yells the third rabbi, "Don't you know! Those are for the other side!!"*

There are two types of Beth Dinim (courts); the *Beth Din kavua*, a "fixed, permanent" body appointed and accepted by the entire community, and a *Beth Din she'eino kovua*, a "non-permanent" group, wherein litigants appoint dayanim to judge their individual case.

Who is qualified to sit on a Beth Din? The Rambam lists seven personal attributes: Wisdom, humility, awe, hatred of money, love of the truth, personal popularity and a good name; in addition, dayanim should have some experience in dealing with communal matters, and must, obviously, be proficient in Halachic rulings (a combination of *yoreh yoreh*, "basic s'micha," and *yadin yadin*, qualified to rule in "diverse areas" ranging from monetary to divorce cases.)

> *Sammy, an engineer, dies and due to a mix up in Heaven ends up in Hell where, dissatisfied with the level of comfort, he starts designing, making improvements, and pretty soon Hell has a working air condition system, toilets that flush, showers that work, even escalators.*
> *One day God calls up Satan on the phone, wanting to rub it in, "So, how's it going down there?"*
> *"Hey, things are going great. We've got air conditioning, flush toilets, working showers, and running escalators. There's no telling what Sammy the engineer is going to come up with next."*
> *"What!?" God shouts, "You've got an engineer?* ▶

> *That's not possible, it's a mistake! He shouldn't be down there; send him up here."*
>
> *"Not a chance! I like having an engineer on the staff, and I'm keeping him."*
>
> *"Send him back up here," God demands, "or I'll sue."*
>
> *"Yeah, right," Satan laughs, "and where are you going to find a lawyer?"*

The Torah's intent, to establish a fair and operative judicial system, now serves as the basis of all Western law that seeks to protect its citizens, but in this new judicial structure there is no mention of the need for a scribe (*sofer*), whose role in enforcing public order appears in Chronicles; nor any opening for attorneys.

> *After an attorney named Bill Strange dies, his partner asks the stonemason to inscribe on his tombstone, "Here lies Strange, an honest man, and a lawyer."*
>
> *"Too confusing," says the inscriber, "people will assume that there are three men buried."*
>
> *"Any suggestions?"*
>
> *"Yeah, if you write, 'Here lies a man who was both honest and a lawyer,' people will read it and say, 'That's Strange!'"*

We know about Jewish kings, but how about Jewish queens? Were there any? Yes: Michal, the wife of David (who Jewish history does not regard highly), and Jezebel, the wife of Ahab (who Jewish history considers a wicked women).

Post-Biblical Jewish queens seemed to do better: respected for their piety, courage, and political abilities were Queen Salome Alexandra (*Sh'lomtzion*), wife of Yannai and sister to Rabbi Shimon ben Shetach who ruled Judea from 76 to 67 BCE; and Queen Helen, wife of Monabazus of Adiabene, a convert in the last century BCE who, with her son Izates helped the Jews stand up to Rome.

What about Sheba, the most famous Biblical Queen? She was not Jewish, and only makes an appearance after hearing "of the name of the Lord [through] the fame of Solomon."

> *When her hospitalized husband was coming out of anesthesia, Queen Malka, his faithful wife, was at his bedside. The king takes one look at her, smiles, and quietly comments, "You're so beautiful," then drifts back to sleep. A few minutes later he opens his eyes and says, "You're looking cute."*
>
> *"What happened to beautiful?" she asks.*
>
> *"The drugs are wearing off."*

The Torah has specific resume qualifications for the king of Israel.

He had to be fair and impartial, beyond reproach or personal compromise, show no favoritism and be able to resist bribes — even if the income was used for "holy" purposes such as a sacrifice, which the Ramban, a classic Medieval commentator on the Torah, calls a "flawed offering (*asher y'h'yeh vo moom.*)"

> *A Washington politician and a Czechoslovakian consulate are walking in the woods when suddenly they bump into two huge bears; one male, one female.*
>
> *While the male bear eats the unfortunate consul, the politician runs back into town and tells the sheriff's office about his Czech friend. The sheriff grabs his gun and they both run back to find the bears still lurking.*
>
> *"He's in that one!" yells the politician, pointing to the male bear.*
>
> *The sheriff immediately shoots the female bear.*
>
> *"Whatdya do that for! I said he was in the other one!"*
>
> *"Exactly...and would you believe a politician who told you that the Czech was in the male?"*

The Judges were the leaders of the Jews after the death of Joshua who had begun the conquest of Israel but did not complete it; prior to the establishment of the monarchy, they were not just arbiters of justice but charismatic heroes and powerful military commanders.

In his pre-death statement Samuel, the last of the Judges, and the reluctant appointee of Saul as the first King of Israel, describes his fears of kingship and the implications of a royal protocol that might want to take away sons to serve in armies or farm for the king, and daughters to work as perfumers, cooks, and bakers. The king would confiscate their best vineyards and olive trees, take a tenth of their crops and sheep, and that they would be, in many ways, the king's slaves.

Despite these warnings the people still insisted on having a king, "That we also may be like all the nations," leading a Midrash to describe them as *am ha'aretz*, a Hebrew expression which means a simpleton or an ignoramus. This description was used to differentiate between the masses of ignorant Jews and the few learned ones who had stopped believing, called *apikorsim*. Remember: there was no such concept in early Jewish religious literature of agnostics and atheists (in contrast to just being "estranged" from Judaism) because in the olden days, everybody believed in some form of supernatural being(s).

A rabbi, a minister, and a priest were playing poker when the king and his men suddenly raid the game.

Turning to the priest, the king demands to know, "Father Murphy, were you gambling?"

Turning his eyes to Heaven, the priest whispers, "Lord, forgive me for what I am about to do," and then lies to the king, "No, your Royalty, I was not gambling."

The king then asks the minister, "Pastor Johnson, were you gambling?" ▸

> *Again, after an appeal to Heaven, the minister replies,*
> *"Oh no, sir; I was not gambling."*
> *"How 'bout you, Rabbi Bornstein," the king then glares,*
> *"Were you gambling?"*
> *Shrugging his shoulders, the rabbi calmly replies,*
> *"With whom?"*

Since the existence of prophecy was an essential precondition for a functioning community the Hebrew prophet is clearly identified as playing a central role in both the spiritual and politico-social leadership of the Jewish nation, usually as part of the vocal opposition.

Concerned that prophecy not be confused with witchcraft ("an abomination"), the Torah, in the middle of this parsha, condemns those who rely on "an augur, soothsayer, diviner, sorcerer, spell caster, ghost consulter..."; instead, the Jew is advised to be *tamim* ("whole-hearted"), a combination of *tam* ("innocent," or "innocuous") and *mu'ad* ("forewarned"), a reference to ones state of mind that God uses in an earlier parsha (*Lech Lecho*), "walk before Me, and be *tamim*," when Avram is about to enter into a lasting covenant via circumcision.

According to Ibn Ezra, 12th century Spanish Biblical commentator, the concept of *temimus* is sheer non-intellectual obedience (the simplistic naiveté of "innocence"); in other words, in the search for a religious consciousness (*avodas Hashem*) God has no need for such phony intermediaries as the necromancer, or those involved in clairvoyance, alchemy, wizardry, magical and gullible voodoo practices which the Rambam, whose entire Torah approach is rooted in rationalism, describes as an insult to "the intelligence and intellect of scholars and pure thinkers (*temimei hada'as*)."

> *Three wizards walk into a bar, and each orders a beer.*
> *They raise their glasses and make a toast: "Here's to 59!"*
>   *After downing their beers, they order another round*
> *and make the same toast: "Here's to 59!"*
>   *This happens again and again. Finally, the bartender*
> *asks them what the significance of the toast is.*
>   *"Well," replies one, "We put a 1,000-piece magic jig-*
> *saw puzzle together in just 59 days!"*
>   *"And that's a big deal?" asked the barkeeper.*
>   *"You betcha! The box said 4 to 8 years!"*

From the word *mishneh,* which implies repetition or duplication, being related to the word *shenayim* ("two"), our rabbis conclude that the king had two Torah scrolls: "One which comes and goes with him, and one which remains in his treasure house;" the former as a visible public symbol, the later at home as a reminder on how to behave in private. This kingly demand, for a Sefer Torah both in the street and at home, was to prevent the split personality of the Jew that appeared in Europe in the 19th century as articulated by Y.L. Gordon, a Russian-Jewish lyricist in his poem *Hakiza Ami,* when the gentile demanded, "Be a Jew at home and a human being in the street!" — and in order to dispel the theory that the Torah is destined "to change" (*lehishtanos,* a word that shares the same Hebrew root as *mishneh*) the king's transportable Torah acted as a constant reminder that he was absolutely subservient to the word of God and to the assemblage of Israel, in front of whom, every seven years at the end of the first day of *Chol Hamoed Succos* (known as *Hakhel*), he had to re-enact Sinai's revelation.

A leitmotif for this weeks Torah portion is the idea, explained by Rashi quoting the Sifrei, that we must listen to the sages in *all* circumstances, even if they claim that "right is left and left is right," not because they are infallible (they are not) but on the basis that their rulings merit *siyata d'shemaya,* "Divine guidance" (the Jewish attitude has always been *Yiftach b'doro k'shmuel b'doro!*, "We must unite behind the less-than-great leader just as we would behind the great leader.")

Both the Rambam and Ramban agree: one is obligated to obey, even if rabbis err. Why? Because spiritual leaders deserve the benefit of the doubt (even if right *is not* left) on the theory that Judaic unity overrules factionalism and religious anarchy.

As Rav Isser from Bobroisk put it: far better to accept a crooked answer from a straight person whose relationship with Torah is of a singular nature than a straight answer from a crooked person.

One day, a judge, having been overruled by the majority on the court, decides to appeal to a higher authority.

"Oh, God!" he cries, "I know in my heart that I am right and they are wrong! Please give me a sign to prove it to them!"

As soon as the judge finishes his prayer, a rumbling storm cloud suddenly moves across the sky above court despite it being a beautiful, sunny day.

"Look!" the judge shouts, "A sign from God! See, I'm right, I knew it!"

But the others disagree, pointing out that storm clouds often form on hot days. So the rabbi prays again: "Oh, God, I need a bigger sign to show that I am right and they are wrong. So please, God, a bigger sign!"

This time several storm clouds suddenly appear, rush toward each other to form one big cloud, sending out a bolt of lightning that slams into a tree on a nearby hill.

"See! I told you I was right!" — but his friends insist that nothing had happened that could not be explained by natural causes.

As the judge gets ready to ask for a "very big" sign, the sky abruptly turns pitch black, the earth shakes violently, and a deep, booming Voice intones, "Heeeeeeeeeeeeee's Riiiiiiiiight!!!!!!!"

The relieved judge turns to the other three rabbis, "You see!"

"Okay, Okay," they shrug, "So now it's two to two!"

This week's Torah portion also reveals the Torah's psychologically profound sensitivity to justice by way of two famous phrases; "an eye for any eye, a tooth for a tooth," a dictate often accused of being too harsh (although, in fact, Jewish tradition reads it as meaning, "the value of an eye and tooth for an eye and tooth" — i.e.: a monetary value was assigned to the loss and the perpetrator was to pay the victim as one would make restitution today); and *Tzedek, tzedek tirdof*, "Justice, justice shall you pursue," a doubling of "justice" that has given rise to much Midrash.

Why "justice" two times?

As a warning to the king: if he neglects to be just, the Prophets will demand that justice be done.

> *Mrs. Guttman is in court charged with failure to pay her share of taxes. After reviewing her case, the judge wags his finger at her, "Mrs. Guttman, we here on the judiciary, and at the IRS, feel it is a great privilege to be allowed to live and work in the USA. As a citizen and member of the community you have an obligation to pay taxes — and we expect you to eagerly pay them with a smile!"*
>
> *"Thank goodness," she sighs, "I thought you were going to make me pay with cash."*

Bachya ben Asher saw the doubling of "justice" to mean, "Justice, whether to your profit or loss, whether in word or action, whether to Jew or non-Jew" — in other words, Jews are to pursue justice by just means, by giving equal justice to all, by ensuring that the "appointed" judges and officers are beyond reproach ("Bribery blinds the eyes of the wise and makes the words of the righteous slippery").

The Torah views justice by itself as insufficient, and demands *mishpat tzedek*, "righteous justice," using the powerful verb "shall pursue" (instead of simply commanding us to "*do* justice" or "*be* just").

But the question is obvious: what's the difference between "justice" and "righteous justice?"

The latter, say our sages, is a "love-tempered" judgment, fueled by compassion, mercy, and an acknowledgement that everybody, even criminals, have a spark of Godliness in them.

> It was Chanukka and the judge was in a benevolent mood as he questions the accused, "What are you charged with?"
>
> "Doing my Yom Tov shopping early," replies Max, the defendant.
>
> "That's no offense. How early were you doing this shopping?"
>
> "Before the store opened."

And another question: although presented as a communal responsibility, why is the pursuit of justice expressed in the singular form, *lecho*?

The Torah knows: the only thing separating anarchy and government is law and order; and thus it is ultimately up to the individual to create an atmosphere of order that respects justice.

The Gaon of Vilna considers "street smarts" a major plus for a Jewish judge. He compares the phrase in this week's parsha, *Y'aveir einei chochomim*, that a judge must be "both a *chochom* (knowledgeable) and a *pikei'ach* (street-wise)" to the verse in Mishpotim (*y'aveir pikchim*), which leaves out the word *einei*. He suggests that this means a *chochom's* wisdom is restricted to what he sees on the surface in both testimony and behavior (*einei chachomim*), whereas the perception of a street-smart adjudicator (*pikei'ach*) goes much deeper, strengthened by instinct to comprehend under the surface (*din m'rumeh*).

This parsha also deals with idol worshippers, rebellious Torah scholars, murderers, false witnesses (*eidim zom'mim*), kidnappers, rebellious sons, adultery, ethics in the course of battle, a diplomacy-before-warfare policy known as "purity of arms" ("When you draw near to a city to wage war against it, you must first call out for peace"), false prophets, and the environmental standard of wastage, known as *ba'al tashchis* ("When you besiege a town for many days, waging war against it, to seize it, you are not to bring ruin on its trees...for from them you eat.")

The importance of preserving trees was such that the Talmud even forbade shifting the course of a stream because that could cause a tree's roots to wither.

This concept may have originated within a military context but was expanded by the rabbis, who saw mankind as caretakers of God's property, to avoid the wanton destruction of anything; whether tangible (clothes, property, water, even to over-tearing ones garment during mourning, or wasting fuel by allowing a lamp to burn too quickly), or intangible (relationships, other's feelings).... and especially food.

> *When Seymour dies, God welcomes the pious Jew in Heaven, "Seymour, are you hungry?"*
>
> *"I could eat," he replies.*
>
> *So God opens a can of tuna, and they share it. While eating his humble meal, Seymour cannot help but notice that down in Hell they are devouring enormous steaks, pastries, and drinking vodka.*
>
> *The next morning, God again asks Seymour if he is hungry, and Seymour replies, "Yes, I could eat." And so God opens a can of tuna and they share it, while down below Seymour sees a huge feast of champagne, lamb, brandy and chocolates.*
>
> *The following day, mealtime arrives and another can of tuna is opened.*
>
> *"God," Seymour meekly says, "Don't get me wrong. I'm very happy to be in Heaven as a reward for my good life but how come all I get to eat is tuna and down there, in the Other Place, they eat like kings?"*
>
> *"To be honest, Seymour, for just two people, does it really pay to cook?"*

Rabbi Chayyim David Halevi of Tel Aviv extended this *ba'al tashchis* concern to the custom of throwing ("wasting") sweets, edible items or peeled nuts in shul on bar mitzva boys and bridegrooms. The rabbi also criticizes any use of food that makes it unfit for consumption, such as cutting vegetables and painting them, inserting vegetables as a decoration in an art work, or even using flour in order to make glue.

Sefer Hachinuch, a compilation of mitzvos by the medieval Jewish pietists, defined a lover of God as one who could not bear to waste a grain of mustard; similar to the declaration of Rabbi Raphael Shimshon Hirsch, the leading Orthodox rabbi of 19th century Germany, who elevated *ba'al tashchis* as the most basic mitzva of them all, a twin acknowledgment: of the sovereignty of God and the limitation of our own will and ego.

> *While passing through a village, Schmulik is stopped by a local man, "Hey, do you know how many cookies you can eat on an empty stomach?"*
> *"Oh, about five..."*
> *"No, no," the man laughs, "You're wrong! You can only eat one. After that your stomach's not empty anymore!!"*
> *When Schmulik returns home he goes running into the kitchen and asks his wife, "Surale, how many cookies can you eat on an empty stomach?"*
> *She thinks and replies, "Two."*
> *"Too bad," he sighs, "If you had said 'five' I would have had a great joke for you!"*

KI SETZEI
A Medley of Morals

For years the rabbi had resisted calls from the local Ammonite priest and Moabite minister to join them for a day of fishing, preferring to maintain a friendly, yet separate, relationship. Finally, one day he relents and finds himself in a boat idling in the middle of a lake.

The priest suddenly realizes that he has left his fishing pole behind so he gets out, walks across the water to his car, grabs his pole, then walks back across the lake and gets into the boat. The rabbi is stunned.

The minister then decides he needs to use the bathroom so he, too, gets out of the boat, walks across the water, finds the nearest men's room, walks back across the water and gets into the boat. The rabbi is dumbfounded — and faces a quandary.

"My faith is as great as theirs!" he thinks to himself and rises to the occasion. He gets up and says, "I'm thirsty. I'll go get us all some drinks."

The rabbi stands up, puts one foot on the water, and, like a rock, sinks instantly.

The other two quickly drag him out but the embarrassed, soaking wet rav brushes them aside, and, determined that his faith is as strong as theirs, steps back out onto the water, only to immediately sink again. Once more, the minister and priest rescue their clerical colleague, who insists on doing it again — with the same disastrous result.

As the rabbi is sinking helplessly for the third time, the minister turns to the priest and says, "Do you think we should tell him where the rocks are?"

The name of this week's parsha, *Ki Setzei*, means "When you go out," and is derived from the Hebrew root "to leave," a reference to having left Egypt and finally standing at the very entry to the holy land.

This parsha seeks the promotion of a unified society in the holy land wherein Jews are not only ordered to interact and care for each other, but also to show concern for such adversaries as the Ammonites, Moabites, Edomites, and even Egyptians.

The Heavens understood the difficulty inherent in this command and so the parsha repeats it twice, calling them not enemies but "brothers" — although God still finds a handful of deviants so objectionable that they are exempt from the Torah's rule of inclusion.

They include Amalek, a genocidal desert raider who is Jewish history's perennial opponent, one whose very memory we are to "blot out from under the Heavens;" and the Moabite, purveyor of assimilation.

> Shmuely hears a commotion coming from his neighbor's house, "Help! Help! Quick, my shvigger said she's going to jump out the attic window!"
> "Nu," yells back Shmuely, "So what's the problem?"
> "It's stuck!"

Sinai envisaged a just community being achieved only through the goodness of the individual towards the powerless, impoverished, dependent, stranger, war captive, child of an unloved wife, fugitive slave, destitute laborer; and, of course, the poor, orphan, and widow.

To act appropriately to the non-Jew was an elevated act of *kiddush Hashem*, the pursuit of raising the "goodness" of the Jewish God in the eyes of the wider world. Thus, the underlying theme of this parsha is kindness and the concept of friendship; in Hebrew *chaver* (from *chibbur*, which means "attached"), as in "joined" in unconditional support, friendship and loyalty.

> *Yossie and Charlie, two close friends, are out in the woods hunting, when Charlie suddenly falls to the ground, stops breathing, with his eyes rolling back in his head. An alarmed Yossie quickly whips out his mobile phone, dials 911, and screams to the operator, "Help me! I think my chaver is dead! What should I do?"*
>
> *"Just take it easy, Sir," she replies in a calm soothing voice, "the first thing we need to do is make sure he's dead."*
>
> *"Okay," says Yossie, as he puts down the phone.*
>
> *The operator hears only silence, then a shot, then Yossie's voice again, "Okay, now what?"*

Yet this is also a "potpourri" parsha: a miscellany teeming with a medley of moral doctrine, ranging from the mitzva of *tzitzis*, a ban on cross-dressing, watching what you say, respect for birds and animals (*tsar ba'alei chayim*), keeping promises, fairness to workers, business issues (is making a profit reprehensible? Absolutely not — but, sings Tehillim, it should be obtained with "clean hands and a pure heart"); labor and management relations (the role model is Boaz who greets his reapers in the field with, "May God be with you" and they respond with, "May God bless you"), and caring for lost property, derived from the term *v'hisalamta*, which means one must "not remain indifferent," as in to "pretend" not to have seen the missing article.

Rabbi Hanina once found some hens that were accidentally left on his doorstep, and soon began to lay eggs. Instead of using them as food for his family, the sage set the eggs and hens aside until there was no more room. So he sold them and used the money to buy goats. When the owner of the hens eventually showed up, Rabbi Hanina presented him with the goats.

This parsha is also the forerunner for today's building safety codes, warning architects, builders and homeowners not to build a flat roof without a railing or parapet, considered "acts of negligence" that invite accidents.

> *The usher finds a strange man lying sprawled across three seats in a theater. Pushing him gently, he whispers, "Sorry, sir, but you're only allowed one seat."*
> *The man groans but does not budge.*
> *"Sir," the impatient usher says, "Please get up otherwise I'm going to call the manager!"*
> *Again, the man just groans, and the manager also tries, with no success, to get him to move. Finally, they summon a cop who sternly addresses the man, "Okay, buddy, what's your name?"*
> *"Morrie Grubinsky," he moans.*
> *"Where ya from, Mo?" the cop asks.*
> *"The balcony."*

Jewish mystics take the Hebrew word for parapet (*ma'akeh*) and see it as a reconstitution of the first initials of *Hirhurei averah kashim me'avodah*, "Sinful thoughts are harder (to control) than the sin itself" — suggesting that each Jew needs to build a personal parapet around himself in order to ensure that careless thoughts do not lead to a fall into sinfulness.

Judaism, no fan of the popular "let the buyer beware (*caveat emptor*)" principle, places the onus of fairness and safety squarely on the seller; meanwhile, Rabbi Joseph Caro, Halachic codifier of the *Shulchan Aruch,* expanded this concept to include an open well, a pit, a broken ladder.

But wait! Doesn't this contradict the words of Psalms, "The Lord protects the simple." No: for it is incumbent on each Jew to ensure the safety of everybody, *including* himself, in fealty to that rabbinic adage, *venishmartem me'od lanafshosechem*, "You shall carefully guard your lives."

However the order of the mitzvot in this parsha still poses a near impossible enigma: they all seem unrelated and disconnect-ed, grouped together in a saturated judicial juxtaposition that, like most mitzvot in Deuteronomy, can be classified under one title, "How to behave in Eretz Yisroel."

But take a closer look and we discover an interesting repeti-tive subtext: a variety of marriage relationships with case histories, ranging from "permissibly desired" women captured in conquest (*ta'avah shel heter*), dysfunctional two-wife families (one loved, one scorned); Levirate marriages (*yibbum*), wife defamation, and so on ("I was married by a judge," says Groucho Marx, "I should have asked for a jury.")

The theme of spousal relationships extends into this weeks Haftarah with Isaiah's vivid *Shivat Zion* poetry, of God-Israel as hus-band-wife metaphors with Jerusalem a "barren woman" (and Israel the "abandoned and brokenhearted" wife, as per Hosea) whose husband had once left her but now returns ("For a brief moment I forsook you; with abiding love I take you back"), the genesis of the inspiration behind the enchanting stanzas of *Lecha Dodi*, the cheery song that ushers in the weekly Shabbat.

Other than the opening chapters of Genesis, there is no legal or philosophical mention anywhere in the Torah of what we, to-day, would describe as the ideal marriage model, the "normal" re-lationship, of one-man and one-woman, united by love. We do, of course, learn much from Avraham, Yitzhak and Yaakov and their relationships.

The laws of Moshe once tolerated more than one spouse, as evi-denced by the many wives and concubines that King Solomon col-lected; however our sages never idealized the situation and instead filled their rabbinic texts with teachings that stressed monogamy as the most satisfying spiritual and physical nourishment.

The Jew goes over to a kosher hot-dog stand in Manhattan and orders one from the bottom. "Why from the bottom?" asks the vendor.

"Well, I'm Jewish, and we always go for the under-dog!"

KI SAVO
Rewards and Warnings

> *"Do you believe in life after death?" the boss asks Beynish, one of his employees.*
> *"Yes Sir, why do you ask?"*
> *"Well, after you left early yesterday to go to your grandmother's funeral, she stopped in to see you!"*

This week's parsha, *Ki Savo*, derives its name from *Ki savo el ha'aretz*, "When you come into the land," a joyous declaration. How do we know?

Whenever a Torah verse begins with *vay'hi* ("and it was") it is a bad sign, however if, as this parsha does, it begins with *v'hayah* ("and it will be") it is a good sign.

And it was: the announcement that their journey was coming to an end must have been a tremendous relief for those who had just spent 40 prolonged years in a desert; an experience that caused all future rabbinic texts to consider *any* "desert," physical or spiritual, the equivalent of an enemy, to be confronted and overcome (Isaiah even defines success as one who "wrestles against a desert and turns it into a Garden of Eden.")

> *"So, where have you chopped before?" the interviewer asks a little ol' Polish Jew who has answered a Help Wanted ad for a woodchopper.*
> *"In the Sahara Forrest."*
> *"The Sahara Forrest! Isn't the Sahara a desert?"*
> *"Yeah, now it is!"*

This parsha begins with promises of rewards if Jews behave

(many children, large flocks, abundant crops, protection from enemies), but then quickly takes a turn for the worse if they don't: a list of 98 brutal, spine-chilling admonitions (famine, disease, military defeat, plagues, slavery) that span nearly half the parsha, surely the most frightening of all Torah clauses.

No wonder this is referred to as the "Warning Chapter (*tochacha*)," causing the *ba'al korei* (Torah reader) to set aside his traditional singsong chanting and rush through the words of terror in hushed fearful tones.

The first and last of the curses deals with one "who does not hold up the words of Torah," a reference perhaps to Jews who cannot relate to *hagbah gliloh*, the public act of lifting, rolling and closing the Torah, an expression whose gematria (98) led Moshe ben Nachman (*Ramban*), one of the leading Torah scholars of the Middle Ages, to suggest that this holy act alone can ward off the ninety-eight exhortations.

> One day a Breslover chassid was bragging about his Rebbe to a litvak, "You know that every Shabbos we give the Rebbe an aliyah, and even though he has been niftar for 200 years we all hear him say the brocho and we still all say "amen.'"
>
> "That's not so impressive," replies the litvak, "let me know when you plan on giving him hagba."

In this, Moshe's third, and final, farewell address, he concludes the parsha with a blueprint for Judaic prosperity that involves a proviso ("If you safeguard this covenant") and a promise ("You will be successful [*taskilu*]."

Torah linguists note that the Hebrew root of *taskilu* is connected to *seichel*, which means common sense, discernment, intelligence. In other words: those who have the *seichel* to occupy themselves with Torah will find prosperity.

Does this mean they will become rich?

Yes, opines Rabbi David Kimchi (*Radak*), but not necessarily in material possessions; for if the road to "success" is paved with the Torah's business ethics, those who walk it do so in a successful atmosphere of well being, merited with *shuttaf l'hakadosh Baruch Hu b'ma'aseh bereshis*, being "partners with God in building the world."

This is why the first question that God asks of the dead is *nasata v'netata be'emunah*, "did you conduct your business affairs with honesty and probity?" — before the next question, "did you set aside time for Torah study;" hard-core proof that of the 613 mitzvos the most important one is simply *Kedoshim tiyu* ("be holy"), in other words, not just obey the letter of the law but also its spirit.

Wishing to be rich is no sin; after all, every month on the Shabbos before Rosh Chodesh we pray for "a life of prosperity and honor," and the Talmud describes how Yehudah Hanasi, editor of the Mishna, used to give honor to rich people.

Yet when Pirkei Avos asks, "Who is rich?" the answer, "He who is content with his lot" comes not in financial, but psychological, terms. This is not a tirade against ambition or drive, but a nod and a wink that fortune is at times measured in such simple things as peace and tranquility with ones lot in life.

That is why laws concerning business were incredibly more difficult than those concerning regular *midos*: the saintly Chofetz Chaim from Radin, Lithuania once asked a student to hold the three volumes of *Yoreh Deah* (the Code of Jewish Law) in one hand and the thicker, heavier three volumes of *Choshen Mishpat* (dealing with business ethics) in the other, to show how more difficult are ethical abuses than ritual neglect (even Moshe was held accountable, pledging, "When the task [of building the tabernacle] is complete, I will give a full account").

> *Jack's grandfather leaves him $10 million dollars and the following week Dina agrees to marry him, but three months later the couple is in a bitter fight.*
> *"The only reason you married me," the husband yells, "is because my grandfather left me $10 million dollars!"*
> *"Don't be ridiculous," she yawns, "It made no difference to me who left you the money!"*

The seeds of the public ratification of Torah are found in this parsha when the Jews, having crossed the Jordan River into Israel, find themselves upon the slopes of two opposing mountainsides (Mounts Gerizim and Ebal.)

The nation stands literally at a crossroads: between wandering and settlement, past and future, blessings and curses.

The first order of the day is a challenge from God; an encouragement of penmanship to "cement the covenant," not by writing on traditional papyrus but by carving on "great stones, coated with plaster."

But write what? "All the words of this Torah." Which "words?" The entire Torah? The Ten Commandments? A list of mitzvot? No one knows for sure; but what is meaningful is that the writing embodies a famous axiom, *lo hamidrash ikar ela hama'aseh*, "It is not the saying that is important, but the doing."

After 40 years of wandering and whining, the time has come to become the world's first Jewish historians; and so the people sit, reminisce and record the momentous events that brought them to this day, the miraculous entry not only into the promised land but onto the stage of Jewish history.

The 15th century Don Isaac Abrabanel, Spanish statesman and keen Torah scholar, compared these stone writings at the national "gateway" into the holy land to *mezuzos* on the door posts of ones home: both texts affirming acceptance of Sinai.

The stone carvings were to be in 70 different languages, one for each nation, to ensure that the message was universal.

> The English professor writes "Woman without her man is nothing" on the blackboard and asks the class to punctuate it correctly.
> The men write: "Woman, without her man, is nothing."
> The women write: "Woman! Without her, man is nothing."

These "great stones" were not just physical billboards of marketing and promotion but emotional and spiritual pillars announcing the border transformation from a loose nation into a strong nationhood. They are the ancient equivalent of today's bumper stickers that specialize on the meaning of life; akin to today's road signs on the freeway; announcing where you are and where you're heading.

Samples?

> "I used to have a handle on life, but it broke."
> "I'm not a complete idiot, some parts are missing,"
> "As long as there are tests, there will be prayer in public schools."
> "Where there's a will, I want to be in it!"
> "Always remember, you're unique, just like everyone else."

This literary surge is appropriate because this parsha falls smack in the pre-Rosh Hashanah month of Elul, an acronym for *Ani l'dodi v'dodi li* from *Song of Songs* ("I am my Beloved's, and my Beloved is mine.")

The subtext of this month is an intensive self-reflection and self-evaluation in order to figure out who we are and what we've been. In this exercise of measuring hopes and intentions, *both* God and Jews write: During this month Reb Nachman of Bratslav would write a list of things he did wrong that day, then read the list over and over until he fell asleep, hoping to improve himself upon the morrow, the first day of the rest of his life.

This week's parsha is read when the Jewish calendar inspires us to sit and reminisce about the past year, to indulge in a "reality check," known as a *cheshbon hanefesh,* taking an inventory of the soul, a checks and balances of our spiritual accounts. And in return, God picks up His own Heavenly quill and writes his beloved chosen into books — of life or death.

At first glance, this parsha appears to be a natural continuation of the previous mitzva-intensive Torah portions, but it is not.

It changes direction and tone; and introduces, right from the start, two new dictates, *bikkurim* and tithing, which "conclude" the cycle of Halachic life.

Bikkurim, the first order of the future, is an inspiring annual mitzva that requires each Jew to bring the season's "first fruits" to the Temple.

What's the importance of the "first?"

That from a good beginning comes good; that in the absence of a strong healthy foundation, cemented with *kedusha* (holiness), all that follows will be manifested with imperfections.

This "First and Foremost" rule applied not just to produce but to wool shearings, dough, man, animal — and to the people of Israel who Jeremiah describes poetically as "the first fruits of God's produce."

What a sight it must have been: a procession of respectful Jews, designated in this parsha for the first time as "His treasured folk," carrying the fruits of the landscape on their shoulders; a token acknowledgment that it was not their farming skills nor strength that produced the abundant harvest but the goodness and decency of the Heavens.

This parsha is thus the parsha of humility and modesty, designed to disengage us of the belief that *kochi v'otzem yadi*, ones achievements are due to ones own power. As such, the first eleven verses are a veritable role model for the Jewish way of saying *Thank You*, a combination of a heartfelt act (*avodas haleiv*) stapled to a prayer of sincerity (*mikra bikkurim*), with an obligatory reminder of our lowly roots ("My father was a fugitive Aramean.")

This falls within the morally enriching rabbinic concept known as *hakoras hatov*, the display of gratitude.

> "*Pheh!*" spits out Moishie after tasting the soup du jour, "*what is this?*"
> "*It's bean soup,*" replies the waitress.
> "*I don't care where it's been,*" he yells, "*what is it now!?*"

NITZAVIM
High Days and Holy Days

> *Cheskel walks into a flower shop and tells the salesgirl,*
> *"I'd like some flowers for my wife."*
> *"Certainly, sir, what do you have in mind?"*
> *"Well I'm not sure, I uh..uh..uh..."*
> *"Perhaps I could help, what exactly have you done!?"*

In this week's parsha, *Nitzavim*, Moshe continues his climactic deathbed speech on the banks of the Jordan, with a simple phrase, *attem nitzavim*, "You are standing," collectively, before God for one reason only: to conclude a *b'ris* (Covenant).

This expression appears nearly 300 times in the Bible in various forms, each reflecting some form of contract, pact, agreement.

> *Josh and his wife Mimi go to their annual Succos charity carnival. Every year Josh wants to go up in a ride on a small airplane, and every year his wife is against it, "It's too expensive, it costs $10, and $10 is $10!" she always screams.*
> *This goes on for nearly fifty years until one year Josh finally puts his foot down, "Look, I'm 81 years old. If I don't ride that airplane now I might never get another chance."*
> *"No Josh!" she shrieks, "The ride costs $10, and $10 is ten dollars!"*
> *For fifty years the same pilot has been listening to this spousal argument, and finally suggests, "Look folks, I'll make you a deal. I'll take you both up for a ride. If you don't fight, and promise to stay quiet for the entire ride, I won't charge you a penny; but if you say one word it's gonna cost you ten dollars!"*
> *Josh and his wife shake hands to cement the agreement — and up they go.* ▶

> *The pilot does all kinds of twists and turns, rolls and dives, up and down, down and up, and is surprised at the total silence behind him. Not a word from Mimi, not a murmur from Josh. And so the happy pilot continues on with all his daredevil tricks, and is pleased not to hear a single sound.*
>
> *Upon landing, he turns around to Josh and says, "By golly, I'm impressed. I did everything I could to scare you into yelling out, but you didn't."*
>
> *"Well," says Josh, straitening himself out, "I was going to say something right there at the beginning when Mimi fell out, but you know, $10 is ten dollars!"*

The multiple Torah pacts, traditionally followed by a festive meal to "sign off" on the contract, range from promises to Avraham (to have offspring as numerous as stars), to Israel (reflected by such binding signs as circumcision, Shabbos, tefillin), to Noach's "covenant of the rainbow" (with the promise that no flood will ever be used again as world punishment), to bond alliances between Yaacov and Lavan, Avraham and the king of Gerar.

However the covenant in this week's parsha, made between God and each and every Jew ("tribal heads, elders, officials, children, wives, strangers, the lowly and exalted") is uniquely different from all the others.

Why? Because this is the first time a bond is bound neither by time nor place: it has everlasting validity ("with those standing here, and those who are not"), making this an unequivocal inherited covenant between a people and their God as permanent as the Heavens and earth; implicitly placing a responsibility on each generation to transmit God's terms and conditions to each subsequent generation.

> *One day an arrogant ol' matron walks into Mrs. Fishbaum's florist shop searching for flowers to decorate her annual* Daughters of the American Revolution *dinner, celebrating the signing of the Declaration of Independence.*
>
> *The snobby woman drones on and on about her* yichus *and stuffy forefathers, "You know, one of my ancestors was present during the presentation of the Declaration of Independence to the Congress."*
>
> *"Really? That's nice," replies a non-chalant Mrs. Fishbaum, "one of my mine was present during the presentation of the Ten Commandments to the world."*

This week's parsha, *Nitzavim*, is always read on the Shabbos before the night of the *Selichos* service, the start of the ten "awesome days" of repentance between Rosh Hashanah and Yom Kippur when God is most accessible, known as *yomim noro'im*.

In English this time period is known as High Holidays, an unfortunate expression derived from the common phrase, "high days and holydays," wherein the two words are used interchangeably.

The word "holy" is derived from the Middle English *hool*, which means not "sacred" but "whole," or "excellent," but none of these accurately reflect the Hebrew term *Yom Kadosh*, a "sacred day." Even Yom Kippur is frequently mistranslated as the "Day of Atonement," a result of the English verb "atone," a combination of *at* and *one*, denoting atonement to reconciliation.

In Hebrew however the word *kippur* is derived from a root that can mean either "to cover, hide," or to "obliterate" (sin), and thus "to expiate."

> *The lawyer rushes into court and breathlessly tells the judge, "Your Honor, we need to reopen the case."*
> *"Why?"*
> *"Because I just discovered new evidence."* ▸

"New evidence!? What possible new evidence could you find after a nine-week trial."
"Well, I just found out that my client still has some money left in his account."

The Levush, a famous authority on Halacha, uses gematria to equate the numerical value of this parsha's first three words, *Atem nitzavim hayyom* (from where the parsha's title comes from) with *la'amod l'selichos*, which mean to get up for Selichos.

Moshe soothes his audience that the Torah is not an insuperable obstacle; on the contrary, that its way of life (*Halacha*) is easily accessible, and advises those who complain they cannot cope ("Keeping kosher is too difficult," "Keeping Shabbat is too inconvenient," etc) with the inspiration of a Psalmist directive, "Taste it and see."

Moshe, in this frightening graphic detail penned more than 3,000 years ago, tries to jolt the people from any false sense of security. The leader eerily predicts how the obstinate and loyal chosen people will survive in a nightmare of history, suffering siege, famine, poverty, war, forced exile, desolation and yet, in contrast to Great Empires who come and go, assures them that their nation would retain its singular identity, distinctiveness and its hope, eventually returning, as it did in May 1948, to its birthplace, the Holy Land.

One dark evening Dovid goes out for his customary walk when without warning an out-of-control bicyclist knocks him over. Dazed, he slowly gets up as passersby rush to help him. Suddenly Dovid starts screaming hysterically and fighting off his helpers until a medic quickly gives him a tranquilizer and calms him down.
"What was the problem," asks the doctor, "why were you struggling so?" ▶

> *"Well, I remember the impact and then blanked out. And then, when I came to, the first thing I saw was a huge, flashing 'Shell' sign, and somebody was standing in front of the 'S.'"*

Commenting on the parsha's opening, "You [*attem*] are standing this day," the charismatic Kotzker Rebbe notes the similarities in the Hebrew letters of *attem* (you) and *emet* (truth), suggestive that truth gives human beings the capacity for endurance and stability — evidenced by the shape of the letters; the *aleph* stands on two legs, the *mem* has a firm horizontal base, and the *tav* has two legs. The word as a whole, and each of its letters, thus has staying power.

In contrast, the opposite, *sheker* [falsehood] *ein lo raglayim*, has "no legs to stand on" — as the *shin* of "*sheker*" swivels in Torah script on a narrow base, and the *kuf* and *resh* each have only one leg.

The usual Hebrew word for "standing" is *omdim*, not *nitzavim*, but this expression connotes an act of will, a physical *hineni* reaffirmation ("Here I am, ready to do Your will!"), a stance described as "steadfast, with permanence." The Torah often compares the body language of angels as *omdim* (standing) in contrast to humans' *holchim* (progressing); in that angels are stationary and, in contrast to mankind, incapable of self-improvement (in other words, there is no such concept of becoming "better angels.")

Nitzavim is similar to *matzeivoh*, a "permanent monument," and a reminder from Moshe that although he is soon to die, the Jewish nation, infused with patience and persistence, will endure and survive "steadfastly" for eternity.

> *One year when cleaning out their attic for Pesach, Arnie and his wife came across an eleven-year-old ticket from the local shoe repair shop. They both laugh and try* ▶

> *to remember which of them might have forgotten to pick up a pair of shoes over a decade ago.*
>
> *"What do you think," asks Arnie, "are the shoes still in the shop?"*
>
> *Although unlikely, he goes to the store and, with a straight face, hands the stub to the man behind the counter.*
>
> *"Just a minute," says the owner, "I'll have to look for these."*
>
> *He disappears into a dark corner at the back of the shop, and returns a few minutes later, "Here they are!"*
>
> *"No kidding? That's terrific! Who would have thought they'd still be here after all this time. Can I have them?"*
>
> *"They'll be ready Thursday," the owner calmly replies.*

This parsha, as is the entire Deuteronomy, is one of chastisement, with Moshe demanding that the Jews not "stand still," lax and stationary, but advance forward and be engaged in a lifelong search for spiritual growth and knowledge for its own sake.

After pointing out that the laws of Sinai are neither difficult nor baffling, nor beyond their reach or capacity to observe, Moshe re-emphasizes the choice: thrive or perish — life and prosperity for those who obey, death and adversity for those who don't.

But wait! Haven't the stakes just been raised?

In a previous parsha (*Re'eh*) the choice was between receiving a blessing or a curse, yet in this parsha it has become a choice between life and death. Why? The chronology has changed: the Jews are reminded that they sinned despite the previous warning, and thus the choices of reward and punishment are now more severe.

> *By the time Yanki and Solly arrive at the football game, the first quarter is almost over.*
>
> *"How come you're so late?" their friends ask.* ▶

> "We had to toss a coin to decide whether to go to ye-
> shiva or come to the game."
> "So how long could that have taken you?"
> "Well, we had to toss it fourteen times."

The Hebrew word for "you shall choose" (*uvacharta*, derived
from the root *bachar*) appears twice in the Torah: when Lot stupidly
chooses Sodom instead of joining his uncle Avraham, and in this
week's parsha. The link between "choosing life" and fidelity to the
laws of Sinai have a lot to do with one's "will to live," a motivated
determination for a certain quality and framework of life based on
a spiritual dedication to Torah (*life* is Torah and *Torah* is life), while
being enveloped in a wardrobe of free-will.

That is why the Hebrew word root *shuv*, which means "to
turn, or "to return" (*t'shuvah*) is repeated in this parsha no less than
seven times (the number '7' having great symbolic significance in
Judaism).

As part of a reconciliation cycle of sincere colloquy, we witness
a dialogue of reciprocity between the Jew and God, an incredible
pattern of redemptive response as acts of returning are immediately
followed by redemption, followed by more returning, followed by
more redemption, and so on.

> "Tata, tata," *the little boy says after his first week in
> cheder,* "I know what the Bible stands for."
> "Okay, son," *smiles the father,* "What does it stand for?"
> "It stands for "Basic Instructions Before Leaving Earth."

As Moshe's career nears its end, this parsha could easily be subtitled, "The Rabbi Can't Win," considering what a hard time the
complaining and criticizing children of Israel gave him. It is re-

markable that he endured so much, with hardly ever a retort.

Since then, it seems to be a Jewish tradition for congregations to "beat up" on their rabbis.

Sigmund Freud claimed (incorrectly) that the Jews actually turned on Moshe in the desert and killed him. Freud was never renowned for his Torah scholarship but his Freudian observation, in that Jews seem to have a need to belittle and destroy their rabbinical leaders, is not far off. Rabbis simply can't win: "If everyone loves the rabbi, he's no rabbi... and if nobody loves him, he's no mensch!"

> *One day a rabbi finds himself on the list of those to be knighted by the British queen. When the big day comes. the rav is in deep anxiety. He knows that the ceremony involves kneeling before the queen, an improper thing for a Jew to do. And worse: he also has to recite a particular verse from the New Testament during the knighting, another violation of Jewish law.*
>
> *And yet, he must go so as not to baleidick her Royal Highness.*
>
> *On the big day the queen enters the room and all kneel, except the rabbi who is sweating profusely. When it is his turn to be knighted the queen waits expectantly for the rav to say a few Latin words.*
>
> *The nervous rabbi starts shaking in the midst of an anxiety attack, cognizant that the whole room is watching him. Suddenly, in a fit of absolute desperation, he blurts out the first words that come to mind, "Ma nishtana halaylah hazeh!"*
>
> *The queen, perplexed and utterly bewildered, turns to her aides and asks, "Why is this knight different from all other knights!?"*

May You Live to be 120 Years!

> The rabbi is giving a lengthy eulogy at Arnold's funeral, and goes into great detail about how the deceased was such a good husband and provider, kind to his wife and children, generous to a fault, always giving them his time and attention, showering his wife with gifts every Yom Tov, bringing her flowers each week for Shabbos, and on and on.
>
> Suddenly, Miriam the widow stops crying, turns to her daughter, and says, "Honey, do me a favor, go see if that's your tata in the coffin."

The title of this week's parsha, *Vayelech*, means "and then he went," a reference to Moshe's appearance amongst the folk to announce that, at the age of 120, he is too old to continue as an active leader — even though his eyes were "not dim" nor "his natural force abated."

But this phrasing, "and then he went," seems odd: it is a verb in the future tense that, by the use of one Hebrew letter (*vav*) is changed to past tense, a practice known as turning a *vav* into a *vav hahipuch*.

This is the shortest parsha of the year, consisting of only one chapter, wherein Moshe prepares his folk and flock for the future, and the transfer of leadership to Joshua ben Nun of the tribe of Ephraim, the charismatic and skilled military leader of the anti-Amalek campaign, a loyal disciple, and partisan follower.

Joshua, the first Jew to greet Moshe upon his descent from Sinai after a patient 40-day wait, becomes the second person to lead the Jewish people in their early history, capturing the city of Jericho, and, eventually, the rest of Canaan.

This is a timely lesson on transition: Moshe, exiting with grace and dignity, knows when to call it quits and sets *the* example on how to pass the torch. The great lawgiver, with thoughtfulness, prudence and no display of any hurt feelings or resentment, bestows blessings, encouragement and affirmation on Joshua ("in sight of all Israel") assuring him, *twice*, that he is perfect for the task. And more: in choosing Joshua over his own two sons (Gershon and Eliezer), the Torah renders the final opinion on nepotism and family favoritism.

> *Chaim, father of five, wins a toy at a raffle and doesn't want to show favoritism, so, to help decide whom to give it to, he gathers them all and asks, "Who is the most obedient? Who never talks back to mummy? Who does everything she says?"*
>
> *"It's okay, tata," five small voices answer in unison, "You get to keep the toy!"*

The Heavens describe Joshua as "inspirational" (literally, "there is spirit in him"); the Midrash locates his exemplary "greatness in his willingness to perform the most menial of communal tasks;" Jewish history honors him by naming the first Book of the Prophets after him.

Within the *ohel mo'ed*, a private tent where only a select few are allowed entry, God advises Joshua to "go with (*tavoh*)" the people, united, so the nation of Israel "be not like sheep without a shepherd."

He is warned against a benevolent dictatorship, and cautioned to seek the counsel of elders and officers; what we today call "consultants."

"Be strong and resolute," is the gentle warning; in that strength of character is necessary for courageous leadership.

Perhaps it helped that he remained single?

Consider: there is not a single reference in the entire Book of Joshua of Moshe's heir apparent ever marrying, nor having any family life; however, a Midrash identifies his wife as Rahab, the harlot who housed the 12 spy scouts, of which he was one, and whose descendants include such famous prophets as Jeremiah and Hulda.

> *Having fired their previous rabbi for excessive alcoholism the shul board is understandably sensitive to this issue when seeking his replacement. So at the end of each interview, the previous rabbi would lean forward, and in a low, confidential tone, ask the applicant, "Tell me, do you partake of alcoholic beverages?"*
>
> *"Rabbi," one young applicant whispers back, "Is this an inquiry or an invitation?"*

After Rabbi Yehoshua ben Gamla became the head of the Sanhedrin in the first century, he confessed that, "Before I accepted this office, if anyone had suggested it to me, I would have tied him up in front of a lion." Is this an admission of humility? Yes, and no, for he goes on to say, "But now that I have this office, if anyone were to ask me to step down, I would pour a pitcher of boiling water on him!"

Ben Gamla learned this from Saul; before he became king he hid from the honor, but afterwards, when David wanted to take it away from him, Saul tried to kill him.

This continuity of leadership is apropos for this parsha. Why?

Because it is usually read with, or "attached" (*mechubar*), to the previous parsha (*Nitzavim*), one derives greater meaning, or important principles, gleaned from two side-by-side texts that are more potent than studying either parsha separately.

One lesson is that *Vayelech* defines who the "you" is in God's previous command, "For this commandment [*t'shuva*] which I command *you* this day." The "you" is inclusive, setting the tone and foundation for the spiritual democracy of Israel: for since Torah "is neither in the Heavens nor beyond the sea," it enters Jewish history as the heritage and destiny of *all* Israel. No priest, prophet, rabbi, or educator can claim exclusivity, not without including children, slaves, aliens. No one was to feel unwelcome, all were to have equal access to God's ear via prayer and study; with or without intermediaries, however, there is no doubt that one inspired leader can influence multitudes of people.

One person, burning with a zest for Torah and mitzvos, can pull along many cold and indifferent people.

> *The first day a train came to their small town, the excited chassidim show their Rebbe this advance of modern civilization.*
>
> *The Rebbe sees a long line of black, cold, somber looking cars attached to one another. The engine in front is belching fire, when suddenly, with an ear-shattering roar, black clouds of smoke rise heavenward, the engine starts to move, and the long line of cars move with it.*
>
> *"Rebbe, rebbe," his chassidim kvel, "What do you say to this wonderful sight?"*
>
> *The Rebbe thinks, and replies, "Just look at how one hot, fiery thing can pull along so many cold ones!"*

As we approach the end of the Torah there appears two more orders: to undertake a public reading of "*this* Torah," and deposit "*this* book of the Torah" in the Ark of the Covenant, a place of permanency.

Does "this" Torah apply only to Deuteronomy, or the entire five Books? It's a dispute, but the latter is the accepted conclusion.

Right in the midst of this parsha, just as we shift uncomfortably with a Godly prediction of apostasy in future Jewish generations, which itself comes on the heels of a harsh order to "proscribe" the seven Canaanite nations to "doom and destruction," we are suddenly exposed to another historic "first" — setting appointed times to teach the Law to the general public; a new mitzva which the Mishna calls *hakhel,* the Command of Assembly.

This required the "assembling" of "all Israel" to publicly read passages of Deuteronomy "on the night following the first day" of Succos of the seventh year (although Rashi claims it took place on the night following the last day, that of Shemini Atzeres).

Why these specific passages?

Because the fifth book of the Torah begins with a summary of history, then proceeds with the premier *Shema,* and on into the second version of the Ten Commandments.

Who actually read the Torah at these assemblies? The king, as God's messenger.

The source of the mitzva is an earlier deuteronomic passage that describes the revelation at Sinai with the same verb, *hakhel,* creating the linkage and equivalence between the two events. Thus the purpose was to re-create and re-live the Sinaitic experience, which is also referred to as "the day of *hakhel*" (making this a parallel parsha, in content and language to *Ki Sisa*), a "return" to an historical experience in order to "awaken and strengthen" the people, a reminder of who we are and where we come from.

> One day grampa Moshe is telling his youngest grandson about his terrifying experience with cannibals, "There I was, lost in the middle of the jungle, surrounded by 20 hungry cannibals."
>
> "But zeidy," interrupts the little boy, "the last time you told me, there were only 5 hungry cannibals."
>
> "Ah, yes, but you were too young then to know the whole horrible truth!"

Clearly the Torah has linked the need for a *hakhel* cycle as an antidote to the creeping custom of idolatry, the lure of deceptive "foreign gods," the catalyst for the time when God "will surely hide His face," the harshest, according to Rashi, of all the cursed 98 prophecies, despite the Psalmist's comforting assurance, "Yet though I walk in death's dark valley, I shall fear no evil because You are with me."

This parsha may be the shortest in the Torah but its dramatic narrative still manages to introduce the Jews, at this late eleventh hour, to many important issues, including the last specific command of them all, number 613, to "write (*kisvu*) down this poem [a Torah scroll]."

This is the genesis of the label, "The People of the Book," namely, its regular public reading.

Moshe jumps at the opportunity, late in his life, to accomplish this mitzva, in the spirit of *zerizim makdimin l'mitzvos,* "Diligent people are quick to observe the commandments as soon as possible;" and, recognizing the potent preserving power of penmanship as the key to the future of Torah, especially when stapled to public teaching, Moshe quickly creates the first written scroll of God's teachings; and in order to permanently dispel any future doubts as to its sanctified authority, he places it in the Holy Ark right next to the tablets of the Law.

Yosef Ber Soloveitchik (the *Rav*) once compared a boy reaching bar mitzva with this command to write a Torah scroll, in that the Jewish education of a young boy to religious maturity parallels the stages of preparing parchment, ink, quill — with the end of childhood equating completion of a scroll in that both attain the appropriate sanctity.

> *The cheder Rebbe was so involved in the text that he never looked up, and every now and then he would call on a student to translate and explain. Without realizing it, the rebbe chose the same boy, Itzi, four days in a row. On the fifth day, the boy is ready.*
> *"Itzi," yells the rebbe with his head in the Chumash, "translate and explain."*
> *"Oh Itzi?" Itzi replies, "He is absent today."*
> *"Okay, then you translate and explain."*

Past and future; future and past: the story ends as it began — we first meet Moshe in Egypt when he "goes out" and sees the oppression amongst his people, and our last image of the great teacher is the same, Moshe going out (*vayelech*), once again, to touch the people with his presence, showing how hard it is to "stand still (*netzavim*)."

It is from here that the popular Yiddish birthday expression, "May you live to be 120 years!" comes from.

Of course, in reality, this age is unreachable for most people which is why the great Sforno, a 16th century Italian Torah commentator, taught that it is simply suggestive of having lived to a good ol' age.

> *The elderly Jewish man walks into an insurance agency and says he wants to buy a life insurance policy.*
> *"How old are you," asks the sales girl.*
> *"I'm eighty."*
> *"Eighty? I'm sorry, sir, but we don't sell life insurance policies to 80-year-old men!"*
> *"Then how come you sold one to my father last week!?"*
> *"Your father!? How old is he?"*
> *"He's a hundred."*
> *"A hundred?" replies the astonished sales girl. "Anyway,* ▶

I don't have that sort of authority. Come back next Thursday and speak to my manager."

"I can't come next Thursday."

"Why not?"

"My grandfather's getting married."

"Your grandfather's getting married! How old is he?"

"Oh, he just turned a hundred and twenty."

"A hundred and twenty!? Why would a 120-year-old man want to get married for?"

"Well, to tell you the truth, he doesn't…but his mother's pushing him into it!"

HA'AZINU
Song, Song, Song

In this parsha, the arch-lawgiver begins his eloquent last words with *Ha'azinu,* which literally means: "Give ear," as in "listen attentively!"

It's human nature: man's attention span is limited, as is this chapter, with only 52 lines, the first 47 consisting of a vivid imagery of song intended for a captive audience, the soon-to-be nation of Israel, as it stands on the threshold of a land promised.

Moshe's choice of communicating his prophetic vision in this week's parsha is not in his usual mode of legal pronouncements but in the form of a valedictory song, a melodic kiss goodbye, which is didactic in prose and style.

Is this the first time Moshe sings? No, he sang together with the entire people at the miracle of the sea splitting, but it is the first time he sings in responsa — first he sings alone and then the people repeat his song.

At first glance this seems like a strange time for song: the generation that left Egypt is dead, and soon Moshe will follow them to the grave, but herein lies his spiritual humility and greatness.

Moshe's ability to sing is not inspired by a wondrous sight, but is present despite personal tragedy which would have broken the spirits of a lesser man.

This summation of Israel's faults, negative yet truthful, is coupled with a reminder of God's power, love and promise of deliverance; indicative not of the dry letter of the law but of its spirit which, in their task of being God's *tikkun* couriers on earth, should be done in song and simcha, happiness and glee, qualities that inspire and invigorate, enliven and animate, in ways that dry scholarship and regimented lectures cannot.

> *One year Harvey is invited to fly to China and give the keynote address at a packed local convention. He goes up to the platform, stands at the microphone, and gives a big bow.*
>
> *The crowd goes wild, clapping and cheering him for several minutes. Harvey is pleased with himself, and bows again. The mood suddenly changes: the audience boos, and starts throwing chairs at the podium.*
>
> *Harvey asks the guy next to him on the dais, "What happened!? What did I do wrong?"*
>
> *"The Chinese don't like long speeches!"*

Moshe, in searching for just the right metaphor to describe God's steadfastness and strength, skips over such stock choices as Redeemer, Creator, Shepherd, Peace Maker, Shield, Healer, Friend, and Father — and chooses "the Rock," comparing God, for the second time in the Torah, to a bird of strength, "an eagle" who lovingly and confidently took the children of Israel out of Egypt on His wings.

It is this particular quality of God (judgment via strength) that made our rabbis choose the verse from this parsha ("He is the Rock, his work is perfect; for all his ways are justice; a God of truth and without iniquity, just and straight is He") as the opening of the *Tziduk Hadin*, the burial service, an acknowledgment that, in finality, the deceased will be judged fairly, by the One "without iniquity."

> *The widow is on the phone to the local Jewish weekly dictating an obituary for her husband, and tells the sales girl to write, "Max is dead."*
> *"But ma'am, for $25 you are allowed to print six words."*
> *"Okay, then print: 'Max is dead. Toyota for sale.'"*

"Jewish life is a symphony whose score is the Torah, whose composer is God, whose orchestra is the Jewish people, and whose most moving performance is on Simchas Torah," writes England's chief rabbi Jonathan Sacks.

Only a Torah that can reach down to the feet is authentic, mused Chassidic Rabbi Zalman Schachter, adding "anything else is just a manipulation of words."

This is why the charismatic founder of Chassidus, Israel ben Eliezer (*Ba'al Shem Tov*), once danced with the Torah, stopped, put it aside — and continued dancing and clutching it in its invisible form. "The purpose of the whole Torah is that each person should become a Torah," was a favorite saying of his.

This ability to perceive something that is not there, and continue as though it is, is the single most remarkable strength of the *Yiddishe folk*. It is confidence personified, *emunah* on a stand, "evidence," according to Menachem Mendel of Kotsk, that "faith is clearer than sight."

Rabbi Moshe Chaim Ephraim once told of "a fiddler who played so sweetly that all who heard him began to dance, but when a deaf man came by, he looked at these dancing people and thought they were madmen, people who had lost their senses." In other words, the music and lyrics of the Torah and our sages are only heard by those willing to dance to them *and* with each other.

> *"Haven't I seen your face before?" the judge asks Beresh Greengarten.*
> *"Yes, your Honor," Beresh answers hopefully, "I taught your son how to play the violin."*
> *"Ah, yes, now I remember. Thirty years!"*

The recent wave of nostalgia for Eastern European music, known as *klezmer*, is a reminder that Jews themselves were once considered walking instruments.

The Yiddish term *klezmer* comes from *klei* ("vessel, instrument") and *zemer* ("song"), metonymically describing the musicians themselves.

Jeremiah would compare the people of Judah to a *k'li rek*, an "empty pot" (for failing to resist King Nebuchadnezzar), the 4th-century CE Rava would refer to himself in his prayers as "a vessel [*k'li*] full of shame," books were titled *k'li yakar*, "a precious vessel," and the Torah uses the expression *k'ley-kodesh*, "holy vessels" (in reference to the Temple's ritual objects).

Those Jews engaged in song (*k'ley-zmorim*) were performing a semi-sacred task, especially since they were performing *together*, in unity. The melodious aspect of Judaism is thus not by accident, but by Divine design.

Where does this idea, that the spirituality of song (*shira*) helps sustain the *ruchnious* ("spirituality") of Torah, come from?

"If two people talk at the same time," writes Reb Nachman of Bratslav, "neither hears or understands the other, whereas if two people sing at the same time, they give each other harmony."

The basis is found right in a Torah that refers to *itself* as an eternal "song;" an acknowledgment of the immense "secular" power of melody and music, powerfully uniting the intellect and the emotions, penetrating into the depths of a person's inner being, known in antiquity as the "language of the heart" (perhaps this is why all countries and peoples create a personalized anthem.)

The song of *Ha'azinu,* which Moshe, as a finishing touch of a life's mission, is ordered to write spontaneously, "on demand" from God, is unlike all the other thanksgiving (*hallel*) songs in the Torah whose common themes are rescue and redemption related: i.e.: like *Shiras Hayam,* "the Song of the Sea," which praises God in response to a supernatural marvel and miracle.

This prerequisite is clearly missing in this parsha that has an acrimonious God declaring, "I shall surely hide My face [*hester ponim*]," a reaction to the befuddled generation of Jews (*dor ikesh ufsaltol*) who flirted with demon-gods "whom your fathers did not know" (*lo se`arum avoseichem*).

The obvious question is this: why match the beauty of "song" with such harsh and scary lyrics ("A fire is kindled in My anger, I will heap evils upon them, I will consume them.")

Because this seemingly peculiar song of Moshe, perhaps the world's first soul symphony, is *not* rejoicing *now* for the Jews of the desert generation but as a witness of destiny, an impending truth when "evils and troubles" will surely arise. This "song" is thus relevant for *future* generations, those who will have life-experiences of despair and triumph, disaster and victory, laughter and tears — and will need to comprehend reward and punishment, good and evil, and how to respond.

> *Sam and Abe are two master pianists who make a pact that whoever dies first, he will contact the other and tell him what life in Heaven is like. Poor Sam soon has a heart attack and dies, but he manages to make contact with Abe the very next day.* ▸

> *"I can't believe it!" says an excited Abe, "Tell me, what's it like in Heaven?"*
>
> *"It's great Sammy, but I've got good news, and bad news. The good news is that there's a fantastic orchestra up here, and in fact, we're playing* Sheherezade, *your favorite piece, tomorrow night!"*
>
> *"So, what's the bad news?"*
>
> *"You're booked to play the solo!"*

Originally, in order to assure its transmission from *dor l'dor* (generational), this poem of Moshe was sung each week in the first and second Temples by the Levite singers, the *meshorer,* descendants of Asaph, the first official singer and poet in King David's court.

In later generations, in order to help internalize the lessons of Jewish history and a sense of Jewish consciousness, Jewish children were taught to memorize the song of *Ha'azinu.*

Moshe's final oration comes not in sad resignation, but in a free-flowing, poetic and passionate crescendo that begins with an unambiguous stirring challenge: to contemplate history (*Z'chor yemos olam, binu shenos dor v'dor,* "Remember the days of old, consider the years of ages past..."). This is why Moshe calls upon *hashomayim v'ha'aretz,* "Heavens and the earth," as witnesses to his valedictorian farewell, because they are immortal and ever-lasting witnesses to Jewish history. What is his message? That the longevity, spiritual resuscitation, and survival of the Jewish people depends on how they act.

That Moshe, who was raised with Egyptian as his mother tongue, was able to compose the song in Hebrew is a testament to its preservation by his followers despite hundreds of years of oppression; one of four metaphysical weapons that the Midrash credits with keeping the Jews Jewish.

The other three? Not giving up their identity (by keeping their

Hebrew names), passing on their traditions to later generations and maintaining their special relationship with God (by not abandoning circumcision.)

This was an important leadership asset of Moshe: impulsiveness, the ability to seize the moment, to react to events with an instinctive sense of urgency and of recognition of the power of timing.

Moshe was not alone: the image of leaders celebrating victories, in their relief and joy, by composing and performing songs appears in this week's Haftarah as well: we have Devorah (whose Hebrew name means "bee," and whose root letters mean "to arrange, speak, motivate, litigate"), a wife (of Lapidoth the candle maker), judge and lawyer (the only judge of Israel who the Torah describes as actually "judging"), and one of only five prophetess in the Torah, sang, together with her Lieutenant Barak, and courageously inspired and united the Jews to defeat the Canaanites and General Sisera.

The Torah says that Moshe sings "until the end," and uses the Hebrew word *tumam* for "end." However *tumam* can also mean "whole," suggesting that the mystical power generated by Jewish singing-a-long creates a people's totality; of unity and harmony and oneness.

In the concluding five lines, God tells Moshe to climb Mount Nebo and view the Promised Land. He will die, *b'etzem hayom ha'zeh*, at midday; an expression that the Torah uses only two other times: when Noach is instructed to board his Ark, in "broad daylight;" and when the Jews leave Egypt "in broad daylight" — in order that all see there is no stopping God's will.

Moshe dies alone; no one knows his burial place, giving extra weight to the "gathered to his people" description. This momentously poignant event, incredibly, receives only a few sparing lines.

The Midrash describes how Moshe, being a mortal man in fear of dying, first reacts lightly, then searches for the right prayer, then scrambles to find a mystical incantation to keep the Angel of Death away and then resorts to trying to get God to change His mind — but nothing helps:

That the constitution of Judaism is not political nor historic but religious is the underlying theme of the entire Book of D'varim, and is why *Ha'azinu* is always read on the Shabbos during the ten-day Rosh Hashanah-Yom Kippur cycle (*aseres yemei teshuvah*), commonly known as *Shabbos Shuvah,* the "Sabbath of Repentance" (or more accurately, the "Shabbos of Turning"), a term chosen from the prophet's opening phrase of the Haftarah, *Shuvah Yisroel,* "Return O Israel."

Hosea, having suffered greatly while living in the Northern Kingdom of Israel during the 8th century BCE, could identify with God's pain of feeling betrayed by His chosen folk and offered the remedy of *Ha'azinu* to the people: assurance that the Heavens forgive those that genuinely change their behavior.

It was *erev* Yom Kippur and Gottlieb has a dilemma: he wants to watch the Yankees start the playoffs. So he calls his rabbi, "Rabbi, I know tonight is Kol Nidre, but I'm a lifelong Yankee fan and I've got to watch the game on TV."

"Gottlieb!" shouts back the rav, "That's what VCR's are for!"

"Really? You mean I can video Kol Nidre?"

Breaking Up is Hard to Do

> *"Yes?" Mrs. Rosenberg asks the needy Jew at her door,*
> *"Can I help you?"*
> *"Please," the schnorrer wails, "My entire house and all my personal belongings have been destroyed in a fire."*
> *"Oy, that's terrible. Tell me, do you have a letter from a rabbi confirming this terrible tragedy?"*
> *"Yes, of course...but unfortunately it was burnt in the same fire."*

The title to this weeks parsha, *Zos Habrocho*, simply means, "This is the blessing," a reference to Moshe's final blessing for health, happiness, prosperity.

Is this brocho original?

No: it made its first appearance in Genesis with Yaacov blessing his children; its reappearance here, at the climax and *finale* of the Torah, is a timely endorsement and reaffirmation, as Yaacov's name "Israel" implies, that he remains *the* progenitor patriarch and founding father of the Jewish people.

The rabbis of the Talmud thus extract from this parsha the first words which parents are to teach their children, usually at age three; "Moshe commanded us to keep the Torah, it is an inheritance (*morasha*) of the community of Yaacov."

Even before the young start their formal Jewish education, this obligatory sentence is intended to give the children of Israel a creedal sense of place, permanency, profound purpose — and respect for a parenthood that has handed down the tradition through the generations.

> *One evening a father and son are sitting together watching the sun set over the ocean. Not a word is spoken as the child witnesses a scene of incredible serenity and beauty. As the sun slowly disappears, the boy turns to his father, and says, "Do it again, Daddy."*

Judaism revolves around children (ever notice that a human baby doesn't walk until it's tall enough to reach a parent's hand?).

King David sang that children were the "heritage of God" and how "happy the man that has his quiver full of them." To Yitzchak Leibush Peretz, 19th century Yiddish poet-novelist, children were "man's eternity," to the Midrash's Rabbi Meir they were "the best surety, better than patriarchs and prophets." To the Yiddishists, insanity was hereditary, gotten from one's kids!

Cementing its ties to children, Simchas Torah is the only time that a special aliyah, under the guise of *kol hana'arim*, "all the children," is given to, yep...all the children.

> *"I'm wasting my time," the little girl says to her mother after her first week of school, "I can't read, I can't write — and they won't let me talk!"*

There is a striking similarity in both the first and last direct Torah commands involving bountiful visions bordered by restrictions: Adam begins his life being shown the Garden of Eden and ordered not to go to a certain tree, while Moshe ends his life being shown the land of Israel's beautiful hills, valleys and fertile plains and being told "you shall not go there."

The Heavens offer no information as to Moshe's whereabouts except to place it in a "valley opposite Beit Peor," in a spot "where no man knows to this very day [*ad hayom hazeh*]." This is a remarkable exception in a religion that stresses the importance of remembering and memorializing those who have died.

Moshe, the most special Jew within Jewish tradition, has no marked grave, and no special *yahrtzeit* ceremony. According to Rabbi Levi ben Gershon, God buried Moshe so that future generations would not come to venerate the burial site and worship him as a deity.

After giving the father of all prophets one last opportunity to see the promised land from afar, God ends Moshe's loyal life in the land of Moav with a soft, gentle kiss (*al pi Adonai*). He then personally buries his loyal disciple, a singular Divine "reward" in return for the respect that Moshe paid to Yosef's last wish to be buried with his ancestors. For of all the acts of *chesed* Moshe performed, only this one is called a *chesed shel emes* (true-kindness), because it was done for a deceased person, and the selfless Moshe could expect no compensation.

The Torah thus begins and ends with an act of Godly *chesed*, from clothing man (Adam) to burying him (Moshe); a trait of *chesed* that became the founding principle upon which the Jewish people were established.

> At the annual yeshiva dinner the rosh yeshiva, the main speaker, suddenly realizes that in his haste to be punctual he has forgotten his false teeth. Turning to the man next to him the rav whispers in a panic, "I forgot my teeth."
>
> "Don't worry, rabbi, it's not a problem," says the man who reaches into his trouser pocket and pulls out a pair of false teeth, "Try these."
>
> "Too loose," the rav replies after trying them on.
>
> "Not to worry. I have another pair, try these."
>
> "Too tight."
>
> "Here's some more," says the unconcerned man as he brings out several more sets of false teeth, "See if they fit."
>
> The rosh yeshiva tries them on, one-by-one, and ▶

> then displays a big smile, "Thank God, this one fits per-
> fectly." With that he finishes his meal, gives his address,
> sits down and leans over to the man, "I must thank you for
> coming to my aid. Where is your office? I've been looking
> for a good dentist."
> "Oh, I'm not a dentist. I'm the local undertaker."

This parsha is unique: it is the only one that does not have a Shabbos unto itself, instead it constitutes the main reading for Simchas Torah, the only time of the year when a Torah reading is permitted at nighttime. Since "breaking up is hard to do," we immediately start reading the Torah all over again. So does Simchas Torah celebrate the end, or the beginning? A bit of each.

The most honored portion is the last aliyah (*acharon*) through whom the entire cycle of Torah readings becomes complete.

Jewish mystics had a field day in closing the circle: they took the last letter (*lamed*) of the last Torah word (*Yisroel*) and added it to the first letter (*bet*, or *vet* without the dot) of the Torah's first word (*Bereishis*). The result? The Hebrew word for heart (*lev*), indicating that Torah is the heart of the Jewish people.

That is why this parsha of Simchas Torah is compared to a concert that resonates with the inspirational symphony of Torah being discussed, dissected, debated, akin to a lyric-free *niggun* that seems endless and infinite; the fertile "noise" of exhilaration, the sounds of excitement, the songs of verbal animation whose lyrics are "the words of the living God."

And since the beat of the heart keeps one alive, there is no time to pause.

This underscores Ezra's premiere canon of Jewish faith: that the study of Torah is, like a circle, a never-ending celebratory "renewal of the covenant."

This parsha also gives us the optimum form of eulogy: when

the Heavens lionize Moshe, the greatest living Jew in Biblical history and the most illustrious rabbi of all time, the one "singled out by God, face to face," they do it in two short and direct words, describing Moshe simply as an *eved Hashem*, "servant of God."

There is no great oratory, no flowering poetry and no tomes of accolades encapsulating a life of outstanding achievements. The Torah focuses instead only on the *raison d'etre* of mortal man, the fidelity to the Divine.

This explains why it is only in this parsha, just before his death, at the last available opportunity, that Moshe is given the ultimate honorific title of being an *Ish Ho'elokim*, a "Man of God," with a name so intertwined with Judaism that the Torah itself becomes permanently referred to simply as *"Toras Moshe,"* the Five Books of Moshe.

> *At his wife's funeral, one of the pall-bearers accidentally bumps into a corner causing the coffin to drop and tumble down the stairs where the body miraculously rolls out, faintly moaning.*
>
> *The fall has brought life back to the corpse and his wife lives on for ten more years — until she dies again.*
>
> *At her next funeral, held in the same hall, the pallbearers are again carrying out the casket. As they approach the same spot, the husband cries out, "Careful, be careful! Watch out for the wall!"*

Every ending also heralds a new beginning, and a lasting message: this parsha makes it clear that Torah began with Moshe, but it didn't end with him.

Rabbi Baruch of Medzibozh, the Ba'al Shem Tov's grandson, by continuing the last words of the last parsha to the first words of this first parsha ("According to the eyes of each of Israel...[is]...*in the Beginning*"), reveals that God has granted a personalized clarity towards comprehending Torah according to the level of each individual's knowledge, faith, and personal experiences.

At the conclusion of the Torah reading, the *hagbah*, the lifting of the Torah scroll, is done differently than the rest of the year. The person lifting the Torah (the *ba'al hagbah*) criss-crosses his hands so that the Torah writing is reversed, facing the congregation. This custom is linked to Pirkei Avos, "Turn it over and over, for everything is in it" (there is also a more practical reason: it is easier to lift since all the weight is on the left side).

But why read the Torah again, and again, and again? Why not just study it once thoroughly, then discuss, debate, dispute it at will?

The answer comes to us from the sage Ben Sira: the Torah's "understanding is wider than the sea, and its counsel deeper than the abyss," to which Yosef Josel Hurvitz adds...

"The Torah is a deep sea, and man a vessel,
to draw water from it, and he draws according to the vessel.
If he comes with a spoon, he will draw a spoonful;
if with a jar — a jarful;
if with a bucket — a bucketful;
if with a barrel — a barrelful.
He may draw as much as he wishes..."

Rav Hurvitz beautifully illustrates how the Torah's rich soil can be "harvested" on so many levels that each time one opens a page of Torah, even the *same* page, one discovers a new experience, a new adventure, "a new Heaven," according to the Zohar.

The more one looks, the more one finds; the more one finds, the more one understands; the more one understands, the more one can grow.

This is why the Torah is called *eitz chayim*, a growing "Tree of Life," a term that comes from the verse in Proverbs, *etz chayim hi l'machazikim ba,* "She is a tree of life for those who hold her tight; a tree of life," buttressed by the esoteric belief that just as a small tree can set a bigger tree on fire, so a Torah student can sharpen the mind of his teacher.

Hold a family tree upside down and you will see how the roots from a single set of ancestors can branch out and multiply into a community; this is why eastern European Jews would plant a tree at the birth of a child (cedars for boys, pines for girls) since both childbirth and Mother Nature were considered miraculous. When the children grew up and married, branches of their trees were cut and used to build the chuppa canopy.

Judaism pays homage to the tree, and salutes its ubiquitous symbolic contribution to the cosmic oasis of life itself; a contribution so esteemed that, in the chronology of creation, God occupies Himself with the tree *before* humans by "planting a garden in Eden," and then extending it to the future: "When you enter the land, occupy yourselves first with naught else but planting."

The symbolism soon surged in Judaic writing: the Jew became the "tree branch" (because as long as a branch is attached to the tree, it can regain its strength; and as long as a Jew is still part of the community, however tenuous the link, his Jewishness can flourish again); Israel was an olive tree (because the olive does not lose its leaves in either summer or winter, so Israel is never abandoned in this world), and the Jewish nation was compared to a vine (which, though plucked up from one place, can flourish in another).

To Job, holder of the Judaic *Guinness Record for Suffering,* the tree is hope, even Messianic: "If it is felled, it will sprout again, its tender branch will not cease. Although its root waxes old in the earth, and its stock dies in the ground, through the scent of water it will bud and bring forth boughs like a plant."

Jewish wisdom is thus eternal, perpetual, never-ending — and sprinkled with a healthy legacy of rabbinic humor.

> *As the elderly rabbi walks by, a young Salvation Army worker asks, "Sir, won't you give a coin to the Lord?"*
> *The rabbi stops, and asks the boy how old he is.*
> *"Nineteen, rabbi."*
> *"Well, I'm past 75. I'll be seeing Him before you, so I'll hand it to Him myself."*

This ends the Book of Deuteronomy, the fifth and final book of the Torah when everyone rises and says, *Chazak, chazak, v'nitchazek,* "Be strong, be strong, and let us be strengthened!" — a roar of encouragement to continue on to Bereishis, the "next" and first book of the Torah, and start all over again.

Why repeat the word *chazak* three times?

To symbolize the past, present, and future.